Black Market Capital

Black Market Capital

URBAN POLITICS AND THE SHADOW
ECONOMY IN MEXICO CITY

Andrew Konove

UNIVERSITY OF CALIFORNIA PRESS

University of California Press, one of the most distinguished university presses in the United States, enriches lives around the world by advancing scholarship in the humanities, social sciences, and natural sciences. Its activities are supported by the UC Press Foundation and by philanthropic contributions from individuals and institutions. For more information, visit www.ucpress.edu.

University of California Press
Oakland, California

Library of Congress Cataloging-in-Publication Data

Names: Konove, Andrew, 1982- author.
Title: Black market capital : urban politics and the shadow economy in Mexico City / Andrew Konove.
Description: Oakland, California : University of California Press, [2018] | Includes bibliographical references and index. |
Identifiers: LCCN 2017049906 (print) | LCCN 2017054559 (ebook) | ISBN 9780520966901 () | ISBN 9780520293670 (cloth : alk. paper) | ISBN 9780520293687 (pbk : alk. paper)
Subjects: LCSH: Black market—Mexico—Mexico City—20th century. | Mexico City (Mexico)—Economic conditions—20th century. | Mexico City (Mexico)—Politics and government—20th century. | Urban economics.
Classification: LCC HF5482.65.M3 (ebook) | LCC HF5482.65.M3 K66 2018 (print) | DDC 330—dc23
LC record available at https://lccn.loc.gov/2017049906

ClassifNumber   PubDate
DeweyNumber'—dc23   CatalogNumber

Manufactured in the United States of America

25   24   23   22   21   20   19   18
10   9   8   7   6   5   4   3   2   1

In memory of my father, Ron, and my brother, Jon

CONTENTS

ILLUSTRATIONS AND TABLES

FIGURES

MAPS

TABLES

ACKNOWLEDGMENTS

This book began in 2006, when I worked at a small microfinance institution in Oaxaca, Mexico. In my role there, I met women and men who operated businesses at the margins of the law—legitimate, yet not fully legal and therefore without all the protections and remedies the law provides. How, I wondered, did that state of legal ambiguity, in which so many people in Mexico and around the world find themselves today, come into being? What, in other words, is the informal economy's history? To answer those questions, I sought to understand how a society draws lines, over time, between legal and illegal and tolerable and intolerable exchange. This book on Mexico City's Baratillo—a marketplace that was illegal but eminently tolerable—is the product of that investigation.

Writing a book requires countless acts of kindness from friends and strangers. A number of people in Mexico City made research on this project possible. The staff of the Archivo Histórico de la Ciudad de México, especially Marlene Pérez, Ricardo Nelson Méndez Cantarell, Alberto Falcón, and Ana Alicia Galindo Méndez, unlocked countless secrets in that archive for me. I am also grateful to the staff at the Archivo General de la Nación, the Archivo General de Notarías, and the Hemeroteca Nacional for their assistance. The Colegio de México offered me an academic home while I was researching the dissertation that became this book. I had the privilege of learning from Marcello Carmagnani, Carlos Marichal, and Sandra Kuntz Ficker while I was there. Guillermina del Valle Pavón, Ernesto Aréchiga Córdoba, and María Eugenia Chaoul became valuable colleagues and friends over the course of this project. Sonia Pérez Toledo was particularly generous, offering thoughtful feedback and access to data that enriched this study. Alfonso Hernández of the Centro de Estudios Tepiteños introduced me to Tepito's rich street cultures and was a vital resource for the neighborhood's history. Linda Arnold's unparalleled knowledge of Mexican archives led me to important finds. Natalia Begún, Cyntia and Sandra González, Armando Martínez, and Sergio Sánchez opened their homes to me on countless occasions while I researched this book. In Oaxaca, I learned from Aurora Vignau, Pablo Albrecht, Caroline Boyd Kronley, and Maureen Keffer, my colleagues and friends at SEFIA.

This project received financial support from the Fox International Fellowship and the MacMillan Center for International and Area Studies at Yale University and the Tinker and Mellon Foundations. The University of Texas at San Antonio's Internal Research Award and travel grants from the College of Liberal and Fine Arts facilitated the project's completion. Parts of chapters 2 and 3 first appeared in the article "On the Cheap: The *Baratillo* Marketplace and the Shadow Economy of Eighteenth-Century Mexico City," *The Americas* 72:2 (April 2015): 249–78. They are reproduced here with permission from the publisher. I am grateful to Abraham Parrish, Nazgol Bagheri, Patrick Keller, and Bill Nelson for their work on the maps in this book, and to Jose Garcia for his research assistance.

As a student, I had the privilege of learning from gifted teachers and scholars. Lisa Jane Graham and Jim Krippner first encouraged me to go down this path and they continue to challenge and inspire me to this day. In graduate school, Jean-Christophe Agnew, Seth Fein, and Steve Pincus pushed me to think more broadly and deeply about my work. Stuart Schwartz has provided sage advice and a model for historical research and writing since my first day of graduate school. Pablo Piccato has been a sharp critic and a generous colleague throughout the life of this project. Finally, Gil Joseph is an unparalleled mentor, advocate, and friend.

Over the years, friends and colleagues provided feedback that made this book immeasurably better. Doug Cope kindly pointed me toward the guild records that helped me reconstruct the Baratillo's history in the eighteenth century. The participants of the Instituto Mora's La Ciudad de México: Pasado y Presente Seminar; the University of Chicago's Latin American History Workshop, particularly Brodwyn Fischer and Mauricio Tenorio; and the UTSA–Trinity University History Workshop helped me think about this project in new ways. Sophie Beal, Julie Kleinman, Eric Frith, Gisela Moncada, and Ingrid Bleynat read and commented on the manuscript, in whole or in part, at key moments in its development. I owe a special debt to Tatiana Seijas and Ted Beatty for their feedback and long-term engagement with this project. This book would not have been possible without Kate Marshall and Bradley Depew, my editors at UC Press.

At UT San Antonio, I have benefited from extraordinarily supportive colleagues, particularly Kirsten Gardner, Jerry González, Pat Kelly, Cathy Komisaruk, Gregg Michel, Catherine Nolan-Ferrell, and Jack Reynolds. Catherine Clinton has been a friend and a mentor since the first day of faculty orientation.

My friends encouraged and inspired me throughout the life of this project. Lisa Ubelaker Andrade, Ana Minian, Leslie Theibert, Luke Bassett, Scott Grinsell, and Caleb Linville made graduate school anything but solitary. Jason Johnson's loyal friendship and spirit of adventure has enlivened my time in Texas. My extended family—Ben Alschuler, Sophie Beal, Anna Bulbrook, Shannon Caspersen, Will Connors, Matt Heck, Prue Hyman, Andy Lapham, and Josh Pressman—has stood behind me for two decades.

Lastly, I thank my family for their unflinching support. My sister, Elissa, has looked after me from day one and provided reasoned advice at every turn. My nieces, Johanna and Miriam, never fail to bring a smile to my face. My mother, Kay, has offered love that knows no bounds. My late father, Ron, was my sounding board and my fiercest advocate. I owe so much to him. No person was a greater source of inspiration than my late brother, Jon. Although he did not get to see me complete this book, I could never have started it without him.

Austin, TX
August 2017

Introduction

IN AUGUST 2016, A GROUP of street vendors in the Mexico City neighborhood of Tepito submitted a request to the capital's mayor: they wanted to be included in the city's new constitution. At the time, a constituent congress was preparing to draft the constitution as part of a political reorganization that turned Mexico's Federal District into the country's thirty-second state, giving the capital city autonomy from the federal government for the first time since 1824. Interest groups from across the city weighed in, pressuring delegates to address their concerns and enshrine new rights. The vendors of Tepito, for their part, wanted the constitution to protect their right to sell in the street. In exchange, they offered the government a compromise: more than three thousand members of their vendor organization would "formalize" themselves—paying all the necessary taxes and submitting to the relevant regulation. That act, they assured the mayor, would produce at least three hundred million pesos in additional revenue to the government every year, a windfall for the administration and the capital's residents. Formalize our rights, the vendors promised, and we will formalize our businesses.[1]

Tepito is Mexico City's iconic *barrio bravo*—its most infamous rough neighborhood—and the reputed hub of its black market. It has a longstanding reputation for crime, poverty, and a culture of lawlessness. Its residents often pride themselves on their fierce resistance to government intrusion; "obstinate Tepito" is one of its monikers. The neighborhood has produced many of Mexico's most famous boxers, and it hosts one of the most prominent shrines to La Santa Muerte, the patron saint of drug traffickers and other criminals.[2] Tepito's oppositional identity is closely linked to the sprawling street market that fills its streets and sidewalks. Six days a week (the vendors rest on Tuesdays), thousands of consumers peruse clothing, electronics, and every type of household good imaginable underneath a web of multicolored plastic tarps. Many of those goods are pirated, which is to say illegally reproduced, or they are contraband, meaning they entered the country without payment of import taxes. This commerce forms part of Mexico's informal economy—the buying and selling that takes place off the books, outside the nation's regulatory system. Behind closed doors, more nefarious transactions unfold. Periodic police raids reveal distribution centers for arms and narcotics.[3] For all these reasons, writers have described Tepito as a place fully outside the law—"the land of no one, the center of uncontainable criminal power."[4] But Tepito does not exist in a world of its own, somehow detached from the rest of Mexican society. In reality, the men and women who make their living in extralegal street commerce have been central to the economic and political life of Mexico City for hundreds of years.

Tepito was not always the nucleus of Mexico City's black market. That reputation developed during the twentieth century, after a market called the Baratillo moved there. For three hundred years, the Baratillo—from the Spanish word *barato*, or cheap—was the city's principal marketplace for second-hand goods and its most notorious thieves' market. New and used manufactured products—including clothing, tools, furniture, and books—circulated alongside stolen jewelry, counterfeit coins, and illegal weapons. The Baratillo's reputation was every bit as sinister as Tepito's is today. Church officials in the eighteenth century called it "the center of wickedness" and "a refuge for lost men."[5] Exposés in Mexico's nineteenth-century press detailed the depravity of the market and the people who gathered there: one author called it "Hell's ante-room."[6] Authorities banned it on a number of occasions, yet the market outlasted every government of the colonial and early-national eras. Indeed, the Baratillo never went away: after moving to Tepito in 1902, the market gradually outgrew the confines of the plaza there and spread through the surrounding streets. By the mid-twentieth century, the Baratillo and Tepito were synonymous. Tepito had become the black-market barrio.

What explains the persistence of an institution that many Mexico City residents saw as a magnet for crime and a threat to the social order? Answering that question requires looking beyond government decrees and impressionistic accounts of the market to explore the shadowy networks that linked the Baratillo's vendors to mercantile and political elites in Mexico City. The Baratillo, it turns out, served far more people than criminals and the poor. In the colonial era, vendors in the market—*baratilleros*, as they were known—traded with some of the wealthiest overseas merchants in Mexico. In the nineteenth century, prominent newspaper publishers sided with vendors in their disputes with local and national authorities (despite the sensational stories those same papers printed about the crimes that took place in the market). Even the local government at times worked to keep the Baratillo in business. The vendors may have traded in stolen goods, but they paid rent to the city—revenue the municipal government, or Ayuntamiento, welcomed.[7] Baratilleros were not passive actors in these relationships. They sent petitions to government officials, filed lawsuits, curried favor with the press, and used the apparatuses of local and national government to assert the legitimacy of their trade and defend their right to practice it in public streets and plazas. Baratilleros possessed political capital—black market capital—that they employed with striking success. The Baratillo flourished for hundreds of years, then, because diverse actors conspired to preserve it. Those individuals forged alliances that extended from the streets to the halls of government to the pages of the capital's newspapers. The Baratillo was not simply a site for illicit economic exchange; it was also a place where men and women from across the social spectrum engaged in Mexican politics. In Mexico City, the black market was as much a political institution as it was an economic one.[8]

This book traces the history of the Baratillo from its first appearance in the historical record in the mid-seventeenth century through its relocation to Tepito at the beginning of the twentieth. In doing so, it sheds light on one of Mexico City's most enduring yet least-understood institutions. The Baratillo, like Tepito today, played an outsized role in the Mexican imagination, symbolizing everything that was criminal, dangerous, and lowly. It was the subject of the first important work of satire written in Mexico, the eighteenth-century "Ordenanzas del Baratillo," and it appears a number of times in José Joaquín Fernández de Lizardi's *El periquillo sarniento*—considered the first Latin American novel.[9] The eighteenth-century *Diccionario de gobierno y legislación de las Indias* defines "Baratillo" as an illicit marketplace in Mexico City, even though many other cities in Spanish America had their own *baratillos* (in this study, I capitalize Mexico City's Baratillo to distinguish it from the others).[10] Indeed, although the Baratillo, in its general form or purpose, was not unique to Mexico or even the Hispanic world—London had its Rag Fair and Lisbon its Feira da Ladra, to name just two examples—few other second-hand markets had the high profile or the staying power of Mexico City's Baratillo.[11] Despite the Baratillo's notoriety, longevity, and importance to the society and economy of Mexico City, this study is the first to reconstruct its history.[12]

In narrating the Baratillo's long history, this book contributes to our understanding of urban life in Mexico and Latin America in several ways. First, it reveals the centrality of extralegal commerce to the broader economy of Mexico City between the seventeenth and the twentieth centuries. The Baratillo was the hub of the city's shadow economy, which incorporated illicit, informal, as well as legal second-hand exchanges and engaged men and women of all backgrounds. These trade circuits flourished in the gray areas, or shadows, of Spanish and Mexican law. Second, the book highlights the multifaceted nature of the state in Mexico City. Baratilleros dealt with local, imperial, and national authorities that pursued different political agendas, some of which coincided with their own. The state in Mexico City was never a single actor but many competing ones, and vendors in the Baratillo used those rivalries to their advantage. Third, the book deepens our understanding of urban politics in Mexico City between the late-colonial era and the Mexican Revolution of 1910. The Baratillo did not survive solely because of the economic benefits it provided to urban residents; it also endured because the baratilleros used the political tools available to them in every era to assert its relevance. Vendors who trafficked in the shadow economy enjoyed a degree of access that historians have rarely observed among non-elite actors prior to the twentieth century. Fourth and lastly, the book offers a new perspective on urban public space in Mexico. The Baratillo's history shows that streets and plazas were not simply venues for conflict between elite and popular groups, as the traditional view holds. Nor did diverse individuals merely rub shoulders with one another in the Baratillo. Instead, the market plaza was a site where men and women from all walks of life exchanged goods and ideas.

THE SHADOW ECONOMY

The Baratillo played a vital role in the local economy. For over three hundred years, it provisioned Mexico City's consumers with textiles, tools, and household goods and provided employment to hundreds of vendors and their families at any given time.[13] While economic policies in Mexico shifted dramatically between the seventeenth and the twentieth centuries—from mercantilism to free trade to industrialization—the Baratillo's product mix remained remarkably constant.[14] No matter what political regime ruled the country or which economic paradigm its leaders adopted, Mexican consumers demanded the kinds of goods the Baratillo offered, regardless of their provenance.[15]

The Baratillo thrived in the contested space between legality and illegality. The market's very existence was a legal contradiction: royal and national authorities repeatedly banned it, yet local officials allowed it to continue, treating it, in some ways, as any other public marketplace. The transactions that took place in the Baratillo do not fit neatly into any single legal category, either. By reputation, it was the city's main distribution point for stolen, prohibited, or otherwise illicit goods—the trade that readers today know as the black market.[16] Yet some exchanges in the Baratillo did not violate any laws. Other transactions might fall under the modern-day category of the informal economy.[17] The Baratillo's opponents routinely complained that baratilleros did not pay taxes on their sales, and, during the colonial era, many vendors in the market sold outside the highly regulated channels of the guild system, which stipulated who had the right to sell a particular good and where. Although such actions were technically illegal, officials generally did not view them as antisocial—as threatening to the social peace.[18] Vendors and their advocates added further ambiguity by routinely challenging authorities' interpretation of the law. The Baratillo's history thus highlights the malleable boundary between legality and illegality and the ways that actors from across the social spectrum helped shape its contours.[19]

The Baratillo and the larger shadow economy of which it formed a part linked diverse individuals and institutions in Mexico City. While the Baratillo may have catered primarily to the city's poor and working classes, urban elites and individuals from the capital's middle sectors also benefited from it.[20] The shadow economy connected the Baratillo to pawnshops, artisans' workshops, import warehouses, and residents' homes. It involved Spaniards, Indians, and people of mixed race. Historians have previously shown that commerce in colonial Spanish American cities created economic and social ties between men and women of different backgrounds; this study suggests that those connections continued well after independence.[21]

The Baratillo's beneficiaries also included government officials. Public marketplaces produced large and relatively consistent revenue streams for Mexico City's Ayuntamiento, and municipal officials fiercely defended their jurisdiction over them. City council members often pushed back against colonial or national officials who tried to disband the Baratillo, fearing the loss of income that would result. Market administrators also had personal investments in the Baratillo. They typically earned salaries for overseeing the market, or a percentage of the fees they collected, and they received *gratificaciones*, or bribes, that vendors paid them to facilitate transfers of their stalls.

These were informal transactions that vendors and municipal officials institutionalized over time. The mere act of categorizing the Baratillo as a public marketplace and collecting rent from its vendors conferred a degree of legitimacy on those businesses. In these ways, agents of the state often did more to sustain the Baratillo than to rein it in.[22]

THE STATE

The involvement of state actors in the Baratillo reveals the limitations of the concept of "the state" itself for the study of Mexican history. There was no consistent state agenda when it came to the Baratillo. From the seventeenth to the twentieth centuries, authorities expressed ambivalence about the market. After furious attempts to disband it in the 1690s, the Spanish Crown made little effort to enforce those prohibitions in the eighteenth century, even as it intervened aggressively in many other areas of Mexico's economy and society. National-era governments followed the same pattern, issuing edicts that ordered the market to disappear only to rescind or forget about them later. Local officials, charged with regulating the day-to-day affairs of the city and providing public services to its residents, rarely shared the same priorities as national ones. Some had personal relationships with the baratilleros, forming patronage networks that mixed business and politics. The varied and often conflicting objectives of authorities in Mexico City meant that baratilleros never confronted a unitary government. This book thus disaggregates the state, seeing it not as a single actor but many competing ones.

Rivalries between government authorities in the capital, particularly between local and national officials, date to the colonial period, when members of the Ayuntamiento, dominated by American-born Creoles, clashed with peninsular officials over local affairs. The friction continued after Mexico's independence from Spain as national officials gradually whittled away at the Ayuntamiento's autonomy. And those same tensions lie at the heart of the twenty-first-century effort to transform the Federal District into a state with its own constitution—the campaign into which vendors in Tepito inserted themselves in 2016.[23] Baratilleros, in fact, found themselves at the center of debates over local autonomy many times over the centuries. Vendors in the market understood those intragovernmental rivalries and used them to their advantage by playing local and national officials against one another. Mexico City's institutional dynamics played an important role in the Baratillo's history, and understanding them is key to making sense of the market's persistence.[24]

This study highlights the importance of municipal government, which often receives short shrift from historians. While national authorities developed the ambitious plans that draw most scholars' attention, local officials enacted many of the policies that had the greatest impact on people's lives. Municipal officials also had the most interaction with subjects and citizens. The Ayuntamiento was the principal vehicle through which vendors in the Baratillo expressed their grievances.[25] Throughout the eighteenth, nineteenth, and early twentieth centuries, baratilleros petitioned, lobbied, and collaborated with officials on the Ayuntamiento. They did not simply resist government attempts to regulate or quash their market; they used Mexico City's institutions to access the urban political arena and exert influence over government decision making.[26]

URBAN POLITICS

The letter the vendors in Tepito sent to Mexico City's mayor in 2016 built on a long tradition of political engagement. Baratilleros had been political players in Mexico City since the colonial era. In the eighteenth century, they petitioned colonial authorities using the political vernacular of the day, asserting that their trade served the common good, and, during the Enlightenment, public utility. They were not pursuing ideological agendas with these efforts; rather, they were using the political tools available to them under the Spanish monarchy to protect or advance their material interests and assert their rights to the city.[27] After Mexico's independence from Spain in 1821, vendors quickly adopted the political mechanisms that republican rule offered.[28] They demanded, as citizens and constituents, that local officials uphold their obligations to provide adequate policing and infrastructure for public markets. They lobbied elected officials on the Ayuntamiento for support when government initiatives endangered their businesses, and they threatened to vote uncooperative council members out of office. Vendors also engaged in the capital's emerging public sphere. In 1842, the baratilleros printed a combative letter to the Ayuntamiento in *El Siglo Diez y Nueve*, the country's leading liberal newspaper of the era, seeking to gain public support in a dispute with the Ayuntamiento. They continued to use the press, forming alliances with sympathetic editors and publishers, throughout the nineteenth century. They deftly navigated both the colonial and republican-era judicial systems.

In charting this course, the baratilleros benefited from important allies. Although critics of the Baratillo penned thousands of pages of diatribes about the market over the centuries, other residents of Mexico City, including elected officials and other members of the political elite, offered quieter but equally consistent support for the vendors. In nearly every controversy that engulfed the Baratillo, individuals raised their voices in defense of the baratilleros. Some had economic interests in the market. They may have owned a business in the Baratillo or a store nearby or had other financial dealings with baratilleros. In other cases, defending the Baratillo advanced a political agenda, as it did for Vicente García Torres, publisher of the newspaper *El Monitor Republicano*, who used the Baratillo as a poster child for the liberal principles of free trade and individual rights in the early 1870s. Baratilleros formed patronage networks that served the interests of elite, middling, and popular actors in the capital.[29]

In other cases, the baratilleros' supporters had no obvious material motivation. Those individuals expressed a paternalistic sympathy for the downtrodden that extended even to vendors in the city's thieves' market. Although historians typically associate those sentiments with the consensual politics of the old regime, they did not disappear after Mexico's independence from Spain. Throughout the nineteenth century, government officials, newspaper editors, and other urban residents expressed a concern for the well-being of the baratilleros. These were attitudes that cut across partisan lines and continued throughout the Porfiriato, a period that scholars often identify with technocratic government and social Darwinism. In their petitions and letters to the press, vendors played to these sentiments. They stressed their poverty and vulnerability and chastised opponents for their callousness. Throughout the Baratillo's history, efforts to eliminate or further marginalize the market competed with these expressions of support, which the vendors themselves engendered.[30]

This discourse of poverty, however, masks a more complicated social reality. Many of the vendors in the Baratillo were not, in fact, poor. Some operated substantial businesses. Many had backgrounds in the skilled trades, and, as a whole, they were relatively well educated.[31] The nature of their trade, which skirted taxes and other regulatory hurdles, offered the potential for significant profit. Those factors, combined with the fact that baratilleros, unlike other street vendors, were predominately male, helped them gain access to Mexico's political arena.[32] While many vendors sent petitions to local and national authorities, only baratilleros seem to have succeeded in getting theirs published in the press in the nineteenth century. That they did so as early as the 1840s, a period when historians generally view the public sphere as restricted to the country's *letrados*, or lettered men, is extraordinary.[33] Other vendors did not have the same clout prior to the twentieth century.[34] This study reveals much about the lives of men and women who made their living on the streets of Mexico City. But it also tells a story that is unique to those who trafficked in the shadow economy.

Baratilleros' political tactics produced a remarkable record of nonviolent resolutions. Indeed, one of the most surprising aspects of the Baratillo's history is how infrequently tensions between vendors and government officials led to physical confrontations. Vendors were able to achieve their goals, or at least mitigate the negative effects of decisions that went against them, by negotiating with authorities. Their success in keeping the market in operation for centuries without resorting to violence may hold clues for understanding how, during eras when much of rural Mexico became embroiled in revolution, Mexico City largely avoided it.[35] The politics of the Mexico City street, where vendors in the thieves' market routinely bargained with local and national authorities, produced compromise far more often than conflict.

THE STREET

In uncovering the political and economic relationships that tied baratilleros to other actors in Mexico City, this book challenges traditional views about the role of public streets and plazas in Latin American society. Historians have long viewed streets and plazas as sites where modernizing elites clashed with recalcitrant popular groups—where the poor resisted, through protest or subtler strategies, elite attempts to assert control over public spaces that were essential to their work and social lives.[36] But the Baratillo's history suggests that a far wider swath of local residents engaged in Mexico City's street economies than the most vulnerable and that vendors did more than protest government policies they found problematic. Furthermore, the capital's governing elites rarely agreed on how to manage its public spaces. While imperial and national authorities wanted clean, orderly streets and plazas where troops could exercise, people and goods could move freely, and leaders could display their power for the public, members of the Ayuntamiento, which depended on rent from the vendors who occupied those public spaces, often saw things differently. They defended the Ayuntamiento's jurisdiction over public markets, plazas, and thoroughfares against interference from higher authorities, which in some cases meant defending the baratilleros. The Baratillo's history provides little support for the idea that urban elites made a consistent or unified effort to eliminate elements of urban popular culture they found distasteful.[37]

Nor were the baratilleros united in opposition to the government. Prior to the twentieth century, vendors in the market were loosely organized, if they were organized at all. There was no guild to create a common identity or common cause among the baratilleros, and no clear leadership structure.[38] Internal dissension was common, and competing vendor factions often sought help from government officials to gain advantage over their rivals within the market. Far from a site that drew neat battle lines between rich and poor, the Baratillo was a venue where elite, middling, and popular actors forged alliances that cut across class and ethnic lines.

If cross-class collaboration helped sustain the Baratillo, it did little to attack the underlying inequalities that created the market in the first place. The seventeenth-century Baratillo, like Tepito in the twenty-first century, was a place where men and women made their living on the street, at the law's margins, with few rights to protect their livelihoods. For hundreds of years, the Baratillo operated in this liminal state—tolerated, but never legal. The Tepito vendors' 2016 request for constitutional protection illustrates the precariousness of their trade and the contingent nature of their rights. The Baratillo's existence was always provisional—a negotiated arrangement that could come apart at any moment.[39]

SOURCES

The shadow economy, by its very nature, leaves little behind for historians to study. Transactions take place off the books and outside the view of regulators and record keepers. But the Baratillo, as a public marketplace and a site that attracted frequent attention from authorities, left a paper trail. Over three hundred years, the market generated thousands of pages of government correspondence, vendor petitions, market censuses, travelers' accounts, newspaper articles, and notarial and judicial records. These sources provide an entry point for the study of individuals and economic exchanges that have long eluded historians. Yet the window they open is frustratingly narrow, and it opens and shuts abruptly with changes to Mexico's institutional landscape. Guild records, for example, paint a vivid picture of the Baratillo's commerce during the eighteenth century. When the guilds lost their monopolies and their investigative authority in the early nineteenth century, however, that documentary trail goes cold. Newspapers and municipal market records fill its place, though inadequately. Indeed, although the extant documentation on the Baratillo provides a glimpse of Mexico City's shadow economy, much remains hidden from view. Quantitative data, beyond inconsistent registers of the rent the vendors paid to the city, are almost nonexistent. Apart from occasional references, there is little record of the prices vendors charged their customers, much less the volume of their sales. Demographic information about the market's vendors and customers is even more elusive.[40] What is evident, however, is that the Baratillo played an indispensable role in Mexico City's economy for centuries—providing jobs for vendors and basic household goods to consumers. The vendors turned that economic clout into political capital, ensuring that the black market never went out of business.

CHAPTER OUTLINE

This book contains six chapters. The first three deal with the late colonial period, from the mid-seventeenth century to the early nineteenth century, while chapters 4 through 6 examine the post independence era to the Mexican Revolution of 1910. This chronology challenges traditional periodizations in the historiography of Mexico and Latin America, which compartmentalize the colonial and national eras into separate fields of inquiry. The Baratillo's history resists such neat divisions. Both the Baratillo and the Ayuntamiento, the body charged with overseeing it, were colonial-era institutions that survived the transition from imperial to republican rule. The *longue-durée* approach of this study provides fresh insight into how nationhood and republican politics transformed old-regime institutions and the people who relied on them—and how they did not.[41]

Chapter 1, "A Pernicious Commerce," examines the efforts of New Spain's last Habsburg viceroys to eliminate the Baratillo in the late 1680s and 1690s, focusing on their response to the 1692 riot that ravaged the Plaza Mayor. Following the riot, Spanish authorities sought to reengineer the Plaza Mayor, forcing the Baratillo out and replacing it with a masonry *alcaicería*—later known as the Parián—that was designed for the capital's elite import merchants. The chapter explores why colonial authorities found the Baratillo so troubling, how they sought to eliminate it, and why that effort ultimately failed.

Chapter 2, "The Baratillo and the Enlightened City," examines the Baratillo's role in eighteenth-century reforms to Mexico City's public administration and its built environment. While New Spain's Bourbon rulers took a number of steps to transform the physical and social worlds of Mexico City's poor, the government never targeted the Baratillo—a site that was synonymous with crime, license, and plebeian sociability. To understand this apparent contradiction, the chapter examines the politics of urban reform in eighteenth-century Mexico City, which saw royal, viceregal, and local authorities jostle for control over urban public spaces.

Chapter 3, "Shadow Economics," moves from an analysis of elite debates over urban renewal policies to an examination of the quotidian transactions that took place in and around the Baratillo in the eighteenth and early nineteenth centuries. The shadow economy linked the baratilleros to some of Mexico's elite overseas merchants while pitting them against the capital's artisan guilds and shopkeepers, who saw them as disloyal competition. In reconstructing these relationships, the chapter reveals the centrality of the Baratillo's commerce to the late-colonial urban economy. It also illustrates the ways that economics and politics intertwined in the market, as vendors pursued multiple strategies to protect their businesses from outside threats.

Chapter 4, "The Dictator, the Ayuntamiento, and the Baratillo," takes readers into the national period with a focus on a largely forgotten urban renewal campaign that the nineteenth-century strongman Antonio López de Santa Anna and the Mexico City Ayuntamiento undertook in the early 1840s. Removing the Baratillo was central to Santa Anna's ambitious, if short-lived, reform agenda. He encountered resistance, however, from baratilleros who pushed back by writing petitions and airing their grievances in the Mexico City press—decades before historians have found popular actors engaging in Mexico's public sphere. The episode shows how the laws and the rhetoric of republicanism gave vendors new tools to defend their businesses against government policies that threatened them.

Chapter 5, "Free Trading in the Restored Republic," focuses on an 1872 court case that divided vendors in the Baratillo and pitted them against the Mexico City Ayuntamiento. The case drew the attention of some of Mexico's most prominent citizens, including Vicente García Torres, publisher of *El Monitor Republicano*, the leading newspaper of the era, and reached Mexico's

Supreme Court, sparking a constitutional crisis. The case shows the improbable range of actors in Mexico City who had stakes in the Baratillo and the degree to which the market's vendors succeeded in turning a debate over its future into a national conversation about individual rights and the rule of law.

The sixth chapter, "Order, Progress, and the Black Market," examines the Baratillo's awkward fit within Porfirian Mexico City, when the country's autocratic president Porfirio Díaz sought to modernize the nation and its capital city in the late nineteenth and early twentieth centuries. It focuses on the events that led to the Baratillo's relocation to the neighborhood of Tepito, in 1902. Facing the threat of the market's closure, the baratilleros bargained with the municipal government, reaching a compromise to move to Tepito—a location the vendors proposed themselves. The chapter contributes to recent scholarship that revises earlier depictions of the Porfiriato as a monolithic dictatorship, emphasizing instead the multiple ways that Mexico's government and citizens maintained a tense and unequal peace for more than thirty years.

The epilogue, "The Baratillo and Tepito," briefly traces the intertwined histories of the Baratillo and the neighborhood of Tepito in the twentieth century. Like many other decisions regarding the Baratillo, its move to Tepito was supposed to be temporary. Yet the market remained, and over the decades it grew into a sprawling marketplace for second-hand, stolen, contraband, and pirated goods that consumed the neighborhood. By the middle of the century, Mexico City newspapers rarely referred to the Baratillo by name; instead, they used the same disparaging language that observers had traditionally employed to describe the Baratillo for the neighborhood itself. Today, Tepito is the most famous barrio in Mexico, with a distinctive oppositional identity that is inextricably tied to its role as the epicenter of Mexico City's black market.

ONE

A Pernicious Commerce

The Baratillo shall be eradicated, banished, and exterminated so that there is not a single baratillero left, under penalty of death.

JUAN ORTEGA Y MONTAÑÉZ,
Viceroy of New Spain, March 30, 1696

ON THE AFTERNOON OF JUNE 8, 1692, a line formed outside of Mexico City's municipal granary. Hundreds of people had gathered there in hopes of buying corn, but there was not nearly enough. After a poor harvest, the city was suffering from an acute grain shortage. Tempers began to flare, so officials allowed some of those waiting outside to enter the granary to verify that it was empty. Inside, an Indian woman fell to the ground after she fainted or, according to other accounts, an official struck her. Members of the crowd, comprised mainly of Indians but also *castas*—people of mixed race—and some Spaniards, picked the woman up and carried her on their shoulders through the city's Plaza Mayor. Claiming she had died from her injuries (a fact elite observers later disputed), they went to the home of the city's *corregidor*, or local magistrate, demanding justice, and then on to the other seats of authority that ringed the plaza. They walked to the home of the archbishop, who refused to see them, and then to the royal palace, where, finding the viceroy not at home, they began pelting the building with stones and chanting "Death to the viceroy and the corregidor!"

According to the most famous account of the riot, by the Creole intellectual Carlos de Sigüenza y Góngora, the crowd then carried the woman through the Baratillo, the sprawling market for second-hand goods located in the middle of the plaza. They did so, according to Sigüenza y Góngora, "in order to incite the *zaramullos*"—the scoundrels who congregated there—and draw them into the fight. With help from the zaramullos, the protest devolved into a full-fledged riot as more than ten thousand people, by Sigüenza y Góngora's estimation, filled the square. Soon the rioters were carting matting from the reed-roofed market stalls to set ablaze in front of the palace door. As the flames spread through the building, the rioters set fire to the Ayuntamiento, the seat of municipal government, and then the markets and shops located in and around the plaza. Looters, led by people from the Baratillo, broke the locks on the stores and took whatever merchandise they could get their hands on before the fire consumed them. By the time it was all over, the riot had taken the lives of at least fifty people and caused more than three million pesos in damage.[1]

The riot, one of only two major uprisings in Mexico City during the colonial era, reverberated through the government. Officials responded with a broad crackdown. They executed fifteen people for their participation in the riot—an extraordinary use of capital punishment in a society where authorities preferred more utilitarian punishments.[2] They shuttered the city's *pulquerias* (taverns that served *pulque*, a Mesoamerican alcoholic beverage); ordered Indians living in the city center to return to the *barrios*, the peripheral neighborhoods designated for native residences; and prohibited Indians from wearing Spanish clothing.[3] And they banned the Baratillo. Officials had long complained that the market's maze of improvised stalls provided cover to criminals. Now, officials worried, those spaces were fomenting acts of subversion—a threat to Spanish rule itself.

In the weeks following the riot, officials with the Spanish Crown and Mexico City's Ayuntamiento began to formulate plans to dramatically reengineer the Plaza Mayor, a design, they hoped, that would prevent a repeat of the events of June 8.[4] Removing the Baratillo was central to authorities' vision of the redesigned plaza. The Baratillo's role in the explosion of violence that June evening lent a new sense of urgency to the government's efforts to stamp out the trade, which authorities had banned at least three times even before the riot. Indeed, when Spain's King Charles II approved plans for a new merchant exchange in the Plaza Mayor, he did so in hopes that "with the greater concourse of merchants, the excesses ... of the zaramullos of the Baratillo will be reined in."[5] Merchants would replace vendors, and respectable subjects would supplant thieves.

The project represented the Crown's first concerted attempt to alter the physical design and social composition of Mexico City's main square since the 1520s, when the Spanish began construction of a new city atop the ruins of the Aztec capital, Tenochtitlán. That undertaking, like the other measures the colonial government adopted immediately after the riot, enjoyed limited and fleeting success. Spanish authorities failed to prevent the Baratillo from returning to the plaza, where it would remain until the end of the eighteenth century. And the markets of the Plaza Mayor continued to attract vendors and consumers of all stripes—from the humblest to the most privileged. Their plan failed because Mexico City elites were not of one mind about the Baratillo, or the Plaza Mayor markets in general. This chapter examines the events leading up to and following the 1692 riot, revealing the fissures that divided agents working at different levels of government in the viceregal capital. Those tensions benefited the vendors of the Baratillo, helping them to weather an effort by Spain's highest authorities to banish their commerce.

THE PLAZA MAYOR AND ITS MARKETS

After the Spanish and their indigenous allies conquered Tenochtitlán in 1521, Hernán Cortés ordered a Spanish plaza constructed in the footprint of the city's ceremonial center. Over the course of the sixteenth century, the Spanish gradually replaced the indigenous structures that ringed the square with their own. On the east side of the plaza, Cortés built his residence, Las Casas Nuevas, on the ruins of the Aztec emperor Moctezuma's palace. The Crown later purchased that property from Cortés's son Martín and converted the building into the viceregal palace. In 1532, the Spanish constructed the Ayuntamiento on the south side of the plaza behind the main canal leading out of the city.[6] On the northern edge of the plaza, Cortés ordered the city's cathedral raised on the site where the Great Temple of the Mexica (the ethnic group that ruled Tenochtitlán and dominated the Aztec Empire) had stood.[7]

Although the Mexica ceremonial center, with its temples, palaces, and rectilinear shape, provided the template for the Spaniards' Plaza Mayor, it lacked one element that became central to the Spanish plaza: a marketplace. Tenochtitlán, like its sister city Tlatelolco, possessed a large and vibrant marketplace. However, that market was located on the southwestern side of the city, not in the ceremonial center.[8] In Spain, however, a town's central plaza had long doubled as administrative center and marketplace.[9] Situating the marketplace within eyesight of local authorities made it easier to oversee.[10] The placement also offered fiscal benefits: the Spanish plaza was a municipal space, owned by the local government, where the ayuntamiento would charge rent to market vendors and shopkeepers and use that revenue to fund its basic functions. With this purpose in mind, in 1527 Spain's King Charles I gave six

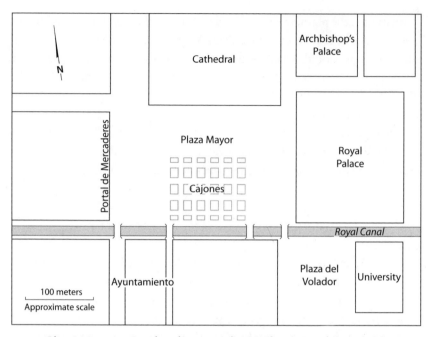

MAP 1. Plaza Mayor, 1596. Based on the 1596 rendering, *Plaza Mayor de la ciudad de México y de los edificios y calles adyacentes*, located in Spain's Archivo General de Indias. Ministerio de Educación, Cultura y Deporte, AGI, MP-México, 47. Map created by Bill Keller.

solares (house lots) to the Ayuntamiento of Mexico City, established five years earlier, so that it could build a consistory, jail, meat market, and shops. The Ayuntamiento subsequently took control of the *portales* (archways) in front of the houses that lined the west side of the plaza in order to build shops there as well, again for the purpose of generating tax revenue.[11] This space came to be known as the Portal de Mercaderes and housed many of the city's finest shops throughout the colonial period. We do not know when, precisely, vendors of food staples and basic household goods began to fill the Plaza Mayor. That transition appears to have occurred gradually, over the course of the sixteenth century, as Spaniards slowly assumed control over quotidian aspects of local governance like food distribution, which had remained in indigenous hands for decades after the conquest.[12]

By the early seventeenth century, however, so many vendors had congregated in the Plaza Mayor that Spanish authorities feared they were sowing chaos. In 1609, the viceroy of New Spain, Luis de Velasco, complained that *buhoneros*, or ambulatory vendors, were crowding the square and leading to "much disorder," leaving it utterly "without policing." Velasco charged the city's corregidor and two representatives from the Ayuntamiento with collecting rent from the vendors—money that would accrue to the municipal government. He made this arrangement possible by transferring ownership of the Plaza Mayor from the Crown to the Ayuntamiento. The viceroy's decree, which King Philip III sanctioned in 1611, ended the practice of granting royal licenses to individual *mesilleros*—the petty merchants who set up tables in the central square—and gave the local government the authority to charge vendors rent so that it could augment "the small quantity of *propios* [income-producing municipal properties] that this city had" and help pay for "the expenses of fiestas and other things that are offered every year" in the city.[13] Street vendors were now the responsibility of the municipal government, not the Crown.

This seemingly mundane bureaucratic transfer had significant ramifications. Rent from the Plaza Mayor markets became the bedrock of the Ayuntamiento's annual budget, and members of the city council became fiercely protective of the site. Yet Crown officials, it turned out, were not willing to surrender full control of the most prominent public space in the viceregal capital to local authorities and continued to dictate how they wanted the plaza used. From this point forward, the Plaza Mayor served as both a venue for the performance of royal power—through public celebrations, Inquisition trials, and executions—and a cash cow for the local government. Those competing roles created tensions between the local and royal governments that endured throughout the colonial era.

When, precisely, the Baratillo became part of the Plaza Mayor's commerce is unclear. There does not appear to have been a precedent for this type of second-hand market in Tenochtitlán prior to the arrival of the Spaniards.[14] Baratillos did exist, however, in Madrid. In the second half of the sixteenth century, there was a baratillo in that city's Plaza Mayor and in other plazas around the city.[15] The first evidence of Mexico City's Baratillo surfaces in a decree that banned the market, in 1635. That document, however, did not survive, and we know of its existence only because a file from the end of the seventeenth century refers to it.[16] The oldest surviving source dates to 1644. This, too, was an order for the Baratillo to disband, or at least for its principal activity of the period—selling ironware—to cease.[17] The Baratillo's history, then, seems to parallel the growth of other forms of commerce in the Plaza Mayor—beginning, perhaps, as early as the second half of the sixteenth century and flourishing in the seventeenth, as the Spanish gradually solidified their control over the production and distribution of basic goods in the local economy. It comprised one section of the sprawling market complex in the plaza that was populated by semi-enclosed wooden stalls with thatched roofs (*cajones*), smaller, open-air *puestos*, portable tables (mesillas), and ambulatory vendors known as buhoneros or *mercachifles*. The impermanent nature of the Baratillo's stands and tables meant that it probably migrated to different locations in the plaza over the course of the seventeenth century.

By the 1680s, the Baratillo had become a major problem for Spanish officials. Its reputation for lawlessness fanned fears that crime in Mexico City was spiraling out of control. It even drew the attention of King Charles II.[18] On August 31, 1688, the king sent a letter to the incoming viceroy of New Spain, the Count of Galve, asking for his recommendation on whether the government should permanently disband the Baratillo. A letter that Simón Ibáñez, an *alcalde del crimen*, or judge on Mexico City's highest criminal court, had sent to the king a year earlier had prompted the inquiry. Ibáñez painted the Baratillo as a grave threat to public welfare. He argued that the tolerance that previous viceroys had extended toward the baratilleros needed to cease, because the market was providing refuge for "idle people and vagabonds" every day of the year, even on the most solemn holidays. Ibáñez urged his superiors to ban the Baratillo immediately to stop further crimes before they occurred.[19] On November 19, 1689, the viceroy rendered his decision, ordering that: "No person of any state or quality, on any day of the year, may attend said Baratillo, nor sell, trade, or contract any good that until now has been bought there, whether new or used, or of any other sort, nor can they do so with the pretext of selling any of the adornments . . . chairs, blankets, stirrups . . . or jewels that were typically furnished there."[20] The consequences for those caught violating the ban were steep: confiscation of their wares, one hundred lashes for the first offense, two hundred for the second, and deportation to the Philippines for six years of hard labor for the third. As for the Indians who sold "*obras de sus manos*" (handmade goods), whom the criminal court had recommended be allowed to remain in the Baratillo, Galve banned them from selling there as well—under punishment of forced servitude in the city's *obrajes*, or textile workshops.[21] No one, regardless of race or ethnicity, could attend this market.

Colonial officials frequently complained that the Baratillo was the city's main distribution point for stolen jewelry, clothing, iron tools, and virtually anything else that had resale value. The viceroy Count of Salvatierra's 1644 prohibition of the Baratillo describes how the market offered a venue for slaves and servants to easily dispose of the items they stole from the houses of their masters and employers, undetected by authorities.[22] There, vendors would pass off those goods to witting or unwitting customers at a fraction of their "true value." Or, as Ibáñez noted sometimes occurred, "the owner would find the thief selling what he had taken" from his victim.[23] The authorities struggled to apprehend the culprits who traded "furtively" in these goods; at first sight of officials, they would simply hide them underneath their cloaks.[24]

The presence of vagabonds in the Baratillo only added to authorities' suspicions that the marketplace was a den of criminal activity. As men who lacked a specific trade or occupation that anchored them in a particular community, vagabonds were a source of anxiety for all European governments in the early modern period. In sixteenth-century New Spain, the Crown saw vagrancy as a threat to the precarious control it exerted over its vast new possessions. To assert its sovereignty over the subject populations of the Americas, Spain needed to establish a permanent settler population. The Crown passed legislation, to little effect, encouraging Spaniards to take up farming in order to create a more lasting attachment to the land.[25] Royal officials worried about what the conquistadors would do once they were no longer needed as soldiers. The single men that the conquest had attracted, if they could not be lured into settling down to work the land, were apt to become rootless and engage in pernicious and exploitative relationships—both economic and sexual—with indigenous people. Thus, although the Crown also worried about indigenous mobility—creating *reducciones* to concentrate Indian populations in new towns—Spanish vagabonds presented a special problem for colonial authorities. Not only did they challenge the permanence of the colonial project; their mixing with Indians and Africans also challenged the coherence of the "two republics" system that Spain had implemented to govern its subjects.

TWO REPUBLICS CONVERGE

The Spanish established the separate *república de españoles* and *república de indios* in the mid-sixteenth century in order to protect the indigenous population from the abuses of Spaniards, Africans, and mixed-bloods and to better provide Indians with a Christian education. Indians were to be governed by their own institutions, though in all cases overseen by Spanish officials and ultimately subject to the authority of the Real Audiencia (the highest court in New Spain) and the viceroy. In Mexico City, a physical segregation accompanied the legal distinction between the Spanish and Indian republics. The Crown stipulated that the Spanish population concentrate in a thirteen-square-block area surrounding the Plaza Mayor, called the *traza*, while the indigenous population would reside in barrios outside the traza, administered by semiautonomous Indian governments.[26] This segregation proved impossible to enforce, however, since Spanish businesses and households depended on indigenous labor and often required their employees to live in their places of work. Some Spaniards also chose to live in the barrios.[27]

Miscegenation created additional problems. To address the rapidly growing population of mixed-race offspring of Indians, Spaniards, and Africans, the Crown developed the *sistema de castas*, a hierarchical ordering of colonial subjects according to their proportion of Spanish blood. At its height, the system identified over forty racial categories, though in practice only eight or so of these saw widespread use: *español* (Spaniard), *indio* (Indian), *mestizo* (offspring of a Spaniard and an Indian), *castizo* (Spaniard-mestizo), *negro* (of African descent), *mulato* (Spaniard-African), *morisco* (mulatto-Spaniard), and *chino* (Asian).[28] Yet the word *sistema*—system—overstates the coherence of those efforts, and recent scholarship has emphasized just how fluid those categories were and how inconsistently colonial authorities applied them.[29] The criteria for belonging to these groups were subjective: dress, occupation, and behavior could be as significant as skin color or lineage in determining who fell into which category. While the Inquisition often looked to parish records to determine the race of an accused subject, local priests tended to rely on the self-declarations of parents when composing birth registries.[30] Over time, miscegenation only made distinguishing between the different groups more difficult. Even if these racial categories were porous and negotiable, however, they nonetheless represented an ideal that Spanish authorities clung to: a society in which they could recognize, and appropriately categorize, all of their subjects.

The Plaza Mayor markets, which brought wealthy Spanish overseas merchants, indigenous food vendors, and baratilleros of every background into the same space, defied that vision. Along with the Baratillo, a nighttime market in the plaza known as the *tianguillo* aroused particular concern among local authorities. In 1680, the Mexico City corregidor worried about the dangerous mix of people that was meeting in this nocturnal marketplace, which "brought together runaway slaves, mestizos, Indians, and even Spaniards into a concourse with women ... and in many cases it was not possible to tell whether they were single or married." The Plaza Mayor markets were supposed to close at eight in the evening, but this one routinely went until ten or eleven, providing cover for many "offenses against God." There were "regular meetings of scandalous women and men carrying weapons."[31] The Baratillo attracted a similarly varied group of people. In virtually every judicial proceeding involving the market, the subjects involved included Indians, Spaniards, and people of mixed race. Authorities frequently referenced the market's diverse composition, describing the *"gente de todas calidades"* (people of all qualities) that gathered there as evidence of the threat it posed to the social peace.[32]

Although the mixing of races and genders in the Plaza Mayor markets unnerved Spanish authorities in Mexico City, for most of the colonial era, they made little effort to stop it. The local economy was too reliant on crosscultural exchanges—with non-Spaniards involved in virtually all aspects of commerce and production—for officials to keep those groups separate from one another. In the wake of the 1692 riot, however, that is precisely what Spanish officials sought to do.

THE BARATILLO AND THE 1692 RIOT

In the months following the riot, Spanish officials, led by Viceroy Galve, conducted an exhaustive investigation into its causes. Galve believed the root problem lay with the comingling of Indians with Spaniards, Africans, and people of mixed race in the traza.[33] Several weeks after the riot, Galve formed a committee of parish priests, which also included Sigüenza y Góngora, to analyze "the difficulties that result from Indians living in the center of the city." The report found that the practice "has impeded the order of the city and the governance of its natives." The priests wrote that, "hidden in back patios and recesses of these houses, where it is not easy to find them, these Indians live in the company of mestizos and vagabonds, secretly scheming such savage iniquities as those that have been recently carried out." In the words of one parish priest, the "bad customs and idleness" of the mestizos, mulattos, and Africans had rubbed off on Mexico City's Indians by living in close proximity to them. The priests wanted to be able to identify their indigenous parishioners to ensure that they fulfilled their obligations to the Church.[34] For Galve and the colonial government, however, distinguishing between colonial subjects of different racial backgrounds was important in its own right. It was essential for the proper policing of the city. Galve gave Mexico City's Indians twenty days to return to their barrios and threatened any resident of the traza who let Indians into his home with a hefty 100-peso fine and two years of exile from the city.[35]

Galve's committee believed that the ethnically heterogeneous Baratillo had provided the spark for the riot. Both Sigüenza y Góngora and another, anonymous, witness suggested that the crowd of Indians that had gathered in the Plaza Mayor only became violent after it passed through the Baratillo. Under interrogation, the witness described how the "contemptible people of the Baratillo—mulattos, mestizos, and other zaramullos" joined forces with the Indians carrying the purportedly dead woman on their shoulders.[36] In his letter to Admiral Pez, Sigüenza y Góngora stated, on more than one occasion, that it was the people in the Baratillo who initiated the looting of the Plaza Mayor shops that night: "I have said that the zaramullos of the Baratillo accompanied [the Indians] from the moment they passed through the market with the *india* who pretended to be dead." "While the Indians set the fire," he continued, the zaramullos "began breaking down the doors and roofs [of the shops], which were very flimsy, and carrying away the cash and merchandise they found there."[37] The baratilleros had taken advantage of the protest to make away with what was not theirs.

Trial records offer further, albeit circumstantial, evidence that baratilleros were participants in the riot. The majority of those convicted for their involvement were artisans. In the seventeenth and eighteenth centuries, Mexico City's artisans simultaneously battled the Baratillo and sustained it, as the market provided an illegal outlet for selling manufactured goods in which both guild members and unaffiliated individuals participated. Indeed, one of the individuals colonial authorities identified as a leader of the riot, an Indian man named Joseph, was a hat maker whom other witnesses had seen selling in the Baratillo. In all, four tailors, seven or eight hat makers, and ten shoemakers were implicated in the riot. These were all professions with a significant presence in the Baratillo.[38]

The multiethnic composition of the riot, which Indians led but involved men and women of every caste, motivated colonial officials to realize the urban plan that Cortés had sought to impose on the ruins of Tenochtitlán nearly two centuries earlier. Galve ordered the city's Indians "back" to their barrios, where many probably had never lived, and enforced sumptuary laws regulating Indians' clothing that residents had similarly ignored for generations. His actions exemplified what Inga Clendinnen called the "chronic utopianism of Spanish colonial legislation"—Spaniards' belief that they could shape American society through laws they had little ability to enforce.[39]

That the viceroy felt the need to delineate the boundaries of the traza, street-by-street, in his July 10, 1692, decree ordering Indians to relocate to the barrios suggests how little meaning that designation held for residents of Mexico City at the end of the seventeenth century.[40] The impracticality of these measures did little to deter Galve; indeed, beyond enforcing imaginary boundaries, he sought to dramatically redesign the Plaza Mayor in order to limit the kinds of dangerous interactions that he believed had led to the uprising.

While the riot and the resulting fire caused extensive damage to the Plaza Mayor markets and the surrounding buildings, they also provided the government with a clean slate—an opportunity to re-create the plaza from scratch. A little more than a week after the riot, Mexico City's Ayuntamiento, charged with carrying out the reconstruction, outlined a plan for rebuilding the Plaza Mayor that called for the construction of two rows of stores with iron doors similar to those that lined the plaza on its southern and western borders. The motivations for replacing the plaza's market stalls with a new structure made of stone were fourfold: to reduce the risk of fire by replacing wooden stands with a more fire-resistant material; to improve the aesthetic appearance of the plaza, leaving it "free, spacious, uncluttered, and controlled"; to attract businesses that would increase tax revenues for the local government; and finally, to change the social composition of the vendors and customers who occupied the space.[41] To achieve all of these goals, the first step was eliminating the Baratillo.

Although the fire of June 1692 had destroyed or badly damaged the stores of the plaza's more established merchants, it had less effect on the Baratillo, where the more portable nature of its stands made them easier to replace. The market appears to have been humming only a month after the riot, and by the summer of 1693 authorities were complaining of an "incomprehensible number of baratilleros" peddling their wares in the plaza "at all hours of the day."[42] In July of that year, Viceroy Galve complained that previous orders for the Baratillo's closure "have not led to the just and proper extirpation of the Baratillo but instead have seemed a motivation for its expansion."[43] In August of 1693, the alcalde del crimen Don Gerónimo Chacón noted that the situation had gotten so out of hand that a policeman had been killed for trying to enforce the ban on the market.[44] Since previous decrees had had little effect in closing the Baratillo, authorities now believed that they could eliminate it by depriving it of its central location and replacing it with a market of a completely different nature.[45]

The project sought to turn the Plaza Mayor into a site worthy of its location at the center of Spanish power in North America. To that end, on December 30, 1694, King Charles II ordered the construction of an imposing new structure, an alcaicería (later known as the Parián), on the western side of the square—a much more ambitious undertaking than the Ayuntamiento's original plan.[46] The new stores, or cajones, would be large enough for the merchants to live in them with their families, which, the Crown believed, would help reduce the risk of fire. The greatest advantage, however, would come from the replacement of the Baratillo with a more reputable commercial institution. With merchants taking the place of baratilleros, "the Plaza will become more beautiful, safer, and the rents more stable."[47]

Half a century before New Spain's Bourbon rulers embarked on a series of sweeping urban reforms in the capital, Spain's last Habsburg ruler, a man historians have described as sickly and incompetent—anything but Enlightened—sought to achieve some of the same goals.[48] The 1694 plan would transform the Plaza Mayor, turning chaos into order and a site of plebeian sociability into one fit for the city's respectable classes.[49] In his letter to Admiral Pez, Sigüenza y Góngora called the Plaza Mayor an "ill-founded village" and a "pigsty." The Plaza Mayor, in his estimation, was no place for improvised markets for foodstuffs and second-hand goods: "Due to bad government, such stands have been permitted there (which, by nature, should be free and clear), making it so easily combustible."[50] A painting of the Plaza Mayor that Viceroy Galve commissioned before leaving office in 1696 sought to capture that vision—depicting a marketplace organized in neat rows and an alcaicería where well-dressed men and women could shop in comfort and style (see figure 1). Local and royal officials seemed to agree that Mexico City's Plaza Mayor could no longer host such a disorderly and heterogeneous commerce. But removing the baratilleros and the other itinerant and semipermanent vendors from the main square would prove more difficult than those men imagined.

THE PLAZA ERUPTS AGAIN

On March 27, 1696, just before sunset, the alcalde del crimen Don Manuel Suárez Muñoz was attempting to remove vagabonds from the Baratillo, which continued to operate in the Plaza Mayor despite the earlier prohibitions.[51] Inside the market, one of Suárez's deputies spotted a man who had helped a prisoner escape from jail a few days earlier. As the deputies took this suspect,

FIGURE I. Cristóbal de Villalpando, *Vista de la Plaza Mayor de México*, ca. 1695. In this depiction of the Plaza Mayor, damage to the palace from the 1692 fire is visible in the background. The alcaicería, later known as the Parián, is in the foreground. Market stalls fill the Plaza Mayor between the alcaicería and the palace. The dating of this painting is somewhat of a mystery. Scholars believe it was commissioned and painted under Viceroy Galve, whose term ended in 1696. Yet it depicts a completed alcaicería, which was not, in fact, finished until 1703. Iván Escamilla González and Paula Mues Orts argue that Galve probably used the painting to show the king a transformed plaza, featuring a completed alcaicería, a palace in the process of reconstruction, and market stalls organized in orderly rows. It was a vision still unrealized when Galve left office in February 1696. See Escamilla González and Mues Orts, "Espacio real, espacio pictórico y poder: 'Vista de la Plaza Mayor de México' de Cristóbal de Villalpando," in *La imagen política*, ed. Cuauhtémoc Medina (Mexico City: UNAM, 2006): 177–204.

one Francisco González de Castro, into their custody, some students who were in the Baratillo demanded with "immodest voices, almost like plebes" that Suárez and his men let González go, for he too was a student.[52] From there, the situation deteriorated. The students snatched the prisoner from Suárez and set fire to the whipping post located in the market, which authorities had placed there "to terrorize the baratilleros," nearly causing the whole plaza to go up in flames as it had four years earlier. The interim viceroy of New Spain, Juan Ortega y Montañéz, perhaps mindful of his predecessor's absence during the

1692 riot (Galve supposedly hid in the Convent of San Francisco while the plaza burned), left the palace that evening to personally oversee the efforts to restore order in the market and apprehend the aggressors.[53]

The incident produced a flurry of correspondence as officials attempted to determine what, exactly, had happened that day and who was responsible. The viceroy, who served simultaneously as archbishop of Mexico, became engaged in a heated, months-long exchange with the rector of the Royal and Pontifical University of Mexico, Juan de Palacios. The viceroy was furious that a group of students preparing to join the clergy had acted with such "grave indecency"—men who in their hair and clothing styles "imitated their inferiors."[54] Ortega y Montañéz complained that, "in their clothes and long hair these men looked secular, profane, anything but disciples."[55] Given their appearance and comportment, how could Suárez and the alcaldes of the criminal court have known that their attackers were students? Ortega y Montañéz urged the rector to adopt stricter dress codes for his students to avoid this type of confusion in the future. He also reminded Palacios of the entrance requirements that he expected the rector to uphold: no one whose parents or grandparents had appeared before the Inquisition, nor anyone who had "any note of infamy" attached to his name could enter the university. Most importantly, blacks, mulattos, chinos, and slaves of any ethnicity were strictly prohibited so that "the evil races do not pervert those of a better nature." The viceroy was careful to make an exception for Indians, "who, as free vassals of His Majesty can and should be admitted"—an opportunity that existed on paper but in practice was rarely extended.[56]

As the investigation into the student uprising progressed in the spring of 1696, it became increasingly unclear whether the instigators were, in fact, students. Eyewitness testimony at first confirmed Suárez's initial impression that his attackers attended the university, but other witnesses were less sure of the men's identity. Both Juan de Morales, a Spanish iron vendor in the Baratillo, and Andrés Martínez, a free mulatto who also sold in the market, stated that they could not see well enough to say for sure whether the men were students. Martínez noted that the vagabonds who lingered around the Baratillo often "took the name of students in order to commit similar crimes . . . and get away with them." Fernando Suárez, another vendor, echoed this last point, telling officers from the criminal court that he doubted the offenders attended the university because he had never before seen students "attempting to impede Justice," as those who freed the prisoner had done on March 27.[57] Within a few months of the incident, Spanish authorities had determined that the offenders were not students after all, but were more likely vendors in the Baratillo.[58]

The March 1696 uprising elicited a quick response from the colonial government. On March 30, three days after the incident, Viceroy Ortega y Montañéz reissued the order banning the Baratillo, this time printing a proclamation that was read aloud and posted around the city. The edict demanded that the Baratillo be "uprooted, banished, and exterminated" from the Plaza Mayor and everywhere else in the city, and that all baratilleros remove their stands from the plaza within two days or face the confiscation and burning of their merchandise. Any vendor who continued to conduct business after this period would now face the death penalty, a significantly harsher punishment than what Galve had ordered in 1689, and an extraordinary measure to prevent the reestablishment of a street market, given the Spanish government's general aversion to capital punishment. Ortega y Montañéz also gave the taverns surrounding the Plaza Mayor two days to relocate to the adjacent Plaza Volador. The Plaza Mayor, apart from the merchants' shops in the alcaicería that was then under construction, would serve from that point forward only for vendors of glass, gravestones (for the adjacent cemetery), and fruits and vegetables. Stands there would not be allowed to have roofs made of the reed matting that had helped spread the fire of 1692; they could only be covered by a canvas, and were forbidden from having sides of any kind (so authorities could see what was happening inside).[59] Ortega y Montañéz ordered the alcaldes del crimen to begin making regular rounds in the Plaza Mayor to ensure that "there is not the same amount of combustible material that can so quickly and effectively cause a fire."[60]

It is difficult to avoid reading a double meaning into these words, for in replacing the more "combustible" stalls of vendors selling used ironware and gold and silver trinkets, the viceroy was also taking steps to avoid the kind of social combustion that had left the palace partially in ruins a few years earlier. The incident of March 1696 made it all too clear to Spanish authorities that despite being located directly under their noses, the Plaza Mayor was still a chaotic and largely unsupervised bazaar, where colonial subjects of every class and ethnic background intermingled. The confusion over the identities of the men involved in the scuffle only reinforced the viceroy's concern that in the Baratillo social and racial hierarchies dissolved and left in their place a great mass of people who were indistinguishable from one another. The backgrounds of the witnesses who testified in the 1696 case attest to the diverse composition of the market: Indians, mestizos, mulattos, and poor Spaniards all bought and sold in the Baratillo. Authorities viewed the mingling of students with other colonial subjects in public spaces with particular suspicion. Even before the 1692 riot, Church officials had prohibited anyone wearing a habit (including students) from entering the Baratillo.[61] Then, just two days after the riot in Mexico City, students led an uprising in Guadalajara. And in 1693, the Crown issued a decree prohibiting Indians and students from meeting with one another.[62] Upon learning of the 1696 uprising, King Charles II reissued many of the same orders from 1692, again focusing on the mingling of Indians and non-Indians in the center of the city and on the Baratillo's continued existence as threats to public order. In the same breath, the Crown decreed that "the Indians who live dispersed in the center of the city and in the houses of Spaniards must return to their barrios . . . and that the concourse that is called the Baratillo cease completely."[63] The king made clear that a "commerce so pernicious and prejudicial to good customs and the public cause" had no business occupying such a privileged site.[64]

The instability Mexico City experienced in the 1690s could scarcely have come at a worse time for the Spanish Crown. By many historians' reckoning, the end of the seventeenth century saw Spain at its weakest. Wounded by expensive European wars, uprisings in Spain, and pirate attacks along the coasts of its American possessions, including New Spain, the Spanish government was ill prepared to deal with a major rebellion in Mexico.[65] Those conditions created a palpable insecurity among Spanish elites in Mexico City. More than any other period before the outbreak of Miguel Hidalgo's revolution in 1810, the years following the 1692 riot saw colonial authorities living in fear of a generalized Indian or casta rebellion. Besides the uprising in Guadalajara, in which the crowd threw stones at members of the Audiencia, a riot had also broken out in Tlaxcala, where six thousand Indians had sacked the municipal palace only days after the riot in Mexico City.[66]

The situation was scarcely calmer four years later. Soon after the March 27, 1696, incident in the Baratillo, colonial officials learned of a meeting of potential conspirators against the Crown in the Jesús Nazareno Plaza. The Mexico City corregidor received word on April 30 that a group had congregated there to plan a revolt in the capital once the Spanish fleet had left Veracruz for Spain. More troubling still, officials also heard that Indians in the *pueblos* (indigenous villages) of San Juan and Santa Clara were hiding guns in their homes in preparation for the rebellion.[67] Viceroy Ortega y Montañéz responded by issuing a decree in May 1696 that prohibited any person, regardless of social status, from buying, selling, or carrying small arms in Mexico

City.[68] Any place where a group of people, particularly individuals from different social or ethnic groups, congregated was a dangerous one. Market plazas, unique in their attraction for men and women from all walks of life, posed a particular threat. As François Rabelais, the sixteenth-century French humanist, had suggested a century earlier, the social mixing that occurred in the marketplace provided the ideal location for the concoction and dissemination of dangerous ideas.[69] The Baratillo, with its infamous combination of vagabonds, thieves, and frustrated artisans and peddlers of every racial background, was the perfect site for plotters to hatch their next rebellion.

The Baratillo represented everything that Spanish authorities feared in colonial society: the indiscriminate mixing of men and women from every class and *calidad*—many of whom engaged in illicit and immoral activities under the cover of the market's jumble of stalls. Yet even the 1692 riot and the sweeping redesign of the Plaza Mayor markets that it precipitated did not lead to the elimination of the Baratillo. If anything, the market only became more vibrant in the aftermath of the riot. So why did it prove so difficult for authorities to eradicate a trade they all seemed to agree was a grave threat to the rule of law? Answering that question requires a deeper examination of the ways the Baratillo was embedded in Mexico City's economy, politics, and society.

A PLACE TO REMEDY THEIR MISERY

When Mexico City residents awoke on March 30, 1696, three days after the incident with González de Castro, the Baratillo had disappeared from the Plaza Mayor. The market was far from vanquished, however. Just three days later, a new decree permitted used clothing vendors back in the plaza.[70] Though there are no other sources documenting the reestablishment of the Baratillo in the next few years, it was substantial enough by December 1700 that Francisco Cameros, the Plaza Mayor's *asentista*, or lessee, had reorganized its vendors, putting sellers of ribbons and *ruanes*—a type of cotton cloth made in the city of Ruan, France—in the center area of the new alcaicería, leaving the market for second-hand goods in the Plaza Mayor itself.[71] These twin Baratillos came to be known as the Baratillo Grande and the Baratillo Chico, and remained in those locations until the end of the eighteenth century. Despite several viceregal and royal decrees banning the market over the previous decade, the imposition of the death penalty for anyone who defied those orders, and hundreds of pages of correspondence dedicated to preventing its reestablishment, the Baratillo remained a fixture in the Plaza Mayor for nearly another hundred years—far outlasting Mexico's Habsburg rulers. The Baratillo's longevity stemmed not only from the perseverance of its vendors, whose livelihoods depended on their continued defiance of royal decrees, but also from more unlikely sources of support: members of the capital's elite.

Throughout the Baratillo's history, Mexico City residents' disdain for the market was tempered by their sympathy for its vendors and customers. Those conflicting sentiments are apparent in the deliberations that took place in 1689, after the Crown asked Galve and the Audiencia for advice on what to do about the market. On November 14, 1689, the members of the Audiencia weighed the benefits and drawbacks of the Baratillo before ultimately deciding to disband it. The report opens by describing the market as a place where the poor could "remedy their misery" by selling their "little jewels and cheap trinkets." It was an institution where, they observed, the "immense number of needy" in New Spain found recourse for their poverty.[72] In a separate investigation in 1693, the Audiencia noted that "Indians and many others" bought and sold in the market each day, where stolen goods were available at irresistibly low prices. In other words, there was significant popular demand for the Baratillo's offerings.[73]

But the market also provided material benefits to middling and wealthier residents of Mexico City, and those connections were instrumental in the market vendors' ability to continually defy eviction orders. In the summer of 1693, after Viceroy Galve had complained that previous decrees banning the Baratillo had merely fueled its growth, three officials on the criminal court sought to find out why those orders had proved so ineffective. The officials made a vague reference to the "many interested parties in this disorder and abuse."[74] One of those men, the alcalde del crimen Gerónimo Chacón, clarified the meaning of that phrase in a subsequent letter to the Crown. He argued that the government needed to issue a decree prohibiting "any merchant who has an *almacén* [import warehouse], or store from selling linen, silk, thread, paper, or other goods to any baratillero," or face a fine of one thousand pesos for each offense. In Chacón's view, it was not only the city's destitute who were sustaining the Baratillo but also some of its most elite merchants—only the wealthiest of whom owned an almacén. Those men were providing the baratilleros with merchandise to sell on the street. Chacón also laid blame with the city's master artisans who made "stirrups, brakes, spurs, candelabras, and other similar things." By trading with vendors in the Baratillo, those artisans flouted colonial regulations that stipulated that artisans could sell their manufactures only from their own workshops.[75] Baratilleros also worked with ambulatory vendors. Chacón sought to ban all petty street vendors from the plaza, "because the buhoneros that are vulgarly called mercachifles on the street lend their hand to the baratilleros and mesilleros of the plaza."[76] The Baratillo thus formed part of a commercial network that spanned from the highest echelons of Mexico City's mercantile hierarchy to the lowest.

In redesigning the Plaza Mayor after the 1692 riot, colonial—which is to say, royal—officials were unanimous in their desire to keep the Baratillo out of the plaza. But they were also cognizant of the challenges involved in realizing that goal. The ties between elite and petty vendors in the Plaza Mayor markets were substantial. Indeed, the *cajoneros*, or store owners, of the Plaza Mayor agreed to help finance the construction of the alcaicería in 1693 only if the local government allowed small traders to sell in the spaces between the cajones. Petty vendors—particularly those that sold fruits and vegetables—had long engaged in a symbiotic relationship with the cajoneros; the vendors paid rent to the cajoneros in exchange for a shaded space to sell their goods while the cajoneros benefited from both that rental income and the additional foot traffic the food vendors drew to their stores.[77]

Mexico City's Ayuntamiento also may have been reluctant to enforce the Crown's ban on the Baratillo. Although no member of the Ayuntamiento seems to have spoken out in support of the market in the period immediately following the riot, the city council had previously defended the Baratillo when royal officials sought to shutter it. The Duke of Albuquerque, viceroy of New Spain from 1653 to 1660, convinced the Ayuntamiento to clear the Baratillo and other freestanding stalls from the Plaza Mayor in 1658, but only after offering the Ayuntamiento a small share of the royal tax on pulque sales in the city to make up for the lost rent. The arrangement lasted for only a decade.[78] Much of the baratilleros' merchandise may have been stolen or otherwise illicit, but the vendors paid rent to the municipal government to ply their wares in the Plaza Mayor—and this was income the Ayuntamiento needed.

Following the destruction of the cajones and mesillas of the Plaza Mayor in the 1692 fire, local officials were scrambling to make up the lost revenue. Without the rental income from those businesses, the city was hemorrhaging more than ten thousand pesos per year.[79] Markets were by far the Ayuntamiento's greatest source of revenue in the late seventeenth century: between 1682 and 1687, rent from puestos, mesillas, and cajones constituted more than half of the municipal government's propios for that period.[80] So local officials may have resisted royal attempts to remove any rent-paying vendors from the Plaza Mayor. In the summer of 1693, the city's corregidor (a royal official, but one who sat on the city council), Teobaldo Gorráez, pushed back against the Audiencia's efforts to clear the plaza of all the mesilleros and buhoneros, arguing that the city simply could not afford to lose the rent those vendors paid to the Ayuntamiento. He also reminded the members of the Audiencia who sought to ban street vending altogether that "selling on the streets is done in Madrid and all great places."[81]

Although local and royal officials initially seemed to agree on the need for a drastically redesigned Plaza Mayor after the 1692 riot, that consensus masked deep and longstanding tensions between the Ayuntamiento and the Crown. The city council, dominated by American-born Creoles, was fiercely protective of its autonomy and its purview over local affairs. Public markets—particularly the ones located in the Plaza Mayor—were among the body's most prized possessions because of the steady revenue they produced. The different branches of government in colonial Mexico City had very different visions and objectives for the city's main square: while peninsular officials increasingly saw the space as a venue for exercising the power and authority of the Spanish Crown, local officials benefited from the heterodox commerce that filled the plaza and often resisted efforts to reform it. The baratilleros were not up against a unified colonial state but a highly fractious one, where official decrees concealed deep disagreements within and between governing institutions in Mexico City.

CONCLUSION

The 1692 riot spurred Spanish officials to readopt Hernán Cortés's original vision for the colonial capital, enforcing ethnic and physical boundaries that miscegenation and the local economy had long since rendered irrelevant. They took advantage of the crisis the riot provoked to do more than simply reissue legislation aimed at keeping Indians and Spaniards apart from one another: they sought to reengineer the city's principal public space. In the Plaza Mayor, where Indians, Spaniards, and castas and men and women of all social classes mixed indiscriminately, the failures of the two-republic model were glaring, and they had led to a frightening attack on colonial authority. Decades before their Bourbon successors sought to transform the city through far more ambitious public works projects, New Spain's last

Habsburg officials acted on a similar impulse to take control of a public space that, despite being located directly under their noses, lay beyond their authority. Spanish officials in the 1690s sought to reconstruct the Plaza Mayor as a site where they could effectively rule over a multiracial population, unencumbered by a maze of market stalls sheltering nefarious activities. They did so by building an ornate new marketplace for the shops of overseas merchants, organizing disorderly food stalls into neat rows, and banishing the Baratillo. Together, those projects represented an attempt to turn a social engineering project into a physical one—the first major effort to do so since the founding of the Spanish city in the 1520s.

Apart from the construction of the alcaicería, however, which stood in the city's main square until 1843, none of those undertakings had any lasting impact. The Plaza Mayor food markets remained disorganized and vulnerable to fire throughout the eighteenth century, and the Baratillo's absence from the plaza was short lived. While governments would continue, in a halting and haphazard fashion, to attempt to turn the Plaza Mayor into a more suitable site for elite consumption and the expression of royal power, those efforts faced opposition from elite and popular groups alike. The persistence of the Baratillo, in particular, highlights how little consensus there was behind urban renewal projects that sought to transform the city's principal public spaces.

TWO

The Baratillo and the Enlightened City

There is in the Plaza of Mexico a traffic prohibited by law . . .
that is so problematic that ending it has eluded me. . . . I have
neither approved nor disapproved its use for the complications
I find with it.

THE DUKE OF LINARES, *Viceroy of New Spain,*
to his successor, the Duke of Arión, on disbanding
the Baratillo (1716)

We live in more freedom than in Geneva.

"ORDENANZAS DEL BARATILLO," *Ordinance 2*

THE "ORDENANZAS DEL BARATILLO" WAS a legal code for a world
turned upside down. Its pseudonymous author, Pedro Anselmo Chreslos
Jache, describes the Baratillo marketplace as a college of mischief, where
"more than four thousand student-vagabonds" congregate each day to receive
instruction from the "doctors in the faculty of trickery." There, attendees
"dress, eat, play, and procreate using only their own devices, lacking any
home or family besides the *tepacherías* and pulquerías . . . of the city."[1]
According to the "Ordenanzas," the vendors, customers, and hangers-on who
gathered in the Baratillo could do exactly as they pleased, and right under the
noses of the highest religious and secular authorities in New Spain. In this
telling, the Baratillo represented all that had gone wrong with Spain's colonial project in Mexico, where racial and social hierarchies had dissolved into
thin air, producing "so many and such distinct castes and tongues that there
is more confusion in this kingdom than in the Tower of Babel." It was a place
that inverted colonial hierarches, where plebeians became nobles, and nobles,
plebeians; where mixed-race castas were in charge and Spaniards suffered
institutionalized discrimination. The rulers had become the ruled.[2]

In the Age of Reason, the Baratillo was its antithesis. "We are not perfectly
rational," Chreslos Jache's baratilleros proclaimed, "or even people at all, but

animals from India that very closely resemble man, like a portrait of him." Though the "Ordenanzas" were a work of fiction, they spoke to real anxieties among colonial authorities. The Baratillo's thicket of improvised stands and portable tables defied any logical organization, challenging reformers' attempts to tame the Plaza Mayor and transform the viceregal capital into a model for Enlightenment urban planning. In the eighteenth century, new ideas about the city crisscrossed the Atlantic World, and comfort, cleanliness, order, functionality, and above all utility became the guiding principles for urban public administration. European writers and architects of the era, applying the work of the English physician William Harvey (1578–1657) to cities, saw the metropolis as a living being in which the free circulation of air, water, and people was necessary to keep the body alive and healthy.[3] Under the Bourbon dynasty, which assumed control of the Spanish Crown after the death of King Charles II in 1700, New Spain's viceroys adopted these ideas and tried to implement them in Mexico City.[4] They pursued projects such as lighting and paving the city's streets and plazas, straightening and extending streets beyond the ordered grid of the central traza, and removing animal and human waste from public thoroughfares to facilitate the flow of people and goods through the city.[5] Officials also sought to reorganize Mexico City's public market system, particularly its main market complex in the Plaza Mayor. Those efforts culminated in the early 1790s when the Count of Revillagigedo II, the most ambitious of New Spain's Bourbon viceroys, removed the food markets from the plaza in order to transform the square into a *plaza de armas*. In Revillagigedo's vision of the city, the main square was as a venue for the performance of royal power, not for the quotidian commerce of the poor.

Despite the Baratillo's seeming incompatibility with eighteenth-century visions of the city, the market attracted relatively little attention from royal officials in this era. Despite the Crown's furious efforts to disband the Baratillo in the late seventeenth century, the market continued to operate in the Plaza Mayor throughout the eighteenth century, before Revillagigedo forced it, along with all other semipermanent market stalls, from the square in 1790. But that decision did not spell the end of the Baratillo, either. The market's vendors, with the blessing of the local government, simply reconstituted the market a few blocks away. Why, then, did Bourbon reformers, in their efforts to transform Mexico City into an exemplar of rational urban planning, not set their sights on such a glaring locus of irrationality?

The Baratillo survived the Bourbon Reforms of the eighteenth century, in part, because Mexico City's elites were deeply ambivalent about it.[6] While many elites certainly shared Chreslos Jache's view that the Baratillo represented Mexico City's worst elements, others saw in the Baratillo a lively bazaar that served the needs of a diverse population. Government officials were similarly divided: some complained about the robberies and other crimes the market seemed to breed while others noted the Baratillo's fiscal benefits for the Ayuntamiento (the vendors may have been trading in stolen goods, but most paid rent to the city for their stands), or simply accepted its existence as a necessary evil. In an era of government activism, authorities' approach to the city's thieves' market was characterized more by inaction than regulatory zeal.

Colonial authorities' ambivalence toward the Baratillo during the eighteenth century forces us to reconsider some longstanding assumptions about the Bourbon Reforms in Mexico City. The prevailing view posits that in the eighteenth century colonial elites sought to control the urban masses by instituting new rules and embarking on ambitious public works projects aimed at changing popular behaviors. According to this interpretation, authorities transformed the social geography of the city and helped create antagonistic new identities between elites and plebeians.[7] Focusing on the implementation of those plans, however, rather than on their design alone, reveals that Mexico City's elites were far from united behind them. Those projects encountered resistance not just from street vendors and other popular actors, as historians have previously shown; they also provoked fierce opposition from local elites. For reasons ranging from the personal to the political, those individuals opposed the broader urban renewal program that successive Spanish viceroys sought to implement. There was no consensus on the part of elites about what an Enlightened Mexico City would look like, or on what role the Baratillo would have in it.[8]

Nor did the colonial state pursue a singular agenda when it came to urban reform. In Mexico, colonial government was characterized by poorly defined and overlapping jurisdictions, personal animosities, and tensions between American-born Creoles and peninsular Spaniards.[9] The friction between the Ayuntamiento of Mexico City and the Spanish Crown was particularly intense. The Ayuntamiento had long enjoyed significant autonomy, and its members zealously guarded their purview over local affairs. Bourbon reformers who sought to shore up the Crown's control over its American colonies and turn the capital of Spain's wealthiest overseas colony into a showcase capital of Enlightened urban planning attempted to curtail those freedoms, and they intervened with increasing frequency in the Ayuntamiento's business. The Baratillo, which stood in the most important public space in Spain's most important American city, found itself at the center of those long-simmering tensions.

Explaining why the Baratillo, a notoriously retrograde institution, survived the Bourbons' modernizing reforms thus requires taking a closer look at the urban politics of eighteenth-century Mexico City, particularly the politics of the street. This chapter, in examining the Bourbon Reforms from the perspective of the Baratillo and the other Plaza Mayor markets, shows that the city's streets and plazas were not simply sites where "the state and the common people clashed," as historians have often argued, but venues that fostered alliances and rivalries that often transcended class lines.[10] As Mexico City's local and metropolitan elites battled for control over the urban built environment, local officials made common cause with vendors in the city's most notorious thieves' market. Those vendors did not sit on the sidelines as the Crown and the Ayuntamiento debated their future. Their actions influenced the outcome of those decisions and helped ensure that the Baratillo would remain part of the urban landscape in Mexico City long after Bourbon rule had ended.

THE BARATILLO AND ITS CRITICS IN THE EIGHTEENTH CENTURY

Despite the efforts of the Habsburg monarchy to eliminate the Baratillo in the 1690s, the market remained in Mexico City's Plaza Mayor throughout most of the eighteenth century. By the middle of the century, the Baratillo had grown into two distinct markets, with one area, known as the Baratillo Grande, occupying the center of the alcaicería, which locals came to call the Parián (after the Chinese-run mercantile district in Manila that it supposedly resembled), and another, the Baratillo Chico, in the plaza itself. A work by Juan de Viera, the administrator of Mexico City's Colegio de San Ildefonso, completed in 1778, offers the best depiction of the two Baratillos. He describes the Baratillo Chico, also known as the "Baratillo de los Muchachos," as a place that offered just about any "curiosity" one could imagine—from keys to knives to little bells—and most of all, used clothes. There were hat sellers, stocking sellers, tanners, and "Indian guitar-makers who sold instruments to other Indians."[11] In José Antonio Alzate y Ramírez's 1769 map of the city, the Baratillo Chico appears just outside the Parián,

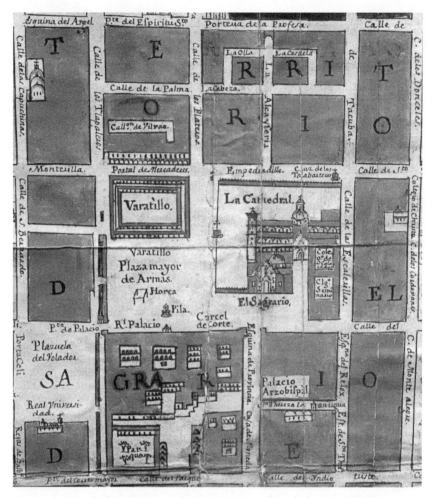

FIGURE 2. Detail of José Antonio Alzate y Ramírez, *Plano de la Ymperial México con la nueva distribución de territorios parroquiales*, 1769. Oriented toward the west, this map shows the two "Varatillos" in the eighteenth century: the Baratillo Grande, in the center patio of the Parián, and the Baratillo Chico in the Plaza Mayor, directly outside the Parián. Colección Museo Franz Mayer, Mexico City.

though it may have migrated to different areas of the plaza over time (see figure 2).

Composed of small *jacales*, or huts, in the central patio of the Parián, the Baratillo Grande offered a similarly broad range of merchandise as the Baratillo Chico, though with a greater selection of upscale items. Viera describes the clocks, glasses, "thousands of things made of silver," swords, shields, firearms, harnesses, books, and "the finest fabrics" that one found there. Two of the aisles on the outer ring of the market housed shoe sellers who offered footwear "for both plebeians and the most polished people."[12] That the Baratillo Grande sold wares for both wealthy and poorer consumers, and appears to have sold new in addition to used goods, means that at times it is difficult to separate it from the Parián itself in the historical record. Indeed, in many places, the Parián is referred to as the "Parián del Baratillo"—a combination that joined a term derived from the word "cheap" with the name of the city's high-end emporium for imported goods from Asia and Europe.[13] The juxtaposition speaks to the heterogeneity of the Plaza Mayor's commerce, where, as one travel writer observed: "one sees two diametrically opposed extremes: supreme wealth and supreme poverty."[14] Despite the differences between the Baratillo Grande and Chico, relatively few writers in the eighteenth century distinguished between the two.

Although Viera viewed the Baratillo as a colorful bazaar that offered something for everyone, other observers saw something more sinister. Some, like the author of the "Ordenanzas," saw the Baratillo as a glaring example of the failures of New Spain's sistema de castas, where miscegenation had created a vast mixed-race underclass that threatened the social stability of the city and viceroyalty. The author's 377 "ordinances" depict an alternate universe where the castas reigned and the gachupines—a pejorative term for Spaniards—were ostracized. This perversion of colonial society had its own police, a Real Audiencia, and lawyers, doctors, and clergy. The Baratillo even had its own racial classification system, an inversion of the sistema de castas that mirrored Mexico's monetary denominations. The system included the categories of half-Spaniard, quarter-Spaniard, tlaco de español (one-eighth Spaniard), and two, four, and eight cacaos of Spaniard. Here, Chreslos Jache satirizes the colonial monetary system, which included both silver coins (pesos and reales) and informal tokens (tlacos) and cacao beans, and suggests the racialized terms in which colonial subjects thought about money. Tlacos and cacao beans were seen as the currency of the multiracial and indigenous underclass, while the larger-denomination peso formed part of an ostensibly Spanish economy.[15]

The "Ordenanzas" go on to explain how the Baratillo was governed by a brotherhood, which admitted Indians, Africans, and every possible combination of mixed-race people—anyone but Spaniards and their purebred offspring.[16] The fictitious guild of the baratilleros (which, to the author's horror, welcomed both men and women) did not just exclude Spaniards; it expressed revulsion toward them. In this author's telling, Mexico's Creoles bore much of the blame for Mexico's degraded condition. They disdained work and diluted Spanish blood and culture by allowing non-Spanish women to wet-nurse their babies and by educating different races in the same schools.[17] The "Ordenanzas" played to Spanish fears of racial degeneration—the idea that in the New World, Spanish domination and Spanishness itself were under threat from Indians, Africans, and castas.

Of course, Chreslos Jache's "Ordenanzas" was a work of satire, not ethnography. Nevertheless, other writers of the era saw similar depravities in the Baratillo. Hipólito Villarroel's treatise, *Enfermedades políticas que padece la capital de esta Nueva España*, written between 1785 and 1787, dedicates a special section to the Baratillo. The author describes the market as "this cave or deposit for the petty theft that apprentices, artisans, maids, and household servants commit, and in sum all the plebeian people—Indians, mulattos, and the other castas that are allowed to live as inhabitants in this city." Villarroel's diatribe suggests that the Baratillo was a melting pot for Mexico's non-Spanish population—a site where the colony's poor blended together into a homogeneous and threatening mass. The *ínfima plebe*, the term Villarroel and his contemporaries employed for this multiracial underclass, "is composed of different castas that have procreated the links between the Spaniard, Indian, and Black; but confusing in this way his first origin, such that now there are no voices to explain and distinguish between these classes of people that make up the greatest number of inhabitants of the kingdom." The poor of New Spain, he went on, "form a monster of so many species that [comprise] the inferior castes, to which are added infinite Spaniards, Europeans, and Creoles, lost and vulgarized with poverty and idleness."[18] Poor Spaniards, a regular presence in the Baratillo, only heightened those anxieties, as their existence further eroded racial hierarchies.[19]

Church officials, too, found much to dislike in the Baratillo. A number of them wrote in support of Viceroy Revillagigedo II's decision to remove the market stalls from the Plaza Mayor in 1789, whose sight, they complained, had "tormented our eyes" before the viceroy reorganized the markets. From their perspective, the Baratillo was a place where "people went naked, others stole to fuel their wickedness, [and] homicides were frequent. It seems as if we are talking about a city without Religion or a King or Government, but all this happened in the Plaza Mayor of the Metropolis of the most Christian North America, in the great Mexico." The Baratillo's bad reputation, they worried, extended far and wide: "In all the Kingdom it was known what went on in that place."[20] In sum, for many eighteenth-century observers, the Baratillo was a hub of criminality and oppositional culture—an obstacle to order, reason, and good governance.

THE BOURBONS REFORM MEXICO CITY'S MARKETS

Even though Mexico City's Bourbon authorities received a litany of complaints about the Baratillo, they did little to address them. They did not make any concerted attempt to enforce the prohibitions that Habsburg rulers had issued throughout the seventeenth century. Nor do they appear to have issued any new decrees banning the Baratillo.[21] Indeed, eighteenth-century authorities were decidedly ambivalent about the Baratillo. The instructions that the viceroy Duke of Linares left to his successor in 1716 capture their indecisiveness. Upon leaving office that year, Linares warned the Duke of Arión: "There is in the Plaza of Mexico a traffic prohibited by law or decree that is so problematic that ending it has been a great challenge for me, being that what is stolen [in the city] is sold there, only disguised. In this way many articles are sold, especially to Indians or hicks, as scoundrels are called here, who are readily provided with the trinkets they need."[22] Faced with this dilemma, Linares found himself unable to render a decision: "I have neither approved nor disapproved its use for the complications I find with it," he wrote, finally, leaving his successor "with the door open to provide what he determines most convenient."[23] The Baratillo may have been an entrepôt for stolen goods, but the city's poor depended on those products, and the viceroy was not eager to take them away.

Making sense of Bourbon-era authorities' relative uninterest in the Baratillo, particularly compared to the attention New Spain's Habsburg rulers paid the market during the seventeenth century, requires understanding the nature of the Bourbon Reforms, which involved multiple and often competing objectives. The Spanish Crown, for its part, focused on increasing revenue. Officials sought to accomplish this goal by establishing government monopolies, raising taxes on various types of transactions, and promoting trade across the Spanish Empire. They also sought to rationalize and centralize the Spanish government, first on the Iberian Peninsula and then in Spain's overseas possessions. They professionalized administrative positions that the Crown had previously contracted out to private parties and created new administrative units. For example, the Bourbons brought the French system of intendancies to Spain in the first half of the eighteenth century and then to New Spain in 1786. In 1782, they divided Mexico City into eight *cuarteles mayores,* each comprised of four *cuarteles menores,* appointing officials to oversee each subsection of the city.[24] These changes attacked what the Bourbons saw as a haphazard structure of government that the Habsburgs had fostered over the centuries. Tighter control over their territories, they believed, would lead to greater tax revenues.

In New Spain, Bourbon authorities also embarked on ambitious urban renewal projects, turning the viceregal capital into a laboratory for Enlightened urban planning. Some of these innovations put Mexico City at the vanguard of the Atlantic World: the city was building sidewalks around the same time as Paris and well before Madrid, for example.[25] However, those public works projects did not always form part of the larger, metropolitan project of increasing tax revenues. Rather, they were often the prerogatives of individual viceroys and, at times, were at odds with the interests of the Spanish Crown because they incurred significant costs and produced no new revenue streams. In 1792, for example, the Crown demanded that Viceroy Revillagigedo II immediately cease his street-paving project because it had run grossly over budget.[26] The Mexico City Ayuntamiento, the body charged with both funding and implementing many of these infrastructure projects, also pushed back—sometimes forcefully. Its members viewed efforts by the Crown and the viceroys to rationalize city finances and remake the city's built environment as an attack on the traditional autonomy of the local government.[27] Thus, the Bourbon Reforms did not constitute a single, coherent project but a series of individual ones, with different objectives and sources of support that produced conflict more often than consensus. Far from a single entity with a common goal, the eighteenth-century colonial state consisted of multiple institutions and many competing interests.[28]

Mexico City's public marketplaces were sites where those conflicts played out. Markets were among the Ayuntamiento's most prized possessions. They contributed as much as 50 percent of the local government's annual tax receipts during the colonial era, leading members of the Ayuntamiento to zealously defend their jurisdiction over these valuable municipal assets.[29] But royal authorities, including viceroys and Crown officials based in Spain, saw marketplaces as ripe for reform. They viewed the city's markets as disorderly and visually unappealing and as public assets that, with some changes, could produce even more income for the local government, helping to wean it off the Crown's support. Royal authorities had been trying to shore up the

Mexico City Ayuntamiento's finances for more than a century. Indeed, ceding the Plaza Mayor to the Ayuntamiento in the early seventeenth century was a step toward this goal: the Crown transferred control of the square specifically so the city could generate income for its operations by renting space to vendors and shopkeepers.[30]

In the eighteenth century, Bourbon authorities implemented new layers of royal supervision over the Ayuntamiento's finances, which incensed the Creole elites who dominated the body.[31] In 1708, King Philip V created a new position, the superintendent of propios and *arbitrios*.[32] Similar to the corregidor, the superintendent, who would be a member of Mexico's Audiencia, was a royal official whom the Crown charged with supervising local affairs, in this case the Ayuntamiento's financial dealings. Then, in the 1740s, Bourbon officials professionalized the position of rent collector for the Plaza Mayor markets. The Ayuntamiento had outsourced that job since 1694, putting the contract out for multiyear bids. The practice was not unusual: the Spanish employed this form of contracting, known as the *asiento*, for everything from collecting tribute to managing the transatlantic slave trade. Upon the death of Francisco Cameros, who held the asiento from 1694 until his death in 1741, Domingo de Trespalacios y Escandón, the superintendent of propios and arbitrios, sought to end the outsourcing of this job, noting that Cameros had administered the plaza "without having put in place rule or method."[33] He demanded that the Ayuntamiento take control of rent collection itself by choosing from its own members a *juez de plaza* (plaza judge) for the Plaza Mayor markets. In theory, the order gave the Ayuntamiento more direct control over its public marketplaces; but it did so in a way that also strengthened royal authorities' oversight of the local government.[34]

Municipal officials took a number of steps in the 1750s and 1760s to address Trespalacios y Escandón's complaints about the Plaza Mayor: they ordered the stands' sides and roofs removed, so that authorities could better monitor what was going on inside them, and cleared the markets' internal passageways to improve the flow of people and goods. In 1753, the plaza judge banned the sale of alcoholic beverages in the Plaza Mayor—an effort to crack down on public drunkenness and the unruly behavior it provoked.[35] But those efforts were short lived, and Trespalacios y Escandón ultimately found the Ayuntamiento's management of the Plaza Mayor markets as unsatisfactory as Cameros's. Upon inspecting the Plaza Mayor in 1760, the superintendent, still in his post, saw "complete confusion, all transit choked, and the whole area . . . filled with puestos [arranged] according to the desires" of each vendor. In that year, Trespalacios y Escandón unveiled a major redesign of the Plaza Mayor (see figures 3 and 4). Under the plan, occupants of the Baratillo Grande inside the Parián would no longer be allowed to live in their cajones, and the market's dense alleyways would be converted into orderly streets. The puestos of the Plaza Mayor, located between the Parián and the viceregal palace, would be reorganized into neat rows separated by product. Vendors would no longer be permitted to congregate in front of the cathedral and palace. Finally, the Plaza Mayor would be paved with cobblestones so the area would not become submerged in mud during the rainy season.[36]

Trespalacios y Escandón was overly optimistic about his ability to bring order to the Plaza Mayor markets. In 1769, one of the municipal rent collectors wrote to complain that the *"vendedores volantes"*—literally, "flying vendors," or street vendors without fixed stalls—continued to operate in the plaza, making it impossible for him to keep an accurate count of all the merchants in the market, much less collect rent from them. These vendors appeared one day and then disappeared the next.[37] By the 1770s, baratilleros, tortilla sellers, and other petty merchants had reoccupied the space in front of the palace and other locations where Trespalacios y Escandón had banned vending.[38] The construction projects he ordered did not proceed according to schedule, either; the Plaza Mayor paving project remained incomplete in 1789 when Viceroy Revillagigedo II assumed his post.[39]

The arrival of the royal inspector José de Gálvez brought additional scrutiny of the Ayuntamiento. Between 1765 and 1771, Gálvez toured New Spain and made a lengthy series of recommendations to the Spanish Crown for reforming the viceroyalty's governing institutions.[40] Like other Bourbon-era reforms, these were aimed at standardizing haphazard or informal practices and professionalizing public services that the local government had long outsourced to third parties. When it came to Mexico City's market administration, Gálvez recommended that the municipal employee who served as the plaza judge receive a salary of 500 pesos per year, rather than 6 percent of the markets' revenues—the existing arrangement. The plan also called for the elimination of gratificaciones—tips that vendors paid market officials to facilitate the sale or transfer of market stalls and other bureaucratic processes. Finally, Gálvez's plan demanded that the city remove the movable stands that were blocking the entrances to the Parián and the ambulatory vendors who clogged the passageways between the market stands in the plaza.[41]

The Ayuntamiento found the plan distressing. Its members claimed that the salary Gálvez proposed for the *regidor* (councilman) who held the plaza

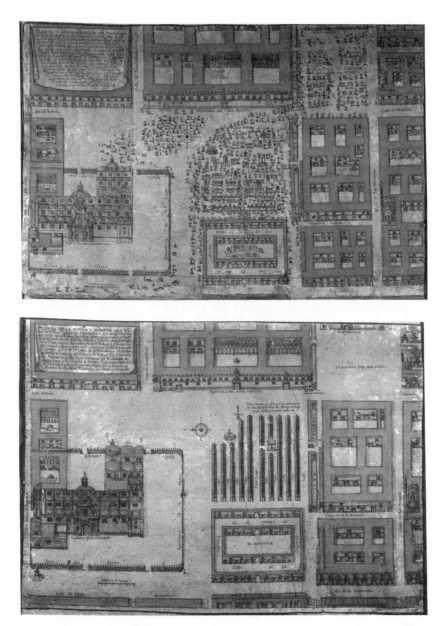

FIGURES 3 and 4. Plaza Mayor, ca. 1760. These two anonymous images depict the Plaza Mayor before and after Domingo de Trespalacios y Escandón's 1760 reorganization project. Both images are oriented toward the east, with the Parián in the foreground and the palace in the background. The first image (figure 3) highlights the chaotic nature of the marketplaces of the Plaza Mayor and Plaza del Volador (which the rendering notes was "as disorganized as the [Plaza] Mayor"). In the second image (figure 4), the Plaza Mayor's stalls are arranged neatly in rows and both the Baratillo Grande (inside the Parián) and the Plaza del Volador are now free of market stands. Like Villalpando's painting of the Plaza Mayor after the 1692 riot, this second image probably reflected Trespalacios y Escandón's aspirations for the space more than reality. Images located in Sonia Lombardo de Ruiz, *Atlas histórico de la Ciudad de México*, ed. Mario de la Torre, 2 vols. (Mexico City: INAH, 1996), 1:27, 29.

judge post amounted to a significant pay cut. They also warned the Crown of the impact the changes would have on impoverished street vendors. They even included in their response written complaints from vendors in and around the plaza who predicted that the changes would lead to their "extinction."[42] The aldermen emphasized that Mexico City was not Madrid, and the Crown could not simply transpose Spanish laws onto New Spain: "the constitution, the customs, and even the laws of this country are different from those of Spanish cities," they argued.[43] This line of reasoning—that what was good for Spain was not necessarily good for Mexico—was one the Ayuntamiento used repeatedly in the second half of the eighteenth century. The Crown's reforms were an attack on the sovereignty of the local government and a threat to the livelihoods of the Creole elites who participated in the often-lucrative business of colonial government. Those families had strong incentives to maintain the existing structure of local government, including its market system.

The baratilleros may have engaged in a nefarious trade, but they also paid rent to the Ayuntamiento, and revenue, regardless of its source, was something royal and local governments alike welcomed. Although the Baratillo was not the market that provided the largest tax revenues (typically the Parián was), its contribution was far from negligible. In 1791, the city collected a total of 7,146 pesos from the stands located in the Baratillo Grande and in the Plaza Mayor—just under 5 percent of the Ayuntamiento's gross revenue that year.[44] The Ayuntamiento suffered from frequent budget shortfalls and its members were loath to eliminate any asset that generated revenue.[45] Indeed, when officials at Mexico City's cathedral, located just off the Plaza Mayor, sought to remove the Baratillo from the square in 1729 because of the "public sins" that people regularly committed there, the Ayuntamiento invoked its jurisdiction over the Plaza Mayor and blocked the proposal.[46]

Frictions between royal and municipal authorities help explain the Baratillo's persistence during a period of ambitious urban renewal projects. Members of the Ayuntamiento resisted royal efforts to limit the body's autonomy and curtail the income that their positions afforded them, which sometimes led them to defend institutions as unsavory as the Baratillo. Furthermore, because the market produced significant revenues for the city, the Spanish Crown may not have been eager to do away with it, either, as it wanted to ensure that its most important American city was a fiscally sound one. Even if some reformers sought to dramatically reengineer Mexico City society in the eighteenth century, not every colonial official, and especially not the members of the Ayuntamiento, was on board with those plans.

Tensions between local and royal authorities continued to rise before coming to a head under New Spain's most ambitious Bourbon viceroy, the Second Count of Revillagigedo.

REVILLAGIGEDO II AND THE APOGEE OF REFORM

More than any other viceroy of New Spain, Revillagigedo II, who governed from 1789 to 1794, was determined to transform the seat of his jurisdiction into a model of Enlightened urban planning.[47] Soon after arriving in the capital, he set in motion a series of administrative changes and public works projects. The scope of Revillagigedo's reforms was sweeping. He began extending the ordered grid of the traza to the city's outlying barrios (see figure 5), minted new coins, and established new regulations on taverns and gambling. He even limited the number of times church bells could ring.[48] Revillagigedo fixated on the unsanitary conditions of the city's public thoroughfares and plazas, picking up the paving project that his predecessors had begun decades before and implementing a property tax that provided a faster and more reliable revenue stream to fund it.[49] Although local elites' frustrations with royal authorities had been brewing for decades, Revillagigedo's term brought a significant escalation of those tensions. The viceroy made unilateral decisions that the Mexico City Ayuntamiento believed drained local resources and posed an existential threat to its autonomy. The project that most incensed local officials was his transformation of the Plaza Mayor.

Upon arriving in Mexico in 1789, the viceroy expressed horror at the state of the plaza that lay in front of his palace. The reforms of previous Bourbon viceroys had failed to turn the Plaza Mayor into a respectable space. The square, in his estimation, was "a confused labyrinth of huts, pigsties, and matted shelters . . . inside of which evildoers could easily hide themselves, day or night, and commit the most horrible crimes." In full view of the viceroyalty's highest authorities were open latrines where both men and women took care of their "corporal needs." Officials routinely removed drunkards who had passed out in the street so stagecoaches did not run them over. Worse still, "with too much frequency, under the shadow of darkness, sins of sensuality were witnessed in the doorways, corners, and cemeteries [surrounding the Plaza Mayor], to the extent that the Fathers considered closing off the atrium in order to avoid sacrileges in the doorways of their Church." In sum,

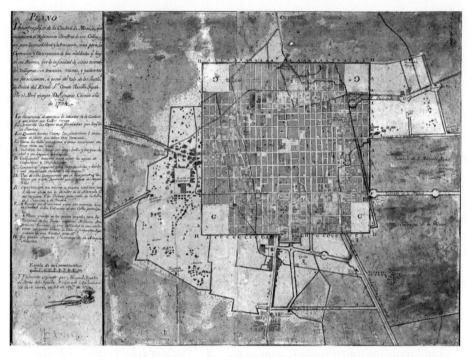

FIGURE 5. Ignacio Castera, *Plano ichnographico de la Ciudad de Mexico . . .*, 1794. Castera was Mexico City's chief architect and the mastermind behind many of Revillagigedo's public works projects. This map, which is oriented toward the east, shows Castera's plan to extend the traza beyond the traditional city center, integrating indigenous barrios and some of Mexico City's hinterlands into the urban grid. The text on the left side of the map discusses how the project will lead to the "correction and extirpation of crimes in the Barrios" by opening up alleys and dead-end streets. Library of Congress.

"all of this made the Plaza so disgusting, and a sight so abominable, that no decent person dared enter it without an urgent motive."[50]

Within months of his arrival in Mexico, Revillagigedo began a two-pronged effort to modernize the distribution of basic staples in the city and transform the Plaza Mayor. To accomplish those goals, he ordered that the city's main food market move from the Plaza Mayor into the adjacent Plaza del Volador. The only market that would remain in the central square was the Parián. The remainder of the plaza would be cleared of all its tables and stands and left for a more dignified public to stroll through at its leisure. The formal process of relocating the food market began on December 14, 1789, when the Ayuntamiento signed a contract to rent the Plaza del Volador from its owner, the Marquisate of the Valley of Oaxaca (the descendants of Hernán Cortés) for five years at a cost of 2,500 pesos per year.[51] This was a steep increase in spending for the municipal government, which owned the Plaza Mayor and thus did not have to pay rent to operate a market there. Over the next two years, the Ayuntamiento, under orders from the viceroy, spent nearly 44,000 pesos paving the Plaza del Volador with cobblestones and building fountains, cajones, puestos, and portable stands. In January 1792, the new marketplace began operation.[52]

Revillagigedo sought to make the Plaza del Volador marketplace the kind of clean, organized, and efficient market that authorities had tried in vain to create in the Plaza Mayor since the 1690s. To that end, he ordered the drafting of an expansive new set of regulations for the city's public markets in 1791. These were as significant as the construction projects themselves because they continued to be in force decades after Revillagigedo's term as viceroy had ended—indeed, long after Mexico's independence from Spain.[53] The rules specified that the Volador market contain rows separated according to the type of product sold and banned all forms of cooking. They also created additional levels of oversight for both the main market and the satellite markets in the outlying barrios that had been under construction intermittently since the 1770s.[54] The plaza judge would continue to oversee the daily operations of the main market and arbitrate disputes that arose within it. Beneath him would be an *administrador*, or rent collector, who would earn 1,200 pesos per year. Finally, the day-to-day policing and cleaning of the markets was left to *guarda-ministros*, paid 15 pesos per month and provided with uniforms of blue wool, black collars, and white buttons. The *Reglamento* specified, for the first time, the responsibilities of the plaza judge, which had previously been dictated by custom and the desires and abilities of the officeholder.[55] The regulations were also printed, adding another layer of formality and permanence.

Revillagigedo's *Reglamento* also banned the practice of the *traspaso*—the transfer of a cajón from one merchant to another. This institution had existed for as long as there were markets in the Plaza Mayor and involved traders paying *guantes* (fees) to merchants to obtain the right to their space in the plaza, and gratificaciones to municipal market officials to facilitate those exchanges.[56] Revillagigedo sought to formalize this process by forcing merchants to go through official channels to transfer their stands to other vendors, leaving the occupant with a license issued by the Ayuntamiento—a written record.[57] The viceroy also sought to make the process of obtaining market stalls fairer, declaring that the spaces occupied by movable stands would now be filled on a first-come, first-served basis.[58] Revillagigedo probably objected to the traspaso because it was done off the books, making it more difficult for the government to oversee, and because gratificaciones lined the pockets of individual officials while depriving the government of fees.

The Ayuntamiento sought to enforce the traspaso ban soon after it went into effect but ran into fierce resistance from the Consulado, the exclusive guild of overseas merchants. The Consulado argued that the prohibition conflicted with the government's stated goal of promoting free trade (*comercio libre*), as the system of guantes and gratificaciones helped smooth the cumbersome process of legally transferring rights to a market stall.[59] The merchants appear to have prevailed in the long run, as the practice resurfaces in documents from the early nineteenth century.[60] Indeed, many of Revillagigedo's innovations would prove difficult to implement or sustain because they encountered entrenched opposition from various quarters.

THE BARATILLO MOVES TO THE PLAZA DEL FACTOR

The Baratillo survived the sweeping transformation of the Plaza Mayor because of the combined efforts of municipal officials and the market's vendors. Revillagigedo made no mention of the Baratillo in his initial plans for the redesign of the Plaza Mayor—a surprising omission, given that the market embodied many of the attributes he found most detestable about the space. The construction, however, must have displaced the Baratillo Chico when the government cleared all of the market stalls from the Plaza Mayor in late 1789. That market all but vanishes from the historical record until the summer of 1792, when a document reveals that it had moved to the Plaza de las Vizcaínas, located in the far southwestern corner of the city.[61] It remained there only temporarily; a year later a plan surfaced to relocate the Baratillo to the Plaza del Factor, located a few blocks northwest of the Plaza Mayor, in the present-day site of Mexico City's legislative assembly.

The Ayuntamiento's desire for revenue led it to relocate the Baratillo to the Plaza del Factor. The original plan for that plaza, which emerged in May 1791, was to build a stone marketplace in the square as part of an ongoing effort to create neighborhood food markets in peripheral areas of the city.[62] By August 1792, however, the Ayuntamiento had run out of money for the project and decided to sell the stones from the half-built structure in order to help pay for wooden stands instead. The proceeds still left the city short of the funds it needed to finish the now more modest project and it was only able to com-

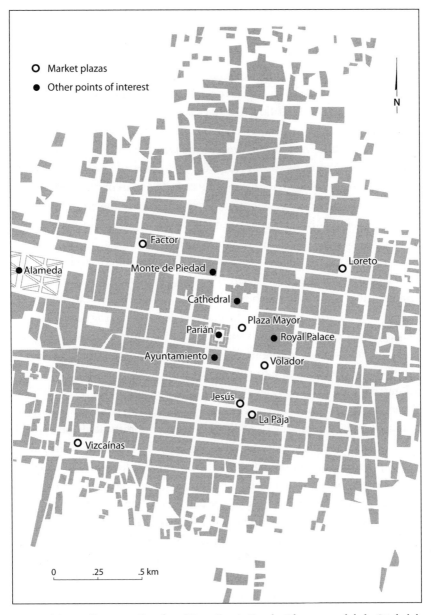

Market plazas
Other points of interest

N

Factor

Loreto

Alameda

Monte de Piedad

Cathedral

Plaza Mayor

Parián

Royal Palace

Ayuntamiento

Volador

Jesús

La Paja

Vizcaínas

0   .25   .5 km

MAP 2. Mexico City, 1793. Based on Diego García Conde, *Plano general de la Ciudad de México* . . . , 1793, engraved in 1807. Reproduced in Sonia Lombardo de Ruiz, *Atlás histórico de la ciudad de México*, 2 vols. (Mexico City: INAH, 1996), 1:340. Map created by Bill Nelson and Andrew Konove.

plete it after receiving an 8,000-peso loan from a local convent.[63] Municipal market officials and Mexico City's corregidor, Bernardo Bonavía, decided that moving the Baratillo to the Plaza del Factor was a better financial decision for the city than putting a food market there. Bonavía ordered "that the Baratillo be transferred to the [Plaza del Factor] in order to populate it . . . [as] the movement of the Baratillo will attract with it the transfer of other puestos [and] I do not doubt that greater rents will be achieved in the Plaza del Factor."[64] The superintendent of propios and arbitrios and the viceroy agreed, and the move was authorized in August 1793.[65] Local and royal officials thus saw the Baratillo not as an intolerable nuisance but as an important source of revenue, even a driver of neighborhood economic development.

By this point, only the occupants of the former Baratillo Chico had moved to the Plaza del Factor. After reorganizing the Plaza Mayor, Viceroy Revillagigedo initially allowed the vendors of the Baratillo Grande to remain in the central patio of the Parián. But then, in March 1794, the viceroy announced a new project to rebuild that space.[66] Officials relocated the occupants of the Baratillo Grande to the Plazuela de Jesús and the catty-cornered Plazuela de la Paja, a few blocks south of the Plaza Mayor. But vendors disliked the location, so, in August 1794, a group of fourteen men who sold in the Plaza del Factor wrote to the superintendent of propios and arbitrios asking that the authorities amend the "distance and disunion" between their Baratillo and the one located across town. Appealing to "both Majesties," temporal and spiritual, the baratilleros offered a sophisticated and compelling case that merging the two markets served the best interests of the public. The superintendent consented to the baratilleros' request and by 1796 the Baratillo was once again a single institution, now located in the Plaza del Factor.[67] It was the first of several times that the vendors of the Baratillo would play a role in determining where their market would be located.

By the mid-1790s the Plaza Mayor had become the clean, orderly, and, above all, respectable commercial center of Mexico City that colonial officials had sought to create for over one hundred years (see figure 6). No used clothing or iron vendors, nor any of the fruit and vegetable, prepared food, or pulque stands that used to clutter the city's main square were in sight. It had become a plaza de armas—a vast open space where the army, stationed in New Spain since the 1760s, could offer public displays of the king's power for his subjects. Religious officials in the capital were ecstatic about the changes the viceroy had brought: "In fewer than four years, the policing of the city was perfected such that even the most sophisticated cities of Europe do not

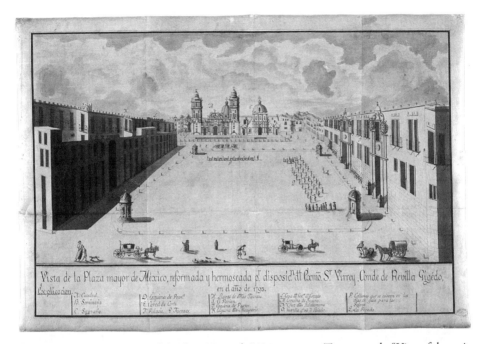

FIGURE 6. Anonymous, *Vista de la Plaza Mayor de México...*, 1793. The text reads: "View of the main Plaza of Mexico, reformed and beautified by order of His Excellency Viceroy Count of Revilla Gigedo in the year 1793." Ministerio de Educación, Cultura y Deporte, Archivo General de Indias, Spain, AGI, MP-México, 446.

surpass it," they wrote.[68] The viceroy's improvements, however, did not sit as well with the Creole elites who controlled the Mexico City Ayuntamiento.

THE AYUNTAMIENTO TAKES THE VICEROY TO COURT

Members of the Ayuntamiento were furious about the viceroy's meddling in local affairs. They complained that the municipal government was responsible for paying for and executing the viceroy's projects but had no say in their design.[69] The cost, scope, and, above all, the unilateral nature of Revillagigedo's reforms so angered Ayuntamiento members that they brought a formal complaint against him in January 1795, shortly after he had left office. The *juicio de residencia*, as the proceeding was called, raised dozens of grievances against the viceroy for undertaking public works projects and enacting fiscal reforms that placed a great financial strain on the city and went against the interests of its residents. The ideas were poorly conceived, the Ayuntamiento argued, and money did not go toward solving the most pressing needs.[70]

No project riled municipal officials more than the renovation of the Plaza Mayor and the relocation of the city's principal marketplace. Indeed, the Ayuntamiento's first accusation in the juicio was that the construction of the new market in the Plaza del Volador "has deprived the City of those fat profits that it earned with the produce and other stands that the Plaza Mayor contained, depriving the public of an annual rent of as much as twelve thousand pesos."[71] Revillagigedo had also raised rents for the cajones and puestos of the new market, provoking an outcry from vendors in 1792, and, the Ayuntamiento argued, ultimately increasing costs for the city's consumers.[72] The complainants also objected to the viceroy's stipulation that the puestos could never return to the plaza, foreclosing the possibility that the city could raise additional revenue in the future from that space. The Ayuntamiento argued that the entire Plaza Mayor project was pointless, since the puestos that were constructed in the Volador were exactly the same as the original ones in the Plaza Mayor, except that they now had roofs made of *tejamanil* (wooden shingles) instead of blankets, ultimately leaving the new market just as vulnerable to fire as its predecessor. Indeed, one had already broken out in May 1794.[73]

The viceroy's public works projects brought the long-simmering tensions between local and peninsular authorities to a boil. In the years immediately preceding Revillagigedo's term, the Crown had stepped up its efforts to chip away at the autonomy of local institutions in the Americas and subject their finances to greater scrutiny by royal authorities. The 1786 establishment of intendancies, in particular, eroded local control by creating a new layer of royal administration throughout New Spain. In the same year, the Crown established the Junta Superior de Real Hacienda, yet another royal body charged with overseeing municipal finances in New Spain.[74] With the creation of that entity, the Council of the Indies ordered that all of the viceroyalty's ayuntamientos submit budgets to royal authorities for review. The Mexico City Ayuntamiento refused. It took a decree from the king himself in 1797 for the Ayuntamiento to comply.[75]

For members of the Ayuntamiento, Revillagigedo's reforms, particularly the public works projects, were a step too far. What most frustrated local elites was that Revillagigedo refused to let the city participate in the decision-making process. Rather than consult with the Ayuntamiento, Revillagigedo relied on outside experts (*peritos*) in planning the projects. There was no transparency in the bidding or construction process; the viceroy gave orders verbally rather than in writing, an "extrajudicial" process, the Ayuntamiento claimed, and nobody knew how much the projects would cost until the money was already spent.[76] Furthermore, the viceroy had intervened in the city's most proprietary sphere of influence and the source of a large part of its annual income: its public markets.[77] Ever since 1609, when the Crown deeded the Plaza Mayor to the Ayuntamiento so it could establish a market there, that space had played a central role in how the Ayuntamiento managed the city.

In its case against the viceroy, the Ayuntamiento pitched itself as the body that had the interests of the broader public in mind. Some projects, the juicio claimed, were "useless and not at all necessary for the public; others were, on the contrary, quite detrimental." Throughout the juicio de residencia, the Ayuntamiento argued that Revillagigedo's reforms were harmful for Mexico City's general population, especially its poorest members, and questioned the "public utility" of projects like sidewalks and curbs—employing the same Enlightenment vocabulary Bourbon reformers used to justify their public works projects.[78] Members of the Ayuntamiento objected to Revillagigedo's description of the Plaza as a "latrine," countering that "the Plaza was not in such decadence as he wants it to appear, and every class of people moved comfortably about it."[79] The heterogeneity of the Plaza Mayor markets, according to this argument, was one of the greatest assets of the space. It offered something for everyone.[80] In the juicio de residencia, Mexico City's Creole elites expressed their resentment for peninsular interference in local affairs, and for the entire Europeanizing project that Revillagigedo and other Spanish viceroys sought to realize in Mexico City.[81] They disputed the notion that their city could or should become a laboratory for Enlightenment ideas, asking: "Because things have been done in Spain and other cities in Europe . . . should the same be done in the Americas?" Their answer to this rhetorical question was a resounding no: "The practice[s] that [are] observed in Madrid and in other capitals of Europe are not adaptable to Mexico."[82]

CONCLUSION

Revillagigedo's reforms left a significant imprint on Mexico City. Above all, he transformed the city's main plaza from a site that had hosted a diverse commerce in foodstuffs and new and used goods into the kind of orderly, dignified space that the Spanish Crown had sought to create since the end of the seventeenth century. The removal of the Baratillo and the food markets from the Plaza Mayor marked the first time in Mexico City's history that the retail activities of the rich and poor were physically separated from one another. By 1795, the main square housed only the commerce of the Parián—without the disreputable Baratillo Grande in its center patio—and the shops in the archways that lined its southern and western sides. Merchants who sold goods that lay beyond the reach of the vast majority of Mexico City's population occupied those spaces. Food vendors now had their own market in the adjacent Plaza del Volador while the market for second-hand goods was relegated to the periphery of the old traza. The process of creating a refashioned, respectable public space at the heart of the viceregal capital did not begin with Revillagigedo or even the Bourbon dynasty. The effort to transform the Plaza Mayor into a safer, more beautiful, and more lucrative commercial space for the local government began in the wake of the 1692 riot with the decision to eradicate the Baratillo and construct the alcaicería, and continued in fits and starts throughout the eighteenth century. Yet, Revillagigedo's efforts were more ambitious than those of his predecessors, and their impact on the urban geography was significant.

Like the urban renewal projects that previous viceroys had spearheaded, however, Revillagigedo failed to accomplish all, or even most, of what he set out to do. By the end of his term, the paving project, begun decades earlier, was still not finished, and the straightening of city streets beyond the traza had barely begun. His attempts to reform the city's market administration were not much more successful. The masonry market in the Plaza del Factor was never built. A fire had broken out in the Plaza del Volador market even before Revillagigedo left office, and the owner of the plaza, the Marquisate of the Valley of Oaxaca, was so dissatisfied with its arrangement with the city that the family threatened not to renew the Ayuntamiento's lease on the land in 1807, nearly forcing the government to relocate the city's principal food market.[83] Although Revillagigedo had successfully cleared the Plaza Mayor of its ramshackle wooden stalls, some vendors continued to defy the ban on selling there. In 1794, officials complained that shoe sellers and other vendors were peddling their wares in the plaza at night, after the doors to the Parián had closed for the evening.[84] Moving the Baratillo to the Plaza del Factor produced a litany of complaints from neighbors and vendors alike, as officials struggled to suppress a troublesome nighttime market on the streets surrounding the plaza.[85] Nor did the reorganization of the city's markets seem to have the desired effect on municipal revenues: Revillagigedo's successor, the viceroy Marquis of Branciforte, worried in a letter from September 1795 that "most of the cajones of the Parián have been abandoned" due to the disappearance of the "crowd of people that for so many years that site attracted."[86]

The Bourbon Reforms, like those of their Habsburg predecessors, failed to realize their objective of reengineering Mexico City's principal public spaces in the eighteenth century because they encountered opposition from various quarters—not only from popular groups but also other elites, who, for reasons both personal and political, took issue with those projects. The fault lines in those struggles often formed between peninsular and local authorities who had very different prerogatives when it came to urban governance. There were also significant conflicts within those groups: while the Crown ultimately supported Revillagigedo in his juicio de residencia, which concluded only after his death, it had opposed many of his initiatives during his time as viceroy due to their high cost.[87] In Mexico City, Bourbon reforms to public administration and the built environment did not represent a coherent program that elites imposed upon the poor; rather, they constituted a diverse set of policy prescriptions and projects that were as controversial among elites as they were among the popular classes.

Those tensions played out in the Baratillo and on the streets of the eighteenth-century city, where both the governing elite's ambivalence about the market and the vendors' strategies for resisting policies that adversely affected them come into focus. Despite the Baratillo's seeming incompatibility with Bourbon reformers' vision of a clean, orderly, and rational city, authorities in Mexico City were far from unified in their desire to disband it, and made little attempt to do so throughout most of the eighteenth century. To observers such as the author of the "Ordenanzas," the Baratillo was the uncontested domain of a multiracial criminal underclass. But other elites were not so sure; the market offered a range of goods for well-to-do and poor residents alike, employed people that might otherwise engage in even more nefarious activities, and provided the chronically cash-strapped Ayuntamiento with a consistent source of revenue.

Disagreements among colonial elites do not, on their own, explain the persistence of the Baratillo during this period of activist government. Understanding the Baratillo's significance to Mexico City society in this era also requires an examination of the quotidian exchanges that took place in the market. Beyond its contribution to the coffers of local government, the Baratillo played an indispensable role in the local economy, and its commerce involved a broad cross-section of society. Vendors leveraged those connections to assert the legitimacy of their trade and defend it from attacks by government officials and rival merchants. The keys to the Baratillo's success in outlasting colonial rule lie as much in the transactions of the shadow economy of the eighteenth and early nineteenth centuries as they do in the power struggles between local and metropolitan elites.

THREE

Shadow Economics

The Baratillo has existed since time immemorial. . . . It is clearly
and manifestly in the common good.

JOSEPH RAMÍREZ, *Diego Rufino and others to
Corregidor Nuño Núñez de Villavicencio,
October 16, 1706*

ON JANUARY 13, 1724, JUAN DE DIOS ANZURES, a lawyer writing on
behalf of a group of shopkeepers in the Plaza Mayor, complained to the viceroy of New Spain that baratilleros and ambulatory vendors were wreaking
havoc on their businesses. The vendors peddled items such as imported
British linen and silver plate, goods that Dios Anzures claimed only Mexico
City's exclusive merchant guild—the Consulado—had the authority to
trade. He reminded the viceroy that royal decrees from the previous century
had banned the Baratillo, and in any case, it was supposed to be the marketplace for second-hand clothing, not new products from Castile and China.
Worse still, the baratilleros engaged in outright fraud, "selling one thing for
another." They peddled less expensive *maná*, or plant oil, for olive oil, and the
cheaper Guayaquil cacao for one of the superior varieties from Maracaibo or
Caracas. In this manner, "they adulterate everything in order to increase
their ill-gotten gain." Dios Anzures pleaded with the viceroy to end those
abuses once and for all. His efforts, like others that targeted the Baratillo in
the late colonial era, gained little traction.[1]

This chapter moves from the elite debates about urban public space that
the previous chapter analyzed to an examination of the quotidian transactions that unfolded in the Baratillo. The Baratillo was the hub of Mexico
City's shadow economy, where circuits of second-hand, stolen, counterfeit,
and contraband goods converged and, on occasion, became visible to authorities. This trade undermined established players in the local economy, especially middling shopkeepers and artisans. But it also created unlikely bedfel-
lows, linking baratilleros to overseas traders and government officials.
Although observers frequently depicted the Baratillo as the exclusive domain

of the underclass, the market in fact served a range of actors—from the most humble to the most privileged. Elites, working people, and members of the city's often-overlooked middle sectors made their living or provisioned their households in the Baratillo.[2]

The baratilleros turned the market's broad appeal to their advantage. Employing the political vernacular of the day, they defended the Baratillo's relevance to urban society and the local economy and asserted their right to practice their trade on the city's streets and plazas. Their actions show that the Baratillo was not just a vital economic institution in eighteenth-century Mexico City; it was also a key site for political expression and negotiation. The Baratillo survived the colonial era because it offered material benefits to many residents of the capital and because its vendors conveyed that fact to authorities.

In reconstructing the circuits of exchange that intersected in the Baratillo, this chapter challenges some of the binaries that scholars have employed to understand urban economies. In the Baratillo, distinctions between legal and illegal commerce blurred. Products that modern-day social scientists might classify as "informal" because they were untaxed or evaded regulation mixed indiscriminately with stolen and other illicit merchandise. If the boundaries between legal and illegal commerce were ambiguous, government officials helped make them so. Although the Baratillo was technically prohibited in the eighteenth century since no one had rescinded the seventeenth-century decrees that had banned the market, local officials continued to collect rents from its vendors and adjudicate disputes among them. Thus, despite widespread fears that crime in late-colonial Mexico City was on the rise, state agents played a key role in sustaining the black market.

THE BARATILLO IN THE ECONOMY OF LATE-COLONIAL MEXICO CITY

The Baratillo occupied one of the bottom rungs of colonial Mexico City's commercial hierarchy. At the top of the pyramid were the import merchants with membership in the Consulado. These were Spaniards who often arrived in Mexico with little money but managed to ascend through the merchant ranks by first working in, and then ultimately acquiring, an import warehouse (*almacén*). The almacenes contained goods from Europe and Asia, shipped to Mexico via Spain or the Philippines, and the businesses were generally worth between 100,000 and 200,000 pesos each. From these warehouses, the importers provisioned retail merchants in the capital as well as provincial traders. The principal retailers of fine imported goods in the capital were the merchants who rented stores, or cajones, in the Parián marketplace and in the arcades that lined the southern and western sides of the Plaza Mayor. Most of these men possessed only one or two cajones, each worth roughly 30,000 to 70,000 pesos. In total, some two hundred stores in the capital offered imported goods in the eighteenth century.[3] Beneath the cajoneros were the owners of *tiendas mestizas* and slightly smaller neighborhood grocery stores, alternatively called *pulperías* or *cacahuaterías*. These stores' values ranged from less than 1,000 pesos to over 25,000 pesos.[4] Their owners were often recent immigrants from Spain who would be considered lower middle class, or near the top of the working class.[5] At the bottom of the mercantile hierarchy were Mexico City's street vendors—men and women who operated small stands or tables in the city's public plazas and ambulatory vendors known as buhoneros or mercachifles. Spanish elites derided those individuals, associating the profession with Indians and castas, though in reality many vendors, particularly in the Baratillo, were Spanish.[6]

Women participated at every level of colonial commerce except the highest, and they were most visible in the humbler establishments.[7] The Baratillo, however, was an exception to this rule. Although women appeared on virtually every list of vendors in the Baratillo throughout the late colonial and early national periods, they always constituted a small fraction of the total. Female vendors were far more common in the markets for foodstuffs. The discrepancy probably stems from the Baratillo's close relationship with artisanal trades in which men predominated.[8]

People of every racial background sold in the Baratillo. Despite frequent assertions by the Baratillo's detractors that the market was a haven for castas, many, if not most, baratilleros were Spanish. A search of marriage records in the eighteenth century, for example, revealed twenty-seven men with the profession of "baratillero" whose race the file identified. Among those men were eighteen Spaniards, three mestizos, three castizos, one indio chino, one morisco, and one mulatto.[9] The relatively high proportion of Spaniards and the absence of Indians in the sample is likely to stem from the ethnic makeup of the trades from which many vendors hailed, namely, metalwork, garment making, and carpentry. Spaniards predominated in all of those professions.[10]

The Baratillo's businesses were also diverse in scale. Cajones inside the Baratillo Grande were expensive: they generally rented for 200 pesos per year during the second half of the eighteenth century—the same price as stores located in the Parián itself.[11] Businesses in the Baratillo Grande were worth anywhere from a couple hundred pesos to several thousand.[12] Vicente Viola, the Genovese owner of a cajón in the Baratillo who died in 1767, sold products such as mirrors, screens, glasses, and other household goods imported from China and Europe, as well as stockings and woolen clothing. He had two employees, and he owned another store in Chalco, a town about thirty kilometers southeast of Mexico City. The contents of his business in the Baratillo were auctioned for a little over 1,500 pesos after his death.[13] Some cajones were worth considerably more: Josef Fianca had two cajones in the Baratillo Grande whose combined value in 1780 totaled 25,000 pesos.[14] Still, many other businesses in the Baratillo were much humbler. An open-air stand, or puesto, rented for around one peso per week in the late eighteenth and early nineteenth centuries, while vendors selling from tables or baskets paid only a couple of reales per week to the Ayuntamiento.[15] Vendors of chía water and prepared foods, usually indigenous women, set up between the stands of the Baratillo Grande and paid little or nothing in rent.[16] Those businesses were much less likely to produce written inventory records.

As in other sectors of the colonial economy, businesses in the Baratillo depended heavily on credit.[17] Import merchants sold baratilleros on credit *avería*—goods damaged in transit—and other products unfit for sale in their own retail outlets.[18] Vendors in the Baratillo also operated a credit system among themselves. In a 1730 case against one Don Santiago Roque, who administered a stand that sold *paño*, a course woolen cloth, several witnesses testified that when clothing sellers in the Plaza Mayor did not have enough money to buy the cloth they needed, the would pawn their clothes to Roque in exchange for fabric. Once they sold the clothes they had made from that cloth, they would buy back the clothes they had left as collateral.[19] The 1767 inventory of Vicente Viola's assets illustrates just how integral credit, and pawnbroking in particular, were to a baratillero's business. The file lists more than twenty individuals who owed Viola money, many identified simply as "Mariano the painter" or "the sugar confectioner in the Plaza de las Vizcaínas." Viola also counted a number of pawned items as assets.[20] More than a household subsistence strategy, pawnbroking was a key lubricant of the urban economy that incorporated street vendors, artisans, shopkeepers, and consumers.[21]

The Baratillo's customers are the most difficult participants in the market to profile because the archives offer few clues about who, exactly, shopped there. Impressionistic accounts from the era suggest that it catered mainly to the destitute and those who cared little about the provenance of the articles they purchased. In a scene in José Joaquín Fernández de Lizardi's 1816 novel, *El periquillo sarniento*, the Baratillo plays precisely this role. When Perico, the protagonist, and Januario, his friend and mentor in mischief, win fifty pesos in a card game, Januario proposes:

> Let's go to the Parián, or better yet, to the Baratillo, so we can buy some decent clothes, which will help improve our lot. They will get us better treatment everywhere . . . because I assure you, my brother, that although they say the habit does not make the monk . . . when a decent person walks around—in the streets, in house calls, in games, in dances, and even in temples—he enjoys certain attention and respect. Thus, it's better to be a well-dressed *pícaro* than an *hombre de bien* in rags.[22]

Here Lizardi plays to popular conceptions that the Baratillo's customers were rogues and lowlifes. With a little cash, those individuals could acquire the castoffs of the wealthy and pass themselves off as respectable people. This theme appears in many late-colonial writings about the Baratillo; it was a place where the identities of both people and goods became unrecognizable, where hierarchies and the categories used to construct them became vulnerable. In the Baratillo, a rogue could turn himself into a gentleman and a casta could become a Spaniard.

Other evidence, however, suggests that the Baratillo also appealed to better-off customers. As Juan de Viera, the administrator of Mexico City's Colegio de San Ildefonso, wrote in 1778, the Baratillo Grande attracted "every class and quality of person" with its dizzying array of goods. Unlike other eighteenth-century writers, Viera saw not a teeming den of thieves and vagabonds but a lively bazaar that offered something for everyone.[23] Archival evidence supports Viera's observations. In 1729, Don Antonio Velasco, a member of the Real Audiencia, sold a relatively expensive cloak, worth twelve pesos, to a vendor in the Baratillo.[24] The cost of such an item was roughly equal to a month's wages for an unskilled worker in the capital in the eighteenth century.[25] Given that historians have shown that members of middling and upper echelons of Mexico City society regularly used pawnshops and the Monte de Piedad, the government-run pawnshop established in 1775, it makes sense that they also would have bought and sold clothing and household goods in the Baratillo.[26] The Baratillo was a commercial institution that offered an array of products—both used and new, cheap and high end—and engaged actors of diverse ethnic and socioeconomic backgrounds.

The Baratillo was also a site where legal and illegal exchanges were deeply entwined. It was the nexus of Mexico City's shadow economy, where the circuits of second-hand, stolen, counterfeit, contraband, untaxed, or otherwise illicit goods intersected. This economy linked some of the most elite traders in New Spain to some of the lowliest and connected pulperías, which often doubled as pawnshops, to artisans' workshops and vendors in the Plaza Mayor. Colonial officials were not of one mind when it came to regulating this trade. While some authorities tried to stamp it out, others condoned or turned a blind eye to it.

An investigation that José Antonio Lince González, Mexico City's chief assayer and a member of the Real Audiencia, conducted into the illegal sale of gold and silver jewelry in the Baratillo in the early 1780s reveals some of the connections between the Baratillo and the city's broader economy. The investigation sought to extinguish the trade in jewelry that lacked the "*quinto*" stamp indicating that the required 20 percent tax had been levied on it. These pieces were often of a lower quality than the twenty-two-carat standard the Crown had imposed. Lince González found that the gold and silver for sale in the Baratillo was coming mainly from three sources: clandestine workshops; pulperías, where the poor pawned such pieces in exchange for short-term loans; and the Real Monte de Piedad.[27] The pieces circulated undetected between those locations and the Baratillo, where they blended in with the market's clothing, tools, and household goods. This trade challenged the rigid barriers the colonial government tried to impose between artisans and merchants, whom colonial law prevented from working together, and linked the Baratillo directly to a government institution—the Monte de Piedad. It also reveals that diverse individuals were involved in the trade: some of the vendors who sold the pieces were single Spaniards, one a married morisco, and another a married Spanish "notable" who had fallen on hard times. Most were clothing sellers who claimed to trade in small valuables on the side, which is to say, they had not manufactured the pieces themselves; they had come into their possession through happenstance. It was a defense that many vendors in the Baratillo used with colonial authorities, with apparent success.[28]

It is tempting to label the shadow economy Lince González uncovered an informal economy, applying a term from twentieth-century social science to the eighteenth century. Indeed, the Baratillo and the semipermanent street markets scattered around late-colonial Mexico City meet several of the criteria that scholars have used to define the informal economy: its transactions were largely unregulated and untaxed, and many of the businesses were relatively small and family owned and operated.[29] Furthermore, one could argue, in the vein of neoliberal approaches to the study of informality, that the trade in unminted gold and silver pieces was a rational response to an overly burdensome regulatory regime. It was a practice that served people's legitimate economic needs; the law simply had not caught up to reality.[30]

Yet, as historians and social scientists have emphasized in recent years, creating a rigid dichotomy between formal and informal sectors obscures the many ways legal and extralegal activities were intertwined.[31] In the Baratillo, untaxed and irregular goods mixed with patently illicit ones. Stolen jewelry and clothes, counterfeit coins, illegal arms, seditious books, and new and used manufactured goods of all kinds circulated alongside one another in the market. The distinction between the antisocial and the merely extralegal breaks down in the Baratillo's dense warren of stands, tables, and ambulatory vendors.

Colonial authorities frequently complained that the Baratillo was a distribution point for stolen goods. Although pilfered items of every kind made their way into the market, stolen clothing was especially common. Clothes were expensive in New Spain, due to the high cost of textile production there, and one could convert them into cash easily by pawning or selling them.[32] The Baratillo was a particularly attractive place for thieves looking to unload stolen clothes. In an 1814 case, police apprehended a nineteen-year-old Indian named Francisco Pineda from the village of Cuautitlán, located about twenty-five kilometers northwest of Mexico City, for his role in the robbery of three Indians. Pineda and his accomplices stole seven or eight pesos from their victims, along with their clothes and bedsheets, "leaving them to go naked to their village." Authorities caught Pineda the next day as he sold one of the stolen sheets in the Baratillo. He was wearing the shirt and underpants of one victim when the police found him, suggesting that the thieves sought not only cash but also the clothes themselves. Pineda received a punishment of 200 lashes and eight years of labor at a fort in Acapulco.[33]

In another case, from 1819, Ángel Ramírez, an indio *ladino* (or Indian fluent in Spanish) and Victoriano Sánchez, a Spaniard, were charged with breaking into a woman's home and stealing four black tunics, three shawls, a shirt, and a tablecloth. The police caught the men as they attempted to sell some of the clothes to a trader in the Baratillo for ten pesos. Ramírez assured the authorities of his innocence, claiming that he was selling the clothes on behalf of another man, a common defense. Sánchez, for his part, claimed he was in the Baratillo not because he was involved in any crime, "but rather to find a woman named Guadalupe whom he says he had seen pass through the Baratillo around this time, because he needed to see her"—an explanation the police quickly dismissed.[34]

These cases illustrate how Mexico City's shadow economy transcended ethnic divisions, bringing individuals from diverse backgrounds together in the business of illicit commerce. They also reveal the geographic reach of that trade, which drew in people like Pineda, who lived in the capital's hinterlands.[35] And they hint at the important social role the Baratillo played in the city. More than just a place to buy and sell, it was a point where men and women from across the city and beyond also gathered to gossip, flirt, and exchange ideas. Authorities worried about those types of interactions, too. Colonial officials repeatedly complained that the Baratillo attracted an unholy mélange that engaged in illicit transactions that extended beyond trading in stolen goods.

The Baratillo also attracted vendors who businesses violated moral and religious laws. Prostitutes gathered there, and, authorities complained, "under the shadow of darkness, sins of sensuality" abounded.[36] The market attracted other vices, too, such as gambling, which colonial authorities repeatedly outlawed.[37] On a number of occasions, vendors in the Baratillo came before Mexico's Inquisition for crimes against the faith. In 1751, the mestiza María del Castillo appeared before the tribunal for practicing witchcraft in the Baratillo Chico—using her supposed powers to save people's souls, make them fall in love, improve their luck in cockfights, "and other such stupidities."[38] As the location of a number of bookshops, the Baratillo Grande was an emporium of dangerous ideas. In 1768, a Spanish poet went before the Inquisition for writing, publishing, and selling a "libelous ballad" criticizing the expulsion of the Jesuits from Spanish America the previous year.[39] In 1791, the Tribunal accused another Spanish bookseller in the Baratillo of "propositions," for telling people that monks and friars served no purpose.[40] To their critics, the baratilleros trafficked not only in pilfered goods but also in seditious thought and moral perversions.

Yet, even as authorities prosecuted some economic exchanges in the Baratillo vigorously, they condoned others. The mere act of collecting rent from vendors in the Baratillo, which the Ayuntamiento did throughout the market's history, conferred a degree of legitimacy on its businesses. Officials also participated directly in extralegal activities in the Baratillo by accepting gratificaciones, the tips or bribes that vendors paid local officials to transfer ownership of a business in the plaza and expedite other bureaucratic processes.[41] On at least one occasion, officials contradicted standing prohibitions of the Baratillo by acknowleding the baratilleros' right to practice their trade. In 1777, the regidor (city councilman) Don Thomás Fernández sought to remove the the baratilleros who trafficked in used iron goods in the Plaza Mayor. His argument was the familiar one: its vendors were selling keys, nails, knives, and other implements that servants had stolen from their masters' homes, in addition to prohibited weapons. This activity gave rise to "drunkenness, stupidity, and other vices" from which the "miserable people" suffered. Fernández acknowledged that the trade in stolen goods required both vendors and customers, and the latter were far from innocent, because they bought "knowing that those pieces [had been] stolen."[42] Fernández's complaint resulted in a new ordinance, in May 1778, from the *fiel ejecutoría*, the branch of the Ayuntamiento responsible for enforcing consumer laws, stating that the sale of new or used iron in the Baratillo was a violation of guild regulations.[43]

Yet the city stopped short of removing the vendors' mesillas altogether, as Fernández had wanted. In fact, the plaza judge determined, in a June 1785 report, that doing so would violate King Philip III's original 1611 decree granting petty vendors the right to practice their commerce in the Plaza Mayor and the Mexico City Ayuntamiento the authority to collect rent from them. Municipal officials, the judge concluded, would have to find new ways of preventing the "inconveniences" these vendors caused. He added, with a note of resignation, that "even if the puestos and mesillas are exterminated, with the hardware, iron, and tin shops remaining open, the evil-doers will never lack a place to buy and sell" their stolen goods.[44]

It was not the only time officials conferred legitimacy on the Baratillo's commerce by acknowledging the limits of their ability to rein it in. Lince González's investigation into the sale of untaxed gold and silver pieces in the Baratillo concluded not in redoubled efforts to root out the purveyors of those goods but in the legalization of the lower-quality, twenty-carat gold pieces.[45] Officials realized that it made more sense to legalize and collect taxes on the smaller pieces than to continue fighting a losing battle to eliminate them.

Colonial officials responded in a similar fashion to the phenomenon of tlacos—the informal tokens that Mexico City shopkeepers created to compensate for the absence of government-issued small change in the capital, and which people traded for silver reales and cacao beans in the Baratillo.[46] Royal authorities never mounted a serious effort to end the trade in tlacos. Instead, they implemented a series of regulations that sought to curtail their abuse, prohibiting loans issued in tlacos and fixing the exchange rate between tlacos and silver reales to halt the slide in tlacos' value. In doing so, they recognized and condoned an extralegal economic practice.[47]

Agents of the government also legitimized informal transactions by mediating conflicts between petty merchants in the capital. Take the 1722 suit that Francisca Magdalena, an Indian clothing seller in the Plaza Mayor, brought against Felipe de Ávila, a man of unspecified racial background, with the city's *mesa de propios*, the tribunal that oversaw public markets. De Ávila had apparently taken possession of Magdalena's stand after she had sold numerous articles of clothing for him but never gave him the proceeds. Magdalena claimed to have acquired the right to the stand from Ana María de la Encarnación, whose mother had received one of the original puestos established after the 1692 riot—a story that witnesses for her side corroborated. De Ávila and his witnesses, however, denied that Magdalena ever had rightful ownership of the stand, contending that de la Encarnación's son and grandchildren had traded de Ávila the stand in exchange for the fourteen pesos he provided for her funeral. The Ayuntamiento's mesa de propios came down with a verdict that attempted to satisfy both parties, ordering Magdalena to pay de Ávila sixty pesos and provide him with seventy-six *naguas de tierra* (Mexican-made skirts) in order to "settle accounts"—but let her remain in the stand.[48] In the absence of written documentation, municipal officials mediated disputes and upheld informal agreements.

The involvement of agents reponsible for enforcing the law in activities that violated it underscores the limitations of the formal-informal model. Government officials helped blur the lines between illicit and legitimate commerce in late-colonial Mexico City by sanctioning, even institutionalizing, exchanges that the law explicitly prohibited.[49] The Baratillo did not operate in a parallel economic sphere outside the formal, regulated economy. On the contrary, its vendors and their businesses had far-reaching ties to other sectors and participants in the Mexico City economy, including the officials charged with policing it. Some of the sharpest conflicts in the Baratillo, in fact, were not between vendors and the government but between baratilleros and rival merchants and artisans.

THE BARATILLO AND THE GUILDS

Throughout the colonial era, the Baratillo had a particularly contentious relationship with Mexico City's artisan guilds. Vendors in the Baratillo flouted regulations that gave the guilds monopolies over the production and distribution of the goods they manufactured and stipulated precisely where they could sell those products.[50] In the eighteenth century, the guilds, with the aid of the municipal government, prosecuted violators of those rules aggressively. Baratilleros pushed back against those efforts by exploiting the ambiguities of colonial law and by playing local and royal officials against each other. When the Ayuntamiento sided against them, the baratilleros appealed to the corregidor, who overturned most of their convictions. The guild investigations underscore that the boundary between legal and illegal in the economy of eighteenth-century Mexico City was anything but fixed and that the vendors of the Baratillo helped determine its contours.

Manufacturing in colonial Mexico City was a tightly regulated affair. Only master artisans, certified by examination, could sell the goods they made, and only from their own workshops. Spanish legislation protected artisanal trades by restricting entry into the professions and by erecting barriers between artisans and merchants. The reselling of artisanal manufactures, known as *regatonería*, by merchants or anyone else was strictly forbidden, and artisans were likewise prohibited from working in merchants' shops or dealing directly with them.[51] The Spanish favored the monopolies of artisan guilds because even if they did not provide consumers with the lowest possible prices, those corporations were relatively easy for the government to oversee. The guilds' stringent regulations, however, created incentives for people to circumvent the system by selling in street markets like the Baratillo.

The guilds' internal regulations also spurred their own members, particularly unexamined journeymen and apprentices, to sell outside the system. Although in theory the guilds offered a means of ascent for poor boys who were able to secure an apprenticeship with an artisan, advance to journeyman, and eventually attain the status of master and open their own workshops, relatively few journeymen made that final leap. The 1788 census reveals that of 1,215 members of the tailor guild, only 94 were masters, while 698 were journeymen and 423 were apprentices.[52] Between 1767 and 1769, an average of just 29 journeymen from all guilds in the capital became masters each year. Furthermore, the average age of those who did was thirty-six, indicating that these men spent the better part of two decades working in someone else's shop before they could open one of their own. The costs associated with becoming a master also presented a significant burden for aspirants. Many were reluctant to pay the six-peso fee for the licensing exam. That amount paled, however, in comparison with the costs associated with opening one's own shop, which included buying a full set of tools—at a cost of 100 pesos or more—and renting or purchasing space for a workshop.[53]

The Spanish Crown had long recognized the threat that the Baratillo posed to the guild system. The oldest surviving document that mentions the Baratillo, in fact, is a 1644 decree that banned the market for this very reason. The viceroy at the time, the Second Count of Salvatierra, claimed that baratilleros were undermining the guild system by selling ornaments, blankets, chairs, and especially iron at prices substantially below those on offer in artisan workshops. Salvatierra explained the harm that Baratillo vendors were inflicting on guild members in stark terms: the baratilleros were "leaving them lost and destroyed because . . . enjoying this liberty, they were leaving the guilds with the burden of the *alcabala* [royal sales tax] and contributions and expenses of their professions, causing such harm that they are not even able to sustain their families."[54] Colonial authorities ordered the Baratillo closed in 1635, 1644, 1689, and 1696 not only because it contributed to the city's crime problem but also because it undermined the economic organization of the colony.[55]

Guild officials, of course, were aware of these issues, and in the first half of the eighteenth century the *veedores* (guild overseers) mounted a campaign to root out people who violated guild rules by selling in the Baratillo.[56] The tailor guild was particularly aggressive. A number of cases they brought before the fiel ejecutoría, the organ of Mexico City's Ayuntamiento responsible for overseeing the guilds as well as all commercial activity in the capital, reveal the extent of clothes-makers' concern that the Baratillo was sheltering many of these contraveners.[57]

The prohibition of textile sales outside the guild system in Mexico dates to a 1613 law barring any person from selling new clothes in "public auctions, tianguises, or anywhere else" under punishment of confiscation of those clothes and a thirty-peso fine.[58] In 1640, the viceroy Marquis of Cadereyta reissued the ban, directing it at the "mestizos, Indians, and mulattos who have as their trade the making and selling of unexamined doublets" in tianguises—racializing a practice that evidence shows Spaniards also engaged in.[59] Since the Crown acknowledged that the price of new clothes left them out of reach of Mexico's vast poor population, it permitted the sale of used clothing by vendors in and around the Baratillo.[60] But in the early eighteenth century, the tailor guild complained that vendors were bending, or in some cases openly flouting, the rules by selling new clothes. They also worried that baratilleros were modifying the appearance of clothing to get around existing regulations. In 1705, a new ordinance complemented the 1613 law by banning the practice of altering new clothes and reselling them. The ordinance was written to stop the sale of stolen clothes, which vendors would refashion to make them more difficult for authorities to identify.[61]

In early October 1706, Ventura Serrano, an alcalde (municipal judge) on the Ayuntamiento, and Domingo de la Moya, a veedor for the tailor guild, wrote to Mexico City's corregidor, Nuño Núñez de Villavicencio, expressing their concern about the widespread practice of selling new clothes from stalls in and around the Plaza Mayor. "Either because of ignorance due to the passage of time [since the 1613 law], or because of the malice of those who know of the prohibition," they wrote, "one sees in the streets and plazas nothing but a crowd of subjects selling . . . various types of clothing, all new."[62] Worse still, many of these vendors were peddling used clothes as if they were new, claiming that they had come directly from Castile, China, or indigenous clothing makers in Mexico, and charging customers accordingly.[63] Serrano and de la Moya pleaded with Núñez de Villavicencio for help in ending these abuses—perpetrated in many cases by members of the tailor guild themselves—which were causing such "pernicious and public harm to the common good and that of the guild."[64]

When the corregidor failed to respond, Serrano and de la Moya took matters into their own hands and went to the Baratillo and the adjacent Plaza del Volador to carry out a series of raids. On October 16, 1706, the officials discovered illegal merchandise in the stands of over a dozen clothing vendors in the two plazas—some of which was new and some of which had been illegally altered or contained imitation silver or gold fibers. Miguel Samudio, one of those apprehended with nonregulation clothing, fought back, taking his case to the court of the fiel ejecutoría. He argued that the clothes the overseers found in his stand were ones he had made for and already sold (for the substantial sum of eighty pesos) to the itinerant merchant Don Joseph de Rivera. He had merely hung those clothes in his stand in the Plaza Mayor to attract the attention of potential customers. Samudio, as his lawyer Domingo de Córdova argued in a subsequent petition, had not violated any ordinances because all of the materials in the clothes were new, and the existing rules prohibited only the reuse of old materials in the fashioning of clothes sold as new.[65] That there was some confusion about the law had not been lost on guild authorities. On March 3, 1706, several months before the confiscation of Samudio's merchandise, a representative of the tailor guild noted in a letter to the Real Audiencia that continuing disputes between tailors (sastres) and clothing sellers (roperos) required a new ordinance to clarify who was allowed to sell what type of clothing and where.[66] That ordinance appears to have been in effect by 1715, when an investigator's report of abuses in the Baratillo cited a rule stipulating that "neither new nor transmuted nor *sangrada* [altered] clothing may be sold in the Baratillo of this city."[67]

Although artisans enjoyed a middling status above that of laborers and the working poor and a common identity based on shared skills and corporate membership, their position was far from secure in the early eighteenth century.[68] Before Bourbon reformers began to break up their monopolies in an effort to promote industry and trade in the latter part of the eighteenth century, the guilds struggled under the weight of their own rules, which proved incapable of insulating members from competition.[69] Even those craftsmen lucky enough to become masters and establish their own workshops sometimes operated side businesses in the Baratillo, or else saw their workshops suffer because of others who did.[70] Market forces, however, were not the only pressures the guild system and its municipal regulators faced in the eighteenth century. Vendors in the Baratillo also engaged in legal maneuvers that proved highly effective in helping them circumvent the law and avoid punishment.

Vendors in the Baratillo employed a number of strategies for resisting the guilds' enforcement efforts. These included operating in networks that seem carefully designed to avoid explicit infractions of the law, or exploiting its ambiguities in ways that allowed them to evade punishment. For example, the practice of a tailor's loaning clothes to a baratillero to sell for him was a common one and seems to have protected the vendor from prosecution since he was not technically the owner of the illicit goods. In 1729, investigators accused Pedro Velázquez, a Spaniard, of selling three new woolen cloaks in his stand in the Baratillo. Velázquez, however, claimed that two of the cloaks belonged to the mestizo tailor Blas de la Rosa, who had asked Velázquez to hold them for him, and that Velázquez had purchased only the third.[71] Velázquez assured the veedores that this was the first time he had ever sold a piece of new clothing, having previously dealt only in used pieces. He got off with a warning and was ordered to return the cloaks to de la Rosa.[72] The practice even appears in Lizardi's *El periquillo sarniento*, when Perico, the protagonist, tries to sell a cloak he has stolen from a doctor named Purgante, only to find that the baratillero to whom he tried to sell it was, in fact, an employee of Purgante, and immediately recognized the cloak. Perico promised the man that he had not purchased the cloak, but had been given it by someone else to sell for him.[73]

Vendors did not limit themselves to defenses based on legal technicalities; they also presented arguments that tapped into a political culture that emphasized leniency toward the downtrodden. Felipe Dávila admitted to selling dozens of articles of new clothing in 1715 because he "did not have enough to eat."[74] Blas de la Rosa stressed that he was a "poor journeyman" who sold the cloak out of desperation. He also defended the quality of his work: for ten years he had made "well-conditioned and not sangrada" cloaks, and that until now no one had questioned the practice.[75] Velázquez claimed that "finding myself a journeyman tailor, poor, and charged with children, I have been obligated to make these cloaks."[76] In making these claims, the vendors played to Spanish officials' customary sympathies for the poor, which played an important role in colonial legal culture. Royal officials were expected to demonstrate compassion for the less fortunate in their administration of justice.[77]

These arguments were remarkably effective. In nearly every case this chapter examines, the accused ultimately succeeded in getting his punishment reduced or tossed out. Núñez de Villavicencio, the corregidor who determined the punishments for those convicted in fiel ejecutoría cases, challenged de la Moya's confiscation of their goods during the October 1706 raids. The corregidor ordered that the veedores return the clothing in question and the thirty-peso fine they had collected from Miguel Samudio.[78] In February 1707, Juan Hernández Chapas, a master in the tailor guild with a stand in the Plaza del Volador, successfully argued, again with the help of the lawyer Domingo de Córdova, that no harm could come from selling new clothing in public spaces. He, too, had his merchandise and his fine returned to him.[79]

The baratilleros also asserted their right to make a living by selling new and used goods on the city's streets and plazas by using some of the same language the veedores leveled against them. On the day of Serrano and de la Moya's raid on the Baratillo in 1709, two Spanish clothing sellers wrote to Corregidor Núñez de Villavicencio in the name of all those who sold clothing in the Baratillo to condemn the tactics of the veedores. Joseph Ramírez, who had been implicated, and Diego Rufino, who had not, claimed that the veedores and alcaldes simply had a grudge against the Baratillo: "They have always tried to destroy it, which has not taken place due to the fact that the Baratillo is clearly and manifestly in the common good, for the poor supply themselves there for much less than they could if they went to those tailors who for their own interest seek to humiliate us and detract from the public good." They pleaded with the corregidor to suspend the orders restricting clothing sales so that they could "with all liberty sell in said Baratillo both new and used clothing" and to "notify those alcaldes and veedors that they may not cause us worry or perturb us."[80] Blas de la Rosa made a similar argument when he defended his wares by noting that "their price is very moderate and of great convenience and utility to the poor."[81] These men asserted that they had a right to practice their trade in a public space because it benefited the larger community.

Street vendors, government officials, and other parties frequently invoked the concepts of *el bien común* (the common good), *el beneficio público* (public benefit), and *la utilidad pública* (public utility) in the eighteenth century. This language stems from the consensual nature of early modern Spanish politics and the notion that although the monarch ultimately determined the common good, he reached that decision through a process of negotiation with his subjects. Theorists of the Salamanca school of sixteenth- and seventeenth-century Spain such as Francisco de Vitoria, Domingo de Soto, and Tomás de Mercado, steeped in the natural law tradition, stressed the popular origins of sovereignty and the limitations on royal power. A social contract bound government and governed, and laws that broke with that agreement were seen as running contrary to the common good. The king, as the head of the "political mystical body," was ultimately responsible for ensuring the welfare of his subjects; his agents on the ground were charged with making everyday decisions that furthered the goal of promoting the widest possible benefit to the political community.[82] Petitions from baratilleros and other petty merchants invoked these principles when they argued that a particular policy threatened not only their livelihoods but the well-being of the community as a whole. Indeed, throughout the Baratillo's history, its vendors routinely employed the same rhetoric that elite opponents used to portray the market as a danger to society to assert the market's social value.[83]

In defending themselves from prosecution, the baratilleros also manipulated the colonial justice system by exploiting tensions between local and royal officials in Mexico City. By appealing the fiel ejecutoría rulings to the corregidor, they gave a royal official the opportunity to show up his local rivals, using his discretion to display leniency to the offenders and perhaps generate good will from the aggrieved vendors.[84] Whatever Núñez de Villavicencio's reasons were for reducing or overruling the fiel ejecutoría's sentences against the baratilleros, his actions helped legitimize the Baratillo's commerce. The guild cases thus reinforce the point that baratilleros never confronted a unified colonial state. Political rivalries and personal animosities among authorities in Mexico City—at the highest levels of government and at the lowest—played an important role in the market's persistence, in part because vendors and their advocates knew how to manipulate them to their advantage.

The Baratillo thrived in late-colonial Mexico City not only because it was vital to the city and region's broader economy but also because vendors made the case for its importance, using the avenues that colonial institutions created for them. With the help of their lawyers, they asserted the legitimacy and necessity of their commerce to the greater community—deploying the political vernacular of the day to defend their livelihoods. In the street markets of colonial Mexico City, even ones sustained by illicit transactions, business and politics were inseparable from one another.

VENDORS, MERCHANTS, AND
THE ART OF COMMERCE

Colonial politics also permeated baratilleros' disputes with rival merchants in the Plaza Mayor in the eighteenth century. Cajoneros in the plaza complained that the baratilleros were underselling them by obtaining the same expensive imported items they sold from their stores through questionable means and offering them to customers at lower prices. In peddling stolen and counterfeit goods, the baratilleros, the cajoneros claimed, were tarnishing the good name of merchants and of the entire mercantile profession. Baratilleros, for their part, adopted that same language in order to defend the social and economic utility of their trade and its contribution to the welfare of the kingdom. In doing so, they tapped into an eighteenth-century political discourse that sought to promote trade as a means of revitalizing Spain's flagging economy.

On July 30, 1709, Don Bacilio de Ribera wrote to the viceroy of New Spain on behalf of the cajoneros of the Plaza Mayor expressing their concern that baratilleros and other petty merchants were robbing the cajoneros of their clients, hurting their sales, and depriving the city of much-needed income by evading rents and taxes. Many baratilleros, he claimed, had begun to sell the same products they offered in their cajones. Visitors to the city were no longer shopping at their stores but going directly to the stalls of the Baratillo. These vendors, according to Bacilio de Ribera, did not pay any of the taxes levied on the cajoneros, and were thus competing unfairly for their business.[85] Tensions between vendors in the Baratillo and the cajoneros continued to rise until they finally came to a head in 1724, when Juan de Dios

Anzures, a lawyer writing on behalf of the cajoneros, lodged his complaint with the viceroy Juan de Acuna.[86]

The cajoneros warned that baratilleros were a threat not just to their own businesses but to the entire merchant profession. Like many opponents of the Baratillo, they described the dangers it posed in racialized terms. "There is not an Indian, mulatto, mestizo, or any of the unidentifiable castas that is not or does not want to be a merchant," one petitioner lamented.[87] These upwardly mobile castas challenged Spanish dominance of high-end trade, tarnishing the profession's reputation. *Mercaderes* (merchants) and *mercancías* (merchandise), he wrote, were fast becoming indistinguishable from mercachifles (ambulatory vendors) and *artificios* (fraudulent goods). True merchants were "honorable" men who held membership in the Consulado and had a personal wealth of at least ten to twelve thousand pesos. The trade that these men practiced was of a completely different order from the "vulgar" work of the baratilleros, who "expel from their commerce the good faith that is the foundation and the principal dogma of the Merchants' Institute," as the Consulado was also known.[88] One writer summarized the cajoneros' argument by explaining that although street vending "seems to be an honest and virtuous application for the many men occupied in this type of commerce," in reality it only "simulates a licit occupation, [hiding] their lack of work ethic and laziness."[89] The cajoneros argued that the difference between merchants and street vendors needed to be formalized by restricting the use of the words *mercader* and *mercancía* to members of the Consulado.[90]

The cajoneros tied the low prices of goods in the Baratillo to the low morals of its vendors. They portrayed the products in their own stores as legitimate because of their higher price, while suggesting that the discounted goods in the Baratillo stemmed from the criminal activities and dirty tricks of the baratilleros. This theme is threaded through colonial-era documents on the Baratillo. In the Count of Salvatierra's 1644 decree banning the Baratillo, he complained of vendors selling stolen goods for a fraction of their "true value."[91] King Charles II worried in a 1688 letter to the viceroy that silver jewelry pieces worth twenty pesos sold for just six or eight pesos in the Baratillo.[92] And in one of their petitions, the cajoneros accused ambulatory vendors of doing nothing but wandering the city trying to sell some "worthless goods."[93] A product with a high price indicated that both it and the merchant who sold it were honorable.[94]

In their efforts to distinguish themselves from lowly baratilleros and ambulatory vendors, the cajoneros also tapped into an eighteenth-century political discourse that sought to promote commerce and elevate the social standing of merchants. The arrival of the Bourbons in Madrid after 1700 brought renewed vitality to Spanish efforts to stimulate commerce. The Junta de Comercio, which the last Habsburg king, Charles II, established in 1679 to foment trade and industrial production, saw its stature raised under King Philip V. In 1724, the same year that the cajoneros' case against the baratilleros began, Gerónimo de Uztáriz, a Spanish economist and member of the Junta, published his *Theórica y práctica de comercio y marina*, which argued that increasing foreign and domestic trade would lead to Spain's resurgence on the world stage. The Spanish Crown tried to elevate the social status of merchants by bringing more of them into the nobility. It also issued decrees that guaranteed that nobles who engaged in commerce or manufacturing would maintain their titles and privileges.[95]

In the minds of Spanish reformers, the commerce that would lift the empire out of its economic rut was long-distance trade, not the quotidian exchanges that took place in the Baratillo and other public markets. Spanish elites viewed petty commerce as "sordid" because they saw it as an extension of manual labor.[96] Spanish observers had long cast scorn on the vendors that filled Mexico's streets and plazas. In 1599, the writer Gonzalo Gómez de Cervantes lamented how few Spaniards in Mexico chose to engage in agriculture and instead preferred to set up small shops and stalls in the streets.[97] King Philip III's 1611 decree granting the Ayuntamiento of Mexico ownership of the Plaza Mayor also expressed disdain for the commerce that filled the square when it noted "the disorder that there was in this city from having the stands of buhoneros in the public plaza . . . occupying themselves in this [trade] many persons who could attend to other industries more important and necessary to the republic."[98]

To restore order to the city's retail sector and repair the damaged reputation of the merchant profession, the cajoneros recommended two remedies. First, the colonial administration should revert to its earlier practice of issuing licenses to purveyors of imported goods, as it had done in the seventeenth century. These permits helped ensure that the government received its alcabala income (which the Consulado collected until the tax farm was abolished in 1754) and that non-Spaniards ("*hombres del color quebrado*") could not participate in this elite trade.[99] The second solution, and the one that became the focus of the cajoneros' efforts as the matter wound its way through the colonial bureaucracy, was the outright prohibition of the Baratillo and the removal of mercachifles from the city's streets. Mateo de Ayssa, Mexico City's *procurador*, or city attorney, at the time, was firmly on the side of the cajoneros. In a letter dated May 19, 1724, he expressed his intention to "extinguish" the Baratillo once and for all, and to ban ambulatory vendors, as the city of Zacatecas had done with apparent success a decade earlier.[100] But the case stalled. On June 22, 1727, King Philip V demanded that Viceroy Acuna make a decision on the fate of the market.[101] He does not appear to have done so. The archival file contains no record of his response, but given that there is virtually no gap in archival evidence related to the Baratillo in the eighteenth century, the merchants' plot to have it eradicated almost certainly failed or at least did not have any lasting impact.[102] The Baratillo continued to exist in the state of legal limbo it had occupied since the seventeenth century.

The cajoneros who took aim at the Baratillo in the eighteenth century positioned themselves as practitioners of the elite art of commerce—as merchants defending an honorable profession from pollution by the vulgar classes. Yet it is unlikely that the men who signed the petitions seeking to outlaw the Baratillo and ambulatory vending were actually members of the Consulado. To gain entrance to the merchant guild, the sole legal importer of overseas goods into Mexico from its incorporation in 1592 until 1778, merchants needed to be at least twenty-five years old and own their own wholesale warehouse that dealt exclusively with imported merchandise. Yet Mexico City's 1816 commercial census reveals that some 150 different merchants owned the Parián's 180 cajones, and few of them also owned warehouses, suggesting that many of these men would not have qualified to join the merchant guild. The Consulado's limited membership (between 100 and 200, depending on the era) also supports that conclusion.[103] Cajoneros and *almaceneros* (warehouse owners), then, probably constituted two separate social groups, with the former rarely becoming the latter. Cajoneros, in reality, were closer in status to the owners of pulperías and tiendas mestizas than they were to the overseas merchants who owned the warehouses. Successful cajoneros were able to buy only small rural properties, not the large haciendas in which almaceneros often invested their fortunes. Others did not even own their own homes.[104]

The language in the cajoneros' petitions against mercachifles and baratilleros reveals the insecurities of an aspirational, middling group of merchants. Their rhetorical strategy was, in all likelihood, an appeal to the Consulado merchants who administered the merchant tribunal and exercised significant influence in colonial government.[105] By highlighting the baratilleros' challenge to the honor of the merchant profession, the cajoneros were defending their own relatively tenuous position in the commercial hierarchy of colonial

Mexico City. They were attempting to open a social and racial distance between themselves and the vendors of the Baratillo because the economic one was small or nonexistent. Their businesses might not have been much more substantial than some of the larger stands in the Baratillo Grande, such as the ones owned by Miguel Samudio and Josef Fianca.[106] Perhaps just as telling, records show that a number of baratilleros used the honorific title "don." Although this term was of declining significance by the eighteenth century, its use nonetheless hints at the baratilleros' aspirations and the concern this aroused for cajoneros.[107] The cajoneros of the Plaza Mayor, like the members of the artisan guilds who waged a parallel attack on the Baratillo during the same period, were middling actors who saw both their economic livelihoods and their social status threatened by the vendors of the capital's most notorious thieves' market.[108]

The cajoneros had good cause for concern; the merchant profession was indeed relatively open to men and women of all backgrounds. While the Consulado had strict entry requirements, the lower rungs of the commercial hierarchy did not. As the cajoneros correctly pointed out, virtually anyone could call himself or herself a "*comerciante*," the general term for any person who owned a mercantile establishment. The 1790 census lists 1,384 comerciantes—a count that far exceeds the 100 to 200 import merchants with membership in the Consulado.[109] Street vending was particularly easy to enter, with little formal regulation and low capital requirements. As historians of Mexico City and other urban centers in Spanish America have shown, commerce offered avenues of ascent for non-Europeans, people of mixed race, and women, and some individuals from those marginalized groups found success in it.[110] At the same time, it was a risky profession, and many merchants, even wealthy ones, saw their fortunes disappear overnight. Competition in the retail sector was intense, and bankruptcies were common among cajoneros and pulperos, who relied heavily on credit from the capital's importers.[111] The instability of their profession led cajoneros to worry that baratilleros, through their shady practices, would put them out of business, so they attempted to introduce new legislation restricting entry into the merchant profession.[112]

Baratilleros did not take those attempts lying down. Although the cajoneros' case file from the 1720s does not include responses from the Baratillo's vendors, in a number of other instances in the eighteenth century, baratilleros defended themselves and their trade by deploying the same political vocabulary that their adversaries used against them, painting their trade as an honest and equally important branch of colonial commerce as any other. In 1713, Spanish mesilleros at the edge of the Baratillo asserted the legitimacy of their trade by claiming, "We work only with almaceneros and mercaderes, without buying anything stolen or from anyone suspicious."[113] They traded exclusively with the most reputable merchants in the capital, so, by extension, their commerce was honorable, too. As cajoneros sought to widen the distance between themselves and street vendors, baratilleros worked to narrow it. In 1796, the baratilleros inside the Plaza del Factor asked permission to place a statue of the Virgin of Guadalupe in the plaza—like the one that the Parián merchants had in their market. Authorities denied the request, citing a prohibition against putting images of Christ, the Virgin Mary, or the saints in "profane places."[114] The vendors in the Plaza del Factor countered that their market was just as legitimate as the city's other retail outlets. In another petition, they explained the commercial significance of their market in the anatomical language that was in vogue among urban reformers in the late eighteenth century. "To deny or doubt," the baratilleros wrote, "that the centers of villages, towns, and cities are the perfect sites for the circulation, or life, of commerce is to doubt or deny that the stomach of man was created for the specific functions or life of the human body." Commerce was the lifeblood of the city, and the commerce of the Baratillo was as essential as any other for its proper functioning. The author, or authors, of the petition are unknown, but fourteen vendors signed the petition. Each, save one, signed his own name (see figure 7).[115]

Baratilleros sometimes deployed that same language against rival street vendors. The aforementioned Spanish mesilleros complained to Francisco Cameros, the asentista who managed the Plaza Mayor during the first half of the eighteenth century, that other vendors in the plaza were blocking the flow of traffic in the market and were selling avería "at very low prices."[116] Baratilleros continued these attacks against their rivals throughout the late colonial period. In 1808, as officials sought to close the nighttime market in the Baratillo, now in the Plaza del Factor, an anonymous letter to the editors of the newspaper *Diario de México* complained that the "tumultuous group of buyers and sellers [that forms outside the Plaza del Factor] is no more than a clandestine commerce in stolen things." Beyond the crimes and frauds that took place there, the market hosted "a multitude of needy people . . . mixed without distinction between sexes or ages." He signed his letter "the Honorable Baratillero."[117]

The conflicts between baratilleros and other merchants and artisans illustrate the Baratillo's centrality in the urban economy. It provisioned Mexico

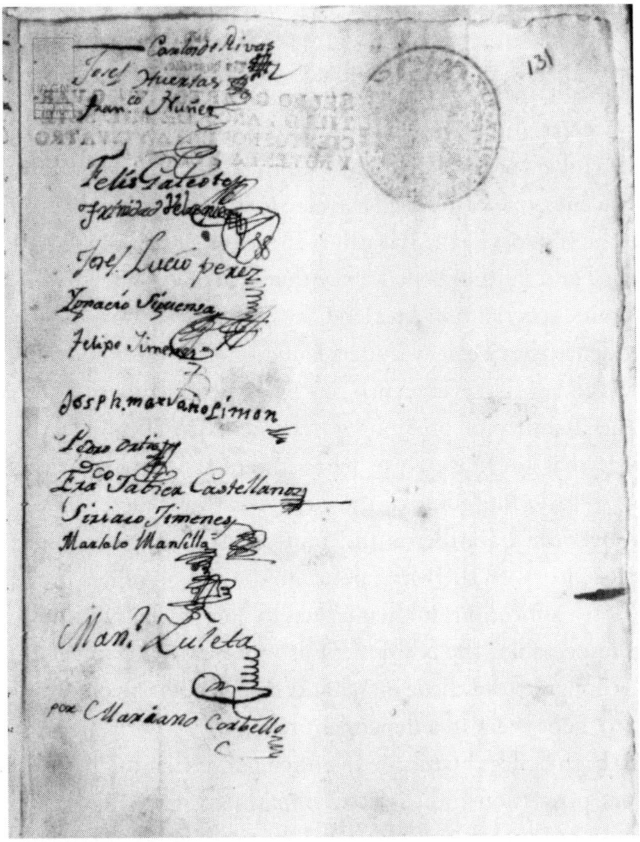

FIGURE 7. Signatures on a petition from baratilleros in the Plaza del Factor to Cosme de Mier y Trespalacios, Mexico City's superintendent of propios and arbitrios, August 1794. All of the signatories except the last one signed his own name. AGN, Indiferente Virreinal, caja 5093, exp. 2, f. 131.

City consumers with clothing, tools, and household goods at prices below those one could find in artisan workshops and retail emporiums like the Parián and the cajones of the Plaza Mayor, and it provided job opportunities to individuals from across the social spectrum. Indeed, while vendors and their critics, for different reasons, often painted the baratilleros as exclusively poor, the Baratillo also drew from professions that served the middle sector of colonial society. The struggles between baratilleros, artisans, and retail merchants highlight the instability of that sector and the efforts of urban residents to obtain and maintain positions within it.

While baratilleros faced hostility from artisans and retail merchants throughout the eighteenth century, they did not encounter the same enmity from the members of the Consulado. To the contrary, the owners of Mexico City's almacenes who comprised the elite merchant guild had extensive dealings with the vendors of the Baratillo. Those relationships speak to the webs of patronage and mutual dependence that entangled actors from across the socioeconomic spectrum in Mexico City's shadow economy.

The evidence that wealthy traders had economic interests in the Baratillo dates to the end of the seventeenth century, when members of the Audiencia blamed the inability of previous governments to eliminate the Baratillo on the fact that there were "so many interested parties in this disorder and abuse"—including some of the city's wealthiest merchants.[118] The relationships between baratilleros and import merchants continued into the eighteenth century. In their 1713 petition, the ribbon sellers in the Baratillo stressed those connections in their efforts to portray their businesses as legitimate and respectable. The petitioners also took care to point out that everything they bought from those merchants they bought on credit, which, they emphasized, kept them in a dependent relationship with their patrons—an attempt to both deflect blame for any illicit goods that might have come into the vendors' possession and to elicit sympathy from colonial officials.[119] The viceroy Duke of Linares also referenced the ties that bound small- and large-scale merchants, writing in 1716 that importers provided the baratilleros with items from their stores to sell in smaller quantities on the street.[120] And in a petition to the merchant tribunal in 1725, the cajoneros of the Plaza Mayor complained that baratilleros were buying the "rotting" goods of the almacenes to sell in the city's streets, plazas, corridors, and homes.[121] That the baratilleros and almaceneros were in business together was common knowledge in the late seventeenth and eighteenth centuries.

On at least one occasion, the members of the Consulado found it advantageous to champion their connections to baratilleros and other street vendors before colonial authorities. In a 1753 petition, they urged the Crown to repeal the alcabala on the resale of goods purchased within the capital, a tax that royal authorities had recently reintroduced.[122] The Consulado argued that the tax was stifling commerce in the kingdom and that it was particularly harmful to poor Indians who were selling the essential goods, such as shoes and candles, on which this tax was imposed. Don Juan de Sierra Uruñuela, the author of the petition, claimed to represent not only the members of the merchant guild but also "the owners of the cajones, tiendas, cacahuaterías, vinaterías [wine stores], and the rest of the cajoncillos and mesillas that are rigorously comprised by, and that can be called, commerce."[123] In this statement, the Consulado broadened the meaning of commerce to include the selling of goods "by hand in the Baratillo and outside of it by the buhoneros, canastilleros [those who sold from baskets], and others that trade in the streets and plazas."[124] This language stands in contrast to the words the cajoneros had used thirty years earlier in an attempt to distance themselves from petty traders and underscores just how flexible the categories of "comerciante" and "comercio" were.

The Consulado's members' motivations, of course, were far from selfless. Their principal concern was that they be able to buy goods within Mexico City for their warehouses and resell them to the small shopkeepers and stall owners without paying taxes. Nonetheless, the merchants of the Consulado found that the utility of grouping themselves with street vendors and shopkeepers outweighed any potential harm to their honor or reputations. They knew that in the realm of colonial politics, arguing that a particular policy benefited poor vendors, in addition to wealthy overseas merchants, made their proposal more compelling. Indeed, the strategy was a success: in 1756, after considering the Consulado's objections, the Crown repealed the resale tax on most goods.[125] The Consulado's actions illustrate how Mexico City's retail economy fostered economic relationships that transcended class lines and were often based more on the pragmatics of business than racial or cultural affinities.

The alliances between the baratilleros and the merchants of the Consulado had their limits, however. Disputes over a militia called the Urban Commercial Regiment near the end of the eighteenth century reveal the fragility of those ties. The Crown ordered this militia formed in the wake of the 1692 riot, which destroyed the Plaza Mayor's shops, and charged the Consulado with staffing and funding it so it could protect the capital's businesses from future attacks. Technically, every person who fell under the category of "comerciante" was required to serve in the corps. This rule, however, left much room for interpretation, and many petty merchants avoided the obligation by claiming, as their adversaries in the Plaza Mayor had long contended, that they were vendedores, buhoneros, or other types of street sellers and shopkeepers, and thus ineligible for the militia. In 1774, Viceroy Antonio María de Bucareli ended the confusion by explicitly requiring all store owners, alcohol vendors, and anyone who had a stand in a market to join the regiment. The Consulado welcomed the clarification, as the move lessened the burden on its members to provide men for the corps, which they typically did by paying substitutes to serve in their place.[126] When Viceroy Revillagigedo II attempted to reverse Bucareli's rule and exclude small shop-keepers and petty merchants from the obligation in the early 1790s, the Consulado objected. Those men, the Consulado argued, were also merchants and needed to do their part to protect the city's businesses.[127] The alliances between the Consulado merchants and baratilleros existed, to a great degree, because they served the merchants' interests; when circumstances changed, those men were quick to discard the petty traders. Even if the networks that comprised the shadow economy transcended divisions of class and race, they did not challenge the fundamental inequalities that undergirded the urban economy.

CONCLUSION

The Baratillo played an indispensable role in the economy of late-colonial Mexico City. In the agglomeration of small shops, stalls, and tables that con-stituted the Baratillo Grande and Baratillo Chico of the Plaza Mayor, the circuits of second-hand, informal, and illicit goods that comprised the city's shadow economy converged. Although many of the Baratillo's transactions broke the law, it was not only criminals and rogues who took part in them. Elite traders, middling artisans, government officials, and consumers of all backgrounds participated in the Baratillo's commerce in different ways. The vendors' dealings with other urban actors challenge the notion that either the black market or the informal economy was a discrete sphere of exchange. In reality, formal, informal, and illicit transactions were all entwined. Agents of the state were often central figures in those exchanges, and not because they sought to stop them. While some officials prosecuted crimes in the Baratillo, others turned a blind eye. Still others, like the market officials who mediated disputes between its vendors or collected rent there, condoned the market's existence. The state was anything but unified in its approach to the Baratillo.

The material advantages the Baratillo provided to Mexico City's residents do not, on their own, explain the persistence of an institution that many pow-erful individuals and entrenched interest groups despised. The market's sur-vival makes sense only when we examine the ways that economics and politics mixed in the Baratillo. Its vendors resisted efforts by rival merchants and artisans to quash their trade by deftly navigating the colonial justice system and employing the most potent political rhetoric of the day—stressing their poverty and asserting the legitimacy of their commerce and its value to the broader community. Rivalries between local and royal officials also benefited the vendors, who played authorities off of another. With Mexico's independence from Spain, baratilleros only became more active players in urban politics as its vendors found new tools with which to assert their rights.

FOUR

The Dictator, the Ayuntamiento, and the Baratillo

So long as there are poor people in the world the rich must tolerate us, just as we patiently suffer the inconveniences of their thunderous carriages and all the other ills that their whims inflict upon us.

Baratilleros in the Plaza del Factor to the Ayuntamiento
of Mexico City, in El Siglo Diez y Nueve, *May 31, 1842*

ON APRIL 12, 1842, JOSÉ MARÍA ICAZA, the prefect of Mexico City, wrote to the members of the city's Ayuntamiento: "It has come to the attention of the Superior Government that the *plazuela* called the Baratillo is the meeting place for the depraved and ne'er-do-wells." The Baratillo, according to Icaza, was "the place where robberies are fomented, where thieves sell the goods they have illegally acquired—the spot where the violent and troublesome are so common for the many pulquerías and vinaterías that surround it, and for the class of people who attend it." By "Superior Government," Icaza meant Mexico's provisional president, Antonio López de Santa Anna— the strongman who played an outsized influence in Mexican politics in the first half of the nineteenth century. Santa Anna wanted the Baratillo's excesses to be "corrected" as soon as possible. To that end, the prefect ordered the Ayuntamiento to report back within the week about how it planned to deal with the situation.[1]

That a high-ranking official in Mexico City wanted to suppress the Baratillo was, by the middle of the nineteenth century, nothing new. Since the seventeenth century, at least one Spanish king and several viceroys had sought to ban the market, to little effect. But the response this 1842 attempt provoked from the market's vendors had little precedent. The baratilleros pushed back forcefully against Santa Anna and the municipal government, asserting their right to practice their trade and lambasting the government, after it decided to evict them, for its callousness.

As the vendors fought to remain in the Plaza del Factor, which the Baratillo had occupied since the 1790s, Mexico's partisans were locked in debate over the shape of the nation's political system. In late 1841 and early 1842, the country was preparing to vote for a constituent congress to draft a new constitution. There was an aura of hope in the capital, as residents awaited a new charter that could quell the political turmoil that had afflicted Mexico since its independence from Spain, in 1821. No Mexican president had successfully completed his term in office. Santa Anna held the post six times during the nation's first three decades of independence, and he had risen to power again in a coup in the fall of 1841.[2] The country vacillated between federalism (which drew support from liberals) and centralism (backed by conservatives).[3] Conflicts over the nature of the Mexican state—particularly questions of whom it would enfranchise and where the equilibrium between government authority and individual rights would fall—did not take place only among the upper-class hombres de bien who occupied high government posts. They involved Mexicans from across the social spectrum, including vendors in the capital's infamous thieves' market. In their response to the government's attempts to uproot them, the baratilleros staked their claims as citizens, threatening to vote municipal officials out of office and printing their petition in the newspaper—perhaps the earliest example of street or market vendors engaging in the capital city's public sphere. As poor people, they argued, they had the same rights to the city's public spaces as anyone else.

In reality, however, the Baratillo brought together more than just the very poor in its trade in second-hand, repurposed, and pilfered goods. As was the case during the colonial era, many of the market's vendors in the mid-nineteenth century were middling artisans and merchants; indeed, some stalls in the Baratillo belonged to wealthier Mexicans. Dozens of vendors were literate enough to sign their own names to petitions. Vendors also received support from members of the urban elite, including the newspaper editors who published their manifesto and a member of the city council who sought, unsuccessfully, to delay the market's relocation. Despite its vulgar reputation, the Baratillo had something to offer Mexico City residents from diverse backgrounds in the 1840s. The streets of Mexico City in the mid-nineteenth century were not simply battle sites between popular groups and elites or venues for power struggles between rival political factions.[4] They also fostered unlikely alliances that transcended the social and political divisions of the era and hosted debates that linked the material anxieties of street vendors to the existential concerns of the Mexican nation. This chapter thus deepens our understanding of Mexico's little-studied early republican era by showing how urban dwellers, including vendors in the Baratillo, engaged in local and national politics.[5]

The chapter focuses on how the members of two old-regime institutions—the Baratillo and the Ayuntamiento—dealt with the changes that republican government and thirty years of instability brought to the Mexican capital. The Ayuntamiento saw the centralist governments that ruled Mexico in the 1830s and 1840s circumscribe its authority. At the same time, it struggled under the dual responsibilities of providing a showcase capital for the Mexican nation and governing a large and diverse city. Mexico's transformation from colony to republic, which turned the capital's *vecinos*, or neighbors and residents, into citizens and voters, further complicated the Ayuntamiento's mandate by expanding its constituency well beyond the elite. The political transition had significant implications for the vendors of the Baratillo; they could now use the levers of local representative government to protect their interests against government decisions they viewed as arbitrary or unfair. As was the case during the colonial era, the baratilleros were not locked in conflict against a monolithic state; rather, they dealt with officials at different levels of government whose roles were in flux in the mid-nineteenth century. Tensions between those institutions and individuals are fundamental not only to the Baratillo's history but also to Mexico City's.

Although sources from the early republican era bring baratilleros' political agency into clearer focus, they tell us frustratingly little about the economic dimensions of the market. The dismantling of the colonial regulatory apparatus, particularly the formal dissolution of the guild system, meant that the government no longer investigated economic activities that violated guilds' rules, since many of those rules were no longer in effect.[6] Freer trade left a thinner paper trail. It did not, however, eliminate the demand for the baratilleros' goods. The market continued to play a vital role in the local economy after independence, benefiting vendors, investors, and consumers from across the social spectrum. It did so even as it persisted in a state of legal limbo—banned by government decree but condoned by municipal authorities who collected rent and adjudicated disputes among its vendors—and retained its reputation as the epicenter of black-market commerce in the capital.

SANTA ANNA'S RETURN AND THE REGENERATION
OF THE REPUBLIC

When Santa Anna returned to power in September of 1841, Mexico was in crisis. The republic had begun to disintegrate after the country's centralists, led by Santa Anna, overthrew the federalist government in 1835 and replaced Mexico's 1824 federal constitution. The centralists' attempt to concentrate power in the capital led various regions to secede—most notably Texas, which achieved independence in 1836.[7] There were eighty-four separate *pronunciamientos*—or revolts—in the country between 1837 and 1841, as regional leaders and rival factions vied for control of the country.[8] Economic crises exacerbated the country's troubles. Mexico had been in fiscal straits ever since the independence wars of the 1810s, when its silver mines flooded and much of its financial capital fled with the Spanish elite.[9] Continuous military operations further drained government resources. To make matters worse, the governments of the 1830s massively overproduced copper coins in a desperate attempt for revenue. Counterfeiting and inflation became rampant.[10] The crisis came to a head in Mexico City in 1837 when Congress devaluated the smallest denomination coins and more than ten thousand people poured into the streets to protest their now worthless currency.[11]

In 1841, Santa Anna joined forces with Mariano Paredes y Arrillaga and Gabriel Valencia to overthrow the unpopular president Anastasio Bustamante and restore order to the country.[12] On September 28, 1841, the three generals signed the Bases de Tacubaya—a two-page document that voided the 1836 Constitution and established Santa Anna as interim president with all of the powers "necessary for the organization of all of the branches of public administration."[13] Bolstered by the virtually unchecked power the Bases gave to him, Santa Anna made this turn as president his most ambitious—"the dictatorship disguised under the handsome name of political regeneration," as one newspaper described it at the time.[14]

Between 1841 and 1844, Santa Anna and his ministers embarked on an expansive set of reforms.[15] The government improved tax collection and invested in infrastructure and social institutions, beginning work on the railroad between Mexico City and Veracruz, rehabilitating the capital's poorhouse, and establishing a national General Directorate of Public Education, which constructed a large number of new schools.[16] Santa Anna brought the copper money saga to a close by amortizing the coins in 1842.[17] The president also sought to leave his mark on Mexico City. In a short-lived period of cooperation with the liberal-dominated Ayuntamiento, the president and the city council worked to rehabilitate a capital that had lost its colonial-era luster.

"Regeneration" was the buzzword of the day, as residents of the capital saw in Santa Anna's newfound enthusiasm for governing signs that the city and nation were turning a corner. Bolstered by the sense of optimism in the capital, the Ayuntamiento adopted an ambitious plan to pave city streets and construct new market halls while the provisional president passed ordinances aimed at improving policing and quality of life in the capital. Rehabilitating Mexico City's public marketplaces was central to the capital's renaissance. In 1841, the Ayuntamiento announced plans to rebuild the city's principal food market in the Plaza del Volador, which the Spanish viceroy Revillagigedo II had erected in the early 1790s but had since fallen into disrepair. The Ayuntamiento also announced plans to build new food markets in the Jesús, San Juan, and Factor plazas. The local government hoped to move the Baratillo from the Plaza del Factor to the Plaza de Loreto, located to the east of the main Plaza de la Constitución (the renamed Plaza Mayor), where it, too, would occupy a new building.[18] But the reconstruction of the Volador market, the first and most high-profile project to move forward, proved highly contentious and ended in a violent confrontation between market vendors and police in December 1841. That episode set the stage for the conflict that would unfold between the government and the vendors of the Baratillo several months later.

A MARKET WORTHY OF ITS CENTURY

By 1841, Mexico City's Ayuntamiento had been trying to replace the Volador marketplace for more than a decade. The building had had problems ever since it opened, in 1792. Only a year later, vendors complained that officials were failing to maintain it. Fires destroyed many of its stands in 1794 and again in 1798.[19] In 1827, the Ayuntamiento sought to replace the dilapidated wooden market structure with one made of masonry. That plan, however, ran into opposition from its vendors. On September 18, 1827, one Gabino Pérez wrote to the Ayuntamiento on behalf of the vendors to protest the market administrator's demand that each vendor contribute 250 pesos toward the construction of the new building, or else lose his or her stand. Some of the language

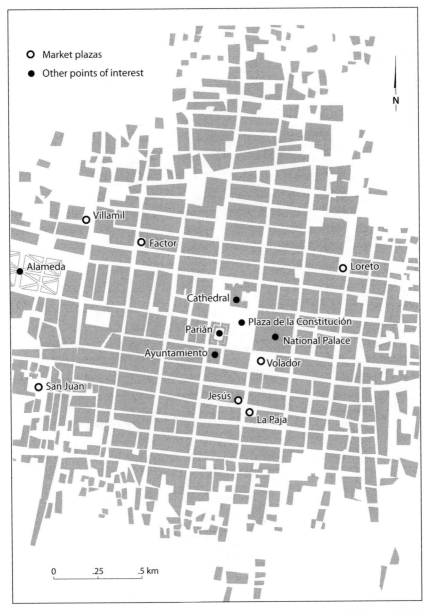

N

O Villamil

O Factor

● Alameda

O Loreto

Cathedral ●

● Plaza de la Constitución

Parián ●

● National Palace

Ayuntamiento ●

O Volador

O San Juan

Jesús O

O La Paja

0   .25   .5 km

MAP 3. Mexico City, 1842. Based on García Conde's 1793 *Plano general de la Ciudad de México*. Mexico City's boundaries had changed so little between the 1790s and the 1840s that the Ayuntamiento reprinted Ignacio Castera's 1794 map (figure 5) for its own urban renewal projects in 1842 (figure 8). Map created by Bill Nelson and Andrew Konove.

this petition contains is familiar: Pérez warned city authorities that if they forced the vendors to hand over such an enormous sum, which many did not have, or ejected them from their stands, they would be sanctioning "the ruin and disgrace of innumerable American families." But he mixed that traditional language with newer, republican rhetoric. The Ayuntamiento's plan, Pérez charged, was "contrary to the principles of equity [and] justice."[20]

Pérez also drew on a more concrete device in his petition: the legal contract. There is no evidence prior to 1817 that petty vendors possessed written rental contracts with the Ayuntamiento for their puestos (open-air stands) or cajones (enclosed stands or small stores). Negotiations were verbal, and vendors typically offered small bribes to officials (gratificaciones) in order to speed the leasing process along and obtain a desirable location.[21] By the 1820s, however, petitions from vendors routinely referenced rental contracts they had signed with the municipal government, as well as other laws that contained protections for their businesses. Pérez argued that the vendors' contract stipulated that as long as the lessees paid their rent on schedule they would be allowed to remain in possession of their stands. Furthermore, their contract said nothing about requiring the market's occupants to pay for repairs. Pérez's argument prevailed, and the project went nowhere.[22]

Gabino Pérez was an *evangelista*, a man hired by individuals or groups with minimal education to argue on their behalf before authorities. Historians know little about these advocates. They rarely signed their names to the documents they produced because the nature of their work often required anonymity.[23] Evangelistas probably assumed a more specific and involved role for their clients than the scribes who gathered in public plazas to write letters for the illiterate. Unlike scribes, evangelistas helped their clients navigate bureaucratic processes, often taking the place of a lawyer. Many contemporaries held a low view of the men who practiced this profession. Fernández de Lizardi, author of *El periquillo sarniento*, portrays evangelistas as sinister characters—men who used their education and position to take advantage of naïve clients.[24] By all accounts, though, Pérez served the vendors of the Volador market well, as he successfully thwarted the Ayuntamiento's plan to make them pay for a new market building. His relationship with the vendors was professional, having been codified in a contract the parties signed a week before he penned the first petition.[25]

Beyond the achievement of their clients' immediate objectives, Pérez and other evangelistas played a broader role in Mexican society: they mediated between illiterate or minimally educated citizens and government institutions.[26] Their work expanded Mexico's political arena by exposing those individuals to political concepts and vocabulary with which they may not have been familiar and facilitating their access to government officials. Yet their role was more complex than as professional intermediaries. Pérez, at least by 1836, was not only the Volador vendors' evangelista; he was also the owner of a business that sold iron goods in the market.[27] The same was true of an evangelista who represented vendors in the Baratillo in a dispute with the Ayuntamiento in 1872. When it came to advocating on behalf of street vendors in Mexico City, political and economic interests were often intertwined.

The Ayuntamiento did not give up on the idea of replacing the run-down Volador market after Pérez and the vendors foiled its first attempt. A new opportunity presented itself in April 1841 when a private citizen named José Oropeza wrote to the Ayuntamiento and asked that it hire him to build a new marketplace in the Plaza del Volador. The building he proposed was a grand structure, with floors made from *tezontle* (a red volcanic rock), stone columns, and large iron doors at the entrances.[28] That design proved too expensive, but the Ayuntamiento reached a deal with Oropeza in October 1841 in which the city would pay the contractor 215,000 pesos for the construction of a scaled-down marketplace.[29] The contract assured that the market's current occupants would have first priority in the new building, but they needed to vacate the plaza during construction.[30]

Everything seemed to be in order to begin construction by the beginning of 1842. On December 14, however, the *junta departamental*, the legislative body that represented the Department of Mexico (which included Mexico City), rejected the contract that the Ayuntamiento had signed with Oropeza.[31] The gross fiscal irresponsibility of the project, the junta members wrote, made it impossible for them to approve it. They noted that the municipal government was deeply in debt—to the tune of almost two million pesos, according to their calculations—and had not conducted a public bidding process for the contract, as the law required. They questioned why the Ayuntamiento did not build the market itself and avoid the costs of outsourcing it to a *contratista* (contractor). Furthermore, the project threatened to destroy a place that was "the asylum and subsistence of a multitude of poor wretches that provision the city like bees maintaining the hive."[32]

Street vendors in nineteenth-century Mexico City found support from elected officials across the political spectrum. Indeed, in their approach to dealing with the urban poor, liberals and conservatives of the era differed little from one another. Although conservatives, like the men who dominated the junta departamental of Mexico, believed that the corporations of the colonial era, especially the Church, were best suited to help the poor, while liberals sought to free the individual from the strictures of those groups and encouraged participation in voluntary associations, liberals and conservatives shared a paternalistic view of the urban poor. A "customary tolerance" of Mexico City residents toward the destitute continued well beyond the colonial era, often stymieing reformers' attempts to institutionalize poor relief.[33] Evidence of this tolerance appears throughout the official correspondence related to the Volador, Baratillo, and other markets in Mexico City in the 1840s.

The junta departamental, however, did not have the final say on this matter. The following day, Santa Anna, as Mexico's provisional president, overruled the junta and ordered that the project move forward. "Taking into consideration this city's need of decoration," he declared, "a handsome new market plaza should be constructed in the Plaza del Volador, removing from sight the deformation that exists today." Santa Anna, who had had no prior involvement in the project, demanded that the Ayuntamiento uphold its contract with Oropeza and called for it to establish a temporary market for the vendors of the Volador market while the new structure was under construction.[34] Privately, Santa Anna notified the Ayuntamiento that it needed to remove the vendors from the Plaza del Volador by December 26 so work could begin on that day—an acceleration of the construction schedule. To some members of the Ayuntamiento, Santa Anna's timeline seemed rushed. In the city council session of December 19, the *hacienda* (treasury) commissioner José Valente Baz warned against removing the vendors before the city had designated temporary markets for them. Plus, he argued, it was almost Christmas and many of these people were already hurting from the recent devaluation of the copper currency.[35]

Baz was not the only individual to raise objections to the sudden eviction of the Volador vendors. Amid the back-and-forth between different governmental bodies, Gabino Pérez, still the representative for the vendors of the Volador market, wrote to Santa Anna and pleaded with him to reconsider the plan. The letter was also printed, and probably posted publicly in the city. As in 1827, Pérez's strategy was two-pronged: appeal to the president's compassion for the poor while also reminding him, and not so gently this time, of his obligation to uphold the laws of the republic. Pérez argued that the government had no right to evict the vendors from their stands in the first place ("Your Excellency knows very well that the laws allow us to conserve our locations"). "We cannot believe," Pérez continued, "that you want to deprive us of the concession which our codes gave us, and which the municipal body [has] conserved for us. Your Excellency, upon putting himself at the forefront of the regeneration of the republic, proposed that he would only respect the laws, [and] never think of destroying them." "Public morality, the interest of society, [and] equality," he argued, all stood in opposition to this project.[36] Despite Pérez's unleashing the full war chest of republican rhetoric, his letter received no response from Santa Anna. A flurry of correspondence between Pérez, the Ayuntamiento, and Santa Anna's government over the next several days similarly failed to delay the project. By December 27, the Ayuntamiento had cleared the plaza in what subsequent correspondence described as a violent confrontation between police and vendors.[37]

Although some elected officials were wary of Santa Anna's methods, the larger project of modernizing Mexico City—beginning with the construction of a new market hall in the Plaza del Volador—enjoyed support from across the political spectrum. On December 31, 1841, the councilman Manuel García Aguirre, a conservative ally of Santa Anna, opened the dedication of the new marketplace with a speech that heaped praise on the dictator and highlighted the historic nature of the event.[38] It was, in his estimation, "the first public work of importance that will be built in this Capital since our emancipation." He thanked Santa Anna for his role in bringing the project to fruition and marveled that "the same generous hand that brandished the sword to achieve the country's independence, that brandished it again to twice repel foreign aggression, and that has always taken it to sustain in the field of battle the sacred cause of liberty and the principles that our Century professes ... does not spurn taking the instruments of the humble artisan and helping him in his work"—an apparent reference to his laying the building's cornerstone. For his unwavering dedication to the Mexican republic, "Santa Anna will be compared by generations to come with the North American General Washington." With that introduction, Santa Anna placed a box containing a copy of the Bases de Tacubaya in the hole that would soon become the building's foundation.[39]

Liberals in the capital were similarly excited about the new marketplace. The moderate-liberal newspaper El Siglo Diez y Nueve, published by the federalist stalwart Ignacio Cumplido, celebrated the start of construction of the new Volador market as an act that "visibly manifests the advance of our society."[40] A group of liberal members of the Ayuntamiento of 1841 joined their conservative colleagues in publishing a pamphlet in the spring of 1842 that defended their decision to build the new marketplace, explaining how the project would contribute to the goal of improving the capital. It was, "in sum, the idea of a civilized city's market, and in truth our miserable and ridiculous Plaza del Volador did not correspond to it." The existing market was "unworthy, absolutely unworthy of a century that looks everywhere for progress and the improvement of things."[41] Though Mexican liberals did not typically look back on the colonial period fondly (the pamphlet authors called the era one in which "barbarity and profound ignorance reigned in Mexico"), local officials from across the political spectrum longed for the time, only forty years earlier, when Mexico City was the largest city in the Americas and the capital of Spain's most prosperous colony.[42] The pamphlet authors expressed a particular nostalgia for the viceroy Revillagigedo II and his ambitious urban reforms. In fact, the Ayuntamiento even reprinted the plans the viceroy had drawn up for the reorganization of the city's streets and plazas in 1794 to use in their own projects in 1842 (see figure 8). They saw themselves as picking up where he had left off.

Foreigners' accounts of Mexico City in the 1840s echoed the councilmen's contention that the capital's sheen had dulled since independence. In Brantz Mayer's travel narrative *Mexico As It Was and As It Is*, the Metropolitan Cathedral served as a metaphor for the city at large: "Its floor is of loose disjointed boards, filled with dirt and filth—the covering of the many dead who lie moldering beneath. But with this, all meanness ends; and whether we contemplate the dimensions of the edifice, or the millions that have been spent upon its decoration, the mind is lost in wonder." The city, in Mayer's view, was a jewel caked in decades of dust. The author agreed, though, that the new Volador market represented a promising new start for the capital. He observed that the marketplace had been built "in a tasteful style" and that it had replaced "shambles and booths built of *bamboo and reeds, sheltered from the rain and sun by thatched roofs!*" (original emphasis).[43] Mexico City's residents and visitors alike agreed that the capital needed a major upgrade—not only to live up to its glorious past but also to meet its promising future.

PROGRESS VERSUS THE BARATILLO

Amid this drive to modernize and rejuvenate the Mexican capital, some residents saw the Baratillo as an obstacle. In February 1842, a contributor to *El Siglo Diez y Nueve* noted, sarcastically, that the market was so "useful and beneficial that it has been respected by imperialists, federalists, centralists,

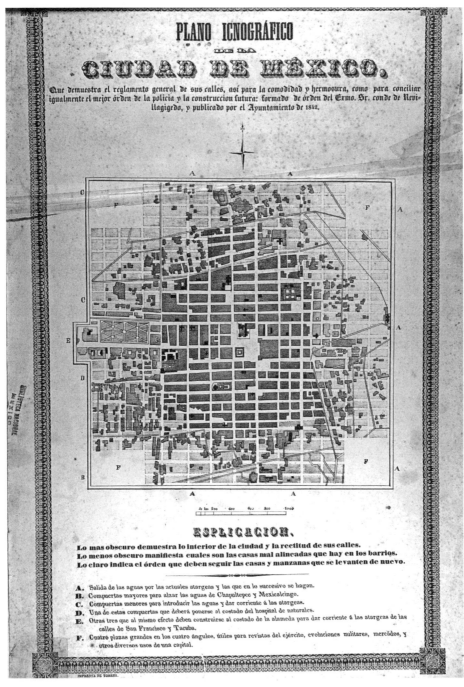

FIGURE 8. *Plano icnográfico de la Ciudad de México*, 1842. The Ayuntamiento of 1842 reproduced the map that Ignacio Castera created for Viceroy Revillagigedo II in 1794 (see figure 5), rotating the map clockwise so that north is now at the top. The text below the title credits Revillagigedo for commissioning the original map and borrows some of the original language that map contained in its description. Biblioteca Nacional de México, Fondo Reservado, R 912.7252F MEX.p.

escoceses, yorkinos—men, in sum, of every era, of ever color, and of every party."[44] In this abominable bazaar, whose origins, the writer declared, were unworthy of investigation, one could find anything and everything, only "scrambled, confused, and transformed." His critique built on colonial-era narratives that insisted that the original states of both goods and people were unknowable in the Baratillo. Something that "in its youthful days was a shirt," the author wrote, "appears converted into white underpants, a cloak into a frock, a frock into a uniform, and a uniform into a vest."[45]

Another citizen proposed a solution to the ills the Baratillo was spreading. On April 19, 1842, a Mexico City resident named José Sánchez wrote to the Ayuntamiento to suggest that it move the Baratillo out of the city center and replace it with a food market. The move would accomplish multiple objectives: it would aid consumers, vendors, and municipal coffers by providing a much-needed market for fruits and vegetables in the Plaza del Factor while also depriving the "filthy Baratillo" of its now-quite-central location, where it had occupied a crude wooden structure since 1793. Relocating the Baratillo to a "distant and unpopulated" area, such as the Plaza de Madrid or San Pablo, Sánchez hoped, would lead to a decline in business that "would equal its extinction" (which, he pointed out, the government had ordered in 1836).[46] In Sánchez's view, the Baratillo simply was not fit for an increasingly civilized and sophisticated city whose residents' tastes were constantly improving. Sánchez saw the Mexican capital as a city on the rise and the Baratillo as representative of the retrograde practices that were holding it back. If reformers could not eliminate those customs entirely, they could at least isolate them from the more civilized sections of the city. In service of that goal, Sánchez demanded that the Ayuntamiento destroy the "ridiculous shrine or chapel" that stood in the market, likely a reference to the statue of the Virgin of Guadalupe that the baratilleros had placed in the plaza. "By no means should there be an object of worship in that place," Sánchez argued.[47]

In the nineteenth-century Mexican press, the word *baratillo* was a euphemism for anything that was vulgar or cheap. A poet deemed to be lacking skill was *"un poeta del baratillo."*[48] One contributor to a newspaper refused to respond to an adversary's "swearwords that have their proper place only in the baratillo."[49] A conservative writer complained in 1833 that "the diabolical invention of popular sovereignty made a king from the baratillo"—an attack likely directed at the radical presidency of Valentín Gómez Farías.[50] The Baratillo was an institution that enjoyed widespread notoriety in the capital and beyond as a signifier of all that was lowly, dishonest, and dangerous in Mexican society.[51]

For local officials in 1842, forcing the Baratillo out of the Plaza del Factor would solve two problems at once: it would remove a troublesome and visually unappealing institution from the city center, and it would provide a temporary home for the vendors that the construction in the Plaza del Volador had displaced. The Ayuntamiento had yet to find a site for those vendors by April 1842, which had led many of them to fan out and clog the city's streets. Others remained in the Plaza del Volador, where they were obstructing work on the new marketplace. Santa Anna's ministers grew frustrated with the municipal government's inaction and demanded that the Ayuntamiento find an appropriate site for the market-less food vendors to sell. The city obliged, offering them the Plaza del Factor. On May 23, 1842, the Ayuntamiento informed the vendors of the Baratillo that Santa Anna's government had given them two days to vacate the Plaza del Factor.[52]

THE VENDORS AND CITIZENS OF
THE BARATILLO RESPOND

The baratilleros did not take this order lying down. Eight of them responded on May 24 in a letter to Mariano de Icaza, the market commissioner. Like the vendors of the Volador market, they appealed to the councilman's sympathy for the poor, asking that officials provide "the same paternal gaze" they had extended to the food vendors of the Volador for the "miserable commerce" of the Baratillo. Also like the vendors of the Volador, they combined this plea with a demand that the government follow the law. "We do not need to remind Your Excellency," the baratilleros wrote, "that the laws concede the same protection to used clothing vendors as they do to merchants and traders in other effects. Nor will we mention that we have a contract celebrated with Your Excellency, which, having not broken on our part, we are in a place to demand that you comply with and receive in good faith [this] petition." Although the vendors believed they were on firm legal footing, they were willing to compromise with the Ayuntamiento. If the government wanted to sell food instead of second-hand clothing in the Plaza del Factor, the vendors were willing to trade their wares for comestibles. But if the government refused to allow them to stay in the plaza, the vendors pleaded for more time and the right to choose the new site for their market. They asked for twelve days, instead of two, and to relocate their stands to the Plaza de Villamil, located two blocks northwest of the of the Plaza del Factor in a sparsely populated area north of the Alameda park—a move the vendors offered to pay for themselves.[53]

The Ayuntamiento responded the same day, agreeing to one of the baratilleros' demands: the vendors could move their stands to the Plaza de Villamil, at their own expense. However, despite calls from one councilman that the government delay the move, the Ayuntamiento gave no extension: the vendors needed to go the following day.[54] In response, a much larger group of vendors—forty in total—sent the Ayuntamiento a letter that reneged on their offer to move themselves to the Plaza de Villamil. They asked the members of the Ayuntamiento to permit them "some reflections on the situation" and allow them to make their case for why they should be allowed to stay in the Plaza del Factor.[55] The letter also appeared in the May 31 edition of *El Siglo Diez y Nueve*—the country's leading liberal daily.[56] It is an extraordinary missive that weaves traditional pleas for magnanimity with political arguments and tactics that had no precedent in street vendor petitions in Mexico City. Unlike the vendors in the Volador market, the petition did not have an evangelista's name attached to it. The baratilleros signed it themselves.

The document begins by warning the city councilmen that forcing the vendors to move to a different plaza will result in their "complete ruin"—a refrain that virtually every petition from street vendors had contained since the colonial period. The vendors then highlighted the impracticality of the move. This larger group of vendors had soured on the idea that the Plaza de Villamil was a suitable site for the Baratillo, noting that it lacked even the most basic infrastructure. The plaza was completely open to the elements, and it had no place for vendors to secure their goods at night after the market closed. The majority of the baratilleros lacked the funds to build storage rooms, especially if they would have to pay for the move themselves.[57]

The tone of the letter then turns more confrontational. The vendors refuted Icaza's claim that Santa Anna's government had ever ordered the baratilleros out of the Plaza del Factor. Somehow, perhaps through an ally on the Ayuntamiento, the vendors had gotten hold of the letters that José María Icaza, the prefect (and the market commissioner's cousin), had exchanged with the Ayuntamiento between April 12 and 18, which they copied in their petition.[58] The letters, the vendors argued, showed that the prefect had never given such an order and that the national government had left it up to the Ayuntamiento to determine the appropriate course of action regarding the

Baratillo.[59] The baratilleros asked the city councilmen—and the readers of *El Siglo Diez y Nueve*—why the Ayuntamiento would turn its back on its own residents when the national government had not compelled it to do so.[60]

The baratilleros also questioned the wisdom of moving food vendors to stalls that from "time immemorial have been occupied by the mattresses of the sick, dirty clothing, and all the other rags of the poor." Who, they asked, would want to eat meat that has been cut "from the same counter that old shoes, used clothing of all classes, and other disgusting objects occupied moments earlier?" This was a clever bit of rhetoric, turning elites' traditional complaints about the Baratillo's unsanitary conditions against those same critics and suggesting that such an unclean place was suitable only for the commerce of the Baratillo. "Public hygiene," the letter instructed, "demands cleanliness, above all with food, as an indispensable condition for health." The Ayuntamiento, they argued, would surely want to consider this issue carefully before moving the vendors of the Volador market to the Plaza del Factor.[61]

The vendors argued that if the Baratillo was unsanitary or unsafe, then it was the government, not the baratilleros, who ultimately bore responsibility. The Ayuntamiento could easily remedy the abuses that the interior minister cited in his letters through "good and well-systematized policing." And would it not be easier, they asked, to protect vendors and consumers by keeping the Baratillo in a central location such as the Plaza del Factor rather than in some remote and unpopulated plaza?[62] It was not the first time that vendors had accused the Ayuntamiento of failing to provide proper oversight of the city's public markets. In 1822, a group of vendors in the Plaza del Volador wrote to the Ayuntamiento to complain that the market administrator was violating several of the 1791 regulations (which were still in effect), including charging arbitrary and extortionist rents and failing to attend the market every day, as he was required to do, resulting in "scandalous disorder" in the plaza.[63]

Vendors were increasingly demanding that authorities comply with their obligations to their rent-paying constituents.[64] Baratilleros asserted that they paid the city on time; now the Ayuntamiento needed to uphold its end of the bargain by providing the basic services it was supposed to offer in exchange for that rent. Indeed, the baratilleros dedicated much of their 1842 letter to reminding elected city officials of their legal and moral responsibilities to Mexican citizens. They took issue with the government's argument that moving the vendors from the Volador market to the Plaza del Factor would augment municipal income. Raising tax revenue, they argued, should always be of secondary consideration to "public utility, the convenience of the majority," and committing the "least prejudice possible" to the city's residents.[65] The Ayuntamiento had a responsibility to promote public works projects that served the city as a whole, including its most vulnerable groups.[66]

If the baratilleros could not convince Icaza and the other members of the city council that relocating their market to the Plaza de Villamil was against both the spirit and the letter of the law, they warned the market commissioner that they had another recourse at their disposal. Mexico's interior minister, they wrote, "did not dare give the order for us to be ruined, and will you, whose existence is of popular appointment?"[67] It was a thinly veiled threat to vote Icaza and his colleagues out of office if they did not cooperate.

Although Santa Anna had won the presidency through a coup and his ministers were not beholden to voters, Mexico City continued to conduct municipal elections in the 1840s, as it had since independence. Interference from the national government, beginning in the 1830s, increasingly challenged the integrity of those elections, but they functioned freely enough in 1841 for the city to elect a liberal-dominated Ayuntamiento that December, to Santa Anna's displeasure.[68] The centralist governments of the latter half of the 1830s sought to limit popular political participation by imposing new restrictions on voter eligibility, including a minimum income, but Santa Anna actually relaxed many of these restrictions in the fall of 1841. In 1842, virtually all adult males except domestic servants, criminals, and members of the clergy were eligible to vote. Under those rules, the majority of the vendors who signed the May 27 letter could vote, according to a municipal census conducted ahead of the 1842 congressional elections.[69] Icaza was not reelected to the Ayuntamiento in 1843, though the reason is not clear.[70]

What is clear from this episode, however, is that the vendors had a voice in local politics, one that they expressed through multiple channels. By publishing their manifesto in *El Siglo Diez y Nueve*, the vendors sought to mobilize public support for their cause and pressure Icaza and other members of the Ayuntamiento to rethink their decision to evict them. That act is likely the earliest example of street vendors participating in Mexico City's public sphere—the intellectual arena where individuals, including not only prominent journalists and politicians but also lesser-known individuals, debated the most pressing social and political questions of the day.[71] The baratilleros' petition tied the material concerns of working- and middle-class actors to existential questions facing the Mexican nation in the early 1840s. Baratilleros may have been at the margins of Mexico's political system, but they were certainly within it. Their market plaza was much more than a center for criminal enterprise; it was a site where diverse actors engaged in the urban political arena.[72]

"THE WHOLE SOCIAL CLASS TO WHICH WE BELONG"

The letter's powerful language raises the question of authorship. Who were the men and women who signed this petition, and who was responsible for composing it? Did one or more of the forty signatories pen the letter? Or did the baratilleros have an evangelista like Gabino Pérez, the man who represented the vendors of the Volador market? If they did, why did he choose to remain anonymous, when Pérez did not? None of the surviving documentation provides definitive answers to those questions. The sources do, however, provide clues about the identities of some of the men and women who signed their names to this missive. Thanks to the census the Mexico City government conducted in 1842 and the database that the historian Sonia Pérez Toledo built from that census, it is possible to ascertain basic demographic and occupational information for most of the individuals who signed this letter. These data shed light on one aspect of the Baratillo that is frustratingly elusive for most of its history: the question of who, exactly, worked there.

The census data reveal that nearly all of the individuals who signed the letter identified as artisans or merchants (see table 1 in appendix). Among the artisans, there was a cobbler, a hat maker, a carpenter, a chair maker, a tailor, and a tanner. These were some of the same professions from which vendors in the Baratillo had hailed during the seventeenth and eighteenth centuries. During the late-colonial period, the market often served as a refuge for unlicensed artisans who found it difficult to enter or ascend the city's guild system. Yet the census data show that the Baratillo continued to serve an important function in the Mexican capital even after those guilds lost their state-sanctioned monopolies over their crafts.[73] The Baratillo was not simply a symptom of an overregulated local economy; it was an outlet that served the needs of a significant portion of the capital's working and middle classes—groups that struggled under the economic turmoil of the decades that followed independence.[74]

Another continuity from the colonial era was the proportion of women among the Baratillo's vendors. Only two of the vendors who signed the letter were women. This gender ratio appears to have been relatively consistent over time: women appeared on virtually every list or census of vendors in the

Baratillo but always constituted a small minority—probably because of the market's close association with artisanal trades that men dominated.[75] In the nineteenth century, as in the eighteenth, women were a significant presence in food vending but played a much smaller role in the market for second-hand goods—at least according to the surviving documentation.[76]

Most of the baratilleros who signed the petition were born in Mexico City and lived close to the Plaza del Factor.[77] In fact, over half of the vendors lived within a one-block radius of the Baratillo. Six of the vendors lived directly across the street from the market, on the Calle del Factor. Francisco Camargo, Gabino Cadena, and Luis Padilla occupied the same address on the Calle del Factor, and Guadalupe Buenrostro and Francisco Solís lived next door.[78] This residential pattern underscores how important the location of the Baratillo was for its vendors; their livelihoods were built around their proximity to the market and to other vendors. The Plaza de Villamil was only a couple of long blocks away, but in 1840s Mexico City that distance was significant—not only because residents viewed the Plaza de Villamil as a peripheral area of the city but also because a move there likely would have disrupted social and economic networks that vendors had cultivated over the five decades the Baratillo had stood in the Plaza del Factor. If the Baratillo was an indispensable part of Mexico City's economy, it was even more essential to its immediate neighborhood.[79]

The census provides few clues about the economic means of individual baratilleros, but other types of sources, including notarial records, partially fill the gap. Some vendors, like Petra Villar, came from very modest backgrounds. Her will, drafted in 1836, lists her only assets as a 50 percent stake in a stand in the Plaza del Factor that sold iron products (her daughter owned the other half) and the clothes in her home. Neither she nor her late husband had brought any assets into their marriage.[80] Other vendors, like Doroteo Franco, had backgrounds in the skilled trades, putting them in a more middling socioeconomic group. Franco was a carpenter who received 1,400 pesos, a substantial sum, to construct an altar in a local church in 1849.[81] Indeed, some of the individuals who signed the 1842 petition seem to have been relatively well off. At least eight of the forty signatories appear on the list of residents qualified to serve on the Mexico City press jury in 1847, which had much stricter eligibility requirements than the 1842 elections.[82] To serve on a press jury one had to be able to read and write and have either capital of at least four thousand pesos or be employed in a trade that produced at least one thousand pesos per year (the typical wage earner in the 1840s earned only around 150 pesos per year).[83] At least one stall owner in the

Baratillo during this era (though not one who signed the 1842 petition) belonged to Mexico's elite. In his 1833 will, Rafael Manzanedo, the owner of a furniture business in the Baratillo, counted among his other assets: a hacienda in Chalco, a wheat-growing area to the east of Mexico City, a country estate in Coyuya, and olive trees in the pueblo of San Juan Ixtayopan.[84] Perhaps a man such as Manzanedo wrote anonymously on behalf of the Baratillo vendors—just as Gabino Pérez, the chief advocate for the vendors of the Volador market and the owner of a business there, had done for those vendors. While the census information may not provide a comprehensive picture of the market vendors' socioeconomic positions, when combined with other evidence from the era, it suggests that the Baratillo continued to host a range of businesses with owners similarly varied in their backgrounds and means, as it had during the late-colonial period.

The presence of relatively well-off business owners in the market did not prevent the baratilleros from portraying the Ayuntamiento's attempts to dislodge them from the Plaza del Factor as an unabashed attack by the rich on the poor. By holding their ground against the Ayuntamiento, the baratilleros were not only defending "our own private interest, but that of the whole social class to which we belong." They warned their local representatives that while "the middle and upper classes would lose nothing, perhaps, with the extinction of the Baratillo, the infinitely more numerous class would find itself extinct."[85]

Never before had a letter from market vendors expressed their predicament so starkly in terms of class conflict. Earlier petitions cited the poverty of both vendors and their customers as a reason the authorities should allow the Baratillo to continue, but such language had always formed part of an appeal to elites' sympathy for the poor. Here, it serves a very different function. The tone of the letter is menacing and self-confident, and although it promises retribution at the polls rather than through violence, it sees conflict between the city's rich and poor as a defining trait of Mexican society. For the letter's authors, the campaign against the Baratillo was part of a broader attack on the poor by an idle and indulgent elite, here represented by the members of the Ayuntamiento.[86]

> The true cause of the war that some have declared against us is the intolerance of the wealthy, which has come to the point at which it cannot stand the aspect of misery, nor that, with its repugnant appearance, it remind them that there are men hounded by hunger and necessity while others live in comfort and abundance and pass their days among feasts and delicacies.[87]

In the baratilleros' telling, the elite's traditional tolerance and accommodation of the urban poor, which had previously played an important role in negotiations between vendors and authorities, had disappeared. To counteract this shifting moral landscape, the baratilleros sought the support of their class—a group whose precise contours, or even whose name, the letter did not specify.[88]

The timing of the baratilleros' petition is striking. Despite the obvious overtones of class conflict, its authors composed it before socialism or the rhetoric of class struggle had a significant presence in Mexico. It appeared before the 1848 revolutions that brought socialism to prominence in Europe, before the first socialist newspapers began to be printed in Mexico in the late 1840s, and before the 1850 uprising by silk workers in Guadalajara—the first collective action by Mexican workers.[89] So how did these ideas make their way into a petition from vendors in Mexico City's notorious thieves' market? Perhaps editors at the newspaper that printed it had a hand in drafting it. Indeed, two of Mexico's leading liberal intellectuals of the 1840s—Mariano Otero and Juan Bautista Morales—were editors at *El Siglo Diez y Nueve*. Otero, in particular, addressed some of the social issues the baratilleros take up in their petition in his influential *Ensayo sobre el verdadero estado de la cuestión social y política*, which he published the same year. In that essay, Otero emphasized the centrality of the proletarian classes in the unstoppable progress of civilization. "Independent of the yokes that need and error have placed on these classes," Otero wrote, "and of the owners of the material and moral resources that create influence, they will come to be the true constitutive base of the republic."[90] In Otero's view, workers, not the educated middle classes that most midcentury Mexican liberals celebrated, formed the backbone of the nation.[91]

Nothing in the writings of Otero, Bautista Morales, or *El Siglo Diez y Nueve*'s publisher, the more moderate Ignacio Cumplido, offers a clear parallel to the language of the baratilleros' petition, leaving the question of authorship unanswered. What is clear, however, is that the vendors of the Baratillo had inserted themselves into some of the most important political debates of the era, and that their fight to determine where they plied their trades in second-hand clothing, tools, and household items formed part of broader struggles over the shape and direction of the Mexican nation. The language they employed in those efforts put them at the vanguard of Mexico's mid-nineteenth-century social movements.

Despite their cogent and strongly worded missives, the baratilleros' appeal fell on deaf ears. By May 30, even before their letter appeared in *El Siglo Diez y Nueve*, they had moved to the Plaza de Villamil.[92] The baratilleros transported their stands, at their own expense, from the market that they and their predecessors had occupied since the 1790s to a remote square in the northwest corner of the city. Santa Anna and the Ayuntamiento appeared to have scored a victory in their efforts to purge the city's core of one of its most unsavory sites in their broader attempts to usher the Mexican capital into the modern era.

The Ayuntamiento's decision, however, was not a unanimous one. As was the case throughout the eighteenth and nineteenth centuries, baratilleros benefited from the support of sympathetic council members. In the city council session of May 27, the conservative councilman Urbano Fonseca urged the Ayuntamiento to delay moving the baratilleros out of the Plaza del Factor until it could build a new market for them either in the Plaza de Loreto, as the plan from the previous December had called for (and near where Fonseca lived), or in the Plaza de Villamil. The other members of the city council, however, voted down the proposal, and the government charged ahead with the move. Fonseca's fellow councilmen did agree to one of his requests: that the Ayuntamiento not use the police to force the vendors out. The government made good on that promise, and the move appears to have taken place without a repeat of the violence that broke out when the police removed vendors from the Plaza del Volador, in December 1841. Fonseca's advocacy on behalf of the baratilleros underscores that support for Mexico City's street and market vendors often transcended partisan politics in the nineteenth century. Just as the projects to build new market halls and undertake other public works in the capital attracted support from both liberals and conservatives, so did the defense of the vendors those projects would displace.[93]

The baratilleros had barely settled into the Plaza de Villamil before members of the Ayuntamiento began to second-guess the decision. On May 30, the prefect relayed public complaints to the Ayuntamiento about a series of robberies that had hit the area surrounding the Plaza de Villamil, including inside the nearby convent of La Concepción. The priests blamed the crimes on the Baratillo's arrival in the area. Icaza, the market commissioner, again proposed building a market for the Baratillo in the Plaza de Loreto, where at least there was a public fountain that could be used in the event of fire.[94] But that marketplace was never built, probably due to a lack of funds but also because of resistance from vendors who were loath to move yet again.[95]

Replacing baratilleros with food vendors in the Plaza del Factor was no more successful. By 1845, rent in the Plaza del Factor had fallen from more than eighty pesos per week, when the Baratillo was there, to only twenty-five or thirty pesos per week.[96] The Ayuntamiento's plans to build a new market structure for vegetables or shoes there never came to fruition, so the plaza attracted few vendors. To remedy the situation, the Ayuntamiento decided to bring the Baratillo—or at least part of it—back to the Plaza del Factor. The Villamil market would continue to host the Baratillo's most disreputable businesses, including the vendors of used clothing and iron and the ambulatory vendors, while the Plaza del Factor would offer larger objects such as used furniture.[97] The Baratillo operated simultaneously in the two plazas until 1850, when the Ayuntamiento sold the Plaza del Factor so a theater could be constructed there.[98] The Baratillo then moved to several different locations on the western edge of the city before settling in the Plaza del Jardín (known today as Plaza Garibaldi) sometime in the 1860s. It would remain in that location until the beginning of the twentieth century. The Ayuntamiento had deprived the baratilleros of their central location but it had not extinguished their trade.

THE AYUNTAMIENTO AND THE REPUBLIC

The Baratillo survived the 1842 regeneration of Mexico's capital, in part, because the Ayuntamiento could not afford to lose it. A chronically indebted institution, the Ayuntamiento depended heavily on the revenue it earned from public markets—even the Baratillo. This fact helps explain why the councilmen were willing to backtrack on their earlier decision to banish the market to the Plaza de Villamil and why there was never any serious discussion among council members of shuttering the market completely, despite pressure from Santa Anna.[99] In the 1840s, the Ayuntamiento was struggling to govern Mexico City as it faced unprecedented threats to its authority from both the national government and private interests. Markets were one area where the municipal government was not willing to cede any ground.

Throughout most of the colonial period, the Ayuntamiento had enjoyed a large degree of autonomy from the Spanish Crown. The creation of the

Federal District in 1824, with its presidentially appointed governor, eroded some of that autonomy when it left jurisdictional boundaries between city and district poorly defined. Still, under the federalist system the Ayuntamiento continued to function largely as it had under the Spanish—with only sporadic interference from the national government.[100] The centralist coup of 1835 and the implementation of the Municipal Ordinances of 1840 altered that dynamic. As part of their effort to consolidate authority under the nation's executive branch, the centralists stipulated in the Ordinances that all ayuntamientos in the Department of Mexico were "directly subordinate and subject in the municipal administration of policing" to the subprefects, prefects, and ultimately the governor and national executive to whom those officials reported.[101] The result was that after 1840 the Ayuntamiento of Mexico City had to run virtually every major decision by the national executive. The president and his subordinates had authority to intervene in the city's internal affairs whenever they saw fit, as Santa Anna did throughout the 1841–1843 period. Since no other regulations replaced them, this set of laws was at least nominally in force until 1903, when President Porfirio Díaz removed the Ayuntamiento's governing powers.

The national government was not the only opposing force with which the Ayuntamiento had to contend. The centralist reforms led to a collapsing of the distinction between the government and private interests in several key areas. Most significantly for the Ayuntamiento, a decree issued in May of 1835 mandated that it contract out all basic municipal services. The *contratas* (outsourced contracts) were ostensibly assigned through public auctions, but transparency in the bidding process was minimal. The contratistas (the people who won the contracts) did little to develop the infrastructure of the city at a time when observers frequently complained of decaying conditions.[102] In an 1840 manifesto, published in the newspaper *El Cosmopolita*, the Ayuntamiento decried the privatization, accusing the national government of turning municipal assets in an "object of speculation."[103] By trading regular income from taxes for one-time payments from contractors, the contratas only made the Ayuntamiento's precarious financial situation worse.[104]

Amid this gloom, the city's markets division was a rare bright spot. It had been one of the most important branches of city government since the colonial period, generating some of its largest and easiest profits, and the centralists had not included it on the list of services that the city needed to outsource.[105] In their 1840 manifesto, the councilmen underscored markets' importance, citing the markets branch of the municipal government as "one of the few . . . that have flourished" in such difficult times—regularly producing 60,000 pesos per year in revenue for the city.[106] Even the rent the Baratillo vendors paid mattered. In 1845, when the Baratillo was divided between the Plaza de Villamil and the Plaza del Factor, the combined markets contributed almost 10 percent of the markets division's total revenue.[107] The baratilleros may have been trafficking in stolen and other illicit goods, but they paid rent, and the city needed their money.

In 1843, a dispute over public marketplaces led to the unraveling of the relationship between the Ayuntamiento and Santa Anna's government. The alliance between the local and national governments in the capital's rehabilitation had always been a fragile one, and it began to show signs of strain shortly after it began. Santa Anna and his ministers repeatedly complained about the Ayuntamiento's slow progress on the new Volador marketplace and other public works projects throughout the spring of 1842.[108] But it was Santa Anna's sudden decision, in 1843, to demolish the Parián, the emporium that had occupied the western side of the Plaza Mayor since the beginning of the eighteenth century, that finally ended the spirit of cooperation. Though it had lost its luster since an 1828 riot sacked its mostly foreign-owned businesses, the Parián was the Ayuntamiento's most prized piece of real estate, continuing to produce around two thousand pesos per month in rent—10 percent or more of the city's total income.[109]

Santa Anna's order caught the Ayuntamiento by surprise. Its members protested vigorously, arguing that the building was municipal property and that the national government had no right to seize it.[110] On July 3, the members of the departmental assembly (the successor institution to the junta departamental) weighed in, publishing a pamphlet that supported the Ayuntamiento's case and warned that the people who would feel the brunt of the building's destruction were not the elite traders who rented shops in the Parián but "those petty merchants, those poor people who take advantage of the gathering of buyers to be able to sell [their products]." To the assemblymen, the gravest danger the president's decision posed, however, was what the liberal Swiss thinker Benjamin Constant envisioned: that such arbitrary action by the government would render the "oppressed classes" incapable of "remaining loyal to the laws of equality."[111] If the president could so easily flout the nation's laws, what, then, would stop the country's millions of suffering poor from doing the same? The members of a conservative-controlled institution, drawing on a liberal intellectual, again came to the defense of petty merchants.[112]

FIGURE 9. Pedro Gualdi, *Vista de la Gran Plaza de México*, 1843. Gualdi's lithograph depicts the planned monument to independence that Santa Anna sought to build in the Plaza de la Constitución after he ordered the destruction of the Parián. The monument was never finished, however, leaving only its pedestal, or *zócalo*, in the plaza. Residents began referring to the plaza itself as the *Zócalo*, which they do to this day. The project's Spanish architect, Lorenzo de la Hidalga, also designed the new market hall in the Plaza del Volador, among other prominent public works in the capital in the 1840s. See Elisa García Barragán, "El arquitecto Lorenzo de la Hidalga," *Anales del Instituto de Investigaciones Estéticas* 24:80 (2002): 101–28. Image courtesy of Mapoteca Manuel Orozco y Berra, Servicio de Información Agroalimentaria y Pesquera, SAGARPA, Mexico City.

Despite a unified opposition from the Mexico City Ayuntamiento, the departmental assembly, the business community, even Santa Anna's own Junta de Fomento—a commission he had established to promote Mexican industry—the president plowed ahead, and by the end of August 1843 the building had been razed. Santa Anna ordered that the Parián's building materials, which he declared property of the Mexican state, be used in the construction of a monument to independence in the capital's main square (see figure 9).[113] The expropriation and demolition of the Parián constituted the most serious single attack on the autonomy of the Ayuntamiento since its founding in the sixteenth century. It was a watershed moment in a longer history of its declining power against the national government.[114] The municipal government's precarious position in the capital's administrative architecture influenced how it dealt with market vendors, including those in the Baratillo. Even if city councilmen did not like the Baratillo, to a certain extent, they needed it.

CONCLUSION

The aura of optimism that permeated Mexico City in the fall of 1841 and the spring of 1842 failed to produce many lasting achievements for the city or the nation. When voters elected a liberal Congress in 1842 that began to draft a constitution that Santa Anna found unacceptable, he disbanded Congress and installed a *junta de notables* composed of men loyal to him. In 1843, they implemented a new constitution, the Bases Orgánicas, which preserved centralism, strengthened the powers of the national executive, and curtailed voting rights.[115] As Santa Anna began making increasingly arbitrary decisions, domestic conditions deteriorated, tensions along the border with Texas mounted, and his support evaporated. In November 1844, Paredes y Arrillaga, Santa Anna's former ally, rebelled and forced him from power.[116]

The regeneration of Mexico City remained similarly unfinished by 1844. Of the major public works projects the Ayuntamiento had begun in 1841 and 1842, it had completed only the Volador market. The other markets never materialized, and the street-paving project had barely begun. The monument to independence that Santa Anna had planned to build in the city's main square consisted only of its base, or *zócalo*, leading residents to call the plaza itself by that name, as they do to this day.[117] Moving the Baratillo to the Plaza de Villamil proved similarly unsuccessful. It brought the Baratillo's problems to a new neighborhood and led to a drop in municipal revenue that forced the Ayuntamiento to backtrack and allow the baratilleros to return to the Plaza del Factor.

Mexico would not overcome its greatest challenges in 1842. But this historical moment—a period of relative stability and an attempt at national rebuilding—provides an extraordinary window onto the politics and society of the mid-nineteenth century. An era that many historians have glossed over as fundamentally chaotic, the middle decades of the century in fact saw impassioned negotiations over the design of the Mexican nation-state—debates that involved not only hombres de bien but also middling and popular actors like the vendors of the Baratillo. The market's vendors mixed traditional and novel methods in resisting the government's attempt to evict them from the Plaza del Factor—writing petitions that stressed their poverty while also threatening retribution at the ballot box and publishing their petitions in the press. They did not achieve their primary aim: to remain in the market plaza the Baratillo had occupied since the end of the eighteenth century. However, the market survived the government's regeneration of the capital in 1842, just as it had weathered the Bourbons' urban renewal projects in the eighteenth century. The baratilleros' tactics illustrate the extent to which republican institutions and ideas had impacted the lives of the capital's artisans and petty merchants, altering the strategies they used to sustain their livelihoods. Much more than an era of elite-led revolts, the middle decades of the nineteenth century were a period in which public debates over the role of government in society, particularly its role in regulating urban public space, expanded to include a much wider universe of stakeholders.

It would be easy to see the Baratillo's move to the Plaza de Villamil as part of an intermittent, centuries-long effort by Mexico's elites to sanitize the capital city's core of its poor and undesirable elements. To be certain, some contemporaries, including elected officials and private citizens who wrote to the city's newspapers, advocated for just such a project.[118] However, there was no elite consensus behind those efforts, much less a lasting commitment to it. In the end, practical concerns motivated the members of Mexico City's municipal government—namely, appeasing Santa Anna, who demanded that they control the excesses of the Baratillo and find a home for the displaced vendors of the Volador market, and maintaining a steady revenue stream from market fees. When it became clear to the councilmen three years later (when Santa Anna was no longer in power) that the move had negatively impacted the municipality's finances, they reversed course and allowed the vendors to return to the Plaza del Factor. Whatever desire local officials had to beautify the area around that plaza, it was secondary to their need to generate tax revenue.

Nor does portraying the baratilleros' efforts to remain in the Plaza del Factor as a struggle between the city's elites and its popular classes, as the vendors themselves did in their May 27, 1842, letter to the Ayuntamiento, accurately capture the complex role the Baratillo played in the Mexican capital. While some vendors and their customers were poor, others were not. Several appear to have operated businesses that produced revenues of thousands of pesos a year. And while the baratilleros had no shortage of detractors among the city's affluent classes, they also had support from within the elite. The vendors found a sympathetic audience at the country's most influential liberal newspaper, *El Siglo Diez y Nueve*, whose editors published their letter to the Ayuntamiento. Support for the vendors of the Baratillo and other markets also transcended the partisanship of the era. In the 1840s, Mexico City's shadow economy continued to unite diverse sectors of urban society, allowing the market to outlast even Santa Anna—nineteenth-century Mexico's most resilient strongman.

FIVE

Free Trading in the Restored Republic

Let the multitude of unhappy people in the Baratillo conduct
their sales in accordance with liberty and equality.

VICENTE GARCÍA TORRES,
in El Monitor Republicano, *April 9, 1872*

ON THE AFTERNOON OF SUNDAY, MARCH 10, 1872, residents of two
Mexico City neighborhoods gathered at a luncheon in the Tívoli del Eliseo,
a recreational spot popular with the capital's upper crust.[1] The guest of honor
was the residents' representative on the Ayuntamiento, Emilio Islas. Several
other members of the city council also attended, in addition to even more
high-profile guests, including Tiburcio Montiel, the governor of the Federal
District, and Vicente García Torres, the publisher of *El Monitor Republicano*,
Mexico's leading liberal newspaper in the 1870s. The newspaper featured the
luncheon on its front page three days later, describing a joyful affair complete
with lengthy toasts from a number of the attendees. The purpose of this event
was to show support for the vendors of the Baratillo, who were facing eviction from their market plaza. A group of vendors in the Baratillo was refusing
to move, and now some of Mexico City's most prominent citizens were rally-
ing behind them. At the luncheon, García Torres gave an impassioned speech,
arguing that it was not only the future of the Baratillo that was at stake in
this dispute but also the causes of "freedom, work, the law, and humanity"
itself.[2]

Thirty years earlier, Antonio López de Santa Anna had claimed that the
Baratillo was incompatible with modernity. To Santa Anna and other critics,
the market was a relic of a bygone era that was holding back the city's progress.
Now a group of Mexico City luminaries were arguing precisely the opposite.
Not only was the Baratillo compatible with modern, republican Mexico; its
very existence was a testament to the nation's commitment to republican values. The Baratillo had no shortage of critics in the early 1870s, as it had had
throughout its history. But what its detractors saw as a hub of chaos and

license, liberal partisans such as García Torres viewed as a humming bazaar whose petty merchants were merely exercising their constitutional rights. In their view, if Mexico were truly committed to protecting the right to assembly, the right to practice the profession of one's choosing, and other liberties that the country's 1857 Constitution guaranteed, then its leaders must allow the baratilleros to sell their wares without interference from the government.

Under the presidencies of Benito Juárez and Sebastián Lerdo de Tejada, in the period known as the Restored Republic that ran from 1867 to 1876, Mexico's republican institutions gained strength after decades of turmoil. Although presidential elections continued to be marred by fraud and limited voter participation, and, in 1871 and 1876, insurrections in the provinces, the period nonetheless saw the emergence of a more independent judiciary and, for the first time, a truly free press.[3] Juárez and Lerdo de Tejada implemented the sweeping liberal reforms known collectively as La Reforma, whose original passage in the 1850s had sparked a war between Mexico's liberals and conservatives and led to the establishment of a French-backed monarchy in the country from 1863 to 1867, under the Austrian Emperor Maximilian.

With Maximilian and the conservatives' defeat, liberalism became both a buzzword and an organizing principle for Mexican society. In the capital city's press, writers espoused the tenets of individual rights, private property, and free trade—going to great lengths to burnish their liberal credentials and to publicly question those of their adversaries.[4] Liberalism's virtues were supposed to deliver political stability and economic growth after decades of internecine strife and foreign interventions. The Liberal Party enjoyed unchecked dominance in the country, relegating conservatives to the margins of political life and branding them traitors for their collaboration with Maximilian. Although there was a broad consensus in Mexican politics on the principles that would guide the country to long-term stability and prosperity, there was no agreement about how officials would apply those tenets to the everyday business of governing. The challenge of reconciling liberal laws, especially those contained in the country's 1857 Constitution, with the quotidian tasks of governance is nowhere clearer than in the 1872 dispute over the Baratillo.

This chapter traces that controversy as it unfolded on the streets, in the halls of government, and in the pages of Mexico City's newspapers in 1872. It illustrates how the vendors of the Baratillo elevated their dispute with local officials into a political standoff that involved the nation's highest authorities. Like virtually every controversy that surrounded the Baratillo, the debate over who had a right to sell in the market was not one that neatly divided elite and popular groups in the capital. It produced alliances between vendors in the city's notorious thieves' market and some of the nation's most prominent political figures. At the same time, it drove a wedge between the Baratillo's vendors, turning those with fixed stands (puestos), who opted to move to the new market plaza, against the ambulatory vendors (*vendedores ambulantes*), who refused. Vendors in both camps used the levers of republican government to advance their case, with one group allying itself with the Ayuntamiento and the other seeking remedy through the nation's courts. Both turned to the press to bring their message to Mexico City's reading public. Thus, the Baratillo was not simply a site of popular resistance; it was a place where elite, popular, and middling actors engaged in republican politics, testing the integrity and stability of Mexico's institutions.

A PROPOSAL DIVIDES THE BARATILLEROS

The controversy began in November 1871 when the city councilman Ventura Alcérreca proposed shuttering the Baratillo. Alcérreca wanted the Baratillo "condemned and demolished" for being a "flagrant infraction of the police orders that prohibit [its] continuous chaos"—a reference to the intermittent bans that authorities had been issuing since the colonial period.[5] The Baratillo of the early 1870s continued to offer the kinds of products it always had, and its critics leveled the familiar complaints. In his *Proyecto higiénico administrativo para los mercados de México*, Lauro María Jiménez, the president of Mexico's Academy of Medicine, wrote of the Baratillo: "In the Plazuela del Jardín, one does not find what its name suggests . . . [a garden]. Underneath the huts that encircle the square, which is completely uncovered and empty, people sell textile fragments, old clothing, pieces of metal, tools with missing parts, and countless other scraps and cast-offs that go out with the trash from people's homes."[6] To observers like Jiménez, the Baratillo was a market for the city's refuse, both human and material.

Alcérreca suggested that if the Ayuntamiento was unwilling to disband the Baratillo, it should move the market from its current home in the Plaza del Jardín (a square known today as Garibaldi), located five blocks north of the Alameda, to a new marketplace that the Ayuntamiento had constructed at the western edge of the city, in the Plaza de Madrid.[7] The city had only recently begun to expand beyond its traditional territory. Developers purchased lands that indigenous communities and religious institutions were

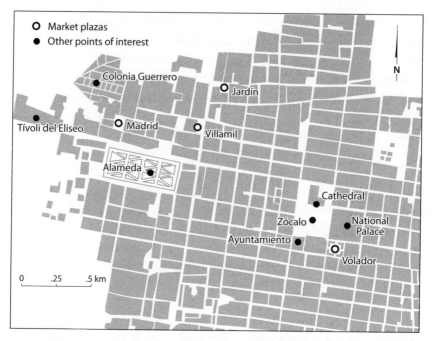

MAP 4. Mexico City, 1867. Based on the *Plano de la Ciudad de México*, ordered by Mexico's Ministry of Development in 1867. Reproduced in Lombardo de Ruiz, *Atlas histórico*, 385. By the late 1860s, the city had begun to push westward. The planned development of Colonia Guerrero is visible in the northwestern corner of the map, at what was then the edge of the city. The map also reflects that by the 1860s residents had begun referring to the Plaza de la Constitución as the Zócalo. Map created by Bill Nelson and Patrick Keller.

forced to sell off following the implementation of the 1856 Ley Lerdo, which mandated that corporate bodies divest themselves of properties that were not directly related to their essential operations. The Colonia Guerrero, where the Plaza de Madrid was located, was one such area. It had been formed from the fields and garden of the Colegio de Propaganda Fide de San Fernando (a school) and the San Andrés Cemetery.[8] The city hoped to develop a new working-class neighborhood there, and the marketplace, also named Guerrero, was part of that plan.[9] Alcérreca's proposal received enthusiastic support from other members of the Ayuntamiento who were anxious to fill the marketplace with additional occupants, as food vendors had been reluctant to move to such a remote part of the city. The Ayuntamiento, one councilman pointed out, was losing nearly 150 pesos per month because so many of the market stalls stood empty.[10] By moving the Baratillo to the Plaza de Madrid, the Ayuntamiento could simultaneously relegate a troublesome source of crime to the city's periphery, boost rental income to the city, and leverage the Baratillo's appeal among poor and working-class consumers to help develop the new neighborhood.

As soon as they received news of the plan, the vendors of the Baratillo wrote a letter in protest. They argued that they could not afford to move again, having only recently built their stands, with their own money, in the Plaza del Jardín. After changing location only once in the two hundred years prior to 1842, the market had become almost itinerant in the thirty years since then—moving to several locations in the northwestern wards of the city before settling in the Plaza del Jardín sometime in the late 1850s or 1860s.[11] The rents, the vendors complained, would also be higher in the Guerrero market—five pesos per month compared to three or four in their current site. The move would be the "death blow" for their "tiny fortunes." In an attempt to mollify concerns about the Baratillo's appearance, they offered to draft a proposal to build a masonry market in the square to replace the ramshackle wooden huts and stands that made the Baratillo such an eyesore.[12] These arguments resonated with at least one member of the city council. Juan García Brito worried that the move would harm the city's poor, who depended on the market. He also noted the benefit of having a central depository for the city's stolen goods, which, he argued, proved quite helpful to the police. When something went missing, they knew exactly where to look for it. But even García Brito saw the wisdom in moving the market to the Plaza de Madrid and seconded Alcérreca's motion.[13]

The Ayuntamiento took no further action on the proposal before municipal elections that December. But on February 9, 1872, the new council took up the issue and passed a resolution ordering the Baratillo to move to the Guerrero market and denying any indemnification for its vendors.[14] A group of baratilleros wrote another impassioned petition to the Ayuntamiento. How, they asked, could the government eject them from a market they had built with their own hands? To make matters worse, the vendors claimed they had learned of the body's decision from the newspaper, not from any official in the government. They implored the councilmen not to implement the order and instead allow the vendors themselves to decide what to do. Some officials in the capital also expressed concern about the plan. Montiel, the Federal District governor, asked the Ayuntamiento to grant those vendors who relocated a two-to-three-month reprieve on rent. Then, Islas, the city councilman for the ward where the Plaza del Jardín was located, temporarily blocked the move.[15] But the Ayuntamiento pressed forward with the plan, and by early March some of the baratilleros had moved to the Guerrero market.

The Ayuntamiento's decision opened a rift between vendors in the Baratillo. While vendors with fixed stalls moved to the Plaza de Madrid, the ambulatory vendors defied the Ayuntamiento's order and stayed behind. Suddenly, there were two Baratillos and two sets of baratilleros. Both groups began sending petitions to the Ayuntamiento, making the case for why they should be allowed to remain where they were. The ambulatory vendors again emphasized their vulnerability—the move would affect them more than it would the "better-off" vendors with fixed stalls who had moved to the Guerrero market. These early petitions hint at the strategies each faction would pursue as the conflict played out over the next several months. Scribbled at the bottom of the ambulatory vendors' letter was the text of Article 9 of Mexico's 1857 Constitution, which guaranteed the right to association. The other group of vendors, now installed in what they called "the true Baratillo" in the Guerrero market, countered that the ambulatory vendors were "laughing at the authority" of the Ayuntamiento, the "representative of the people."[16]

FREE TRADE ON THE STREETS OF MEXICO CITY

In their petitions and letters to the editors of Mexico City's newspapers, the rival vendor factions advanced two distinct visions for the role of government in Mexican society. One held that individual liberty, outlined in the articles of the 1857 Constitution, was inviolable and trumped the municipal government's jurisdiction over urban public spaces. The other saw the need for the government to place reasonable limits on the activities of urban dwellers to benefit the wider public. The baratilleros' legal wrangling shows how little consensus existed in the Restored Republic over where the line between individual rights and government authority should be drawn.

The 1872 case was not the first time vendors in Mexico had raised these issues. Soon after the country's independence from Spain in 1821, Mexico City's vendors began invoking the principle of free trade to assert their right to sell on city streets. In doing so, they forced municipal officials to consider what free trade meant in the context of the local economy. In the early- and mid-nineteenth century, free trade proponents in Mexico focused mainly on breaking up monopolies like the colonial-era merchant and artisan guilds.[17]

The 1857 Constitution also guaranteed every citizen's right to practice the profession of his or her choosing and the right to free assembly. Given these limitations on the government's authority, to what extent could local authorities intervene to determine who could sell their wares in urban public spaces?

An early test for Mexico City's authorities on this issue occurred in 1824, when a group of vendors who sold *rebozos* (a traditional Mexican shawl) outside the Parián marketplace asked the Ayuntamiento to remove the ambulatory vendors that were blocking access to their stalls and peddling what the petitioners alleged were imitation rebozos. The municipal market commission declined to take action on the petition, noting that it "does not find it within its powers, nor in accordance with Justice, to prevent each person from bringing and selling his merchandise in the location he desires and finds most advantageous." Doing so, it determined, would "attack his liberty."[18]

The issue was far from resolved on a national level, however, and a similar dispute between merchants and street vendors in the city of Puebla, located roughly one hundred kilometers miles east of Mexico City, shows local authorities taking a different approach. Puebla, like other major cities in Mexico, had both its own baratillo and an emporium for finer goods, which, like the one in Mexico City, was called the Parián. In October 1844, the merchants of Puebla's Parián wrote to the ayuntamiento of that city asking it to remove the ambulatory vendors who congregated in front of their stores and force them to return to the baratillo.[19] The Parián merchants argued that by blocking access to the their stores, the ambulatory vendors were insulting the honor of the wealthier merchants and depriving them of their individual rights. The merchants claimed that although they paid rent to the city for their space, "we do not have the free and clear use of it, but rather suffer insults to our persons and a general discredit to our commerce."[20] The petitioners were careful to note, however, that "we do not seek to deprive anyone of his rights, nor to increase our wealth by hurting others." On the contrary, it was the ambulatory vendors who were impeding the rights of the Parián merchants by obstructing access to their shops and preventing a "free commerce" in the plaza. Those vendors sought to take individual liberty "beyond its just limits and true character" by selling wherever they pleased and without any regard for the rights of other merchants.[21] Puebla's market commission, in May 1845, agreed with the complainants and ordered the baratilleros to vacate the area.[22] Free trade, in this case, signified the free circulation of goods, not a person's right to sell wherever he or she pleased.

By the time the Ayuntamiento of Mexico City voted to move the Baratillo to the Guerrero market in early 1872, there was still no consensus about how local governments should interpret the nebulous principle of free trade when it came to regulating commerce in public streets and plazas. If anything, the political and institutional environment of the Restored Republic only complicated matters for local governments: petitioners had new legal tools to support their cause, especially the bill of individuals' rights included in the 1857 Constitution, a stronger judiciary, and a vibrant free press that they could use to pursue their claims. The ambulatory vendors in the Plaza del Jardín adeptly, even systematically, used the different institutional mechanisms available to Mexican citizens to make their case for their right to remain in that plaza. First, they protested by writing petitions to the Ayuntamiento. When that strategy did not yield the desired results, they turned to the courts, and finally to the press. They did not take those actions on their own, however. They had help from influential friends.

ALLIES

After the Ayuntamiento voted on February 9, 1872, to move the Baratillo to the Plaza de Madrid, the ambulatory vendors approached Emilio Islas, their representative on the Ayuntamiento, to ask for his support. While the details of that encounter are not known, it produced results for the vendors, as Islas used his veto in the city council session of February 13 to suspend the move. Recognizing that Islas's veto had bought them time but had not forced the Ayuntamiento to abandon its plan to relocate the Baratillo, the ambulatory vendors spent the following weeks cultivating support for their cause among the city's other elected officials. Roughly a month later, on March 10, the residents of wards two and four hosted the luncheon at the Tívoli del Eliseo for Islas and other potential allies, including Governor Montiel. *El Monitor Republicano*'s article on the event does not state explicitly whether any of the baratilleros attended, but the "artisans and residents" (*artesanos y vecinos*) it referenced probably included vendors in the market. By all accounts, it was a heterogeneous gathering at a space that historians have described as a leisure spot for the rich.[23]

In their attempts to block the Ayuntamiento's plan, the ambulatory vendors mobilized a neighborhood-based political network. At least thirteen individuals who signed petitions or wrote letters to the capital's newspapers during the 1872 dispute lived within one square block of the Plaza del Jardín, illustrating how closely the Baratillo and its neighborhood were intertwined.[24] That the residents of the neighborhood around the Baratillo hosted the luncheon suggests how important the market was for the economy of that section of the city—an argument that vendors and neighborhood residents made in support for the Baratillo throughout the nineteenth century. The baratilleros tapped into a working-class political network that linked neighborhood residents, municipal officials, and members of the press.[25]

According to *El Monitor*'s account, the governor did not speak at the March 10 luncheon. Instead, two other men held the spotlight. The first was José Rosales Gordoa, the ambulatory vendors' *evangelista*, or advocate. Rosales Gordoa was an invalid former commander in the army and the son of Víctor Rosales, a hero of Mexico's independence wars.[26] Rosales Gordoa was a public figure in his own right, known mostly for his advocacy of veterans' issues and for his role in recovering a Spanish flag that Mexican soldiers had captured during the wars for independence but was later sold to the Spanish ambassador—by a baratillero. Rosales Gordoa was himself the owner of a hardware store in the Baratillo.[27]

Rosales Gordoa sent a petition to the Ayuntamiento on behalf of the ambulatory vendors in the Baratillo on March 9, the day before the luncheon, outlining their argument for staying in the Plaza del Jardín. He then read the letter aloud for the guests at the event. It began by thanking the Ayuntamiento for offering the vendors such an elegant structure as the Guerrero marketplace. Rosales Gordoa then presented three main arguments for why the city council should let the ambulatory vendors continue to sell in the Plaza del Jardín, even if for only two hours per day. The first was that preventing them from doing so was a violation of Article 9 of the 1857 Constitution's Rights of Man, which declared that: "no one may restrict the right to associate or to meet peacefully with any licit objective."[28] Second, the "luxurious" Guerrero marketplace was simply more suited to the "better-off" baratilleros who had already snatched up all the prime locations there. Lastly, Rosales Gordoa assured the city council that allowing the ambulatory vendors to stay in the Plaza del Jardín would cost the city nothing; on the contrary, with some vigilance on the part of municipal authorities, the vendors could make a significant contribution to city coffers through their payment of the *viento* tax that the city levied on vendors without permanent stalls. Rosales Gordoa hoped that the men of "elevated social position" who sat on the Ayuntamiento would consider this request from their fellow citizens at their next meeting.[29] It was an argument that employed the rhetorical strategies that vendors had long used in their petitions to government officials—expressing deference toward members of the governing elite, stressing the vendors' vulnerability, and appealing to officials' common sense. But the letter also contained the thinly veiled threat of legal action if the plea for magnanimity did not succeed.

Though Rosales Gordoa was the ambulatory vendors' primary representative, it was García Torres, the long-time owner and publisher of *El Monitor Republicano*, who seems to have been the principal architect of the vendors' case. García Torres was one of the most important liberal voices of the era. Throughout the second half of the nineteenth century, his newspaper was the most consistent advocate for a progressive liberalism, giving more attention to social issues, especially the plights of workers and peasants, than its main rival, the more moderate *El Siglo Diez y Nueve* (the paper that printed the baratilleros' petition in 1842).[30] García Torres is well known today for his role as a publisher and editor, but less so for his brief stint on the Mexico City Ayuntamiento—which lasted less than six months but coincided with the 1872 controversy over the Baratillo.[31] García Torres was thus doubly valuable to the ambulatory vendors: he possessed a vote on the city council as well as a platform, through his newspaper, to build public support for their cause. Indeed, he made it his signature issue during his short time in office.

García Torres became the most vocal supporter of the Baratillo's ambulatory vendors during the spring of 1872, acting as what he called "the organ and interpreter of [their] sentiments."[32] In his advocacy, he articulated a liberal vision that was at once orthodox and progressive. García Torres expressed a reverence for the Constitution of 1857 and its enshrinement of individual liberties, seeing the charter as the most capable mechanism for delivering both economic development and social justice to a country that had seen little of either since its independence from Spain. He viewed the ambulatory vendors' dilemma as a struggle to defend three rights, in particular, whose protection he believed was fundamental for the construction of a more modern society: the rights to free trade, to work, and to free association.

In the article that *El Monitor* published about the luncheon, the author introduced García Torres as "a staunch partisan of all of the franchises and of the freedom of commerce."[33] Like other liberals, García Torres believed that expanding trade was key to jumpstarting the country's long-suffering economy. For that to happen, liberals advocated what was called "*la libertad de comercio*"—an expression that suggested both the lifting of internal and external duties on goods and the right of all people, regardless of stature or political connection, to freely engage in commerce. García Torres took an even more expansive view of commerce than many of his contemporaries. In a speech at a city council session in early April 1872, he explained that "although I support large-scale foreign trade . . . I am a more decided partisan of the commerce which engenders the work of the poor—mixed, of little value, and ambulatory, but generalized [and] extended throughout the Republic."[34] Few, if any, writers had ever associated petty commerce with economic development. If street selling had attracted the attention of political economists, which it rarely did, those writers generally portrayed it negatively. García Torres, on the other hand, disregarded concerns that street vending blocked traffic, dirtied public spaces, and fomented crime. He wanted to encourage petty commerce in order to involve as many members of the poor as possible in the buying and selling of inexpensive articles, thus bringing them into a larger, more inclusive commercial sector.

For García Torres, encouraging commerce, both large and small, required lifting the impediments that had historically constrained trade in Mexico. These measures included reducing or eliminating import tariffs and the internal duties (alcabalas) that had outlasted Spanish rule, and prohibiting monopolies. He also sought to limit the government's say in who could trade and where—advocating the freedom *to* trade in addition to free trade. García Torres argued that the ambulatory vendors' "right to trade wherever they wanted, without having to ask permission, is absolute." At one point, he allegedly told the group of baratilleros in the Guerrero market that he was so committed to the principle of free trade that he would let petty vendors sell anywhere in the city, "even if it were in the Cathedral or Palace."[35] García Torres claimed that this right was one respected "in all societies, even in monarchies, but especially in our most liberal one."[36] The state simply had no business telling its citizens where they could trade.

Commerce was the economic activity that had the capacity to bind the Mexican nation and propel it forward, but it was also, at its base, a form of labor. In the view of many leading Mexican liberals, the right to work, and to benefit from the fruits of one's own labor, constituted the very foundation of the individual's relation to society.[37] It was the second major theme that García Torres addressed in his public comments on the Baratillo. García Torres asserted the legitimacy of a baratillero's work, arguing that it was useful—contributing to the expansion of commerce—and honest. The distinction mattered: Article 4 of the 1857 Constitution declared that "Every man is free to embrace the profession, industry, or work that suits him, so long as it is useful and honest, and to benefit from its fruits." The Constitution also made having "an honest way of life" a prerequisite for Mexican citizenship.[38] If the ambulatory vendors' profession was viewed as criminal or dishonest, they had little constitutional grounds for their case.

The third liberal principle that García Torres sought to advance through the ambulatory vendors' cause was the freedom of association. Absent from the 1824 and 1836 Constitutions, the right was first mandated in 1857 but not enforced until after the overthrow of Maximilian and the establishment of the Restored Republic in 1867. During the two decades that followed, an "associationist fever" took hold in the country, with hundreds of workers' associations, scientific congresses, and artistic societies bringing together thousands of "free and juridically equal individuals" in voluntary pacts with their fellow citizens.[39] García Torres was a consistent advocate for voluntary associations. On the Ayuntamiento he served on the Fomento de Artesanos commission, which promoted artisans' associations in the capital. He argued that workers' associations, which caused "horror among the conservative classes," were perfectly compatible with Mexico's "democratic code." Unlike the guilds they replaced, its members enjoyed equal standing and voting rights in the organizations.[40] Voluntary associations, in liberals' view, empowered individuals in a way that also stimulated economic activity in the country.[41] Although it is not clear whether baratilleros ever formed a voluntary association—nothing in the records suggests they did—García Torres argued that they had every right to gather in the Plaza del Jardín to conduct their business without harassment from the government.

In two speeches in early 1872, one at the luncheon with the baratilleros and another before the city council, García Torres made the case that the dispute over the Baratillo was testing Mexico's commitment to the values that lay at the heart of its Constitution. He argued that the Ayuntamiento, in its haste to fill a new public marketplace, failed to see the implications of its actions, which had deprived some of the nation's most vulnerable citizens of their most basic rights. García Torres used his position within Mexico City's government to try to persuade his fellow council members to reverse their plans, or at least reach a compromise. At the same time, he utilized the pulpit of *El Monitor Republicano* to make what might have been a local, administrative issue into one that posed existential questions about the Mexican republic.[42]

Although García Torres was the ambulatory vendors' most high-profile advocate, he was far from their only supporter. During the month of March, they secured the backing of other important allies, including in the police. On March 18, 1872, the police inspector of the fourth ward, where the Plaza del Jardín was located, wrote to the Ayuntamiento to warn the government that a conflict with the ambulatory vendors was impending. He believed that there were "an infinite number" of these men and women who were unwilling to move. The Guerrero market was simply too far away to be practical; the Plaza del Jardín, on the other hand, was at the center of the barrios "where all of these unhappy people live." Most concerning, however, was the "antipathy between the baratilleros . . . which we will call the rich ones and the poor ones." The inspector repeated the ambulatory vendors' claim that they, unlike the wealthier baratilleros, lacked the funds to move to the Plaza de Madrid. Clearly sympathetic to the ambulatory vendors, he noted in his letter to the Ayuntamiento that he had asked his superiors in the office of the Federal District governor, to whom the city's police reported, whether he would be forced to remove the vendors against their will. He even relayed the ambulatory vendors' claim that such a move might violate their constitutional right to free assembly. The governor's office responded that the matter fell under the Ayuntamiento's jurisdiction and that the inspector must obey its orders.[43]

In another show of support for the aggrieved vendors, an anonymous contributor wrote to the newspaper *El Ferrocarril*, lamenting that, "in our country, instead of being protected, the poor are oppressed in a cruel manner, being buried in desperation and misery." The Ayuntamiento, the letter argued, was acting irresponsibly by not finding a more convenient location for the ambulatory vendors and for extracting rents from them that would fill the city's treasury without providing a wider benefit to the city, "as the public desires."[44]

By mid-March, the combination of public and private lobbying by the ambulatory vendors and their supporters seemed to be paying off. At the urging of García Torres, José Núñez, the city's market commissioner, agreed to let the ambulatory vendors sell in the Plaza del Jardín for two hours every day.[45] But on March 19, the Ayuntamiento, including Núñez, voted to reverse that decision and move all the vendors of the Baratillo to the Guerrero market once again. The establishment of the two-hour selling window in the Plaza del Jarín had apparently emptied the Guerrero market and led to the reestablishment of a full-fledged Baratillo in its previous home, which the city council found unacceptable.[46] This time, the government executed the order and the police removed everyone, including the ambulatory vendors, from the Plaza del Jardín.

THE BARATILLO, THE AYUNTAMIENTO, AND THE LAW

By the end of March, the ambulatory vendors had exhausted their efforts to win over the members of the Ayuntamiento. In 1872, unlike in 1842, however, they had other channels through which they could pursue their grievance against the city. On April 8, twenty-eight vendors, including both men and women, filed a writ of *amparo* with a judge in the federal district court in Mexico City, claiming that the Ayuntamiento had violated Articles 1, 4, 9, 15, and 28 of the 1857 Constitution.[47] The vendors' legal case was essentially the one Rosales Gordoa and García Torres had outlined at the luncheon on March 10: they argued that the Ayuntamiento had infringed on their rights to free association and to practice the profession of their choosing. Moreover, in stipulating that the Baratillo could operate only in the Guerrero market, the Ayuntamiento had created an illegal monopoly.

Similar to the U.S. writ of habeus corpus, Mexico's amparo became a bulwark against the government's infringement of personal liberties. It was a legal innovation that legislators introduced in 1847 as an amendment to the 1824 Constitution, but it was not regularly in force until 1867.[48] Baratilleros had filed an amparo petition before. In 1850, in one of Mexico's earlier amparo cases, a group of vendors in the Plaza del Factor sued the Ayuntamiento for violating their rights when the government evicted them to build a theater there. (The Baratillo had returned to the Plaza del Factor after the vendors' move to the Plaza de Villamil in 1842 proved to be a failure.) The baratilleros lost that case; indeed, few of the early amparo suits succeeded due to the absence of enacting legislation.[49] By 1872, however, the institutional environment in Mexico had evolved. During the Restored Republic, legislators created a legal framework that opened the door to a flood of amparo cases. It was the ambulatory vendors' last legal recourse to regain access to the Plaza del Jardín.

A majority of Ayuntamiento members, led by the body's president, Eduardo Arteaga, and market commissioner Núñez, adamantly denied that the Ayuntamiento's decision overstepped its authority or violated the constitutional rights of the vendors. On the contrary, they argued, it was the ambulatory vendors who had chosen to flout the law by ignoring an eviction order. The municipal government, they asserted, had clear authority to determine where public markets could operate—a right the body had possessed since colonial times. In their response to the amparo petition, the councilmen cited the federal Ley de Dotación, signed by President Benito Juárez in 1867, and the 1871 Civil Code of the Federal District and Territory of Baja California. The Ley de Dotación established the Ayuntamiento of Mexico's jurisdiction within the Federal District of Mexico, specifying which areas of government it was responsible for overseeing and what assets it could call its own. The section dealing with markets read: "The right to establish markets, of any class, belongs exclusively to the Ayuntamiento."[50] This law repeated a centralist-era decree that had codified what had been custom since the establishment of the Plaza Mayor markets in 1609: that the Ayuntamiento was responsible for regulating public marketplaces and would be the sole beneficiary of the rents it collected there.

Markets continued to be among the Ayuntamiento's most prized assets in the 1870s. They were among the few properties that municipalities were able to maintain after the enactment of the 1856 Ley Lerdo, and they constituted some of the Ayuntamiento's largest revenue sources in the early 1870s, contributing between 5 and 10 percent of its annual budget.[51] Even the vendors of the Baratillo, who generally avoided paying other taxes, paid rent to the city for the space they occupied in public plazas. The Ayuntamiento had spent the better part of the nineteenth century wresting control of market plazas from private hands—buying the land on which they were situated, as it did with the Plaza del Volador in 1831, and pushing back against national authorities' incursions, such as Santa Anna's decision to demolish the Parián in 1843.[52] Given this long struggle to establish and maintain its authority over public markets, the Ayuntamiento of 1872 was not willing to let a rag-tag group of ambulatory vendors dictate policy.

The controversy over the Baratillo exacerbated longstanding tensions between the Ayuntamiento and national authorities. During the Restored Republic, the federal government began to take a more active role in the organization of public space in the Mexican capital. It used the new powers it had obtained under the laws of the Reforma to open alleyways and straighten and extend streets—rationalizing the urban landscape in a project that picked up where the Bourbons had left off (and which the Ayuntamiento of 1842 had also sought, unsuccessfully, to continue). Federal officials, either through the Federal District governor's office or the Ministry of Justice and Development, selected public works projects that would require expropriation, designated the contractors that would execute them, and authorized indemnifications. Yet, as was the case under Bourbon rule, the Ayuntamiento was generally responsible for paying for those projects, and for managing the backlash from affected residents. This arrangement led to repeated clashes between municipal and national authorities over the jurisdictional, financial, and constitutional issues that arose from these projects.[53] In the Ayuntamiento's 1868 annual report, municipal officials complained that even under the "absolute monarchy" of the Spanish Crown, ayuntamientos had enjoyed many *fueros*, or traditional rights, that the federal government was now impinging. They argued that the city barely had sufficient funds to manage its existing responsibilities, much less take on the new ones that the national government was imposing.[54]

In 1872, street vending itself became another source of contention. In January of that year, the Ayuntamiento, at the initiative of Arteaga, wrote to President Juárez to ask that he exempt the viento vendors of tortillas, vegetables, and flowers in markets and adjacent streets of all taxes. He did so because these poor women, who "almost without exception belonged to the Indian race," were suffering continuous abuse at the hands of the tax collectors. Arteaga, however, got more than he had bargained for: on February 14, 1872, Juárez exempted a long list of vendors from all taxes and rent obligations—not just sellers of the aforementioned products, but also vendors of poultry, herbs, peanuts, baskets, brooms, palm leaf mats, and various other goods. The order also stated that the Ayuntamiento must permit the vendors to sell in any public thoroughfare.[55] Juárez had simultaneously eliminated a significant source of revenue for the city and opened the door to chaos by curtailing the Ayuntamiento's ability to limit the areas in which vendors could sell their products. The list of vendors exempted from paying rent, however, did not include the ambulatory vendors of the Baratillo. This omission, the Ayuntamiento argued, left those vendors firmly under its jurisdiction.

The Ayuntamiento found unwavering allies for its interpretation of the law among the baratilleros who had moved to the Guerrero market. Those vendors strongly opposed the ambulatory vendors' attempts to remain in the site of the old Baratillo because they believed that splitting the market in two would hurt their businesses, which they had moved to the new, more remote, marketplace. They had every interest in maintaining a monopoly on the name and trade of the Baratillo. These vendors, led by one Ramón Escalante and one Jesús Farfán, dismissed the notion that the Mexican Constitution granted their rivals the right to sell wherever they pleased.[56] After sending a letter to the president of the Ayuntamiento on March 10, in which they

claimed that those who were still in the Plaza del Jardín were flagrantly disobeying the government's orders,[57] they penned a letter to the editor of the
newspaper *El Correo del Comercio*, which it printed on March 27. In it, the
Guerrero vendors argued that the Baratillo had always operated in a locale
designated by municipal authorities, where the police could adequately
supervise its activities. Only in such a location could the work of a baratillero
be considered "useful and honest."[58] The vendors of the Guerrero market
never claimed that the ambulatory vendors' business itself was dishonest or
not useful to society—a charge that the Baratillo's opponents had frequently
leveled against vendors in the market throughout its history and which street
and market vendors sometimes used against their rivals.[59] Instead, they
argued that it was the ambulatory vendors' flouting of the government's
orders that made their trade dishonest and therefore undeserving of Article
4 protection. The Guerrero baratilleros also claimed that the real opponents
of the move were the owners of the pulquerías, pawnshops, and other properties around the Plaza del Jardín, who worried that the Baratillo's relocation
would hurt their businesses by reducing foot traffic. The ambulatory vendors,
according to Escalante and Farfán, were merely their proxies.[60]

The Guerrero baratilleros also challenged García Torres's claims that he
and the ambulatory vendors held the moral high ground in the case and that
their position was the one more in keeping with liberal values. Escalante and
Farfán felt betrayed and belittled by García Torres, who, they point out, originally voted *for* the Baratillo's move before becoming the most vocal opponent
of it. They claimed that García Torres told them, condescendingly, that he was
a "true liberal" and a defender of people's right to sell wherever they pleased,
and that the baratilleros were "stupid" to agree to move to the Plaza de
Madrid.[61] Escalante and Farfán did not agree that it was a prerogative of a
liberal government to allow vendors to situate themselves wherever they
wanted. They cited the example of Juan José Baz, a former governor of the
Federal District, "whom nobody could brand as anti-liberal," who had successfully removed the shoe-sellers from the Portal de Mercaderes at the edge
of the Zócalo. "This he did because ... he needed to do so for the good of
society."[62] Acting on behalf of the public interest was the true prerogative of
the liberal state, and this is what the Ayuntamiento had done by moving the
Baratillo to a more modern facility, where the police could better oversee it.

The Guerrero baratilleros allied themselves with the Ayuntamiento
because its decision to consolidate the baratilleros in the Guerrero market
offered a clear material benefit to them; its reversal would have harmed their

businesses by creating a rival Baratillo in a more central location. Yet the Guerrero vendors, like their adversaries, were able to cast their argument in a political language that spoke to some of the most pressing questions that Mexico faced under the Restored Republic: how to balance individual rights against the government's need to ensure stability and promote economic growth—two goals that had eluded Mexico ever since the nation's independence, more than fifty years earlier.

A DECISION, AND A CONSTITUTIONAL CRISIS

The district judge who received the ambulatory vendors' amparo petition agreed with the Ayuntamiento and the Guerrero vendors: the government was within its rights to force the baratilleros out of the Plaza del Jardín.[63] But Rosales Gordoa and the ambulatory vendors quickly appealed to Mexico's Supreme Court, where their case found a sympathetic audience. On May 13, the Court, led by Chief Justice Sebastián Lerdo de Tejada, sided unanimously with the ambulatory vendors, after deliberating for less than a day.[64] The Ayuntamiento, by forcing all baratilleros to congregate in the Guerrero marketplace, had violated Articles 1, 4, 9, and 28 of the Constitution (all but one of the articles the complainants argued the government had breached). The Court opined that although the 1867 Ley de Dotación gave the city the exclusive authority to establish markets, the Ayuntamiento had "no right whatsoever to obligate the merchants to meet in said plazas, nor impede them from trafficking in the places they see most fit, so long as they do not build a market, because this would be an attack on the freedom of commerce guaranteed by the Pact of the Republic." The justices reversed the district court's decision. By May 25, the ambulatory vendors were back at work in the Plaza del Jardín.[65]

García Torres celebrated the Supreme Court decision in the pages of his newspaper, printing a story on May 31 that recounted the events of the previous several months in a dramatic fashion. The story was complete with a hero, played by himself, and a villain, played by Núñez, the market commissioner and "enemy of the merchants," who, with the governor's support, had deployed the police to violently remove them from their market, hauling many off to jail. García Torres cheered the Supreme Court for recognizing that the Ayuntamiento had violated rights guaranteed by the Constitution, and, more importantly, by "natural liberty." These liberties were "absolute and un-legislatable."[66] García Torres expressed his deepest disappointment with the Ayuntamiento. It was supposed to be "the most immediate protector of the *pueblo*, but had [instead] shown itself to be its evil stepmother."[67] He also lambasted the district judge, who, "without legal or justified motive, has gone on record that ... liberty has no guarantees." The episode, in *El Monitor*'s view, had put Mexico's precarious democracy to the test—and both the Ayuntamiento and the local courts had failed. Their actions had not only deprived the vendors of their rights; they had "opened the doors to disorder and even revolution."[68] Were it not for the intervention of Lerdo de Tejada and the justices of the Supreme Court, chaos might have prevailed.[69]

El Monitor's victory celebration proved premature, however. On May 31, the same day the paper printed García Torres's article and only a week after the ambulatory vendors had returned to the Plaza del Jardín, Jesús Farfán and the baratilleros in the Guerrero market wrote to the Ayuntamiento to ask, once again, that it force the ambulatory vendors to vacate the plaza. On June 7, the Ayuntamiento, from which García Torres had since resigned over a separate dispute, did just that, voting 11 to 3 to ban the ambulatory vendors from forming a market in the Plaza del Jardín—an outright repudiation of the Supreme Court's order.[70] According to Rosales Gordoa, the police had not even waited until the council approved this motion before entering the plaza and harassing the vendors there. Then, on the afternoon of June 7, after the resolution passed, the police returned with a larger force and tried to force all the vendors to move to the Guerrero market, "under the threat of arms." Rosales Gordoa claimed that the police officer who led the operation, "after vociferating in public that I was a con man for what I wrote to the baratilleros [in the Guerrero market] and that he should have sent me to prison," began hauling vendors who resisted off to jail. He began with three female relatives of Rosales Gordoa who were tending his small hardware store in the plaza. Since the shop was left unattended while the women were in jail, thieves made away with most of its merchandise.[71]

In response to the Ayuntamiento's action, Rosales Gordoa and the ambulatory vendors filed another complaint with the Supreme Court, in which they claimed that the municipal government was playing semantic games.[72] In its original ruling, the Court had determined that residents possessed the right to sell their wares in any of the city's public spaces so long as they did not build a market—which the Court recognized that only the Ayuntamiento had the authority to do. To avoid creating a market, with the kinds of fixed stalls and roof coverings that had existed in the plaza prior to their eviction, the vendors had been sitting on the ground, without any type of shade or market stand. This, Rosales Gordoa pointed out, was how many other vendors sold on the streets of the capital, without interference from the government. Yet these efforts did not satisfy the Ayuntamiento and the police, who insisted that the Court had only authorized "ambulatory baratilleros" to conduct their "commercial traffic." The words *ambulante* and *tráfico,* according to the Ayuntamiento's interpretation, meant that the vendors could sell only if they were "walking without interruption, in continuous movement."[73] To Rosales Gordoa and the ambulatory vendors, it was an unreasonably literal interpretation of the Court's decision. Rosales Gordoa implored the Court to clarify its ruling to "both sustain the authority of the foremost power of the Federation" and reach out to "the poor, the most needy children of the pueblo, and the targets of the hateful vengeance of the powerful."[74]

While the Court considered the ambulatory vendors' petition, some vendors had returned to the Plaza del Jardín. On June 13, the police, acting on orders from the Ayuntamiento (and apparently Governor Montiel), entered the Plaza del Jardín once again, this time using an unprecedented level of violence in arresting the ambulatory vendors and bringing them to the municipal jail.[75] A broadside went up the next day, accusing the Ayuntamiento of dragging off to prison the "unhappy ambulatory baratilleros and the poor women owners of the bazaars in the Plaza del Jardín." The poster appealed to the public's sympathy for the downtrodden, focusing on the police's brutalization of its female vendors in order to emphasize their vulnerability (see figure 10). The Ayuntamiento, in taking these actions, was "laughing at the judgment of the Supreme Court."[76] A contributor to the conservative Catholic newspaper *La Voz de México* declared the Ayuntamiento "in complete rebellion" against the nation's highest court and blasted its members for "governing by arbitrary means" and denying people's basic rights.[77]

On June 28, the Supreme Court reaffirmed the right of the ambulatory vendors to practice their trade in the Plaza del Jardín. The justices denounced both Governor Montiel and the Ayuntamiento for the abuses the police had committed in removing the vendors.[78] The Ayuntamiento, however, responded again with defiance, convening on June 30 and voting to ignore the ruling. They instructed the police to prevent vendors from reconstituting the Baratillo in the Plaza del Jardín.[79] A stalemate ensued, and Mexico found

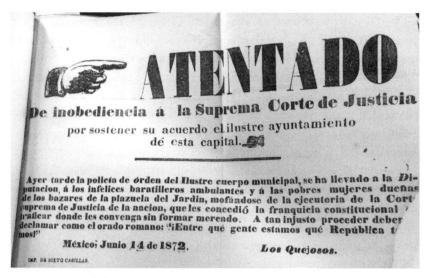

FIGURE 10. Broadside criticizing the Ayuntamiento for disobeying the Supreme Court and violently evicting the baratilleros from the Plaza del Jardín, 1872. AHCM, Ayuntamiento, Rastros y Mercados, vol. 3734, exp. 554, f. 64.

itself in a constitutional crisis over the rights of vendors in the country's most infamous thieves' market.

FROM THE COURTS TO THE PRESS

During the summer of 1872, with the Ayuntamiento in open rebellion against the Supreme Court and the ambulatory vendors barred from reentering the Plaza del Jardín, the two sides took their cases to the public. Though both groups of vendors had used the press throughout the controversy, the frequency and intensity of their appeals increased during what became a months-long stalemate. The back-and-forth took place largely in the pages of the daily *El Ferrocarril*, as García Torres and *El Monitor Republicano* disappeared from the debate after the publisher resigned from the Ayuntamiento.[80]

The exchange began with a letter from Jesús Farfán and the Guerrero baratilleros that appeared in *El Ferrocarril* on July 29. Having failed to persuade the Supreme Court using federal law, they employed a new approach: they publicly challenged their adversaries' honor. The Guerrero vendors claimed that the ambulatory vendors were lying about being poor. They accused them of being puppets of the "capitalist owners of [the] stores, pawnshops, pulquerías, and properties that surround the Plazas del Jardín," asserting that the vendors there had taken the "false pretense" of being poor ambulatory vendors when the truly poor were the vendors in the Guerrero marketplace. They reserved their harshest comments for Rosales Gordoa, whom they called *"un hombre de negocios sin título"*—a businessman without a university degree, which, technically speaking, he was.[81] They suggested that he took on the ambulatory vendors' case not for the principles involved but for money. "The profits that his gullible clients provide him every day are for our adversary a commercial business so lucrative that we are sure that since the year 1867 none so profitable could possibly have presented itself to him," they wrote. They smeared his war record, submitting six documents that purported to show evidence of his misconduct in the war against Maximilian and the conservatives in 1867, and even questioned whether he was a Mexican citizen.[82]

In a harsh-tongued response in *El Ferrocarril*, Rosales Gordoa claimed that Farfán and the other baratilleros had "slanderously wounded my person" by calling him, in so many words, a "tinterillo," or unqualified lawyer. Furthermore, the idea that the property owners around the Plaza del Jardín had "fomented resistance" among the ambulatory vendors was, in Rosales Gordoa's words, "such an obvious vulgarity, and an assertion so improbable that it does not deserve any time being wasted on debating it." As to the assertion that Rosales Gordoa was representing the vendors only for the money, he replied that this, too, was a lie; he took on the work pro bono. Besides, he was a baratillero himself, as the owner of a hardware store there.[83]

The attacks on Rosales Gordoa's character might have reflected the Guerrero baratilleros' belief that they were losing the battle for public opinion. After all, their adversaries in the Plaza del Jardín had secured the early support of both Rosales Gordoa and García Torres and the sympathies of a number of contributors to both liberal and conservative newspapers. The Guerrero baratilleros did not have a prominent evangelista of their own, perhaps because they were allied with the Ayuntamiento and did not believe one was necessary. As they now found themselves on the wrong side of a Supreme Court decision, the vendors in the Guerrero market may have felt that their only option was to attempt to swing public opinion in their favor. Their attacks on Rosales Gordoa illustrate an important characteristic of Mexico's public sphere in the nineteenth century: it was not only the substance of an argument that mattered but also who was making it.

Honor was an essential component in the construction of Mexico's nineteenth-century public sphere. Members of the political elite legitimized their claims to speak on behalf of the nation and their fellow citizens by establishing their status as honorable men. This conception of honor was determined not through inherited status but through public negotiation, particularly through the press.[84] As the number of newspapers in the country proliferated under the Restored Republic—in 1873 there were fifty-seven periodicals in Mexico City alone—and all restrictions on free speech, save for the laws against calumny and slander, were removed, the public sphere became more democratic.[85] That a group of baratilleros was able to publicly, and at times viciously, challenge the honor of Rosales Gordoa, the son of an independence hero and a well-regarded soldier himself, underscores this point. Even the fact that vendors were penning letters in the capital's press is significant: other street and market vendors in Mexico do not appear to have done the same.[86] In attacking each other's honor, the dueling vendors in the Baratillo were jockeying for dominance within the capital's public sphere.

Yet there appear to have been two different standards of honor operating in this case. The Guerrero vendors suggested that Rosales Gordoa was practicing law without a degree and challenged his reputation as a respected veteran. His honor, and his credibility as a public figure, depended on his military service to the nation and his credentials as a man of letters. The honor of the baratilleros, however, was put to a different test. Here the question was which group of baratilleros was more impoverished and therefore more deserving of the public's sympathy. The ambulatory vendors called their rivals in the Guerrero market "better-off" and asserted that those vendors could afford to move their belongings to the new marketplace. Meanwhile, the Guerrero vendors accused the ambulatory vendors of being "fake baratilleros" who, because of their relationship with the property owners around the Plaza del Jardín, were actually rich, and could afford to bring their case all the way to the Supreme Court.[87]

Despite the fact that all sides in this dispute claimed to be carrying the liberal torch, advocating solutions that liberated the individual from artificial constraints, such views did not conflict with contemporary actors' belief that the poor needed and deserved the sympathies of the fortunate. Indeed, as scholars of nineteenth-century Mexico have previously suggested, an embrace of liberalism and a traditional tolerance for the poor coexisted with one another.[88] García Torres, who vigorously defended the individual rights of the vendors, nonetheless described his relationship with them in paternalistic terms. In his April 9 speech before the city council, he urged his fellow councilmen "not to sound in this room the trumpet of war in the ears of the poor who, following the law, and more so because they consider us their fathers and never their executioners, came to ask us for protection, mediation, and remediation."[89] Rosales Gordoa, in his initial appeal to the Ayuntamiento, recognized the "elevated social position" of the Ayuntamiento members.[90] The advocates for the ambulatory vendors thus saw no conflict between their efforts to protect the constitutional rights of vendors and their request that governing elites fulfill a traditional, unwritten obligation to care for the downtrodden. Vendors' poverty made them more deserving of government protection, but it also bestowed them with a kind of honor and social standing in Mexico's expanding public sphere. In the baratilleros' printed letters, older sentiments mixed seamlessly with new rights and novel means of expression.

RESOLUTION

On September 14, in an abrupt turnaround, the Ayuntamiento convened an extraordinary session and voted, 5 to 1, to "permit the baratilleros to conduct their commerce in the Plazuela del Jardín." They also agreed to allow ambulatory vendors to sell in public streets anywhere they did not impede traffic.[91] What had led the body to suddenly reverse itself after openly defying the Supreme Court for months? According to the newspapers *La Voz* and *El Monitor Republicano*, the order to let the ambulatory vendors return to the Plaza del Jardín came from the interim president of the republic Sebastián Lerdo de Tejada, who had succeeded Benito Juárez in office after Juárez had died on July 18. That only six of the twenty members of the Ayuntamiento voted on the measure suggests that many councilmen did not change course willingly.[92]

Persistent instability and shifting alliances make it difficult to determine precisely why Lerdo de Tejada might have forced the Ayuntamiento to accept the Supreme Court's decision, when Juárez had not. One possible explanation is that the ambulatory vendors had gained the support of the Mexico City public, and the interim president sought to use the issue to rally support for his election to a full term in October 1872. Yet Lerdo de Tejada's intervention in the dispute also may have stemmed from a desire for retribution. In the run-up to the presidential election of 1871, Mexico City's electorate was largely divided into two camps: Juaristas, who supported Juárez's bid for reelection (in violation of constitutionally mandated term limits), and Lerdistas, who backed Lerdo de Tejada. The municipal elections of December

1870 were highly contested and each faction ended up forming its own city council. Because the Mexico City Ayuntamiento determined voter eligibility and managed presidential elections in the capital, its political composition mattered immensely to national politics. Juárez initially let Congress resolve the impasse in the Ayuntamiento, but after its members chose the Lerdista contingent as the legitimate government, Juárez, via the governor of the Federal District, ordered the Ayuntamiento disbanded and replaced it with the Ayuntamiento of 1870, which was comprised of members of both factions.[93] Following Juárez's successful reelection in July 1871, control of the Ayuntamiento passed to his supporters—who included Arteaga.[94]

After gaining control of the presidency, Lerdo de Tejada may have sought to punish his adversaries on the Ayuntamiento, who, in addition to supporting Juárez, had also defied his authority as chief justice of the nation's Supreme Court when they refused to let the ambulatory vendors back into the Plaza del Jardín. Indeed, shortly after Lerdo de Tejada's election to a full term as president in October 1872, he had Arteaga suspended from his post as Ayuntamiento president (again via the intermediary of the Federal District governor) for allegedly conducting official government business outside the Ayuntamiento's offices. *El Monitor Republicano* saw the episode as a fitting end to a terrible year for the municipal government.[95]

The ambulatory vendors, of course, were elated by the Ayuntamiento's decision. When they received the news, they and the residents of the neighborhood surrounding the Plaza del Jardín responded "with jubilation," setting off fireworks and playing music.[96] On September 24, the ambulatory vendors even wrote a letter of appreciation to the Ayuntamiento, praising its members' change of heart.[97] The baratilleros in the Guerrero market were naturally disappointed by this course of events. They wrote to the new Ayuntamiento in January 1873 to request that it designate their market as the city's only Baratillo—a last-ditch attempt to regain control of the Baratillo brand and attract customers to their remote location. Their letter never received a response.[98] References to the Baratillo for the remainder of the nineteenth century find it in the Plaza del Jardín.

It is difficult to say with certainty why the Ayuntamiento had so dramatically and resolutely defied an order from the nation's highest court. The reasons could have been political, stemming from the factional disputes of the previous year, or even personal. Yet the councilmen also might have been trying to preserve the municipality's autonomy against what they saw as the unlawful or unjust encroachment on its jurisdiction by private parties (the ambulatory vendors, in this case) and the federal judiciary. The trend that had begun under the centralist regimes of the 1830s continued unabated under the liberal governments of the Restored Republic: the federal government was gradually eroding the authority of the Ayuntamiento. As the nineteenth century wore on, national authorities came to see Mexico City as too important, too symbolic, to be self-governed and took steps to curtail the autonomy of the Ayuntamiento. This case shows that for federal authorities Mexico City was a showcase not only for the nation's material progress but also for its republican institutions and the rule of law.

CONCLUSION

Vendors in the Baratillo had used Mexico's institutions to sustain their businesses since the colonial period. But the 1872 controversy was different: the vendors became the protagonists in a conflict that involved the highest authorities in the nation, turning a debate over the location of the capital's most notorious thieves' market into a conversation about the nature of the Mexican republic. They did not accomplish this feat on their own; they had powerful allies who facilitated their access to the public sphere and the halls of justice and helped them couch their arguments in the rhetoric of liberty and individual rights. Yet the evidence suggests that it was the vendors who led the effort to forge those patronage networks.

For the Ayuntamiento members who sought to move the Baratillo out of the Plaza del Jardín, this case was not about protecting individual rights but maintaining order in urban public spaces. They derived the authority to regulate those spaces from federal law but also from a particular interpretation of the meaning of "*el público*"—the public. The Plaza del Jardín, like all streets and plazas under the domain of the Ayuntamiento, was a public space, and the members of the Ayuntamiento, as the elected representatives of Mexico City's residents, saw themselves as responsible for determining how those spaces would best serve the greater good. The Ayuntamiento used that authority to determine which activities, and therefore which people, were suitable for which spaces. Yet, under the Restored Republic, just as under the Spanish Bourbons a century earlier, there was no consensus among the capital city's elites about what purpose those spaces would serve or who had the right to use them. Prominent members of Mexico's political establishment— including city councilmen, newspaper publishers, and the justices of the nation's Supreme Court, argued that the individual rights of street vendors to ply their trades trumped the local government's authority to regulate urban public spaces.

The events of 1872 reveal the diverse set of actors in Mexico City who had interests in the Baratillo. Members of the capital's elite, street vendors with businesses of varying sizes, and an array of other merchants all benefited, in different ways, from the capital's infamous second-hand market. For the ambulatory vendors and shopkeepers, that interest was material in nature; moving to the remote Guerrero market could have destroyed their businesses. Vendor petitions and municipal records from the mid-nineteenth century suggest that relocating markets to peripheral areas often led to a decline in sales volume, which hurt individual vendors. Furthermore, many vendors lived very close to the street or plaza on which they sold. Moving the market would have caused serious disruptions to a family's business and livelihood.

Rosales Gordoa's involvement in the case illustrates just how intertwined political and economic objectives were in the Baratillo. Rosales Gordoa passionately defended the baratilleros through petitions to the local government and in the press, translating their material concerns into the political vernacular of the day. In some respects, he was a member of Mexico City's elite—a man with a famous father and a military hero in his own right. Yet, as the owner of a hardware store in the market, he was a baratillero himself, and had an economic interest in the market's survival.

Despite its unsavory reputation, the Baratillo served a broad and heterogeneous swath of Mexico City's population, drawing elite, popular, and middling actors into alliances and rivalries that scrambled those categories as often as they reinforced them. The Baratillo was not always a pacific place, as the violent removal of the ambulatory vendors in the spring of 1872 demonstrates. The threat of police action always lurked behind vendors' negotiations with authorities. By all accounts, however, that confrontation was an outlier in the history of the Baratillo, a rupture in a much longer tradition of legal and political debate between the baratilleros, the government, and the public. That pattern continued under the authoritarian presidency of Porfirio Díaz.

SIX

Order, Progress, and
the Black Market

We had heard much about this center of rapacity and moral
misery . . . but the reality is even grimmer than what others had
described: it is hell's anteroom.

"UNA VISITA AL BARATILLO,"
La Patria, *October 15, 1891*

The Baratillo is not a warehouse of misery; it is a resource for life
for a multitude of people who live off the garbage of others—off
the vanity of the rich and the superfluous luxury of others.

*"El palacio de la miseria: El Baratillo, lo
nuevo y lo viejo,"* La Patria, *March 4, 1897*

WHEN WRITERS FOR THE NEWSPAPER *La Patria* visited the Baratillo
in 1891, they found a horrifying scene. "People [were] strewn across the
ground, stupefied by Bacchus and revealing their nauseating flesh." Vendors
peddled old blankets and dirty clothes, "cloaked in fear that someone might
strip them of the disgusting garment they were trying to sell." Even the children in the Baratillo were depraved: a "dirty, ragged little boy" the authors
allegedly met "had the twinkle of criminal desire in his eye: that of obtaining
what was not his." After relating this spectacle to its readers, the paper concluded: "To visit the Baratillo it is necessary to be one of three things: a
writer, to study the degree of immorality and abjection that those people
possess; a doctor, to propose hygienic measures that may save us from conta-
gion; or a policeman, to prevent crimes." The reporters resolved "never to lay
our eyes on that horrific site again."[1]

To many residents of Mexico City at the end of the nineteenth century,
the Baratillo was a relic of a bygone era and an obstacle to the "order and
progress" that President Porfirio Díaz promised Mexico's citizens. Under
Díaz, who ruled directly or indirectly from 1876 to 1911, the country experienced a period of political stability and sustained economic growth for the

first time since its independence from Spain, in 1821.[2] The nation's capital became a showcase for this newfound prosperity. An upscale department store, the Palacio de Hierro, opened just off the Zócalo in 1891 and offered the finest European fashions. In the first decade of the twentieth century, the federal government spent lavishly to construct ornate new public buildings like the national post office and the Palace of Fine Arts. To the west, mansions sprouted along the Paseo de la Reforma, the boulevard that Emperor Maximilian had constructed to connect the city center to Chapultepec Park. With its tree-lined streets, luxurious homes, and lavish cultural events, more than a few visitors compared this part of Mexico City to Paris.[3]

The Baratillo was an awkward fit for this gleaming, modern city. Its vendors continued to ply their trades in used clothing, tools, and curiosities from their ramshackle wooden stands, as the Baratillo still lacked a formal market hall. Its detractors complained, as they always had, that the market was a magnet for stolen and counterfeit items. Throughout the 1880s and 1890s, calls mounted for the government to relocate the Baratillo from the centrally located Plaza del Jardín, which was only a few blocks from the stately Alameda park. The impetus to do so finally came in 1901. To prepare the capital to host the Second Pan-American Congress, a new hemispheric trade organization, the federal and municipal governments embarked on a series of ambitious public works projects. As in the 1790s and the 1840s, the Baratillo was in the way. In January 1902, the Ayuntamiento relocated the Baratillo to Tepito, a poor neighborhood in the northern reaches of the city while it conducted work in the Plaza del Jardín. Although the government assured the vendors the move would be temporary, the Baratillo never left Tepito.

The move had significant ramifications for the vendors of the Baratillo, for the residents of Tepito, and for Mexico City as a whole. It deprived the baratilleros of their market's central location and helped transform Tepito into the capital's most infamous barrio bravo—its wildest neighborhood. Yet the process through which that dislocation occurred is as important as the outcome. Unlike the tactics it employed in 1842 and 1872, the Ayuntamiento never tried to force the vendors out of the Baratillo. The 1902 move instead resulted from a negotiation between the baratilleros and the elected officials of the Ayuntamiento. While the Baratillo had many detractors at the turn of the twentieth century, as it had throughout its history, there was no consensus that the market was incompatible with Porfirian modernity. Mexico City's elites continued to express ambivalence about the market. As the epigraphs to this chapter illustrate, the same newspaper—in this case the pro-Porfirian *La Patria*—could declare the Baratillo a threat to society in one moment and defend it in another.[4] While some residents wanted to expunge the market from the city center, others sought instead to *improve* it through modern infrastructure and closer government oversight. Indeed, the Baratillo's move to Tepito coincided with an ambitious campaign by the Ayuntamiento to bring modern public services, including paved streets and sidewalks, drinking water, and sewers to the city's impoverished barrios.[5]

The negotiations surrounding the Baratillo's move to Tepito complicate our understanding of the Porfiriato. Historians, particularly in the Anglophone world, have often portrayed the Porfiriato as a period when elites worked systematically to marginalize the urban poor—both physically and politically.[6] This chapter, by contrast, highlights the divergent views Mexico City's prominent citizens held of the Baratillo and their lack of agreement over how to address the broader problem of urban poverty.[7] Official policies designed to punish or exclude undesirable populations coexisted with efforts to provide education and public services to the poor.[8] At the same time, some elites argued, with equally paternalistic overtones, that the poor needed the support and protection of the government, which required allowing the less fortunate to live and work as they always had. According to this view, the Baratillo, whatever its faults, was an essential piece of the urban fabric.[9]

This chapter also reveals that working-class and popular actors in Mexico City continued to engage in urban politics, despite the authoritarian tendencies of the Porfirian regime. Baratilleros worked within, not against, the political institutions of the era, using the apparatuses of local government and the press to defend their interests and shape public policy. Indeed, while the impetus for the Baratillo's move came from the municipal government, it was the vendors who suggested Tepito as the temporary site for their market. They expressed that desire through petitions and by personally lobbying city council members and newspaper editors. Under that pressure, the Ayuntamiento listened and negotiated. Porfirio Díaz may have weakened many of Mexico's political institutions by 1900, including both the press and the Mexico City Ayuntamiento, which the president increasingly packed with loyalists.[10] But this incident shows that the vendors of the Baratillo continued to utilize those same institutions with relative success, as they had throughout the nineteenth century.[11] While the baratilleros and the government never shared a level playing field, the vendors had clout, and they used it to exert control over their fate.

That influence waned in the first decade of the twentieth century, however. In 1903, Porfirio Díaz removed the Ayuntamiento's governing powers, effectively folding it into the Federal District. Though the body continued to exist, it lost its autonomy, becoming a purely consultative institution to the Federal District governor, an official appointed by the president of the republic. The 1903 political reform fundamentally altered the Baratillo vendors' relationship with authorities. When vendors found that the Ayuntamiento had failed to uphold its end of the bargain it had struck with them in 1901, they had few avenues for appeal. Without formal representation in municipal government, the vendors resorted to the centuries-old practice of petitioning authorities—a strategy that depended principally on the magnanimity of government officials. With less ability to influence Mexico City's government, the baratilleros stayed in Tepito, where they occupied a provisional and improvised marketplace throughout the twentieth century.

THE BARATILLO IN PORFIRIAN MEXICO CITY

Mexico City changed dramatically in the last two decades of the nineteenth century. As the country's economy expanded, migrants left the countryside to take advantage of new opportunities in the capital, swelling its population and pushing the physical boundaries of the city.[12] In 1858, roughly 200,000 people occupied an area of 8.5 square kilometers; by 1910, the city had grown to 40.5 square kilometers and its population had more than doubled to 471,066.[13] Building construction in the capital doubled in the 1870s from the previous decade, and tripled during each of the next two decades.[14] As the city grew, however, so did its wealth disparities.

Rural migrants settled in unincorporated *colonias populares*—makeshift neighborhoods that sprang up along the city's northern, eastern, and southern periphery and ringed the indigenous barrios that for centuries had lain at the margins of urban life.[15] These areas enjoyed few if any of the modern features that increasingly characterized the city's central and western areas. Many of these colonias' residents lived in *vecindades*—tenements formed from colonial-style buildings that were originally built to house a single family and servants but were now divided into dozens of tiny rooms, each housing as many as ten people. In 1895, an estimated 100,000 people lived in Mexico City's vecindades—almost a third of the city's total population.[16] Other residences were even cruder and more improvised, such as the simple wooden huts that dominated the unincorporated colonias on the city's out-ermost edge. The guidebook *Terry's Mexico* warned travelers to avoid "slums" such as La Bolsa, located to the east of Tepito, "as it is a ghetto with dirty and microbic streets, repulsive sights, and evil smells." The area hosted "the most ferocious fights . . . terrible vengeances, and . . . the most horrible crimes."[17]

At the same time, as John Lear has described, the center of Mexico City transformed from a place where a diverse population had lived and worked to one devoted mainly to government administration and high-end retail and banking. Throughout the 1870s and 1880s, the streets running between the Zócalo and the Alameda hosted both the ornate homes of the country's elite and the residences of much humbler people. Foreigners frequently com-mented on the contrasts they witnessed in the city center, such as a doorman living with his many children and animals under the staircase of a colonial mansion. Those mansions stood adjacent to vecindades, which were often socially diverse themselves. For example, a lawyer might have occupied a spa-cious front apartment while soldiers and domestic servants lived in the rear.[18] Around the turn of the century, however, the city center began to lose popu-lation as wealthier residents moved to the higher, drier lands located to the west, and businesses and government agencies took their place. Large new department stores like the Palacio de Hierro and government buildings such as the ornate central post office replaced vecindades and crumbling colonial houses. A 1907 map shows few residences and no vecindades on the principal Cinco de Mayo and San Francisco streets. In 1900, 50 percent of the total tax paid by businesses to the city came from the blocks between the Zócalo and the Alameda.[19] By this time, the city center also benefited from the amenities of modern city life: asphalt streets, sidewalks, street lighting, sewers, and a system to provide clean drinking water.

To some observers, the Baratillo, located just north of the city center, looked out of place. In 1898, *El Universal* wrote: "It seems incredible that only a few blocks from the Alameda . . . there exists a fetid plaza, sown with foul-smelling stores formed from dirty planks, straw, and blackened and torn fabrics."[20] The Plaza del Jardín, where the Baratillo had stood since the 1860s, still lacked a formal market building, and its vendors continued to sell from improvised wooden stalls and tables. One newspaper worried in 1883 that the market was in such bad condition that it was "ready to blow down at any moment."[21] And while Mexico's economy underwent significant changes in the last two decades of the nineteenth century, the core businesses of the Baratillo remained the same as those in the colonial period. In the 1880s and

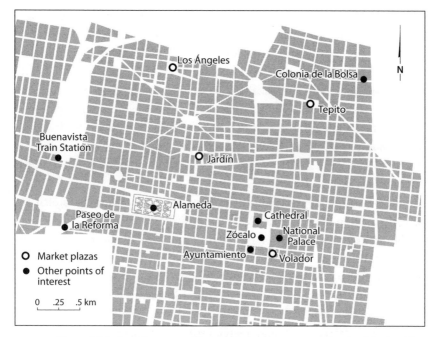

MAP 5. Map of Mexico City, 1901. Based on the map created by the Mexico City Ayuntamiento Commission for Improvements and Beautification, located in *Discurso . . . y Memoria documentada de los trabajos municipales de 1901* (Mexico City: J. Aguilar y Compañía, 1902). By the turn of the century, the city had grown significantly, pushing well beyond the boundaries of the colonial-era traza. Map created by Bill Nelson and Patrick Keller.

1890s, the vast majority of the Baratillo's stands sold metal tools, clothing, and shoes.[22]

For its critics, the Baratillo embodied all that was backward and dangerous in Mexican society. In a single, confined space, they argued, one encountered thieves, prostitutes, vagabonds, and children and old women dressed in rags—people who lacked education, morals, and even the most basic personal hygiene. The Mexico City press, which increasingly trafficked in sensational coverage of crime and other social ills in the capital, showed a particular fascination with the Baratillo. The number of stories about the market surged in the last two decades of the nineteenth century.[23]

The Porfirian-era press painted the Baratillo as an exceptionally violent place. Among the physical confrontations Mexico City's newspapers chronicled in a sample year, 1897, were: a woman beaten by her husband; another woman whom authorities found "bathed in blood" after she tried to protect a female friend from a man who had sought to kill her; and a fight between iron vendors, in which they threw stones, hammers, and other tools at each other, forcing bystanders to run for cover.[24] When *México Gráfico*, a news magazine, ventured into the Baratillo for an exposé, it found that "for the most insignificant motive, passions ignite in a moment.... One cent is, on many occasions, the origin of a fight that ends in the hospital or prison."[25] One man was allegedly beaten to death for stealing a guitar. Such writing drove home the impression that the people who bought and sold in the Baratillo lacked the ability to control their passions and coexist peacefully in Mexican society.[26]

The Baratillo's reputation as the city's principal emporium for stolen and illicit goods endured in the Porfiriato. While some of the stolen items authorities recovered in the market were of a traditional nature—the jewelry and household furnishings that had surfaced in the Baratillo since the seventeenth century—others were unmistakably new—products of Mexico's nascent industrialization at the end of the nineteenth century. Among the pilfered goods police recovered in the Baratillo were bolts, screws, bearings, ammunition cartridges, a manometer, various pharmaceutical products, telegraph wire, train rails, and even the type from the printing press of the newspaper *El Tiempo*.[27] Police discovered counterfeit coins circulating in the market and a house nearby that was manufacturing them.[28] Books, which had their own section in the Baratillo Grande in the eighteenth century, still had a place in the market in the late nineteenth century. They, too, had dubious origins. A writer for *La Patria* wondered how books from the personal libraries of Lucas Alamán, Basilio Arrillaga, and José Joaquín Pesado, all famous and deceased Mexican men of letters, had ended up in stands in the Baratillo. Surely, the writer noted, these men did not bring the books to the Baratillo themselves.[29]

The tone of these articles alternates between horror and a kind of admiration for the criminal genius of the baratilleros—"*talento mal empleado*" (talent poorly employed), as one paper described it.[30] Many complaints about the Baratillo focused on the vendors' extraordinary capacity for trickery. For example, one vendor's scheme allegedly consisted of placing an old change purse in the pocket of an article of clothing. If the article was worth two reales, the vendor would charge the customer six. The hapless buyer would eagerly pay the inflated price, thinking he was about to get a purse full of coins, only to return home to find that the purse was empty.[31] These anecdotes built on colonial-era narratives of the Baratillo that painted the market as a refuge for fraudsters. Now, instead of a "school of trickery," as the "Ordenanzas del Baratillo" called the market, it was a "corporation established among mercachifles and *rateros*"—ambulatory vendors and thieves—an analogy more befitting of the Porfirian economic boom.[32] In these accounts, the Baratillo was the headquarters for Mexico City's rateros. Those individuals, the thinking went, inhabited migrant barrios like Tepito and the neighboring Colonia de la Bolsa (as rateros were deemed to be outsiders), and spent their days in the Baratillo.[33]

Authorities in Porfirian Mexico City sought to rein in these behaviors by strengthening the criminal justice system. An 1879 reform professionalized the capital's police force and rationalized jurisdictional responsibilities by dividing the city into eight police districts. The Porfirian-era police were supposed to implement order and education—enforcing laws and instilling law-abiding habits in the city's residents.[34] Those people who could not coexist peaceably in society, however, were removed from the city and placed in prisons, like the new federal penitentiary at San Lázaro, or distant penal colonies. This category of criminals included convicted thieves, whom the government began to send to penal colonies after the passage of an 1894 law.[35]

The government also outlawed some of the everyday habits officials associated with criminality. It prohibited public drinking and imposed new regulations on the city's pulquerías. Reducing alcohol consumption among the poor was of particular interest to Guillermo de Landa y Escandón—the president of the Mexico City Ayuntamiento from 1900 to 1902 and governor of the Federal District from 1903 to 1911.[36] Landa y Escandón enacted laws forcing pulquerías to close earlier and personally bought many of them in order to shut them down.[37] Through education and policing, Porfirian technocrats—known as *científicos*—believed they could improve the morals of the urban poor, which, in turn, would lower crime rates and improve public health.

Mexico City residents worried that the Baratillo, in addition to fomenting crime and immoral behavior, was a health hazard. Local leaders believed that Mexico City was one of the unhealthiest places in the world. Chronic flooding, stemming from the city's location on a former lakebed and exacerbated by the city's limited drainage infrastructure, combined with what many elites viewed as the poor sanitary habits of the lower classes to turn it into a ripe environment for infectious disease. A typhus epidemic ravaged the city in 1884, and cholera, smallpox, and other air- and water-borne diseases were constant threats to the capital's population. In the first decade of the twentieth century, Mexico City's mortality rate was over five times higher than that

FIGURE II. "Rumbos y Concurrentes," *Frégoli*, August 8, 1897, 8. The image depicts *rumbos* (directions) of Mexico City and the people (*concurrentes*) one would be likely to find there. The caption below the image of the Baratillo, on the bottom right, reads: "*cuando se siente la necesidad*" (when one feels *need* [emphasis original]). Note the juxtaposition with the image directly to its left, which shows an upper-class man and woman on Plateros Street, in the central business district of the capital, "*a la hora del aperitivo*" (at cocktail hour). The title of the image suggests that it was not only Mexico City's poor who conceived of the city in terms of rumbos. Hemeroteca Nacional Digital de México, Mexico City.

of London or Paris—the cities to which Mexicans increasingly compared their capital.[38]

If Mexico City's poor were one of the primary sources of the capital's ills, the Baratillo was a veritable petri dish—"a morbific laboratory of scarlet fever, typhus, diphtheria, [and] smallpox," and "one of the most important, if not the principal center of infection that there is in Mexico," as one newspaper wrote.[39] To many observers, the Baratillo was pulsating with infection. In its 1891 "Visit to the Baratillo," *La Patria* wrote: "The streets adjacent to the Plazuela del Jardín, which is the one the Baratillo occupies, are completely abandoned; they are truly dumps; the water pipes that are in its center give off miasmas that must undoubtedly contribute to the awful sanitary conditions of that part of the city; everywhere one sees filth and open-air latrines."[40] Visitors to the Baratillo complained that organic waste from humans, animals, and decomposing fruits and vegetables covered the area.[41]

Another, equally serious source of concern was the Baratillo's trade in used clothing. News outlets complained that the clothing, bed sheets, and mattresses of those who had recently succumbed to illness ended up in the Baratillo, where the poor would purchase them. In 1899, one newspaper reported about a family that had bought a mattress from a vendor in the Baratillo. Only days later, typhus sickened the mother and one of her children. It was soon discovered that the baratillero had bought the mattress from the family of a pulque vendor who had recently died of the same disease.[42] The press implored the government to either ensure the proper disinfection of all used clothing or ban its sale in public markets altogether.[43]

These lurid depictions paint the Baratillo as an anachronism in turn-of-the-century Mexico City—a traditional relic in an increasingly modern and prosperous city. The market's continuing existence threatened the moral and economic order that Porfirio Díaz's regime promised. Yet, despite repeated calls for the government to abolish the market, authorities in Mexico City showed little interest in doing so. Officials continued to express ambivalence about the city's thieves' market, as they had for more than two centuries.

"A RESOURCE FOR LIFE"

The Baratillo may have been unsightly, but it was economically vital to Porfirian Mexico City. The market's product mix in the 1880s and 1890s, which still consisted mainly of second-hand clothing and metal tools, highlights the limitations of Mexico's manufacturing sector, which was not yet capable of providing working-class or poor consumers with affordable new manufactured goods at the end of the nineteenth century. As economic historians of the era have shown, Mexican manufacturers faced small and fragile markets for their goods. The consumption of cotton cloth remained sensitive to fluctuations in the price of corn, the mainstay in the diet of Mexico's poor. Bad harvest years, when the price of corn rose, led to crises in the domestic textile industry because of the sudden drop in demand for its products.[44] Thus, while the trade in second-hand goods in major European cities declined significantly in the latter half of the nineteenth century as a growing working class gained access to inexpensive new manufactured goods, no comparable trend took place in Mexico during the same period.[45] Urban consumers still demanded the second-hand products the Baratillo offered.

To satisfy that demand, dozens, if not hundreds, of vendors sold their wares in the Baratillo during the Porfiriato.[46] In the 1880s and 1890s, the market had two tiers of vendors, those who occupied smaller *tinglados*, located in the center of the Plaza del Jardín, and those who sold from larger puestos that ringed its edges. Some of those who sold from the tinglados were women who offered prepared foods like enchiladas, tamales, and quesadillas, while men who dealt in second-hand goods occupied the larger stands. The tinglado vendors seem to have been more transient than those who occupied the larger stalls.[47] Most businesses in the Baratillo—whether puestos or tinglados—were not very substantial. A sheet containing the values of the Baratillo stalls that burned in a fire in 1888 reveals that of the eighteen affected stands, none was worth more than 500 pesos. Several were worth only 40 or 50 pesos.[48] Pawnshops, by comparison, had capitalizations that ranged from 600 to almost 9,000 pesos during the Porfiriato.[49] The majority of vendors on the 1894 market roster owned only one stand and all but a few of the vendors operated their stands themselves.[50]

Yet not all of the baratilleros in this era were poor. At least two vendors' households had live-in maids in 1882. And although the majority of vendors owned and operated only one stall, it was not uncommon for one individual to own several stands in the market. A woman named Luisa C. de Herrera owned seven stalls in the Baratillo in 1894.[51] Furthermore, if the baratilleros were a corporation of thieves, as their detractors alleged, they were particularly educated thieves. An analysis of the census data for a sample of twenty-six baratilleros who lived on the blocks adjacent to the Plaza del Jardín in

1882 (see table 2, appendix) reveals that those vendors were much more literate than the typical resident of Mexico City. Twenty-three of the twenty-six baratilleros could read and write, including twenty-one of twenty-three men and two of three women. In Mexico City as a whole, by contrast, fewer than half of all men and only about one-third of women could read and write in 1895—more than a decade later and after significant government investment in public education.[52] The census data corroborate anecdotal evidence of baratilleros' literacy from the petitions they sent to authorities, in which the majority of vendors had signed their own names since the colonial era.[53] Far from rootless criminals, the baratilleros who lived on the blocks surrounding the Plaza del Jardín in 1882 were mainly married, middle-aged men with backgrounds in the mercantile and artisanal trades.[54]

Some writers in the Mexico City press recognized the market's economic and social importance.[55] Those authors argued that the Baratillo was indispensable to the city's poor. In 1897, the newspaper *El Mundo* visited the Baratillo and found more than just "a museum for antique dealers and the curious." The market, they noted, was also where a resident of a vecindad would go "in search of pants and shoes that elegant people with homes in the capital's center have discarded."[56] The article featured a rendering of the Baratillo (see figure 12) on its front page that provides a slice-of-life portrait of the market, rather than the caricature *Frégoli* offered the same year (see figure 11). *El Chisme*, for its part, claimed that the market was "too useful and beneficial to the poor" to be eliminated.[57] *La Patria*, which called the Baratillo "hell's anteroom" in an 1891 article, offered a full-throated defense of the market in 1897, criticizing the semiofficial *El Imparcial* for its callous treatment of the baratilleros. *La Patria* emphasized that there could be honor in a baratillero's work—an argument that the vendors and their allies had made during their dispute with the Ayuntamiento in 1872 but which few authors echoed at the turn of the century. "There are honorable people in the Baratillo, believe it, *El Imparcial*," *La Patria*'s writers insisted. If there was a problem with crime in the market, then fault lay with the government for its inadequate policing of the Baratillo, not with vendors or their customers.[58]

Indeed, despite widespread concerns about crime in the capital, the Baratillo appears to have been chronically underpoliced. In 1891, *La Patria* asked the government to provide at least two *gendarmes*, or officers, for the Baratillo, since the market administrator was routinely breaking up fights himself. The government complied ten days later but then reassigned the

El Baratillo de México
(Escenas tomadas del natural por E. Olvera)

FIGURE 12. "El Baratillo de México," *El Mundo*, January 17, 1897. The image shows a bustling market-place and lacks the disparaging portrayal of the people who attended the market that *Frégoli* offered in its depiction (figure 11). Hemeroteca Nacional Digital de México, Mexico City.

officers shortly thereafter, leaving the market without police supervision once again.[59] Vendors in the Baratillo also complained about the poor policing and administration of the market.[60]

Nor did Porfirian authorities attempt to regulate the Baratillo's trade in second-hand goods, even though they intervened in other areas of the urban economy. Officials implemented a number of policies that minutely regulated the pawnbroking industry, going so far as specifying how pawnbrokers should fold and organize clothes within their stores, and limiting their profits.[61] Local officials also made repeated efforts to rein in street vending.[62] Yet they directed those efforts at vendors of prepared foods and fruits and vegetables, not those who sold second-hand goods. The Baratillo continued to operate as it had throughout the nineteenth century: with minimal oversight from authorities. Even the trade in second-hand clothing, which members of the press and the government saw as contributing to the capital's notorious insalubrity, remained unregulated until 1911.[63]

Porfirian officials' ambivalence toward the Baratillo speaks to the paternalistic undertones that continued to influence Mexico's political culture at the end of the nineteenth century—sentiments that extended even to the alleged criminals of the Baratillo. Those views survived not only the transition from colonial to republican rule but also the evolution of Mexican liberalism in the second half of the nineteenth century, which gave rise to a more autocratic and interventionist state, guided by the supposed expertise of the científicos.[64] Traditional expressions of sympathy for the less fortunate continued to play an important role in urban politics under the Porfiriato and existed uneasily with the concurrent efforts to aggressively police or even extirpate the poor from the city. Vendors in the Baratillo exploited those sentiments. In a 1901 petition to the Ayuntamiento, for example, they appealed to "the benevolence, the philanthropy, and the consideration of the enlightened assembly."[65] They made a case for themselves and their trade using a political vernacular that still held sway, even in an era of technocratic governance.

Yet baratilleros had other tools at their disposal, beyond appealing to the compassion of elected officials. They also cultivated allies on the Ayuntamiento and in the press. Despite Díaz's gradual strangling of Mexico's republican institutions, baratilleros still enjoyed a degree of access and clout in Mexico City's political arena. The vendors' influence becomes clear in the 1901 dispute that ultimately led to the market's relocation to Tepito.

A BARATILLO FOR THE TWENTIETH CENTURY

In the spring of 1901, Mexico City was preparing for an auspicious event: the city had been selected as the site for the Second Pan-American Congress. Hosting the Congress, to take place between October 1901 and January 1902, was a testament to Mexico's rise and to the caliber of its capital city (the first meeting had been held in New York). The event would bring high-profile visitors from across the hemisphere to marvel at the progress the city and nation had made under the steady hand of President Porfirio Díaz.[66] To prepare the capital for this event, Díaz provided a two-million-peso subsidy to the Ayuntamiento to modernize the infrastructure of the city center. Using those funds, the city paved streets, built sidewalks, and extended the street grid to outlying neighborhoods such as Tepito. The city methodically swept its streets, by hand and with new electric street-sweepers, and installed electric lighting throughout the city center. The Ayuntamiento even required residents of the city center to paint the facades of their houses to give visitors the best possible impression of Mexico's capital.[67]

Landa y Escandón, the president of Mexico City's Ayuntamiento, used the opportunity to pursue an even more ambitious agenda of urban renewal— one that looked beyond the city center to focus on its long-neglected barrios.[68] In the city council session of May 21, 1901, Landa y Escandón argued that while the government was "spending large quantities of money on paving and other important projects in the center of the city and in the luxurious neighborhoods," it was equally important to extend those improvements to the city's impoverished periphery. The poor, he argued, "live in such awful conditions ... in narrow alleyways without ventilation, without cobblestones, without drainage, without the smallest comfort in their unhealthy bedrooms, making necessary the immediate and active intervention of the authorities to remedy such a grave situation." To improve conditions in the marginalized barrios, he proposed widening and paving streets, bringing potable water, installing sewers, and planting trees and gardens in the barrios of the northern, eastern, and southern quarters of the city.[69] Unlike urban renewal projects elsewhere in this era, it did not involve large-scale demolition.[70] The project received praise in both establishment and working-class press outlets. *La Convención Radical Obrera*, a workers' publication, noted that since the founding of Mexico City in 1521 no Ayuntamiento had focused so much attention on the barrios.[71] Indeed, maps the Ayuntamiento published in its annual reports for 1902 and the first half of 1903 demonstrated substantial progress in extending public services beyond the city center.[72]

The municipal government believed that bringing modern services to the squalid and overcrowded areas of the city could fundamentally change the behavior of the people who lived there. In its official *Boletín Municipal*, the Ayuntamiento explained how paving streets and building sidewalks would lead residents of poor neighborhoods to "acquire the habit of cleaning." They would now "wait for the garbage cart to pass instead of throwing [their trash] into the creek." "The benefits," it touted, "that our barrios receive from the realization of these works are incalculable." They would "put the principles of hygiene into practice," and "bring [with them] notions of education, which little by little are moralizing our popular masses."[73] The project stemmed from the idea that the nation's elite could inculcate in the poor the values and habits necessary for them to enter modern society.[74] In Landa y Escandón's view, infrastructure could serve as a pedagogical device, improving the physical surroundings of the poor so the poor would improve themselves.[75]

The idea that the government could use infrastructure to remedy the low morals and bad habits of the poor also spurred the Ayuntamiento to dedicate greater attention to its public markets. In March 1901, the Ayuntamiento created the Markets Improvement Commission, led by Miguel Ángel de Quevedo, Mexico's premier urbanist of the era and a man who became known as "the apostle of the tree" for his focus on creating and protecting green spaces.[76] The Ayuntamiento tasked Quevedo, who also led the citywide Commission for Improvements and Beautification, with developing a more organized and sanitary market system. The commission began instituting new regulations that governed where and when vendors could sell their products, focusing initially on comestibles.[77] Then, in July 1901, the commission turned its sights on the Baratillo. The Council of Health needed a space to build a new municipal Office of Disinfection to house a plant for sanitizing used clothing, and the Ayuntamiento had selected the Plaza del Jardín as the site. The Ayuntamiento directed Quevedo's Markets Improvement Commission to determine what it should do with the Baratillo.

On July 19, 1901, Quevedo issued his report to the full Ayuntamiento. After a long and thoughtful rumination on the role of the Baratillo in the twentieth-century capital, Quevedo determined that not only was the market out of place in the centrally located Plaza del Jardín; the market itself was an anachronism in modern, prosperous Mexico. He thought it "inappropriate that the authorities exploit and foment those miserable trades when our flourishing shoe, fabric, and clothing industries permit the poor to provide themselves, at an economical cost, with entirely new objects." Quevedo, overestimating the ability of Mexican manufacturing to provision the urban poor with affordable goods, was convinced that the Baratillo was a relic of bygone era, unworthy of the city and country in which it stood. He recommended that the Ayuntamiento disband it and the smaller baratillos that operated in other parts of the city within two months. The Baratillo, as both a physical marketplace and a genre of commerce, would finally disappear from the city. Quevedo argued that many of the vendors in the Plaza del Jardín had more than sufficient resources to open proper stores, and he urged them to do so. He promised to provide the truly destitute merchants with space in one of the city's market halls, provided they sold comestibles, not "*baratijas*" (knickknacks). Quevedo did recognize that the city needed a market for second-hand goods that are "burdensome or unusable for their owners but usable for other people." But the Baratillo, with its jumbled mass of stands and ambulatory vendors, met this need "very incompletely." What the city required was a modern second-hand "bazaar."[78]

The plan to transform the city's barrios and modernize its public markets, including the Baratillo, formed part of the same ambitious project: to improve the material conditions in which the urban poor lived in order to mold them into citizens fit for life in twentieth-century society. But Landa y Escandón and Quevedo's vision for Mexico City faced a number of obstacles. Chief among these was opposition from the vendors of the Baratillo.

THE BARATILLEROS PLAY PORFIRIAN POLITICS

Quevedo's proposal was not the first time the Porfirian-era Ayuntamiento had considered shuttering or moving the Baratillo. Its members had discussed the topic on several occasions throughout the 1880s and 1890s and even relocated it, briefly, in 1884, to another plaza. In each instance, however, they reversed course after vendors in the market protested.[79] In 1901, the baratilleros pushed back again. Two different groups of baratilleros sent letters to the Ayuntamiento on July 26, 1901. Those vendors also appointed commissions to approach members of the Ayuntamiento and attend public city council meetings to express their grievances.[80] The first letter, signed by one Primo Giles and twenty-two other vendors, claimed that the Baratillo's shortcomings stemmed not from the nature of its commerce but from the poor infrastructure the city provided it. If the municipal government would only invest in widening the surrounding streets, building sidewalks, paving the plaza, and adding sewers, they argued, the Baratillo would cease to be a public health hazard and an eyesore for the capital. They couched their argument in terms they believed would resonate with the Ayuntamiento—the same language of urban renewal the councilmen used in their own plans.

The baratilleros also warned that the plan threatened their livelihoods. Closing the Baratillo, they warned, would convert over three hundred merchants into beggars. Merchants like themselves, they asserted, conducted their businesses "not so much by the class of merchandise they sell but rather by their personal credit and their stability in a fixed place, where the consumer knows to look for them. . . . To move these shops from one place to another is to lose the credit acquired."[81] The newspaper *La Patria* agreed, noting in an August 1901 article that "People are accustomed, when they live in a large city, to live within a specific rumbo and there are many who are born, raised, and die there." The vendors of the Baratillo were among those who possessed a "love of their rumbo, an attachment to their barrio"; displacing them would lead to enormous disruption in their lives.[82]

The term *rumbo* connoted not just a physical place but also a way of life in which work, home, and social lives were all intertwined.[83] Indeed, the market possessed an important relationship with its surrounding neighborhood during the Porfiriato, as it had throughout the nineteenth century. The 1882 census suggests that many baratilleros continued to live close to the market—a pattern that dated at least to the 1840s and which would continue during the twentieth century.[84] The baratilleros' professions also mirror those of their rumbo: like the vendors of the Baratillo, the male residents who lived on the blocks immediately surrounding the market were primarily craftsmen and merchants.[85] The census also lends supports for one of the Baratillo's critics' frequent complaints—that the market was a magnet for pulquerías. There were sixteen pulquerías in the blocks adjacent to the Plaza del Jardín—more than any other type of business.[86] Those businesses likely relied on the foot traffic the Baratillo generated.

While Primo Giles and his cosigners emphasized the economic consequences of dissolving the Baratillo, the vendors' supporters in the press attacked the Ayuntamiento for its callousness. The newspaper *El Popular*, the self-described "comic-serious" mouthpiece of the working class, emerged as the most outspoken critic of the decision.[87] On July 23, 1901, the paper exclaimed, "The Baratillo is dead! Or better said, the Ayuntamiento has killed it because it is disgusted by it, it finds it repugnant, it irritates its aristocratic nerves." It asked, "Does Madrid, the great capital of Spain, not have its Rastro (which is what they call the Baratillo there) in which old things are bought and sold. . . . And does Paris not have one as well?"[88] The editors of *El Popular* portrayed the issue as one about social class, not crime or public health. In several articles in 1901 and 1902, the paper criticized the Ayuntamiento's reasoning behind the project and for what it viewed as its attempt to "aristocratize" an institution that was so fundamental to the city's poor. In seeking to shutter the Baratillo, the government, *El Popular* argued, was deflecting blame for its own shortcomings. "That the police cannot keep watch over some open-air booths is a fantastic thing," the newspaper wrote.[89] For defenders of the Baratillo in the working-class press, which included *El Hijo del Trabajo* and *El Diario del Hogar*, in addition to *El Popular*, the market was an indispensable part of the urban social fabric. It was an institution that provided a source of employment for the poor and offered them access to inexpensive consumer goods. Moreover, it was a tradition—a part of the capital's history that the Ayuntamiento could not simply erase by remaking the market as a bazaar.[90]

Not all of the vendors in the Baratillo, however, agreed with Primo Giles and his cosigners' strategy. The other letter that baratilleros sent to the Ayuntamiento on July 26, signed by a group of over one hundred vendors and led by a man named Macedonio Ruiz, took a different, and perhaps savvier approach. It embraced the idea of converting the Baratillo into a bazaar, enthusiastically adopting the language of modernity in their praise of the Ayuntamiento's plan.[91] "It is indubitable," the baratilleros wrote, "that an appropriate building, of a modern style, and subject to European customs and models, beyond beautifying the place in which it will be installed, will be one more demonstration of our progress and civilization." They assured the city council that "we do not seek, in any manner, even for a moment, to block the improvements that will enrich our architecture, give a better appearance to our commerce, and will be one more step toward the civilization and prosperity of our City." They did, however, worry about how long it would take the city to complete the marketplace, a process, they imagined, that could stretch for months or even years. Surely the Ayuntamiento did not want 200 baratilleros to scatter around the city's streets and plazas in the meantime. That situation would also impede the Ayuntamiento's ability to collect rent from the vendors, costing the city at least twenty-five pesos per day in lost revenue, in the vendors' estimation. So they proposed a solution: allow the vendors to stay in the Plaza del Jardín while construction began and then, when it became necessary for them to move, permit them to set up temporarily in the Plazuela de Tepito or the Plaza de San Sebastián.[92]

It was an idea that Quevedo and Luis Riba y Cervantes, the head of the markets and slaughterhouses division of the Ayuntamiento, quickly embraced—over the objections of the smaller group of baratilleros led by Primo Giles, who claimed in an August 8 letter that they did not even know Macedonio Ruiz.[93] Residents of Tepito had proposed the idea of moving the Baratillo to the neighborhood more than a decade earlier. In January 1889, a group there petitioned the Ayuntamiento asking for the Baratillo to relocate there, noting that their "extensive plaza" was better suited to the business of the Baratillo than the Plaza del Jardín.[94] In fact, residents of several northern barrios vied for the Baratillo in the summer of 1901, including neighbors of the Plazas de la Lagunilla and del Carmen. Those individuals believed that the market would generate new economic opportunities for their barrios. The idea that the Baratillo could help develop poor neighborhoods was not new; members of the Ayuntamiento had suggested as much on a number of occasions over the course of the nineteenth century.[95]

The other group of vendors strenuously objected to the Macedonio Ruiz proposal, insisting that their families had occupied their stands in the Plaza del Jardín for over sixty years and that forcing them to move would destroy their businesses. If it proved absolutely necessary for them to abandon their stalls, they preferred to move to the Plaza de los Ángeles (see map 5), which they found much better suited for their commerce. Just as Mexico City's elites were far from united on how to deal with the Baratillo, the market's vendors disagreed on how to respond to Quevedo's proposal. As in 1872, rival camps emerged, each advocating its own solution. And as before, those divisions were fluid. One E. Arrellano López signed both of the July 26 petitions. Another vendor, Zeferino Martínez, signed both the Macedonio Ruiz letter on July 26 and the August 8 letter that claimed its signatories did not know Macedonio Ruiz.[96] These shifting alliances highlight the tensions that existed within the Baratillo and its seeming lack of internal organization. They also underscore the degree to which disputes over urban public space did not always pit poor vendors against modernizing elites. Many times, alliances and rivalries cut across class lines, even if they did little to challenge them.[97]

Despite the efforts of the vendors who sought to move the Baratillo to the Plaza de los Ángeles, a proposal that also enjoyed substantial support in the press, the Ayuntamiento chose Tepito as the market's provisional home while it constructed the new bazaar. It gave the baratilleros two months to vacate the Plaza del Jardín, during which time it hoped to pave the plaza in Tepito. The market commissions used the opportunity to further rationalize the distribution of second-hand goods in the city, ordering all of the city's vendors of "trinkets and used iron" to congregate in the temporary market in Tepito. After the Ayuntamiento agreed to two extensions that the vendors requested, and a further delay in paving the plaza, the market finally opened for business in Tepito in January of 1902.[98]

The events of 1901 demonstrate that vendors in the Baratillo continued to use the institutions of local government and the press, with remarkable success, to advance their interests.[99] They did so in an era when Mexico's national government had curtailed the autonomy of both. The baratilleros protested Quevedo's proposal to dissolve the market not only by writing petitions but also by showing up at public meetings of the Ayuntamiento in July 1901. After they did, Quevedo and the Ayuntamiento compromised.[100] The vendors' strategy did not rely on protest alone: it also involved courting allies.

One such ally was Pedro Ordóñez, an important figure in Mexico City's urban politics in the last decades of the nineteenth century. A labor leader whom voters reelected to the Ayuntamiento continuously for more than two decades and who also edited the newspaper *La Convención Radical Obrera*, Ordóñez served as an influential power broker between the Porfirian regime and the city's working classes. Through representatives like Ordóñez, urban workers enjoyed substantial access to Porfirian-era leaders—primarily through the organ of the Ayuntamiento. Although Díaz had circumscribed the Ayuntamiento's autonomy by stacking it with loyalists like Landa y Escandón, the municipal government continued to be an important venue for working-class political engagement at the turn of the century.[101] In 1901, Ordóñez, under pressure from vendors and their supporters in the press, objected to the deal the market commission had struck with the Macedonio Ruiz faction, arguing that: "The Baratillo is a market that is part of the customs of our pueblo and is necessary for the poor of our society; nor is it prudent to strip from so many merchants the way of life that they have established."[102] He and two other members of the Ayuntamiento voted against moving the market to Tepito.[103]

The baratilleros also curried favor with the press. The group that sought to move the Baratillo to the Plaza de los Ángeles instead of Tepito wrote to *El Popular* asking them to back their plan, which the paper's editors did.[104] *El Popular* also leaned on Pedro Ordóñez to support those baratilleros ahead of the August 2 vote on the move to Tepito, asking whether he remembers that he, too, was a *"Perico de los Pelotes"* (a nobody) before he became a councilman. Would he now turn his back on his own people?[105] That pressure seems to have worked, since Ordóñez voted to reject the plan. Porfirio Díaz may have increased censorship of the press when it came to issues related to national politics, but in the orbit of local politics, periodicals like *El Popular* still felt free to criticize the Ayuntamiento, and actors like the vendors of the Baratillo still had access to their writers and editors. Baratilleros were not only a subject of press coverage; they also helped shape it. Despite the restrictions the Díaz regime had imposed on Mexico's political sphere by 1901, the baratilleros still had multiple political channels available to them to pursue their agenda, and they did so with a great degree of success.[106]

Still, the question arises of whether the vendors' politicking merely facilitated the outcome that the Ayuntamiento had sought all along—to force the Baratillo out of the city center. In his initial report, Quevedo noted that the goods its vendors sold—used iron, shoes, and clothes—were not objects of necessity for the surrounding neighborhood but ones that benefitted the lower classes throughout the city. In his view, there was no particular reason why it needed to stay in the Plaza del Jardín, where it gave an "ugly look" to a central area of the city.[107] Nothing in the city council minutes from the summer of 1901 suggests that the city planned to build the bazaar in the Plaza del Jardín. In fact, there was little discussion of *where* the new structure would be located, raising the question of whether the Ayuntamiento ever intended to build it.[108]

Furthermore, as a fast-growing neighborhood on the city's northeastern fringe, Tepito probably looked like an appropriate site for the Baratillo. Originally part of the *parcialidad*, or indigenous district, of Santiago Tlatelolco, it was lightly populated before 1880, and most of its residents worked in agriculture. Around 1880, however, as migration to the capital increased, the area's population surged—from less than 5,600 in 1879 to more than 21,000 in 1890.[109] Although portable stands had occupied the neighborhood's plaza since the early 1890s, from which vendors sold food, used clothing, and metal tools, Tepito lacked a formal marketplace in 1901.[110] Furthermore, relocating the Baratillo to Tepito brought an institution that many viewed as a gathering place for rateros to an area of the city where people believed rateros lived.[111]

But leaving the Baratillo in an uncovered, undeveloped site went against the broader project that Landa y Escandón and Quevedo were undertaking in the capital—to modernize and improve the living conditions of the poor. Throughout 1901, the Markets Improvement Commission emphasized that the Baratillo's move to Tepito would be temporary. In its official report to the Ayuntamiento on August 2, 1901, it recommended that the government "tell the merchants of the Baratillo established in the Plazuela del Jardín that they are permitted to establish their puestos or stores, in a provisional and transitory manner, in the Plazuela de Tepito."[112] Newspapers like *La Voz de México* lent their support to the move only under the condition that its existence in Tepito was "transitory" while the Ayuntamiento constructed a new bazaar.[113] Officials were still calling the Baratillo a "provisional market" in 1907.[114] But the bazaar never materialized, and the Baratillo never left Tepito.

Soon after the vendors arrived in Tepito they began to second-guess their decision to move there. The Ayuntamiento was not holding up its end of the bargain. In March 1902, the vendors accused the Ayuntamiento of reneging on its promise to charge them two cents per square *vara* for their stands by charging them three instead.[115] The government had already rejected the vendors' request for a four-month rent abatement, which the vendors argued was only fair since they had moved to Tepito at their own expense.[116] *El Popular* continued to criticize the Ayuntamiento's treatment of the baratilleros, asking the government how it could justify demanding from these poor men and women a rent that was higher than that of a small store or a room in a vecindad—especially when the Ayuntamiento had contributed nothing toward the cost of building the vendors' stands.[117] The paper's writers were not impressed with the plaza's infrastructure, either. In May of that year, they complained that the uneven cobblestone paving had created pools of stagnant water and that garbage was accumulating on the streets outside the market, which neither property owners nor the police seemed interested in collecting.[118]

Despite its promises, the Ayuntamiento made little effort to improve the conditions of the Baratillo over the next decade. Visits by *La Patria* in 1903 and the Council of Health in 1906 found the same wooden huts that the vendors had made or transported from other plazas when they moved there in early 1902.[119] Some vendors were even living in those huts. The Council of Health urged the Federal District government to build a proper market in Tepito to address "the very bad hygienic conditions" there.[120] But neither that market nor the bazaar that Quevedo had envisioned for the Baratillo was ever built, so it continued to operate in Tepito as an improvised assemblage of stands. It would become a permanent fixture in Tepito—central to the neighborhood's economy and its identity—without ever losing that temporary character.[121]

The project to transform the city's barrios similarly languished. After making substantial progress in paving streets, building sidewalks, and bringing water and sewer lines to the city's northern, eastern, and southern peripheries between late 1901 and early 1903, the project stalled in the second half 1903. While Landa y Escandón simply may have lost interest in the project, particularly after he became more involved in a campaign against the city's pulquerías, two other factors almost certainly contributed.[122] One was the deteriorating financial conditions in which the Ayuntamiento found itself.

By 1902, it had exhausted the two-million-peso subsidy it had received from the federal government. At the same time, the price of Mexican silver was falling in global markets, which made the Ayuntamiento's significant foreign debt more expensive.[123] Its spending on public works declined precipitously after 1901 as a result of those two factors.[124]

But another event probably had the greatest impact for both the residents of the city's barrios who awaited public services and the vendors of the Baratillo who expected a new marketplace. On March 26, 1903, Porfirio Díaz signed the Law of Municipal and Political Organization of the Federal District, which removed the governing powers of all of the ayuntamientos within the territory of the Federal District. As of July 1, 1903, the Ayuntamiento of Mexico City, a nearly 400-year-old institution, would cease to exist as an autonomous political body. The law transferred the assets of the ayuntamientos in the Federal District to the national government and turned them into advisory bodies for the new Consejo Superior de Gobierno del Distrito Federal (Superior Council of Government of the Federal District). That body was comprised not of elected officials but three men—the governor of the Federal District, the president of the Superior Health Commission, and a new director general of Public Works. The president of the republic appointed all three.[125]

While the Ayuntamiento was far from a perfectly democratic institution before 1903, its members were nonetheless accountable to at least some portion of Mexico City's residents and citizens.[126] Its members included working-class labor leaders like Ordóñez, continuing a tradition of artisan representation on the Ayuntamiento that dated to the colonial period. In the 1880s and 1890s, the president and vice president of the moderate Congreso Obrero were both members of the Ayuntamiento and sat on its Artisan Development Commission. After the 1903 law went into effect that commission disappeared.[127] Before the reorganization, poor and working-class residents were able to take their concerns to their representatives on the Ayuntamiento, as vendors in the Baratillo repeatedly did. Those men could then lobby the other councilmen on behalf of their constituents. Furthermore, most city council sessions were open to the public; residents had the ability to attend the meetings and voice their concerns in person, as the baratilleros did to protest Quevedo's proposal to close the market in 1901.

After Porfirio Díaz stripped the Ayuntamiento of its powers, however, Mexico City's citizens no longer had a formal role in local government. The meetings of the Consejo Superior were not open to the public, and its members were accountable only to the president and his interior minister. To voice their grievances to officials, poor and working-class residents now had to rely on the support of the press, which itself suffered from increasing government censorship, and petitions—the same mechanism that street vendors and other members of the urban popular classes had employed since the colonial period.[128]

CONCLUSION

Although Mexico City experienced a great deal of change during the Porfiriato, much about the Baratillo remained the same. Its vendors came from the same types of backgrounds as they always had, and they continued to offer the same kinds of goods. Despite the country's expanding economy and growing manufacturing sector, Mexico City's residents still sought second-hand clothing, shoes, tools, and consumer goods—regardless of their provenance. Furthermore, baratilleros continued to use the levers of local government and the Mexico City press to protect their interests. They relied not just on the centuries-old practice of petitioning authorities to resist attempts to relocate them and demand adequate policing and better infrastructure; they also delegated representatives to attend public city council sessions. Those tactics yielded results; their negotiations with the local government in 1901, in fact, went far more smoothly than they had in 1872, despite the constrictions that had taken place in Mexican politics in the intervening decades. The vendors also found support for their cause in the capital city press, including not only outlets dedicated to working-class issues, like *El Popular* and *El Hijo del Trabajo*, but also establishment papers like *La Patria*. While Porfirio Díaz's regime may have curtailed press freedom by the turn of the century, it did not prevent the capital city's papers from openly advocating on behalf of vendors that many residents viewed as career criminals, or from openly criticizing the Ayuntamiento.[129]

Mexico City's elites, both inside of government and out, expressed ambivalence about the Baratillo during the Porfiriato. During the 1880s and 1890s, the municipal government vacillated over how to deal with the market. On several occasions, the Ayuntamiento attempted to relegate it to a peripheral neighborhood of the city, only to backtrack when the vendors protested to their councilmen. The federal government, despite its aggressive intervention in many areas of Mexican society, including in other spheres of the urban economy, largely ignored the Baratillo. This ambivalence stemmed in no small part from the patronage networks that the vendors forged with government officials and newspaper editors during this era. Far more than a "palace of misery," the Baratillo was an important site of political negotiation during the Porfiriato, one where elite and popular interests aligned as often as they clashed.[130] The Baratillo was more compatible with Porfirian modernity than the market's critics acknowledged; indeed, this chaotic and dangerous site thrived under the regime of Order and Progress.

Amid these continuities, however, the baratilleros also experienced significant ruptures at the beginning of the twentieth century. Regardless of how the vendors and local officials reached the decision to relocate the market to Tepito, the result was the permanent removal of the Baratillo from the city center. The dislocation of a market that had served a heterogeneous clientele from a central location for well over two hundred years had significant consequences for the Baratillo's vendors and for the capital's broader population. It helped solidify a perception—if not the reality—that Mexico City's core was a space for the privileged while the vulgar and criminal classes populated its barrios. And by relegating an unseemly institution to a peripheral neighborhood that many viewed in the same negative light, the Ayuntamiento helped fuse Tepito's identity with the Baratillo's.

The vendors of the Baratillo had agreed to move to Tepito only temporarily, while the Ayuntamiento built them a modern, new bazaar. But when that structure did not materialize, the vendors found that they had less leverage with their government than they had historically enjoyed. Although the Ayuntamiento continued to hold elections for its members after 1903 and still oversaw some aspects of public market administration, the body had no formal governing powers, no autonomy, and little accountability to its constituents.[131] For more than 250 years, the Baratillo's history had been tied to the Ayuntamiento's. On a number of occasions, the municipal government had resisted eliminating the Baratillo because even the relatively meager rents its vendors paid contributed to the Ayuntamiento's bottom line. Vendors had extensive dealings with municipal officials throughout the eighteenth and nineteenth centuries. The 1903 law altered that dynamic. That reform, along with the sweeping changes that the Mexican Revolution brought to Mexico City during the following decade, led baratilleros to find new ways of defending their interests and asserting their rights.

Epilogue

THE BARATILLO AND TEPITO

Extremely powerful interests and organizations are behind the
alleged contrabandists of Tepito.

El Informador *(Guadalajara), August 22, 1996*

IN THE TWENTIETH CENTURY, TEPITO became the most famous
neighborhood in Mexico. Today, it is synonymous with poverty, crime, oppositional culture, and above all, the black market. Tepito had a bad reputation
even before the Baratillo arrived there in 1902. Newspapers chronicled the
crimes that took place on its streets throughout the 1880s and 1890s, and it
formed part of a rumbo, or direction, of the city that the Porfirian-era press
described as "the cradle of crime."[1] The neighborhood's infamy only
increased, however, when it became the home of the capital's notorious
thieves' market. Over the ensuing decades, the identities of Tepito and the
Baratillo gradually fused. By the middle of the twentieth century, the word
"Baratillo" faded from use as residents of Mexico City began referring to the
market simply as "Tepito."[2] Tepito had become the black-market barrio.

In Tepito, the Baratillo continued to offer second-hand clothing, household goods, and other products of uncertain provenance, playing as vital a
role in the local economy as it had for centuries. After a 1913 fire in the market
reduced many of its stands to ashes a broadside appeared with an image of the
flames and a *corrido*, or ballad, lamenting the loss of the market:

> Don Luis the saddle-maker
> and don Carlos the typesetter

and don Alfonso the coachman
and little Pedro the motorman

Who bought his shoes
his shirt or his overcoat
they were so cheap there!
Now where will they shop?[3]

But the corrido's eulogy was premature. The Baratillo survived the fire, just as it had endured so many other existential threats over the centuries. The baratilleros reconstituted their stalls from the debris and provisioned Mexico City residents through the darkest days of the Mexican Revolution, selling decomposing horsemeat to the hungry and offering arms and ammunition to those who engaged in the fighting.[4] It thrived in the postrevolutionary landscape as well, cementing its notoriety as the city's principal emporium for black-market goods (see figures 13 and 14). In the 1930s, police apprehended vendors selling everything from stolen radio parts to marijuana there.[5] When the anthropologist Oscar Lewis published his ethnography of Tepito, *The*

FIGURE 13. View of the Baratillo in Plaza Fray Bartolomé de las Casas, Tepito, 1927. The Plaza de Tepito was officially known as the Plaza Fray Bartolomé de las Casas. Centro de Estudios Tepiteños, Mexico City.

FIGURE 14. Shoppers in the Baratillo, 1928. Centro de Estudios Tepiteños, Mexico City.

Children of Sanchez, in 1961, he called the neighborhood's market "the largest second-hand market in Mexico City, also known as the Thieves' Market."[6]

As Mexico's economy transformed over the course of the twentieth century, however, the Baratillo changed with it. The import substitution industrialization policies that the country implemented in the middle decades of the twentieth century imposed high tariffs to protect domestic industry, creating new markets for extralegal commerce. The vendors of Tepito stepped in to satisfy that demand.[7] In the early 1970s, *fayuca*—contraband clothing and electronics—began to appear on the streets of Tepito. Contraband quickly displaced many of the second-hand goods that had long been the market's staples. Land values in the neighborhood surged as merchants from across the city clamored for a piece of the trade.[8] When Mexico opened its borders to freer trade in the 1980s and 1990s, allowing for cheaper legal imports, Tepito's commerce evolved again. *Piratería*—pirated, or illegally reproduced, music and movies and knockoff clothing and accessories—soon filled Tepito's stands.[9] Today, the second-hand market in Tepito is confined to a few blocks of Calle Tenochtitlán and the Plaza de la Concepción, in the northern reaches of the barrio, where used clothing, cell phone chargers, and shoes pile high along the streets and sidewalks.[10] Across the rest of the

FIGURE 15. Shoppers in Tepito, 2017. Photo by Andrew Konove.

neighborhood, contraband, pirated, and legally imported merchandise circulate alongside one another, as indistinguishable to the consumers who gather there today as they were to the Baratillo's customers in the eighteenth century (see figure 15).[11]

Tepito's commerce provides economic benefits that extend well beyond the market's immediate neighborhood. Thousands of vendors from across Mexico City labor on its streets every day, where they sell to diverse consumers.[12] In the 1970s and 1980s, Tepito's *fayuqueros* thrived, in part, by supplying the capital's middle classes with inexpensive electronics, clothing, and accessories, particularly during the prolonged economic crisis of the 1980s.[13] On the supply side, large-scale importers and individual merchants from Tepito have all partaken in this illicit trade. What began with *tepiteños* (residents of Tepito) packing contraband into suitcases in Laredo, Texas, and traveling by bus back to Mexico City has expanded into far-reaching trade circuits that involve Asian exporters, Mexican customs officials, large retail chains, and street vendors in Tepito. Tepiteños pioneered this trade and continue to be major players in it. They travel abroad to deal with suppliers, and in recent years even established a community in Beijing to facilitate the export of Chinese manufactures to Mexico.[14] As in the colonial era, when the Baratillo served as an outlet for Mexico City's overseas merchants, the city's principal "thieves' market" continues to provision local consumers through global networks—links that have only multiplied over the centuries.

The shadow economy has thrived in Mexico City for centuries because diverse actors profit from it. Although critics routinely cast the Baratillo as an institution that served the city's criminal classes and the very poor, in reality, its benefits accrued to a wide swath of the urban population and beyond. In the colonial period, elite merchants of the Consulado, master artisans, and many others traded with or set up shop in the Baratillo because it provided the potential for profit. Government officials, too, saw the value in the Baratillo. They collected fees from its vendors that helped fund the basic operations of municipal government and bribes that lined their own pockets. Some political elites defended the market for reasons that had nothing to do with money. They argued it was an essential piece of the urban fabric, indispensable to those who made their living in the market or furnished themselves and their households with its wares.

Those arguments speak to the fundamentally political nature of the shadow economy in Mexico City. It has not endured for hundreds of years simply because of the material benefits it offers; rather, vendors and their allies fought to preserve the Baratillo using the institutions available to them in every era. Throughout the eighteenth and nineteenth centuries, baratilleros signed collective petitions that employed the prevailing political vocabulary of the day—whether it was the common good, public utility, hygiene, or progress—to assert their rights as subjects and citizens. Baratilleros exercised their political muscle through some avenues that do not appear to have been open to other street and market vendors. In the nineteenth century, they lobbied their local elected officials and threatened to vote those who failed to support them out of office. They also developed relationships with members of the capital's press, including some of the most prominent newspaper publishers of the nineteenth century. Time and time again, they used those relationships to resist efforts to shutter or relocate the market. Baratilleros harnessed their market's noxious reputation and turned it into an asset. They repeatedly made the case that the Baratillo was vital to their city's economy and society and deflected blame for the Baratillo's problems onto their government for failing to provide it with adequate infrastructure or policing.

The market's perseverance attests to the success of those arguments and to the vendors' ability to bring them to an audience that extended far beyond the city's market administrators.

In the twentieth century, baratilleros found new ways to express their political will. They did so, in part, to cope with changes to the structure of government in the capital. In 1914, Venustiano Carranza, the general whose forces emerged victorious from the Mexican Revolution, restored the governing powers of Mexico City's Ayuntamiento, overturning the 1903 law that had effectively federalized government in the capital.[15] But the Ayuntamiento's return was short lived. In 1928, as Álvaro Obregón and his supporters consolidated their power over the nation's capital, Mexico's Congress dissolved the Ayuntamiento for good.[16] An institution established in the 1520s ceased to exist. Mexico City's residents and citizens would have no formal role in local governance again until 1988.[17] Vendors who were unhappy with official decisions could no longer appeal to their aldermen for support or attend open meetings of the city council. They continued to write petitions to authorities, as they had since the colonial era, but those missives carried little political weight. So the vendors found a new instrument to negotiate with government officials: the labor union.

Mexico's 1917 Constitution enshrined workers' right to organize, and beginning in the 1920s, vendors in Mexico City and elsewhere began to form unions.[18] By the early 1930s, newspapers in the capital were reporting on negotiations between the Unión de Comerciantes en Pequeño (Union of Petty Merchants) and local authorities over where vendors could sell, what materials they could use in the construction of their stalls, and other issues related to their trade.[19] By 1932, the baratilleros in Tepito had their own section of that union—the Unión de Comerciantes en Pequeño del Mercado Bartolomé de las Casas (the Plaza de Tepito was officially known as the Plaza Fray Bartolomé de las Casas).[20] Membership in vendor unions blossomed over the following decades, and by the early 1950s there were at least six umbrella unions for street and market vendors in the Federal District.[21]

Labor unions became one of the central pillars of the postrevolutionary regime that coalesced into the Party of the Institutional Revolution (PRI), which ruled Mexico from 1929 to 2000 and which voters returned to power in 2012. They constituted an important component of the corporatist state— a new mechanism that Mexican authorities used to assemble patronage networks they hoped would undermine popular resistance to the regime. Yet Mexico's postrevolutionary governments never succeeded in controlling vendor organizations, and unions became effective instruments for vendors to articulate their demands and resist policies that adversely affected them.[22]

Tepito's vendor organizations, in particular, became a political force in the capital and for decades frustrated government efforts to force vendors off the neighborhood's streets.[23] Their clout is still evident in 2017. In response to vendors' demand that Mexico City's new constitution recognize their right to sell in the city's streets, the charter's authors included language that acknowledged the right of unsalaried workers, including petty merchants, "to conduct decent work and possess a formal [legal] identity in Mexico City." The constitution calls for the establishment of special zones designated for street selling and new guidelines for "a gradual process of regularization, formalization, and regulation" for street vendors.[24] While the practical implications of those articles are not yet clear, their political significance is obvious: vendors who traffic in the shadow economy helped shape the constitution of Mexico's thirty-second state. Their political capital did not emerge from a vacuum. It grew out of a long tradition of vendor engagement in urban politics.

The links between vendors in Mexico City's shadow economy and other economic and political players in the capital created a conundrum for the capital's authorities. On the one hand, baratilleros openly flouted the law by peddling illicit merchandise and operating a market that was technically illegal for much of its existence. On the other hand, their trade benefited a wide swath of the urban population, including not only the poor but also middling and elite groups and even the government itself. For these reasons, authorities in Mexico City have always been ambivalent about the shadow economy. Officials such as the viceroy Duke of Linares weighed the Baratillo's costs against its benefits and found themselves unable to render a decision. Even when authorities at one level of government banned the market, other officials ignored or repudiated those orders by collecting rent from its vendors, adjudicating their disputes, or acknowledging the vendors' right to practice their trade. For much of the Baratillo's history, it operated in legal limbo—outlawed and sanctioned at the same time. The state never offered a coherent policy toward the Baratillo because the state in Mexico was never a single entity. Intragovernmental rivalries and competing political visions have complicated governance in Mexico's capital since the colonial era. Those conflicts created a space for the Baratillo and the shadow economy to thrive.

The pattern continues in Tepito in the present day. Though many, if not all, the transactions that take place on the neighborhood's streets occur off the books and beyond the reach of the nation's regulatory regime, the government intervenes only sporadically to disrupt the trade and confiscate illicit merchandise.[25] While those raids produce dramatic images in the Mexican press, they mask the patronage networks that link Tepito's vendors and residents to local and national authorities. Today, dozens of vendor and neighborhood organizations in Tepito help channel local demands to Mexico City authorities. Those officials, in turn, depend on vendors for political support. The Mexican state does not mount a concerted effort to rein in the shadow economy because so many of its agents rely on it.[26]

Seeing the Baratillo as a key site of political and economic exchange offers a new perspective on the history of public space in Mexico City. The capital's streets and plazas were not merely venues for class conflict, where recalcitrant popular groups resisted the disciplinary projects of modernizing elites. They also hosted networks that linked vendors to elites in government, business, and the press. More than rub shoulders with one another, men and women from diverse backgrounds engaged in far-reaching alliances and rivalries that extended from the market plaza to the city's import warehouses and its halls of government. Those connections become visible only by looking beyond impressionistic sources of street life to archival evidence of the quotidian activities that took place in public streets and plazas.

From this perspective, the urban renewal schemes that sought to remake Mexico City's public spaces between the seventeenth century and the twentieth, which almost inevitably took aim at the Baratillo, come into new relief. From the redesign of the Plaza Mayor in the aftermath of the 1692 riot to the Baratillo's relocation to Tepito in 1902, members of the city's governing elite repeatedly sought to modernize the capital by displacing its most unsavory marketplace to the urban periphery. Those projects, however, were always contentious, and they encountered resistance from vendors and members of the capital's upper classes alike. The Baratillo's history shows that there was no single elite vision for the city.

Nor did popular groups who made their living on the streets unite in opposition to modernizing reforms. Within the confines of the Baratillo, rival vendor factions often advanced very different agendas—some that aligned with those of local or national officials and others that vociferously opposed them. Those tensions still exist in present-day Tepito, where vendor organizations compete for space on the street and influence in local politics.[27] For at least three hundred years, the shadow economy has been a venue for negotiating competing views of the city—ideas that did not always hew to ethnic or class-based identities.

One of the most remarkable aspects of the Baratillo's long history—and a contrast with Tepito's more recent past—is how rarely relations between vendors and authorities turned violent.[28] Violence played a role in the market in other ways, usually in the form of fights that broke out between vendors or among customers who gathered there. But there is little evidence of congregants in the market sparring with authorities prior to the late twentieth century.[29] The shadowy networks of illicit, informal, and second-hand goods that converged in the Baratillo brought diverse actors into relationships with one another. Those webs of patronage and mutual interest may offer clues for understanding how Mexico City mostly avoided the revolutionary violence that rural areas of the country suffered during the period this book has examined. Baratilleros sustained their trade not through violent resistance or public protest but through their deft use of Mexico's institutions. The Baratillo's history thus sheds light on an urban political system that was routinely capable of producing compromise.

Yet the arrangements that system produced have always been unstable. They seldom yielded enforceable compacts or acknowledged inalienable rights. The Baratillo was an improvised marketplace whose continuing existence depended on personal relationships and unwritten rules. Tepito's market today maintains that provisional quality. Walking the neighborhood's deserted streets on a Tuesday afternoon, when the vendors rest, one is struck by the ephemeral nature of its commerce. Although the shadow economy has undergirded Mexico City's society for centuries, its existence still depends on quiet deals and blind eyes. Perhaps Mexico City's new constitution will alter that dynamic by providing vendors firmer legal footing. Until the government implements that charter's provisions, however, vendors' rights will remain as informal as their businesses. Here one day, they could be gone the next.

APPENDIX

TABLE 1 Census Data for Signatories to May 27, 1842, Letter to Mexico City Ayuntamiento

Last	First	Sex	Age	Marital Status	Profession	Birthplace	Vote
Alcantara	José	M	46	W	Commerce*	Otumba	Y
Álvarez	Juan	M	50	M	Commerce	Querétaro	Y
Álvarez	Pedro	M	40	M	Merchant	Mexico City	Y
Argumedo	Ignacio	M	42	—	Merchant	Puebla	N
Ayala	Joaquín	M	50	—	Merchant	Mexico City	Y
Buenrostro	Guadalupe	M	28	—	Merchant	Zamora	Y
Cadena	Gabino	M	39	M	Hat maker	Mexico City	Y
Camargo	Francisco	M	40	—	Merchant	Mexico City	Y
Casillas	Felipe	M	47	—	Tailor	Mexico City	Y
De La Paz	José	M	40	—	Tanner	Mexico City	N
Franco	Doroteo	M	36	—	Carpenter	Mexico City	Y
Gálvez	Ignacio	M	16	S	—	Mexico City	N
García	Joaquín	M	35	—	Barber	Mexico City	Y
Gómez	Tomas	M	38	—	Merchant	Celaya	Y
Guerrero	Francisco	M	23	—	Merchant	Mexico City	Y
Guerrero	Saturnino	M	50	M	Muleteer	Guanajuato	Y
Leal	Juana	F	50	—	Merchant	Mexico City	N
Malo	Mariano	M	40	M	Merchant	San Luis Potosí	Y
Martínez	Vicente	M	36	—	Merchant	Mexico City	Y
Molina	Dionisio	M	21	M	Carpenter	Mexico City	Y
Morales	Trinidad	M	35	M	Butcher	Mexico City	Y
Osorio	José María	M	50	M	Collector	Mexico City	Y
Padilla	Luis	M	30	—	Merchant	Mexico City	Y
Párraga	Manuel	M	42	M	Merchant	Mexico City	Y
Rivera	Lino	M	41	W	Merchant	Mexico City	Y
Rubio	Nabor	M	30	—	Merchant	Puebla	Y
Salinas	Francisco	M	57	M	Chair maker	Los Remedios	Y
Solís	Francisco	M	15	—	Merchant	Mineral del Monte	Y**
Solís	José María	M	34	M	Merchant	Valle de Santiago	Y
Sumalla	Manuel	M	40	S	Merchant	Mexico City	Y
Vara	Miguel	M	34	M	Cobbler	Mexico City	Y
Vidal	Joaquín	M	30	—	Merchant	Puebla	Y
Villar	Petra	F	60	—	—	Mexico City	N

SOURCES: AHCM, Ayuntamiento Rastros y Mercados, vol. 3730, exp. 161; "Representación hecha al Escmo. ayuntamiento el día 27 del corriente por los individuos que la suscriben," *El Siglo Diez y Nueve*, May 31, 1842, 2–3; Sonia Pérez Toledo, "Base de datos del Padrón de la Municipalidad de México de 1842," 2005.

KEY:
Marital Status: M=Married; S=Single; W=Widowed
Vote = Voting Eligibility: Y = Eligible to vote; N = Ineligible to vote
*Some individuals' professions appear as "*comerciante*" (merchant) and others as "*comercio*" (commerce). The reason for the distinction is not clear.
** The census listed fifteen-year-old Francisco Solis as eligible to vote, so there was an error either in his age or his voter eligibility designation.

Using Pérez Toledo's database, I was able to locate thirty-three of the petition's forty signatories in the 1842 census. Three signatories' names do not appear in the census, suggesting that those individuals may not have resided within the municipality of Mexico City at the time. While it is also possible that someone signed the names of people who did not exist, it seems unlikely that forty signatories would have had a much greater impact than thirty-seven. There are some discrepancies between the original petition the baratilleros sent, preserved in Mexico City's municipal archives, and the version that *El Siglo Diez y Nueve* printed on May 31, 1842. The newspaper staff appears to have copied two names incorrectly: "Luis Rivera" in the print version is most likely Lino Rivera; "Benigno Molina" is almost certainly Dionisio Molina. In addition, one name, Vicente Padillas, appears in the newspaper but was not on the original petition (he also is absent from the 1842 census). In four cases, multiple names in the census matched a signatory's name, and it proved impossible to determine which corresponded to the baratillero. For names that corresponded to multiple individuals in the census, the results were narrowed based on age (at least thirteen years old); profession (one traditionally represented in the Baratillo or which could plausibly have served a purpose there); and location of residence (once a residential pattern began to emerge from the data, individuals who lived closer to the market were chosen over ones with more distant residences). This methodology is imperfect, and some individuals were matched to census entries with greater confidence than others. Any errors are my own.

TABLE 2 Census Data for Baratillo Vendors Residing within a One-Block
Radius of the Plaza del Jardín in 1882

Last	First	Sex	Age	Marital Status	Profession	Read	Write	Year(s) in Baratillo
Aguilar	Rafael	M	50	M	Merchant	Y	Y	1872
Alvarez	Rafael	M	50	M	Cobbler	N	N	1872
Araujo	Román	M	22	M	Cobbler	Y	Y	1894
Campuzano	Guadalupe	F	58	M	—	Y	Y	1901
Campuzano	Lusano	M	62	M	Merchant	Y	Y	1901
Castro	Ygnacio	M	40	M	Blacksmith	Y	Y	1886, 1889
Chávez	Ancieto	M	48	M	Cobbler	Y	Y	1894
De la Luz Vida	José	M	57	M	Merchant	Y	Y	1872
Delgado de López	Carmen	F	40	M	—	N	N	1893, 1894
Díaz	José María	M	50	M	Merchant	Y	Y	1889, 1893
Farfán	Félix	M	50/	—	Carpenter/	Y/	Y/	1872
		M	58	W	Merchant	Y	Y	
González	Jesús	M	34	M	Merchant	Y	Y	1889, 1983
Grimaldo	Santiago	M	43	W	Cobbler	N	N	1889, 1894
Guerra	Antonio	M	64	S	Merchant	Y	Y	1872
Herrera	Felipe	M	40	M	Merchant	Y	Y	1894
López	Apolonio	M	50	M	Merchant	Y	Y	1886, 1889
López	Manuel	M	29	S	Tailor	Y	Y	1886, 1889, 1893, 1894
Montoya	José	M	43	W	Merchant	Y	Y	1872, 1889, 1893
Moreno	Hermenegildo	M	25	S	Merchant	Y	Y	1872
Olvera	María Soledad	F	47	W	Merchant	Y	Y	1872
Orozco	José	M	45	W	Merchant	Y	Y	1886, 1889, 1893
Rangel	Francisco	M	27	S	Tailor	Y	Y	1872
Ríos	Julián	M	45	M	Merchant	Y	Y	1893, 1894
Sánchez	Antonio	M	41	M	Carpenter	Y	Y	1886, 1889, 1893, 1894
Solís	José	M	50	M	Merchant	Y	Y	1872, 1886, 1889,
Yslas	Loreto	M	50	M	Chair maker	Y	Y	1872

SOURCES: 1882 municipal census, located in AHCM, Ayuntamiento, Padrones, vol. 3425; market rosters from 1886, 1889, 1893, and 1894, located in AHCM, Ayuntamiento, Rastros y Mercados: Padrones, vol. 3750, exp. 2; and signed vendor petitions from 1872 and 1901, located in AHCM, Ayuntamiento, Rastros y Mercados, vol. 3734, exp. 554 and AHCM, Ayuntamiento, Rastros y Mercados, vol. 3740, exp. 1256, respectively.

To identify these individuals, I searched the four blocks adjacent to the Plaza del Jardín (*manzanas* 36, 37 [1st and 2nd parts], and 38 [1st part]) for the names of baratilleros who signed petitions or appeared on market censuses between 1872 and 1901. This methodology may have led to false positives—people with the same names as baratilleros who were not, in fact, the same person. I attempted to control for this problem using the age and profession of the vendor (eliminating potential matches that included a vendor under the age of thirteen or over the age of ninety, for example). Despite the potential for producing false positives, the method almost certainly undercounts the number of baratilleros living on these four blocks, as the absence of a digital database like the one Pérez Toledo built from the 1842 census meant that the search could not be comprehensive. The census may contain errors of its own. For example, it lists two individuals named Felix Farfán (a participant in the vendors' 1872 dispute with the Ayuntamiento)—one aged fifty and the other aged fifty-eight. While it is possible these were two different people, perhaps cousins, the fact that one entry was a residence and the other was a workshop and the closeness of the men's ages and other key details suggest it was probably the same person.

NOTES

ABBREVIATIONS

ACSCJN	Archivo Central de la Suprema Corte de Justicia de la Nación
AGI	Archivo General de Indias
AGMP	Archivo General Municipal de Puebla
AGN	Archivo General de la Nación
AHAGNCM	Acervo Histórico del Archivo General de Notarías de la Ciudad de México
AHCM	Archivo Histórico de la Ciudad de México
AHMNA	Archivo Histórico del Museo Nacional de Antropología
CIDE	Centro de Investigación y Docencia Económicas
CIESAS	Centro de Investigaciones y Estudios Superiores en Antropología Social
CONACYT	Consejo Nacional de Ciencia y Tecnología
exp.	*expediente* (file)
f.	*foja* (sheet)
INAH	Instituto Nacional de Antropología e Historia
para.	paragraph
SEP	Secretaría de Educación Pública
TSJDF	Tribunal Superior de Justicia del Distrito Federal
UAM	Universidad Autónoma Metropolitana

UNAM	Universidad Nacional Autónoma de México
v.	verso
vol.	*volumen* (volume)

INTRODUCTION

1. Alejandro Cruz Flores, "Comerciantes de Tepito proponen regular su activi-dad y pagar impuestos," *La Jornada*, August 15, 2016, http://www.jornada.unam .mx/2016/08/15/capital/037n2cap, accessed August 20, 2016; and María de Lourdes Torrano, "Presentan comerciales de Tepito propuestas de Leyes Secundarias para la Constitución de la CDMX," *Noticias MVS,* August 14, 2016, http://www .noticiasmvs.com/#!/noticias/presentan-comerciales-de-tepito-propuestas-de-leyes-secundarias-para-la-constitucion-de-la-cdmx-654, accessed August 20, 2016.

2. Tepito's fame extends beyond Mexico. The neighborhood was the setting for Oscar Lewis's 1961 book, *The Children of Sanchez*, in which the American anthro-pologist developed his influential theory of the culture of poverty. That book was also the basis for a 1979 feature-length film of the same title, which starred Anthony Quinn and Dolores del Río. U.S. media outlets regularly feature stories about Tepito. See, for example, Hector Becerra, "Mexico City's 'Barrio Bravo' Refuses to Be Conquered," *Los Angeles Times*, July 21, 2014, http://www.latimes.com/world /la-fg-c1-mexico-tepito-20140721-37-story.html, accessed November 23, 2016.

3. Alejandra Sánchez I., "GDF expropia La Fortaleza, enclave de 5,000 m2 del narcomenudeo en Tepito," *La Crónica,* February 15, 2007, http://www.cronica.com .mx/notas/2007/285936.html, accessed November 22, 2016.

4. Carlos Martínez Assad, "Presentación," to Ernesto Aréchiga Córdoba, *Tepito: Del antiguo barrio de indios al arrabal, 1868–1929, historia de una urbani-zación inacabada* (Mexico City: Ediciones ¡Uníos!, 2003), 11.

5. Juan Vicente Güémez Pacheco de Padilla Horcasitas y Aguayo, Conde de Revillagigedo and Ramón Mena, *El Segundo Conde de Revilla Gigedo (juicio de resi-dencia)* (Mexico City: Talleres Gráficos de la Nación, 1933), 494.

6. "Una visita al Baratillo," *La Patria*, October 15, 1891, 1–2.

7. The terms *ayuntamiento* and *cabildo* have similar meanings. This study uses "Ayuntamiento" for the institution of municipal government in Mexico City and "cabildo" for the city council sessions in which the members of the Ayuntamiento met. I capitalize "Ayuntamiento" when referring to the government of Mexico City to distinguish it from ayuntamientos in other cities.

8. This book draws on the work of Karl Polanyi and the economic anthropolo-gists known as "substantivists" who challenged the notion that the economy consti-tutes an autonomous sphere, separate from and unaffected by politics and social and cultural practice. See Karl Polanyi, *The Great Transformation: The Political and Economic Origins of Our Time* (1944; rpt. Boston: Beacon Press, 2001); and Karl Polanyi, Konrad Arensberg, and Harry M. Pearson, eds., *Trade and Market*

in the Early Empires: Economies in History and Theory (Glencoe, IL: Free Press, 1957).

9. Ilona Katzew, *Casta Painting: Images of Race in Eighteenth-Century Mexico* (New Haven, CT: Yale University Press, 2004), 56; José Joaquín Fernández de Lizardi, *El periquillo sarniento* (Mexico City: Editorial Época, 1986), 151, 248, 273.

10. *Diccionario de gobierno y legislación de Indias*, Archivo Histórico Nacional de España, Consejo de Indias, Códices, L.728 (BAL–BUZ), Imagen 14 (16th–18th C.). In Mexico, Puebla, Guadalajara, Zacatecas, Guanajuato, and other cities had their own baratillos by the late colonial period. Madrid had several baratillos by the late sixteenth century. See José Nieto Sánchez, *Historia del Rastro* (Madrid: Vision Net, 2004), 21. Historical documents relating to Mexico City's Baratillo inconsistently capitalize the first letter, in keeping with a lack of standardization in Spanish orthography prior to the late nineteenth century.

11. Second-hand markets have received little attention from historians of Mexico or elsewhere. On Madrid's Rastro and baratillos, see Nieto Sánchez, *Historia del Rastro*. On London's Rag Fair, see Madeleine Ginsburg, "Rags to Riches: The Second-Hand Clothes Trade 1700–1978," *Costume* 14:1 (1980): 121–35. See also: Patricia Allerston, "Reconstructing the Second-Hand Clothes Trade in Sixteenth- and Seventeenth-Century Venice," *Costume* 33:1 (1999): 46–56; Luiz Mott, "Subsidios a história do pequeno comércio no Brasil," *Revista de História* 27:105 (1976): 81–106; and Laurence Fontaine, ed., *Alternative Exchanges: Second-Hand Circulations from the Sixteenth Century to the Present* (New York: Berghahn Books, 2008). Many second-hand markets, including Madrid's Rastro and Guadalajara's Baratillo, ultimately transformed into Sunday flea markets popular with tourists and residents alike.

12. While no historian has traced the Baratillo's entire history, references to the market appear throughout the historiography of Mexico City. See, for example, Jorge Olvera Ramos's work, including a chapter in his book, *Los mercados de la Plaza Mayor en la Ciudad de México* (Mexico City: Cal y Arena, 2007), and his essay, "El Baratillo de la Plaza Mayor: La crítica ilustrada al comercio tradicional," in *El impacto de las reformas borbónicas en la estructura de las ciudades: Un enfoque comparativo*, ed. Sonia Lombardo de Ruiz (Mexico City: Gobierno de la Ciudad de México, 2000), 381–92. The Baratillo also receives brief attention in Katzew, *Casta Painting*, 56; R. Douglas Cope, *The Limits of Racial Domination: Plebeian Society in Colonial Mexico City, 1660–1720* (Madison: University of Wisconsin Press, 1994), 37, 41, 141; and Gabriel Haslip-Viera, *Crime and Punishment in Late Colonial Mexico City, 1692–1810* (Albuquerque: University of New Mexico Press, 1999), 40–41. Aréchiga Córdoba describes the Baratillo's move to Tepito in 1901–1902 and its role in transforming the nature of the neighborhood in the early twentieth century in *Tepito*, 215–29.

13. The number of people who worked in the Baratillo varied by era and according to who was counting and for what purpose. In disputes with the government, vendors often inflated the number of people who worked there, while officials seeking to disband the Baratillo might similarly have underestimated the number of

vendors to minimize the impact of closing the market. Municipal records tracking rent collection from the city's public markets provide some of the best estimates. In 1771, the Baratillo Grande, one of two Baratillos located in the Plaza Mayor at the time, had 142 stands. In the 1880s and 1890s, the number of stalls remained relatively constant at around 120. See AGN, Indiferente Virreinal, caja 1428, exp. 26; AHCM, Ayuntamiento, Rastros y Mercados: Padrones, vol. 3750, exp. 2.

14. Those same records indicate that clothing, shoes, jewelry, and metal tools—particularly ones made of iron—were the Baratillo's principal offerings between the mid-seventeenth century and the mid-twentieth.

15. The study thus provides anecdotal support for Stephen Haber's argument that Mexican industry was still not capable of producing manufactured goods for a mass market in the early twentieth century. See Stephen H. Haber, *Industry and Underdevelopment: The Industrialization of Mexico, 1890–1940* (Stanford, CA: Stanford University Press, 1989), 28.

16. Economists employ a narrow definition of the black market as: "trading which violates rationing or price control laws, or both." See s.v. "Black market," in John Black, Nigar Hashimzade, and Gareth Myles, eds., *A Dictionary of Economics*, 5th ed. (Oxford: Oxford University Press, 2017). In common usage, however, the black market can encompass trade in prohibited goods of virtually any kind, regardless of the regulatory regime in place. See, e.g., *Cambridge Academic Content Dictionary*, which defines the black market as "an illegal trade in goods or money," or the Wikipedia entry for "Black Market," which offers an even broader definition: "A black market, underground economy, or shadow economy is a clandestine market or transaction which has some aspect of illegality or is characterized by some form of noncompliant behavior with an institutional set of rules." See *Cambridge Academic Content Dictionary* (Cambridge University Press), http://dictionary.cambridge.org /us/dictionary/english/black-market; and https://en.wikipedia.org/wiki/Black_ market, accessed April 14, 2017.

17. Although social scientists typically see the phenomenon of the informal economy as a product of twentieth-century industrialization, the Baratillo's history illustrates that many of the issues that define the informal sector, including struggles among street vendors, shopkeepers, and governments for control over urban public space and the challenges of regulating exchanges that take place in ephemeral street markets, pre-date industrial capitalism by centuries. For the prevailing view, see "Black Markets, Underground Economies, and the Informal Sector," in the *Oxford Encyclopedia of Economic History*, ed. Joel Mokyr (Oxford: Oxford University Press, 2005), which describes the emergence of the informal economy in the twentieth century. For examples of historians who have pushed that periodization back, see: Amy Chazkel, *Laws of Chance: Brazil's Clandestine Lottery and the Making of Urban Public Life* (Durham, NC: Duke University Press, 2011), which situates the Brazilian *jogo do bicho*, an illegal lottery, in the context of the late nineteenth and early twentieth-century urban informal economy. On Mexico City, see R. Douglas Cope, "The Marvelous and the Abominable: The Intersection of Formal and Informal Economies in Eighteenth-Century Mexico City," *Diacronie* 13:1 (2013): 1–20.

Outside of Latin America, Sheilagh Ogilvie describes the emergence of a "black-market informal sector" that operated outside the guild system in early modern Germany. See "The Economics of Guilds," *Journal of Economic Perspectives* 28:4 (2014): 169–92.

18. There is little scholarly consensus on the definition of the informal economy. Keith Hart, who coined the term in the 1970s, focuses on the nature of the firm and whether it employs wage or nonwage labor. Other scholars focus on the nature of regulation—whether the activities in question are subject to government oversight and tax collection. John Cross, in his study of street vendors in Mexico City, describes the informal economy as "economic strategies that contravene laws regulating *how* business should be conducted, but not laws specifying *what* business may be conducted." Hernando de Soto, who helped popularize the concept of the informal economy, draws a distinction between practices that are technically illegal but widely accepted versus "antisocial" ones. See Keith Hart, "Informal Income Opportunities and Urban Employment in Ghana," *Journal of Modern African Studies* 11:1 (1973): 61–89; Ray Bromley, "Introduction: The Urban Informal Sector: Why Is It Worth Discussing?" *World Development* 6:9/10 (1978): 1033; Basudeb Guha-Khasnobis, Ravi Kanbur, and Elinor Ostrom, "Beyond Formality and Informality," in *Linking the Formal and Informal Economies: Concepts and Policies*, ed. Guha-Khasnobis, Kanbur, and Ostrom (Oxford Scholarship Online, 2006), 4; John C. Cross, *Informal Politics: Street Vendors and the State in Mexico City* (Stanford, CA: Stanford University Press, 1998), 29–30; and Hernando de Soto, *The Other Path: The Invisible Revolution in the Third World*, trans. June Abbott (New York: Harper & Row, 1989), 11.

19. This statement reflects a growing consensus in the social science literature that the informal and formal sectors do not constitute self-contained spheres of exchange, but, as Guha-Khasnobis, Kanbur, and Ostrom write, "a continuum of the reach of official intervention in different economic activities." "Beyond Formality and Informality," 16. Of course, some scholars have expressed skepticism about the utility of the formal-informal model since the 1970s. See, for example, Jan Breman, "A Dualistic Labor System? A Critique of the 'Informal Sector' Concept," *Economic and Political Weekly* 11:48 (1976): 1870–76.

20. This study resists categorizing the Baratillo as part of a distinct "popular economy" because elite actors also had stakes in it. On the concept of the popular economy, see Rossana Barragán, "Working Silver for the World: Mining Labor and Popular Economy in Colonial Potosí," *Hispanic American Historical Review* 97:2 (2017): 193–222.

21. See, for example Cope, *Limits*; and Jane Mangan, *Trading Roles: Gender, Ethnicity, and the Urban Economy in Colonial Potosí* (Durham, NC: Duke University Press, 2005). Gisela Moncada traces elite involvement in Mexico City's food markets into the early decades of Mexico's independence. Gisela Moncada González, *La libertad comercial: El sistema de abasto de alimentos en la ciudad de México, 1810–1835* (Mexico City: Instituto Mora, 2013). See also Richard Graham, *Feeding the City: From Street Market to Liberal Reform in Salvador, Brazil, 1780–1860* (Austin: University of Texas Press, 2010).

22. Recent scholarship on twentieth- and twenty-first-century informal economies has also stressed the centrality of the state in sustaining extralegal economic practices. See Patricia Fernández-Kelly and Jon Shefner, eds., *Out of the Shadows: Political Action and the Informal Economy in Latin America* (State College: Pennsylvania State University Press, 2006); Daniel Goldstein, *Owners of the Sidewalk: Security and Survival in the Informal City* (Durham, NC: Duke University Press, 2016); and Chazkel, *Laws of Chance*, 71.

23. In early 2016, Mexico's Congress voted to turn the Federal District into the country's thirty-second state. The sixteen delegations in the capital will revert to being municipalities, as they had been before a 1903 political reorganization of the District. See Georgina Saldierna and Roberto Garduño, "Desaparece el DF: Se llamará Ciudad de México y será el estado 32," *La Jornada*, January 20, 2016, http://www.jornada.unam.mx/ultimas/2016/01/20/constitucional-la-reforma-politica-del-df-1697.html, accessed August 20, 2016. See also Andrew Konove, "Will Mexico City Become a State?" *The National Interest*, January 8, 2013, http://nationalinterest.org/commentary/will-mexico-city-become-state-7939, accessed August 20, 2016.

24. This book builds on an institutional historiography of Mexico City, published primarily in Spanish by historians working in Mexico. See, in particular, the work of Ariel Rodríguez Kuri, including *La experiencia olvidada: El ayuntamiento de México: Política y gobierno, 1876–1912* (Mexico City: El Colegio de México, 1996), and the edited volume *Historia política de la Ciudad de México (desde su fundación hasta el año 2000)* (Mexico City: El Colegio de México, 2012). See also the work of Carlos Illades, Mario Barbosa Cruz, Fausta Gantús, and Sonia Pérez Toledo, including essays the last three authors contributed to *Historia política*.

25. See Rodríguez Kuri, *La Experiencia olvidada*, 14, where he describes the Ayuntamiento as an "argumentative body."

26. As Charles Walker has warned, "Historians should be careful not to categorize every behavior that contradicted the state's social project as resistance." See "Civilize or Control? The Lingering Impact of the Bourbon Urban Reforms," in *Political Cultures in the Andes, 1750–1950*, ed. Nils Jacobsen and Cristóbal Aljovín de Losada (Durham, NC: Duke University Press, 2005), 86.

27. James Holston calls these "contributor rights"—"claims on the basis of [residents'] contribution to the city itself." Holston, *Insurgent Citizenship: Disjunctions of Democracy and Modernity in Brazil* (Princeton, NJ: Princeton University Press, 2008), 260, cited in Sophia Beal, *Brazil Under Construction: Fiction and Public Works* (New York: Palgrave Macmillan, 2013), 7. See also Patricia Acerbi, "'A Long Poem of Walking': Flâneurs, Vendors, and Chronicles of Post-Abolition Rio de Janeiro," *Journal of Urban History* 40:1 (2014): 97–115. Acerbi describes how chroniclers constructed an "alternative urban citizenship" that included street vendors whom Brazilian authorities sought to exclude.

28. Historians have found similar patterns among other rural and urban citizens in Mexico who appropriated liberal and conservative ideas to advance their own interests. See, for example, Richard A. Warren, *Vagrants and Citizens: Politics and the Masses in Mexico City from Colony to Republic* (Lanham, MD: Rowman & Littlefield,

2007); Peter Guardino, *"The Time of Liberty": Popular Political Culture in Oaxaca, 1750–1850* (Durham, NC: Duke University Press, 2005); Florencia Mallon, *Peasant and Nation: The Making of Postcolonial Mexico and Peru* (Berkeley: University of California Press, 1995); and Benjamin T. Smith, *The Roots of Conservatism in Mexico: Catholicism, Society, and Politics in the Mixteca Baja, 1750–1962* (Albuquerque: University of New Mexico Press, 2012).

29. On patronage networks in nineteenth-century Mexico City, see Sonia Pérez Toledo, "Movilización social y poder político en la Ciudad de México en la década de 1830," in *Prácticas populares, cultura política y poder en México, siglo XIX*, ed. Brian Francis Hanley (Mexico City: Casa Juan Pablos, 2008), 335–67; and David W. Walker, "Porfirian Labor Politics: Working-Class Organizations in Mexico City and Porfirio Díaz, 1876–1902," *The Americas* 37:3 (1981): 257–89. On artisans' political participation in the nineteenth century, see Carlos Illades, *Hacia la república del trabajo: La organización artesanal en la Ciudad de México, 1853–1876* (Mexico City: Colegio de México, 1998); and Vanesa E. Teitelbaum, *Entre el control y la movilización: Honor, trabajo y solidaridades artesanales en la ciudad de México a mediados del siglo XIX* (Mexico City: El Colegio de México, 2008).

30. Michael Scardaville has described "the Habsburg notion of a paternalistic and benevolent state," which expected the sovereign, through his agents in the courts and elsewhere in the royal bureaucracy, to be both just and compassionate toward his subjects, particularly the poor. See "(Hapsburg) Law and (Bourbon) Order: State Authority, Popular Unrest, and the Criminal Justice System in Bourbon Mexico City," *The Americas* 50:4 (1994): 514. Scholars have shown that those sentiments persisted beyond colonial rule. Silvia Marina Arrom describes a "customary tolerance" for the poor that existed well into Mexico's liberal era. See *Containing the Poor: The Mexico City Poor House, 1774–1871* (Durham, NC: Duke University Press, 2000), 284. See also Marie Eileen Francois, *A Culture of Everyday Credit: Housekeeping, Pawnbroking, and Governance in Mexico City, 1750–1920* (Lincoln: University of Nebraska Press, 2006), 223. On paternalistic relations between street vendors and authorities in Mexico City, see the work of Juan Olvera Ramos, who traces the origins of those relations to the late seventeenth and early eighteenth centuries, when petty vendors in the Plaza Mayor began paying rent to the Ayuntamiento. Ricardo Gamboa Ramírez has noted that municipal officials continued to express paternalistic sentiments for poor vendors in the first half of the nineteenth century, and that those feelings influenced their enforcement of local market regulations. Judith Martí finds that vendors played to those same sentiments during the Porfiriato, noting that "goodwill, mercy, and compassion" were standard tropes in their petitions. More recently, Ingrid Bleynat has argued that the specific combination of the Ayuntamiento's fiscal needs and the elite's duty of compassion for the poor framed relations between market vendors, the elite, and the Ayuntamiento in the last third of the nineteenth century. See Gamboa Ramírez, "Las finanzas municipales de la ciudad de México. 1800–1850," in *La ciudad de México en la primera mitad del siglo XIX*, ed. Regina Hernández Franyuti (Mexico City: Instituto Mora, 1994), 1:35; Olvera Ramos, *Mercados*, 131; Martí, "Nineteenth-Century Views

of Women's Participation in Mexico's Markets," in *Women Traders in Cross-Cultural Perspective: Mediating Identities, Marketing Wares*, ed. Linda Seligmann (Stanford, CA: Stanford University Press, 2002), 39; and Bleynat, "Taxes and Compassion: Public Markets between 1867 and 1880" (Paper presented at the Mellon Latin American History Conference, Chicago, May 2–3, 2008); and "Trading with Power: Mexico City's Public Markets, 1867–1958" (Ph.D. diss., Harvard University, 2013), ch. 1.

31. Census records from the late nineteenth century show that many baratilleros could read and write. Indeed, throughout the market's history, most vendors signed their own names to petitions.

32. Although women were present on virtually every petition the baratilleros signed and in nearly every census the Ayuntamiento conducted of the market, they were always a minority. In contrast, women played a much more significant—or at least more visible—role among vendors of fruits and vegetables and prepared foods in Mexico City. The difference likely stems from the fact that many baratilleros were artisans by training—tailors, blacksmiths, cobblers, and craftsmen in other trades in which men predominated. For comparison, see Susie Porter, "'And That It Is Custom Makes It Law': Class Conflict and Gender Ideology in the Public Sphere, Mexico City, 1880–1910," *Social Science History* 24:1 (2000): 113, where Porter analyzes the gendered dynamic of street vending in the late nineteenth century.

33. Ángel Rama famously described writing in Latin America as an "instrument of state power." In Jürgen Habermas's original conception of the public sphere it was a bourgeois venue for discourse. See Rama, *The Lettered City*, trans. John Chasteen (Durham, NC: Duke University Press, 1996), xi; and Habermas, *The Structural Transformation of the Public Sphere: An Inquiry into a Category of Bourgeois Society*, trans. Thomas Burger (Cambridge, MA: MIT Press, 1989). James Sanders has described a "public sphere of the street" in mid-nineteenth-century Latin America, an argument for expanding the concept of the public sphere beyond the canon of Latin America's letrados to include sources such as public speeches. This study's conception of street politics similarly seeks to broaden the Latin American political sphere but it does by focusing specifically on a group of citizens who made their living on the streets of the city. See Sanders, *The Vanguard of the Atlantic World: Contesting Modernity in Nineteenth-Century Latin America* (Durham, NC: Duke University Press, 2011), 15.

34. Scholars who have studied vendors in late nineteenth- and twentieth-century Mexico have also found that those actors engaged in local and national politics. This study contributes to that scholarship by demonstrating that baratilleros participated earlier and more extensively in the urban political arena than other types of vendors. See Christina M. Jiménez, "From the Lettered City to the Sellers' City: Vendor Politics and Public Space in Urban Mexico, 1880–1926," in *The Spaces of the Modern City: Imaginaries, Politics, and Everyday Life*, ed. Gyan Prakash and Kevin M. Kruse (Princeton, NJ: Princeton University Press, 2008), 214–46; and idem, "Performing Their Right to the City: Political Uses of Public Space in a Mexican City, 1880–1910s," *Urban History* 33:3 (2006): 435–56; Porter, "And That It Is Custom";

Martí, "Nineteenth-Century Views"; Bleynat, "Trading with Power"; and Sandra C. Mendiola García, *Street Democracy: Vendors, Violence, and Public Space in Late Twentieth-Century Mexico* (Lincoln: University of Nebraska Press, 2017).

35. On the relative absence of revolutionary violence in Mexico City, see Eric Van Young, "Islands in the Storm: Quiet Cities and Violent Countrysides in the Mexican Independence Era," *Past & Present* 118:1 (1988): 130–55, and John Lear, *Workers, Neighbors, and Citizens: The Revolution in Mexico City* (Lincoln: University of Nebraska Press, 2001), intro.

36. A good example of this interpretation is Juan Pedro Viqueira Albán's *Propriety and Permissiveness in Bourbon Mexico*, trans. Sonia Lipsett-Rivera and Sergio Rivera Ayala (Wilmington, DE: Scholarly Resources, 1999). Viqueira Albán describes how "the state and the common people clashed over control of the streets" (100, 103). Anton Rosenthal notes that the historiography of urban Latin America paints the plaza as both a point of contact between different social classes and a site of popular protest. See "Spectacle, Fear, and Protest: A Guide to the History of Urban Public Space in Latin America," *Social Science History* 24:1 (2000): 33–73. On the role of the plaza in modern-day protest movements in Latin America, see Setha M. Low, *On the Plaza: The Politics of Public Space and Culture* (Austin: University of Texas Press, 2000).

37. Pamela Voekel notes that in the eighteenth century, "The *gente culta* strove to drive popular culture out of the streets and plazas—to marginalize it geographically—and to replace it with a display of their rational organization of public space." See "Peeing on the Palace: Bodily Resistance to Bourbon Reforms in Mexico City," *Journal of Historical Sociology* 5:2 (1992): 193. Susie Porter discusses attempts by authorities in the Porfiriato to redefine public spaces in the capital by excluding certain populations, including female street vendors. See "And That It Is Custom," 135. See also William H. Beezley, Cheryl English Martin, and William E. French, eds., *Rituals of Rule, Rituals of Resistance: Public Celebrations and Popular Culture in Mexico* (Wilmington, DE: Scholarly Resources, 1994), intro.

38. There is no evidence that baratilleros ever had their own guild, or, in the nineteenth century, a mutual aid society. Vendors in the market began to form labor unions after Mexico's 1917 constitution was enacted.

39. On the notion of "rights poverty" and legal inequality in urban Brazil, see Brodwyn Fischer, *A Poverty of Rights: Citizenship and Inequality in Twentieth-Century Rio de Janeiro* (Stanford, CA: Stanford University Press, 2008).

40. Colonial-era documents that deal with the Baratillo mention race inconsistently. After independence, however, when Mexico dissolved its racial classification system and stopped identifying people's race in official documents, those references all but disappear.

41. This study forms part of a growing body of work in Mexico and other regions of Latin America that bridge the colonial-national divide. See, for example, Guardino, *"Time of Liberty"*; Smith, *Roots of Conservatism*; and Pamela Voekel, *Alone Before God: The Religious Origins of Modernity in Mexico* (Durham, NC: Duke University Press, 2002). On Mexico City, specifically, see Arrom, *Containing the*

Poor; Francois, *Everyday Credit*; and Sonia Pérez Toledo, *Los hijos del trabajo: Los artesanos de la ciudad de México, 1780–1853* (Mexico City: El Colegio de México, 1996). Beyond Mexico, see Sarah Chambers, *From Subjects to Citizens: Honor, Gender, and Politics in Arequipa, Peru, 1780–1854* (University Park: Pennsylvania State University Press, 1999).

CHAPTER 1. A PERNICIOUS COMMERCE

1. For centuries, Carlos de Sigüenza y Góngora's August 30, 1692, letter to Admiral Pez was the authoritative account on the riot. Sigüenza y Góngora blamed the city's Indians, whom he called "the most ungrateful, thankless, grumbling, and restless people that God ever created." For an English translation of the letter, see Irving A. Leonard, *Don Carlos de Sigüenza y Góngora: A Mexican Savant of the Seventeenth Century* (Berkeley: University of California Press, 1929), 251–56 (the text's quote is found on page 244). In recent decades, however, historians have turned to the trial records and official correspondence housed in Spain's Archivo General de Indias in order to paint a fuller picture of the events, using witness testimony. R. Douglas Cope argues that the riot stemmed from a breakdown in the traditional lines of communication between the urban poor and authorities—a protest that "began as a political message but degenerated . . . [into] an 'every man for himself' orgy of looting" (Cope, *Limits*, 160). Natalia Silva Prada argues in *La política de una rebelión: Los indígenas frente al tumulto de 1692 en la Ciudad de México* (Mexico City: El Colegio de México, 2007) that the riot was a premeditated attack on colonial authority, led by members of Mexico City's indigenous nobility. The summary of the events that appears in the above paragraphs draws on Sigüenza y Góngora's letter, reprinted in Leonard, *Don Carlos*, 233–277; Silva Prada, *Política de una rebelión*, 235–43; and Cope, *Limits*, 125–60.

2. Cope, *Limits*, 155–56.

3. Silva Prada, *Política de una rebelión*, 247.

4. The colonial-era Ayuntamiento consisted of *alcaldes* and *regidores*. Regidores were appointed by the Crown, and their positions were permanent and hereditary. In the seventeenth century, they became purchasable. The regidores (who numbered between 12 and 30 during the colonial era) elected two alcaldes (sometimes known as *alcaldes ordinarios*) annually, and these officials served as judges of first instance. The corregidor was the local magistrate, a royal official, who sat in on the cabildo sessions. For more analysis of the Ayuntamiento in the seventeenth century, see María Luisa Pazos Pazos, *El Ayuntamiento de la Ciudad de México en el siglo XVII: Continuidad institucional y cambio social* (Seville: Diputación Provincial de Sevilla, 1999). See also Iván Escamilla González, "Inspirados por el Espíritú Santo: Elecciones y vida política corporativa en la capital de la Nueva España," in *Las elecciones en la ciudad de México, 1376–2005*, ed. Gustavo Ernesto Emmerich (Mexico City: Instituto Electoral del Distrito Federal/UAM, 2005), 83–84.

5. AHCM, Ayuntamiento, Cédulas y Reales Ordenes, vol. 2977, exp. 13, f. 2v.

6. María del Carmen León Cázares, *La Plaza Mayor de la Ciudad de México en la vida cotidiana de sus habitantes (siglos XVI–XVII)* (Mexico City: Instituto de Estudios y Documentos Históricos, 1982), 91–93.

7. The Mexica, who originated in the north of present-day Mexico, founded the city of Tenochtitlán in the fourteenth century. From there, they built the polity known as the Aztec Empire, which incorporated different ethnic groups from the Valley of Mexico and beyond. Work on the original Spanish cathedral finished in 1532, but the church underwent significant renovations and expansions over time and the exterior was not completed until 1813. Ibid., 98–100.

8. Barbara Mundy, *The Death of Aztec Tenochtitlan, the Life of Mexico City* (Austin: University of Texas Press, 2015), 80. The Spanish conquistadors marveled at Tlatelolco's marketplace. See Bernal Díaz del Castillo, *The History of the Conquest of New Spain*, ed. David Carrasco (Albuquerque: University of New Mexico Press, 2008), 173.

9. Robert Ricard, "La Plaza Mayor en España y en América española," *Estudios geográficos* 11:39 (1950): 321–27. Ricard notes that Spanish plazas did not typically include churches; this was a New World innovation.

10. Ricard contrasts the Spanish practice of placing the market in a town's main square with the Muslim tradition that dominated in medieval Iberia, in which local leaders placed markets, viewed as sites of potential criminality or violence, outside city walls. Ibid., 323–24.

11. Luis González Obregón, *México viejo* (Mexico City: Promexa Editores, 1979), 404; Jesús Galindo y Villa, *La Plaza Mayor de la ciudad de México* (Mexico City: Museo Nacional de Arqueología, Historia y Etnología, 1914), 327.

12. After the fall of Tenochtitlán in 1521, the city's principal food market remained in the heavily indigenous western and southern sections of the city and continued to be governed by indigenous nobles throughout much of the sixteenth century. It was probably not until the late sixteenth or early seventeenth century that indigenous food vendors began relocating in significant numbers to the Plaza Mayor, turning that site into the main distribution point for staples—a transition, as Mundy has argued, that paralleled the gradual Hispanicization of Mexico City. See Mundy, *Death of Aztec Tenochtitlan*, 81–94.

13. AHCM, Ayuntamiento, Cédulas y Reales Ordenes, vol. 2977, exp. 10, fs. 2v–3. The two principal sources of income to municipal governments in Spanish America were propios, income derived from selling or renting municipal assets, and *arbitrios*, a share of taxes that the Crown collected and passed on to the municipal government.

14. On the Aztec economy, see Kenneth Hirth and Deborah L. Nichols, "The Structure of Aztec Commerce: Markets and Merchants," in *The Oxford Handbook of the Aztecs*, ed. Nichols and Enrique Rodríguez-Alegría (New York: Oxford University Press, 2016), 281–98.

15. Nieto Sánchez, *Historia del Rastro*, 21.

16. AHCM, Ayuntamiento, Rastros y Mercados, vol. 3728, exp. 2, f. 4v.

17. AGN, Reales Cédulas, Duplicadas, vol. D15, exp. 168, f. 127–28. A 1602 decree banned the selling of used iron in "public plazas and *tianguises*," but does

not reference the Baratillo by name. The *tianguis* is a rotating, weekly market—an indigenous institution that continues to this day in Mexico. See AGN, Ordenanzas, vol. 2, exp. 107, fol. 120v. Iron goods were imported from Europe and therefore expensive in Mexico, spurring a vibrant secondary market in used and stolen iron tools. Although such markets were common throughout the preindustrial world, the absence of a local iron-smelting industry in Mexico probably contributed to the Baratillo's appeal. See Alexander von Humboldt, *Political Essay on the Kingdom of New Spain* (New York: I. Riley, 1811), 110–12. On the reuse of iron products in early modern England, see Donald Woodward, "'Swords into Ploughshares': Recycling in Pre-Industrial England," *Economic History Review* 38:2 (1985): 183–86.

18. On Spanish concerns about crime in late seventeenth-century Mexico City, see Haslip-Viera, *Crime and Punishment*, 40.

19. AGN, Reales Cédulas Originales, vol. 22, exp. 73, f. 2. The alcaldes del crimen served on the criminal court of the Real Audiencia. See Haslip-Viera, *Crime and Punishment*, 44.

20. AHCM, Ayuntamiento, Rastros y Mercados, vol. 3728, exp. 2.

21. Ibid., fs. 6–8. The decree did, however, give indigenous vendors the option of applying for a spot in another location, provided they did so within fifteen days. The Spanish often granted Indians exemptions from economic regulations.

22. AGN, Reales Cédulas Duplicadas vol. D15, exp. 168, f. 127–28.

23. AGN, Reales Cédulas Originales, vol. 22, exp. 73, f. 2. In Hispanic society, where the natural law tradition remained dominant throughout the early modern period, the "just price" (here referred to as the "true value") was based on the "common price" of the marketplace, which in turn was considered "natural" and "reasonable." Prices that diverged from the norm—whether considerably higher or lower—drew the attention of authorities. See Pierre Vilar, *A History of Gold and Money, 1450–1920*, trans. Judith White (London: NLB, 1969), 158.

24. AHCM, Ayuntamiento, Rastros y Mercados, vol. 3728, exp. 2, f. 9v. Given authorities' frequent complaints about the Baratillo's trade in stolen goods, criminal records documenting those acts are surprisingly scarce. This issue stems from the loss of many archival documents during the 1692 riot and the limited cataloging to date of the criminal records that have survived, making it difficult to locate cases dealing specifically with the Baratillo. For two sample cases, see: AGN, TSJDF, Corregidor de México, vol. 16, exp. 57; and AGN, Inquisición, vol. 1575, exp. 12.

25. Norman F. Martin, *Los vagabundos en la Nueva España: Siglo XVI* (Mexico City: Editorial Jus, 1957), viii, 41, 46.

26. Haslip-Viera, *Crime and Punishment*, 13.

27. Parish priests conducted censuses between 1690 and 1692 of Indian barrios in the capital and found that hundreds of skilled Indian laborers were living in the traza. See Cope, *Limits*, 89–90.

28. Cope, *Limits*, 24. For a detailed investigation into the relationship between the medieval Spanish concept of *limpieza de sangre*, or purity of blood, and the sistema de castas as it developed in New Spain, see María Elena Martínez, *Genealogical*

Fictions: Limpieza de Sangre, *Religion, and Gender in Colonial Mexico* (Stanford, CA: Stanford University Press, 2008). On the construction of categories of difference in the sixteenth century, prior to the evolution of the sistema de castas, see Robert C. Schwaller, Géneros de Gente *in Early Colonial Mexico: Defining Racial Difference* (Norman: University of Oklahoma Press, 2016). In the seventeenth century, the term *chino* referred to Asian slaves who arrived in New Spain via the Spanish Philippines. See Tatiana Seijas, *Asian Slaves in Colonial Mexico: From Chinos to Indians* (New York: Cambridge University Press, 2014).

29. For an overview of the scholarship on the sistema de castas and New Spain's racial hierarchies, see Jake Frederick, "Without Impediment: Crossing Racial Boundaries in Colonial Mexico," *The Americas* 67:4 (2011): 497–98. See also Seijas, *Asian Slaves*, who shows how Asian slaves in New Spain effectively turned themselves into Indians, making them free vassals of the Spanish Crown.

30. Cope, *Limits,* 55–56.

31. AGN, Bienes Nacionales, vol. 546, exp. 7.

32. AHCM, Ayuntamiento, Rastros y Mercados, vol. 3728, exp. 2, f. 9v. References to the diversity of the market's participants abound. See, for example, the letter from the alcaldes del crimen to the corregidor of Mexico City complaining of the "Indians and many others" who bought and sold there. AHCM, Ayuntamiento, Rastros y Mercados, vol. 3728, exp. 2, f. 19v (August 14, 1693).

33. Cope and Silva Prada have argued that the trial records support Sigüenza y Góngora's contention that Indians led the riot, noting that the lists identifying those individuals who were wounded or killed on June 8 indicate that the majority of those who took part in the riot were indigenous. Silva Prada estimates that just over 77 percent of the rioters were indigenous. Although Sigüenza y Góngora highlights the role of indigenous women in the riot, the trial records suggest the majority of the rioters were male. See Cope, *Limits,* 157; and Silva Prada, *Política de una rebelión,* 251–52.

34. Anna More, *Baroque Sovereignty: Carlos de Sigüenza y Góngora and the Creole Archive of Colonial Mexico* (Philadelphia: University of Pennsylvania Press, 2013), 164–67.

35. "Sobre los inconvenientes de vivir los indios en el centro de la ciudad," *Boletín del Archivo General de la Nación* 9:1 (1938): 22, 33.

36. Silva Prada, *Política de una rebelión,* 329.

37. Carlos Sigüenza y Góngora, *Relaciones históricas* (Mexico City: UNAM, 1940), 152–53.

38. Silva Prada, *Política de una rebelión,* 373; 600–601; 381–82. While there are no market censuses of the Baratillo from the late seventeenth century, investigations that guild overseers conducted in the early eighteenth century reveal that artisans from those trades often sold in the Baratillo.

39. Inga Clendinnen, *Ambivalent Conquests: Maya and Spaniard in Yucatan, 1517–1570* (New York: Cambridge University Press, 2003), 58.

40. "Sobre los inconvenientes," 33.

41. AHCM, Ayuntamiento, Rastros y Mercados, vol. 3728, exp. 3, f. 2.

42. Ibid., exp. 2, f. 9v, 13v.

43. Ibid., exp. 2, f. 13.

44. Ibid., exp. 2, f. 21.

45. Ibid., exp. 2, f. 13v.

46. AHCM, Ayuntamiento, Cédulas y Reales Ordenes, vol. 2977, exp. 13, fs. 2–2v. The word *alcaicería* historically referred to the structure in the cities of Moorish Spain where growers brought silk to be taxed.

47. Ibid.

48. John Lynch described Charles II as the "last, most degenerate and the most pathetic victim of Habsburg inbreeding." Lynch, *The Hispanic World in Crisis and Change, 1598–1700* (New York: Basil Blackwell, 1992), 348. Henry Kamen offered a more tempered view, noting that Charles II "showed considerable independence and initiative, but never ruled in any real sense," while a revisionist assessment by Christopher Storrs highlights the significant administrative reforms the monarchy undertook under the last Habsburg king. See Kamen, *Spain in the Later Seventeenth Century, 1665–1700* (New York: Longman, 1980), 20–22; and Storrs, *The Resilience of the Spanish Monarchy, 1665–1700* (New York: Oxford University Press, 2006), 188–89. Juan Pedro Viqueira Albán has observed the paradoxical nature of the reforms the Habsburgs enacted after the riot. On the one hand, they sought to reinforce the old hierarchies of the caste system. On the other, they presaged some of the Enlightenment-inspired reforms the Bourbons implemented in the eighteenth century. See Viqueira Albán, *Propriety and Permissiveness*, 9–10.

49. The Bourbons' urban reform projects in Mexico City have received attention from a number of historians, including: Voekel, "Peeing on the Palace"; Viqueira Albán, *Propriety and Permissiveness*; and Sharon Bailey Glasco, *Constructing Mexico City: Colonial Conflicts over Culture, Space, and Authority* (New York: Palgrave Macmillan, 2010).

50. Leonard, *Don Carlos*, 260; Sigüenza y Góngora, *Relaciones históricas*, 149.

51. Several historians have suggested that the Baratillo was in the Plaza del Volador in this period. Given the centrality of students at the university—located on one side of that plaza—in the events that transpired in March 1696, that location seems logical. However, contemporary sources suggest that the Baratillo was still in the Plaza Mayor. The gallows and whipping post that the students attempted to burn were in the city's main square. There was at least one attempt, in April 1696, to reestablish the Baratillo in the Plaza del Volador, but authorities quickly thwarted it. See AGN, TSJDF, Corregidor de México, vol. 16, exp. 58. María Rebeca Yoma Medina and Luis Alberto Martos López, *Dos mercados en la historia de la ciudad de México: El Volador y la Merced* (Mexico City: Secretaría General de Desarrollo Social, Departamento del Distrito Federal/INAH, 1990), 59; and Haslip-Viera, *Crime and Punishment*, 40, locate the Baratillo in the Plaza del Volador in this period.

52. AHCM, Ayuntamiento, Rastros y Mercados, vol. 3728, exp. 4, f. 78v; AGN, Reales Cédulas Originales, vol. 28, exp. 11, f. 25v.

53. AHCM, Ayuntamiento, Rastros y Mercados, vol. 3728, exp. 4, f. 79–80; AGN, Reales Cédulas Originales, vol. 28, exp. 11, f. 24v. Gerónimo Chacón blamed

Galve for the riot, claiming that if he had come out of the convent he might have halted the uprising. See "Memorial ajustado de acusaciones, enviadas por Don Jerónimo Chacón Abarca, Alcalde del Crimen más antiguo de la Real Audiencia de México a Don Baltasar Tovar, del Consejo de su majestad y fiscal de la Real Audiencia de México, Juez de Residencia del conde de Galve," in María Pilar Gutiérrez Lorenzo, *De la Corte de Castilla al Virreinato de México: El conde de Galve (1653–1697)* (Guadalajara: Excma. Diputación Provincial, 1993), 186.

54. AHCM, Ayuntamiento, Rastros y Mercados, vol. 3728, exp. 4, fs. 95, 97.

55. Ibid., exp. 4, f. 96.

56. Ibid, exp. 4, fs. 113, 99–99v. Enrique González González, "La universidad: Estudiantes y doctores," in *Historia de la vida cotidiana en México*, vol. 2: *La ciudad barroca*, ed. Antonio Rubial García (Mexico City: FCE, 2005), 262.

57. ACHM, Ayuntamiento, Rastros y Mercados, vol. 3728, exp. 4, fs. 115–16v.

58. AGI, México, 64, R. 2, N. 21, f. 13.

59. AGN, General de Parte, vol. 17, exp. 182, f. 192; AGN, Reales Cédulas Originales, vol. 22, exp. 73, f. 2. Interestingly, Charles II had issued a new order on January 6, 1696, to ban the Baratillo—three months before the incident involving González de Castro. It is unlikely that the order reached Mexico City before March 27. A typical trip from Seville to Veracruz, New Spain's principal Atlantic port, took ten to thirteen weeks, but additional time was necessary to travel from Madrid to Seville and then up the mountains from Veracruz to Mexico City. See J. H. Elliott, *Empires of the Atlantic World: Britain and Spain in America, 1492–1830* (New Haven, CT: Yale University Press, 2007), 50; AGN, Reales Cédulas Originales, vol. 27, exp. 42.

60. Juan Ortega y Montañéz, *Instrucción reservada que dio a su sucesor en el mando, el Conde de Moctezuma*, prologue and notes by Norman F. Martin (Mexico City: Editorial Jus, 1965), 174.

61. In 1690, the vicar Don Diego de la Sierra ordered that no man could enter the market wearing his habit. AGN, Matrimonios, vol. 255, exp. 15.

62. Silva Prada, *Política de una rebelión*, 50–53.

63. AGN, Reales Cédulas Originales, vol. 27, exp. 67, f. 155 (October 2, 1696).

64. Ibid., exp. 42, f. 1.

65. Sigüenza y Góngora describes Galve's success at beating back the pirates along Mexico's coasts. See *Relaciones históricas*. Silva Prada argues that these unstable conditions facilitated a "reconstruction of ethnic identity" in Mexico, which, in turn, led Mexico City's Indians to plan and execute the riot of 1692. See Silva Prada, *Política de una rebelión*, 28–32.

66. "Memorial ajustado de acusaciones," 117.

67. AGN, Reales Cédulas Originales, vol. 28, exp. 11, f. 24v (February 24, 1698).

68. ACHM, Ayuntamiento, Rastros y Mercados, vol. 3728, exp. 4, fs. 118–21v.

69. Mikhail Bakhtin, *Rabelais and His World*, trans. Hélene Iswolsky (Bloomington: Indiana University Press, 1984), 154, 160.

70. Antonio de Robles, *Diario de sucesos notables, 1665–1703* (Mexico City: Porrúa, 1946), 41.

71. AHCM, Ayuntamiento, Plaza Mayor, vol. 3618, exp. 4, fs. 1 and 2. Beginning in 1694, the city auctioned off the right to collect rent from vendors in the Plaza Mayor, including the merchants of the Baratillo. For more on Cameros, who held the asiento until his death in 1741, see AHCM, Ayuntamiento, Plaza Mayor, vol. 3618, exps. 1, 9, 10.

72. AHCM, Ayuntamiento, Rastros y Mercados, vol. 3728, exp. 2, fs. 4–5.

73. Ibid., exp. 2, fs. 18v–19 (August 14, 1693).

74. Ibid.

75. Ibid., exp. 2, fs. 21–21v (August 17, 1693).

76. Ibid., exp. 2, f. 22.

77. Olvera Ramos, *Mercados*, 29.

78. Pazos Pazos, *Ayuntamiento*, 175; AHCM, Ayuntamiento, Rastros y Mercados, vol. 3728, exp. 3.

79. AHCM, Ayuntamiento, Rastros y Mercados, vol. 3728, exp. 3, fs. 1–1v. Another estimate put the loss at fifteen thousand pesos per year. See AHCM, Ayuntamiento, Alcaicería, vol. 343, exp. 1, f. 1.

80. Pazos Pazos, *Ayuntamiento*, 186–87.

81. AHCM, Ayuntamiento, Rastros y Mercados, vol. 3728, exp. 2, fs. 19–22. Gorráez did agree with Gerónimo Chacón and other members of the Audiencia, however, that the Baratillo needed to be relocated.

CHAPTER 2. THE BARATILLO AND
THE ENLIGHTENED CITY

1. Pedro Anselmo Chreslos Jache, "Ordenanzas del Baratillo," AHMNA, Colección Antigua, MS 292, prologue, para. 3; para. 2, 52. The manuscript has been digitized and is available on the website of the Biblioteca Nacional de España. One of the satirical letters in the manuscript is dated 1734, but the work itself is undated. Ilona Katzew dates it to 1754. The work was never published, but some people in eighteenth-century Mexico seem to have been familiar with it. In his 1763 travel narrative, *Diario del viaje a la Nueva España*, Francisco de Ajofrín includes a section on the Baratillo in which he notes that he lacks sufficient space to describe the "tangles and sophistications of the Baratillo" and instead directs his reader to consult the market's "constitutions, which are in manuscript, and he will enjoy himself with its beautiful method and salty style"—an all-but-certain reference to the "Ordenanzas." See Katzew, *Casta Paintings*, 56; and Francisco de Ajofrín, *Diario del viaje a la Nueva España* (Mexico City: Secretaría de Educación Pública, 1986), 65. Pulquerías served pulque, a Mesoamerican alcoholic drink made from the maguey plant; *tepacherías* served a version of that drink with sugar. See Augusto Godoy, Teófilo Herrera, and Miguel Ulloa, *Más allá del pulque y el tepache: Las bebidas alcohólicas no destiladas indígenas de México* (Mexico City: UNAM, Instituto de Investigaciones Antropológicas, 2003), 21–22, 42.

2. Chreslos Jache, "Ordenanzas," paras. 4, 10.

3. Regina Hernández Franyuti, "Ideología, proyectos y urbanización en la ciudad de México, 1760–1850," in *La ciudad de México*, ed. Hernández Franyuti, 1:119–20.

4. Charles II's attempts to hand over Spain and its empire to a French ruler sparked the War of Spanish Succession, which engaged the French, British, Dutch, and other powers in Europe. It ended in 1713 with the French-born Philip V retaining control of Spain and its American possessions but ceding Sicily, the Spanish Netherlands, and other European possessions to its rivals. See Iván Escamilla González, Matilde Souto Mantecón, and Guadalupe Pinzón Rios, eds., *Resonancias imperiales: El Tratado de Utrecht de 1713* (Mexico City: UNAM, 2015).

5. María Dolores Morales, "Cambios en la traza de la estructura vial de la ciudad de México, 1770–1855," in *La ciudad de México*, ed. Hernández Franyuti, 1:163. For a look at the projects themselves, see AHCM, Ayuntamiento, Calles: Alineamientos, vol. 444.

6. R. Douglas Cope has noted that colonial elites found petty commerce in Mexico City "both remarkable and dismaying." See "The Marvelous and the Abominable," 3.

7. Pamela Voekel, for example, describes a "new antagonism between elite and popular cultures" that arose from the Bourbon reforms of the late eighteenth century, while Cope describes the formation of an oppositional, multiracial plebeian subculture in the late seventeenth and early eighteenth centuries. Juan Pedro Viqueira Albán describes the Bourbon elite's attempt to fashion a new identity for itself through new regulations on popular behavior after 1750. Sharon Bailey Glasco argues that Bourbon urban renewal projects in Mexico City in the late eighteenth century sought to "quell [elite] anxieties through a reshaping of plebeian culture." Sites of popular sociability that received increased scrutiny under the Bourbons included pulquerías, ball games, and festivals. See Voekel, "Peeing on the Palace," 202; Cope, *Limits*, 163; Viqueira Albán, *Propriety and Permissiveness*; and Glasco, *Constructing Mexico City*, 1.

8. Charles Walker, in his study of eighteenth-century urban reforms in Lima, similarly observes that historians often make broad generalizations about the upper classes, when, in reality, that social category contained diverse viewpoints and agendas. Walker, "Civilize or Control?," 84.

9. This system, if inefficient at times, held many advantages for the Spanish Crown, which sought to prevent individuals or interest groups in the Americas from gaining too much power at the expense of the king.

10. Viqueira Albán, *Propriety and Permissiveness*, 103.

11. Juan de Viera, *Breve y compendiosa narración de la Ciudad de México* (Mexico City: Instituto Mora, 1993), 32–34.

12. Ibid., 34–35.

13. AHCM, Ayuntamiento, Rastros y Mercados, vol. 3728, exp. 34, f. 48. The Parián also offered some Mexican-made goods.

14. Ajofrín, *Diario*, 68.

15. Chreslos Jache, "Ordenanzas," prologue, para. 12. In New Spain, the coins in circulation were the silver *peso* (known in the Anglophone world as the "piece of

eight"—because it was worth eight reales) and silver coins valued at four, two, one, and one-half real. As New Spain had no coins worth less than a half-real until the end of the eighteenth century, and that coin was too large for many of the goods sold in the city's markets and general stores, shopkeepers made their own tokens out of wood, metal, or even soap that were called *tlacos* (worth one-eighth of a real) and *pilones* (worth one-sixteenth of a real). Indigenous food vendors frequently traded in cacao beans, whose worth fluctuated based on the price of cacao. Tlacos and cacao beans did, in fact, circulate in the Baratillo, where they were exchanged for silver pesos. See AGN, Archivo Histórico de Hacienda, vol. 1152, exp. 1, f. 3 (1768); and José Enrique Covarrubias, *La moneda de cobre en México, 1760–1842: Un problema administrativo* (Mexico City: UNAM/Instituto Mora, 2000).

16. Chreslos Jache, "Ordenanzas," paras. 29–31. The list of eligible races reads like an encyclopedia of New Spain's eighteenth-century caste system—a literary counterpart to the casta paintings Katzew explores in her book.

17. Chreslos Jache, "Ordenanzas," prologue, paras. 21–22.

18. Hipólito Villarroel, *Enfermedades políticas que padece la capital de esta Nueva España . . .* (Mexico City: Editorial Porrúa, 1999), 213–14. Here Villarroel quotes an unnamed source, which he describes only as "a certain report."

19. Many Hispanic elites in eighteenth-century Mexico, including the author of the "Ordenanzas," worried about the downward mobility of Spaniards. In her study of Mexico City's poor house, Silvia Arrom argued that one of the motivations for establishing the poorhouse (in 1774) was to reinforce the sistema de castas by supporting Spaniards who had fallen on hard times. See Arrom, *Containing the Poor*, 157.

20. Revillagigedo and Mena, *El Segundo Conde*, 454–55.

21. In their defense of Viceroy Revillagigedo II in his juicio de residencia at the end of the eighteenth century, a group of religious officials cited two royal decrees from earlier in the century that banned the Baratillo—one from December 21, 1735, and another from October 22, 1744. I did not locate those decrees, nor did I find any other references to them. Furthermore, the dates closely resemble those of two seventeenth-century decrees that banned the market (December 24, 1635, and October 22, 1644), suggesting that the authors may have misstated the date on which those decrees were issued (see Revillagigedo and Mena, *El Segundo Conde*, 454). It is entirely possible that the Bourbon Crown issued one or more decrees prohibiting the Baratillo that I did not uncover or that did not survive. If it did give such an order, however, it could not have had any lasting impact, as there is a nearly continuous record of the market's existence throughout the century.

22. Ernesto de la Torre Villar, *Instrucciones y memorias para los virreyes novohispanos*, 2 vols. (Mexico City: Editorial Porrúa, 1991), 2:776. Spanish viceroys typically left a formal set of recommendations for their successors.

23. Ibid.

24. See Viqueira Albán, *Propriety and Permissiveness*, 175–76. Viqueira Albán notes that the system was based on René Descartes's mathematical hypotheses.

25. Esteban Sánchez de Tagle, "La remodelación urbana de la ciudad de México en el siglo XVIII: Una reforma virreinal," in *El impacto de las reformas borbónicas*, ed. Lombardo de Ruiz, 135.

26. Esteban Sánchez de Tagle, " La remodelación urbana de la ciudad de México en el siglo XVIII: Una crítica de los supuestos," *Tiempos de América* 5/6 (2000): 12–14.

27. Ayuntamientos were technically autonomous institutions, and no law explicitly subordinated them to the Crown. They were not formally integrated into the hierarchy of government until the founding of a federal republic in Mexico in 1824. Sergio Miranda Pacheco, "La fundación del Distrito Federal y los avatares de su régimen político institucional (1808–1857)," in *Poder y gobierno local en México, 1808–1857*, ed. María del Carmen Salinas Sandoval, Diana Birrichaga Gardida, and Antonio Escobar Ohmstede (Mexico City: El Colegio Mexiquense/El Colegio de Michoacán, 2011), 109. See also Hernández Franyuti, "Ideología, proyectos y urbanización."

28. Recent scholarship on the Bourbon Reforms elsewhere in Spanish America has emphasized their contested nature. Kenneth Andrien notes that the reforms lacked a "consistent, coherent ideological vision," while Gabriel Paquette has stressed the "idiosyncratic and uneven nature" of the reforms. Charles Walker, in examining Bourbon-era urban reforms in Lima, finds that the state failed to successfully take control of key urban public spaces because of reformers' lack of commitment to their own plans and to the resistance they encountered from various quarters. This scholarship challenges studies of Mexico City, by Viqueira Albán, Voekel, and others that viewed the reforms as a coherent, and to some extent successful, attempt by elites to reshape the urban built environment. See Kenneth Andrien, "The Politics of Reform in Spain's Atlantic Empire during the Late Bourbon Period: The Visita of José García de León y Pizarro in Quito," *Journal of Latin American Studies* 41:4 (2009): 637–62; Gabriel B. Paquette, *Enlightenment, Governance, and Reform in Spain and Its Empire, 1759–1808* (New York: Palgrave Macmillan, 2008), 153 (cited in Andrien); Walker, "Civilize or Control?"; Viqueira Albán, *Propriety and Permissiveness*; and Voekel, "Peeing on the Palace."

29. On the fiscal importance of markets to the Ayuntamiento in the colonial era, see Pazos Pazos, *Ayuntamiento*, 186–87; and Timothy E. Anna, "The Finances of Mexico City during the War of Independence," *Journal of Latin American Studies* 4:1 (1972): 57–59. On tensions between royal and municipal authorities over the Baratillo and Plaza Mayor markets, see Pazos Pazos, *Ayuntamiento*, 175, and Olvera Ramos, *Mercados*, 99.

30. The Spanish Crown wanted the Ayuntamiento's finances in good order to promote stability in the viceregal capital and so the local government could fund public works and other projects that the Crown wanted.

31. In the 1770s, the Spanish Crown sought to reduce the influence of wealthy Creole families on the Ayuntamiento by requiring a minimum number of peninsular-born Spaniards on the body. The reforms had only a limited impact. See John E. Kicza, "The Great Families of Mexico: Elite Maintenance and Business Practices in

Late Colonial Mexico City," *Hispanic American Historical Review* 62:3 (1982): 450–52; and Timothy E. Anna, *The Fall of Royal Government in Mexico City* (Lincoln: University of Nebraska Press, 1978), 27.

32. AHCM, Ayuntamiento, Cédulas y Reales Ordenes, vol. 2977, exp. 13, fs. 6–6v.

33. AHCM, Ayuntamiento, Plaza Mayor, vol. 3618, exp. 10, f. 1v. Cameros won the first contract with a bid of 1,300 pesos for one year and went on to win every subsequent bidding process, paying between 700 and 1,400 pesos per year, with successively longer contracts, until his death in 1741. After Cameros died, his executor Juan de Sau took over the asiento until the practice was abandoned in 1745, and the lessee was replaced by the *juez de plaza*. AHCM, Ayuntamiento, Plaza Mayor, vol. 3618, exps. 1, 9, 10.

34. The phasing of these projects is also significant: as Esteban Sánchez de Tagle points out, they began well before the reign of Charles III (1759–1788), the period historians generally associate with the Bourbon Reforms in the Americas. Scholars are increasingly looking at the reforms that began under Philip V (1700–1746) and Ferdinand VI (1746–1759) and at the continuities between Habsburg and Bourbon rule. See Sánchez de Tagle, "Reforma virreinal"; and Francisco A. Elissa-Barroso and Ainara Vázquez Varela, eds., *Early Bourbon Spanish America: Politics and Society in a Forgotten Era (1700–1759)* (Leiden: Brill, 2013).

35. AHCM, Ayuntamiento, Plaza Mayor, vol. 3618, exp. 11; AHCM, Ayuntamiento, Plaza Mayor, vol. 3618, exp. 12, fs. 1v–2.

36. AHCM, Ayuntamiento, Plaza Mayor, vol. 3618, exp. 12, which also contains a rendering of the proposed project.

37. Ibid., exp. 13.

38. Ibid., exp. 14 (1776).

39. Ibid., exp. 19, f. 2.

40. Gálvez created a new fiscal bureaucracy in New Spain that professionalized tax collection. For more information on Gálvez's reforms, see Herbert Ingraham Priestley, *José de Gálvez: Visitor-General of New Spain 1765–1771* (Berkeley: University of California Press, 1916); and Linda Salvucci, "Costumbres viejas, 'hombres nuevos': José de Gálvez y la burocracia fiscal novohispana (1754–1800)," *Historia Mexicana* 33:2 (1983): 224–64.

41. AHCM, Ayuntamiento, Justicia, Ordenanzas, vol. 2984, exp. 21.

42. AHCM, Ayuntamiento, Rastros y Mercados, vol. 3728, exp. 9, f. 3.

43. AHCM, Ayuntamiento, Justicia, Ordenanzas, vol. 2984, exp. 21, fs. 78v–79.

44. The city's total income in 1791 was 148,058 pesos. The Parián contributed 25,448 pesos, or slightly more than 17 percent. Colonial-era governments reported income from the Plaza Mayor markets using different methods, so it is difficult to plot the Baratillo's fiscal contributions over time. The line in the 1791 budget that includes the Baratillo reads "Puestos del centro del Baratillo y Plaza Mayor." In 1791, Viceroy Revillagigedo II had begun the process of removing the market stands from the Plaza Mayor, so the 7,146 pesos would have come almost entirely from the Baratillo Grande. The figure thus probably underreports the total rent the city was collecting from the two Baratillos in this era. Indeed, reports from the 1780s suggests

that the market produced over 20,000 pesos per year. See AGN, Indiferente Virreinal, caja 629, exp. 3; AHCM, Ayuntamiento, Propios y Arbitrios, vol. 576, exp. 1.

45. Pazos Pazos notes that the viceroy Duke of Albuquerque struck a deal with Mexico City's Ayuntamiento in 1658 to provide it with a small percentage of sales from the royal pulque monopoly in exchange for eliminating the Baratillo, but the arrangement lasted for only a decade. See Pazos Pazos, *Ayuntamiento*, 175.

46. AHCM, Actas de Cabildo, vol. 55A, fs. 46v–50 (September 26 and October 24, 1729). Olvera Ramos argues that street vendors who paid rent to the Ayuntamiento became clients of the local government and benefited from the aldermen's paternalism. See *Mercados*, 131.

47. Revillagigedo II was the son of Francisco de Güemes y Horcasitas, Conde de Revillagigedo I, who served as viceroy of New Spain from 1746 to 1755 and was himself an important Bourbon-era reformer. Interestingly, Revillagigedo II was a Creole, born in Havana in 1740 while his father served as captain-general of that colony.

48. On Revillagigedo's reforms of popular behaviors, see Voekel, "Peeing on the Palace," 188–89. For details of Revillagigedo's plan (spearheaded by his chief architect, Ignacio Castera) to reform the barrios by extending the street grid of the traza, see AGN, Obras Públicas, vol. 2, exp. 1; Regina Hernández Franyuti, *Ignacio de Castera: Arquitecto y urbanista de la Ciudad de México, 1777–1811* (Mexico City: Instituto Mora, 1997); and Sonia Lombardo de Ruiz, "Ideas y proyectos urbanísticos de la Ciudad de México, 1788–1850," in *Ciudad de México: Ensayo de construcción de una historia*, ed. Alejandra Moreno Toscando (Mexico City: SEP/INAH, 1978), 169–88.

49. The previous method of funding the paving project involved requesting that each property owner pay for the cobblestone paving in front of his or her address. Revillagigedo introduced a tax of two granos per square vara, which seems to have helped speed up the process but, as Sánchez de Tagle has noted, the tax was regressive because it required property owners in poorer outlying areas, whose streets would not be paved, to pay for paving in the wealthier central zone of the city. Sánchez de Tagle, "Reforma virreinal," 131–32.

50. AGN, Archivo Histórico de Hacienda, vol. 550, exp. 35. These descriptions of the Plaza Mayor come from the interrogatory Revillagigedo and his lawyers produced to defend the viceroy in his juicio de residencia.

51. AHCM, Ayuntamiento, Rastros y Mercados, vol. 3728, exp. 16.

52. Yoma Medina and Martos López, *Dos mercados*, 69; AHCM, Ayuntamiento, Rastros y Mercados, vol. 3728, exp. 21.

53. In 1822, a group of vendors used these regulations to bolster a complaint about a market administrator's poor job performance. AHCM, Ayuntamiento, Rastros y Mercados, vol. 3730, exp. 120, fs. 1–2.

54. AHCM, Ayuntamiento, Rastros y Mercados, vol. 3728, exp. 10; and AHCM, Ayuntamiento, Rastros y Mercados, vol. 3729, exp. 53. This project began under Viceroy Antonio María de Bucareli, who governed New Spain from 1771 to 1779.

55. For a copy of the printed *Reglamento* see AGN, Impresos Oficiales, vol. 18, exp. 40. Correspondence related to the issue of the new regulations is located at AGN, Obras Públicas, vol. 8, exp. 4–5.

56. Usually conducted informally, these transactions left little evidence of how they functioned. For two examples, see AGN, Indiferente Virreinal, caja 5288, exp. 55, which contains a balance sheet for one such traspaso, in 1767; and AHCM, Ayuntamiento, Hacienda, Propios y Acreedores, vol. 2231, exp. 64.

57. Officials and vendors frequently used the term "ownership" in the documents, even though the Ayuntamiento was the actual owner of the space a stand occupied; its occupants were lessees.

58. AGN, Impresos Oficiales, vol. 18, exp. 40.

59. AHCM, Ayuntamiento, Hacienda, Propios y Acreedores, vol. 2231, exp. 64, fs. 4v–6v.

60. See AGN, Indiferente Virreinal, caja 1838, exp. 35. AGN, Consulado, vol. 245, exp. 7; AGN, Consulado, vol. 10, exp. 15.

61. AHCM, Ayuntamiento, Rastros y Mercados, vol. 3728, exp. 17, f. 3.

62. Ibid., exp. 10, fs. 24–25.

63. AHCM, Ayuntamiento, Fincas: Mercados, vol. 1100, exp. 2; AGN, Mercados, vol. 1, exps. 7–9. Religious institutions, including convents, were indispensable financial institutions in colonial Spanish America. See Asunción Lavrin, "The Role of the Nunneries in the Economy of New Spain in the Eighteenth Century," *Hispanic American Historical Review* 46:4 (1966): 371–93; and Kathryn Burns, *Colonial Habits: Convents and the Spiritual Economy of Cuzco, Peru* (Durham, NC: Duke University Press, 1999).

64. AGN, Indiferente Virreinal, caja 5093, exp. 2, fs. 32–32v.

65. Ibid., f. 33.

66. AHCM, Ayuntamiento, Rastros y Mercados, vol. 3728, exp. 34, fs. 4–4v.

67. AGN, Indiferente Virreinal, caja 5093, exp. 2, fs. 130–31. The word *plazuela* was a diminutive term for *plaza*.

68. Revillagigedo and Mena, *El Segundo Conde*, 451. It is important to note that the word *policía* had a broader implication in eighteenth- and nineteenth-century Spanish than "policing" does in English. The policing of a city in that era involved providing not only public security but also a general assurance of well-being for its residents, including cleaning and maintenance of public spaces and facilities. See Rodríguez Kuri, *La experiencia olvidada*, 21, 33.

69. Under Spanish law, ayuntamientos were responsible for the police and any public works projects that needed to be undertaken in the locality. See Sergio Miranda Pacheco, *Historia de la desaparición del municipio en el Distrito Federal* (Mexico City: Unidad Obrera y Socialista, 1998), ch. 1.

70. For example, Revillagigedo apparently took 120,000 pesos from the *desagüe* project that sought to solve the city's flooding problem and applied it elsewhere (AHCM, Ayuntamiento, Historia: Juicio de Residencia del Virrey Revillagigedo, vol. 2289, exp. 1, f. 120). For a more detailed examination of the Ayuntamiento's complaints, see Sergio Miranda Pacheco, "El juicio de residencia al virrey Revilla-

gigedo y los intereses oligárquicos en la ciudad de México," *Estudios de Historia Novahispana* 29 (2003): 49–75.

71. AHCM, Ayuntamiento, Historia: Juicio de Residencia del Virrey Revillagigedo, vol. 2289, exp. 1, f. 24. The source of this figure is not clear. In his instructions to his successor, Revillagigedo claims to have increased the yearly income from the city's main marketplace from 12,500 pesos to 24,800 pesos. Data located in the AGN show that after a dip in 1790–91 while the Volador market was under construction, overall income from the city's marketplaces (excluding the Parián) surged to 20,876 pesos in 1792 from an average of around 12,000 pesos in the 1780s. In 1792 and 1793, the Volador market produced roughly 13,000 pesos per year, a modest increase from the 11,000 pesos per year the Plaza Mayor markets brought in prior to 1790. See Juan Vicente Güemez Pacheco de Padilla Horcasitas y Aguayo, *Informe sobre las misiones, 1793, e instrucción reservada al Marqués de Branciforte, 1794* (Mexico City: Editorial Jus, 1966), 179–80; AGN, Indiferente Virreinal, caja 5093, exp. 2.

72. AGN, Indiferente Virreinal, caja 5093, exp. 2., f. 42. For the petition that vendors in the Volador market sent to authorities asking them to moderate their rents, see AHCM, Ayuntamiento, Rastros y Mercados, vol. 3728, exp. 22. Revillagigedo listed the new, higher rents in his 1791 *Reglamento*, located at AGN, Impresos Oficiales, vol. 18, exp. 40. In his instructions to his successor, the Marquis of Branciforte, Revillagigedo defended his decision to raise rents by explaining that vendors no longer had to pay for night watchmen, as that post was now held by a municipal employee. See Güemez Pacheco de Padilla Horcasitas y Aguayo, *Informe sobre las misiones*, 179–80.

73. AHCM, Ayuntamiento, Historia: Juicio de Residencia del Virrey Revillagigedo, vol. 2289, exp. 1, fs. 27–29v.

74. Miranda Pacheco, "Juicio de residencia."

75. Anna, "Finances," 69. Anna argues that the Ayuntamiento went broke during the wars for independence in part because it was forced to absorb extraordinary costs (bearing the entire burden of an epidemic in 1813), but mostly because of its own gross mismanagement of funds.

76. AHCM, Ayuntamiento, Historia: Juicio de Residencia del Virrey Revillagigedo, vol. 2289, exp. 1, fs. 46, 92–94v.

77. In 1791, only the *sisa*, or wine tax, contributed more to the municipal treasury than the Plaza Mayor markets. AGN, Indiferente Virreinal, caja 629, exp. 3.

78. See, for example, their claim that the higher rents in the Volador market harmed consumers by raising prices and that the relocation of certain items to the new markets in the Plazas del Factor and Santa Catarina required residents to travel to distant parts of the city to buy what they needed. They also criticized Castera's project to straighten streets in the Indian barrios, which required demolishing the homes of "miserable people, where they maintained the trades that they subsist on." AHCM, Ayuntamiento, Historia: Juicio de Residencia del Virrey Revillagigedo, vol. 2289, exp. 1, fs. 42, 174, 57.

79. AGN, Archivo Histórico de Hacienda, vol. 550, exp. 35. AHCM, Ayuntamiento, Historia: Juicio de Residencia del Virrey Revillagigedo, vol. 2289, exp. 1, f. 73.

80. Certainly, the Ayuntamiento's concerns for the city's poor could have been disingenuous. Yet the fact that they believed that this argument would resonate with the Crown nonetheless suggests that "traditional" notions of the common good still held sway at the end of the eighteenth century. Rationality had not replaced earlier sentiments. On the persistence of Habsburg-era customs in the Bourbon period, see Scardaville, "(Hapsburg) Law."

81. The Ayuntamiento's hereditary structure allowed Creoles, many of whose families had purchased their seats on the council in the sixteenth or seventeenth centuries, to maintain control of the body despite the Bourbons' efforts to stack it with peninsular Spaniards in the eighteenth century. See Anna, *Fall of Royal Government*, 26.

82. AHCM, Ayuntamiento, Historia: Juicio de Residencia del Virrey Revillagigedo, vol. 2289, exp. 1, fs. 115, 147.

83. AHCM, Ayuntamiento, Rastros y Mercados, vol. 3729, exp. 91.

84. Ibid., vol. 3728, exp. 41.

85. Ibid., vol. 3729, exp. 92.

86. Ibid., vol. 3728, exp. 34.

87. In addition to the viceroy's overspending on public works projects, the Crown was annoyed that Revillagigedo refused to abolish the Intendancy of Mexico, as it had demanded. Some members of the Ayuntamiento went around the viceroy to improve relations with peninsular authorities in the 1790s, obtaining the right to name honorary members to the body. See Miranda Pacheco, "Juicio de residencia," 48.

CHAPTER 3. SHADOW ECONOMICS

1. AHCM, Ayuntamiento, Hacienda, Propios y Acreedores, vol. 2230, exp. 12. Chreslos Jache makes the same accusations in "Ordenanzas del Baratillo," paras. 54 and 60.

2. On the middle sectors of late-colonial Mexico, see Francois, *Everyday Credit*, 2–3; and Arrom, *Containing the Poor*. On the subject of social mobility within Mexico's middle sectors, see Brígida von Mentz's edited volume, *Movilidad social de sectores medios en México: Una retrospectiva histórica (siglos XVII al XX)* (Mexico City: CIESAS, 2003).

3. John E. Kicza, *Colonial Entrepreneurs: Families and Business in Bourbon Mexico City* (Albuquerque: University of New Mexico Press, 1983), 4, 101–2, 107. On the merchants of the Consulado, see Louisa Schell Hoberman, *Mexico's Merchant Elite, 1590–1660: Silver, State, and Society* (Durham, NC: Duke University Press, 1991); and Guillermina del Valle Pavón, ed., *Mercaderes, comercio y consulados de Nueva España en el siglo XVIII* (Mexico City: Instituto Mora/CONACYT, 2003).

4. Kicza, *Colonial Entrepreneurs*, 112. See also Jay Kinsbrunner, *Petty Capitalism in Spanish America: The Pulperos of Puebla, Mexico City, Caracas, and Buenos Aires* (Boulder, CO: Westview Press, 1987).

5. Francois, *Everyday Credit*, 49.

6. Juan de Solórzano y Pereyra, *Política indiana* (Madrid: Atlas, 1972), Book 6, ch. 14, 63, quoted in Guillermina del Valle Pavón, "El régimen de privilegios de la Universidad de Mercaderes de la ciudad de México," in *Cuerpo político y pluralidad de derechos: Los privilegios de las corporaciones novohispanas*, ed. Beatriz Rojas (Mexico City: CIDE, 2007), 165.

7. Kicza, *Colonial Entrepreneurs*, 101.

8. Although demographic data on street vendors is hard to come by, most references to fruit and vegetable sellers, as well as to vendors of prepared foods such as tortillas, *atole*, and *chía*, a popular drink, show that they were typically women. See Cope, "The Marvelous and the Abominable," 14–15.

9. The term *indio chino* referred to a native of the Philippines. See Seijas, *Asian Slaves*, 5–6. For marriage records that mention baratilleros, see: AGN, Matrimonios, vol. 6, exp. 77; vol. 23, exp. 10; vol. 23, exp. 21; vol. 23, exp. 29; vol. 34, exp. 59; vol. 32, exp. 8; vol. 32, exp. 18; vol. 32, exp. 48; vol. 71, exp. 47; vol. 71, exp. 78; vol. 78, exp. 53; vol. 84, exp. 9; vol. 89, exp. 4; vol. 89, exp. 115; vol. 99, exp. 18; vol. 103, exp. 67; vol. 104, exp. 77; vol. 108, exp. 8; vol. 108, exp. 21; vol. 108, exp. 44; vol. 109, exp. 35; vol. 141, exp. 19; vol. 162, exp. 38; vol. 165, exp. 100; vol. 174, exp. 94; vol. 221, exp. 2. These records span from 1722 to 1778. The files identify the ages of twenty of those men; the median age in that sample is 38.5 years, suggesting that baratilleros were, on average, middle-aged and Spanish.

10. According to the 1811 census, the blacksmith, tinsmith, and tailor guilds had large majorities of Spanish members. Carpenters and weavers, two other professions represented in the Baratillo, had pluralities of Spanish members. See Jorge González Angulo Aguirre, *Artesanado y ciudad a finales del siglo XVIII* (Mexico City: Fondo de Cultura Económica, 1983), 153–55.

11. AGN, Indiferente Virreinal, caja 5979, exp. 72; AGN, Indiferente Virreinal, caja 1321, exp. 24. Owners of the cajones typically signed three-month leases for fifty pesos with the Ayuntamiento.

12. AHAGNCM, Fondo Antiguo, Sección Notarías Siglos XVI–XIX, Miguel de Castro Cid, vol. 842bis; AGN, Indiferente Virreinal, caja 4520, exp. 35.

13. AGN, Intestados, vol. 32, exps. 10–11.

14. AGN, Indiferente Virreinal, caja 4520, exp. 35.

15. AHCM, Ayuntamiento, Fincas: Mercados, vol. 1100, exps. 3, 9. A man described only as "Don Valentín" paid thirteen reales per week for two puestos in the Baratillo in 1782. AHCM, Ayuntamiento, Hacienda, Propios: Parián, vol. 2237, exp. 28. Unfortunately, there do not appear to be any comprehensive lists of either rental prices or the values of individual businesses in the Baratillo during the colonial period.

16. AGN, Indiferente Virreinal, caja 5610, exp. 52.

17. The demand for Mexican silver abroad meant that the vast majority of silver coins left the colony. For a general discussion of the centrality of credit to the colonial Mexican economy, see Jeremy Baskes, *Indians, Merchants, and Markets: A Reinterpretation of the* Repartimiento *and Spanish-Indian Economic Relations in*

Colonial Oaxaca, 1750–1821 (Stanford, CA: Stanford University Press, 2000), 93–94.

18. AHCM, Ayuntamiento, Hacienda, Propios y Acreedores, vol. 2230, exp. 7. Owners of import warehouses in New Spain bought merchandise that arrived on ships from Spain and the Philippines in bulk, including a large variety of goods, not all of which may have been suitable for sale in their warehouses. Carmen Yuste notes the wide range of economic actors who had a stake in Spanish overseas trade, including petty merchants. See Carmen Yuste, ed., *Comerciantes mexicanos en el siglo XVIII* (Mexico City: UNAM, 1991), introduction.

19. AHCM, Ayuntamiento, Real Audiencia, Fiel Ejecutoría, Veedores, Gremios, vol. 3832, exp. 46.

20. AGN, Intestados, vol. 32, exp. 10.

21. On the centrality of pawnbroking in the economy of eighteenth-, nineteenth-, and early twentieth-century Mexico City, see Francois, *Everyday Credit*.

22. Fernández de Lizardi, *El periquillo sarniento*, 151. A *pícaro* is a rogue, usually a mischievous young man, around which the picaresque, a Spanish literary genre, grew in the early modern period. An *hombre de bien*, in the simplest terms, was a gentleman. For a more extensive discussion of the latter term, see Michael P. Costeloe, *The Central Republic in Mexico, 1835–1846: Hombres de Bien in the Age of Santa Anna* (New York: Cambridge University Press, 1993), 16–17.

23. Viera, *Narración*, 32–35.

24. AHCM, Ayuntamiento, Real Audiencia, Fiel Ejecutoría, Veedores, Gremios, vol. 3832, exp. 40.

25. In the second half of the eighteenth century skilled workers made between four reales and one peso per day, while unskilled workers generally made three reales. See Amílcar Challú and Aurora Gómez-Galvarriato, "Mexico's Real Wages in the Age of the Great Divergence, 1730–1930," *Revista de Historia Económica Journal of Iberian and Latin American Economic History* 33:1 (2015): 96; and Francois, *Everyday Credit*, 24.

26. See Francois, *Everyday Credit*.

27. AGN, Industria y Comercio, vol. 5, exp. 2, f. 15v. The Monte de Piedad was established to rein in the excesses of private pawnshops. See Francois, *Everyday Credit*, 70. See also Esperanza Cabrera Siles and Patricia Escandón, *Historia del Nacional Monte de Piedad, 1775–1993* (Mexico City: Nacional Monte de Piedad, 1993).

28. Carlos Rubén Ruiz Medrano, *El gremio de plateros en Nueva España* (San Luis Potosí, Mexico: El Colegio de San Luis, 2001), 19, 57–58.

29. See Bromley, "Introduction: The Urban Informal Sector," 1033; and Guha-Khasnobis, Kanbur, and Ostrom, "Beyond Formality and Informality."

30. Hernando de Soto makes this argument most forcefully in *The Other Path*.

31. See, e.g., Guha-Khasnobis, Kanbur, and Ostrom, "Beyond Formality and Informality"; and Cope, "The Marvelous and the Abominable."

32. Textiles produced in Mexican obrajes, or workshops, were relatively expensive and generally of inferior quality to imported European fabrics. See Richard

Salvucci, *Textiles and Capitalism in Mexico: An Economic History of the Obrajes, 1539–1840* (Princeton, NJ: Princeton University Press, 1987), 9. As Marie Francois (*Everyday Credit*) has shown, both lower-class and middle-class residents used clothes as investment vehicles. See also Beverly Lemire, "The Theft of Clothes and Popular Consumerism in Early Modern England," *Journal of Social History* 24:2 (1990): 270. Lemire notes that a good wardrobe in early modern England was "akin to a savings account."

33. *Diario de México*, February 24, 1816, 2.

34. AGN, Indiferente Virreinal, caja 148, exp. 43. In January 1821, the prosecutor recommended five years of labor in a fort in Veracruz for both men. The archives also abound with criminal cases against soldiers accused of selling their uniforms. See, for example, AGN, Indiferente Virreinal, caja 6544, exp. 33; caja 5076, exp. 26; and caja 6445, exp. 79.

35. Martha Few similarly finds that the illicit economy of healers in colonial Santiago de Guatemala linked urban and rural areas. See Few, *Women Who Live Evil Lives: Gender, Religion, and the Politics of Power in Colonial Guatemala* (Austin: University of Texas Press, 2002), 7.

36. AHCM, Ayuntamiento, Rastros y Mercados, vol. 3728, exp. 11, f. 1v; AGN, Archivo Histórico de Hacienda, vol. 550, exp. 35.

37. See AHCM, Ayuntamiento, Rastros y Mercados, vol. 3728, exp. 12 (1780); AGN, Indiferente Virreinal, caja 5828, exp. 37 (1813); and AHCM, Ayuntamiento, Fincas: Mercados, vol. 1100, exp. 11 (1819).

38. AGN, Inquisición, vol. 993, exp. 2.

39. Ibid., vol. 1043, exp. 10.

40. Ibid., vol. 1381, exp. 2. This category of crime referred to reckless or inadvertent expressions that challenged Catholic orthodoxy. For more on booksellers in eighteenth-century Mexico City, see Olivia Moreno Gamboa, "Hacía una tipología de libreros en la ciudad de México (1700–1778)," *Estudios de Historia Novohispana* 40 (2009): 121–46.

41. Occasionally, traspasos in the Baratillo show up in notarial records. In 1754, Manuel González paid 800 pesos to Pedro de la Lama for his cajón in the Baratillo (the price included only the stand itself, with no merchandise inside). But it turned out that de la Lama did not actually own that cajón, and he was forced to return the guante to González. AHAGNCM, Fondo Antiguo, Sección Notarías Siglos XVI–XIX, Juan Amador de Estrada, vol. 193, fs. 444–44v, 472v–73v.

42. AHCM, Ayuntamiento, Rastros y Mercados, vol. 3728, exp. 11, fs. 1–2.

43. Ibid., fs. 4–4v.

44. Ibid., f. 5v.

45. Ruiz Medrano, *El gremio de plateros*, 19, 57–58.

46. AGN, Archivo Histórico de Hacienda, vol. 1152, exp. 1 (1768).

47. In 1758, the viceroy Marqués de Amarillas ordered that shopkeepers must accept tlacos issued by their competitors, and he fixed the exchange rate between silver reales and tlacos at 1:8. See "Ordenanzas para el régimen y govierno de los tenderos y tiendas de pulpería . . ." reprinted in Miguel L. Muñoz, *Tlacos y pilones:*

La moneda del pueblo de México (Mexico City: Fondo de Cultura Económica, 1976), 159–74; Covarrubias, *Moneda de cobre*, 48.

48. AHCM, Ayuntamiento, Hacienda, Propios y Acreedores, vol. 2230, exp. 10.

49. Historians and social scientists who study street markets in the twentieth and twenty-first centuries have similarly found that state actors, particularly police and municipal officials, have often done more to perpetuate informality than to rein it in. See Goldstein, *Owners of the Sidewalk*, 75; Chazkel, *Laws of Chance*, 71; and Mario Barbosa Cruz, *El trabajo en las calles: Subsistencia y negociación política en la ciudad de México a comienzos del siglo XX* (Mexico City: El Colegio de México/ UAM Cuajimalpa, 2008), 262.

50. For background on the development and evolution of the guild system in colonial Latin America see: Lyman Johnson, "Artisans," in *Cities and Society in Colonial Latin America*, ed. Louisa Schell Hoberman and Susan Migden Socolow (Albuquerque: University of New Mexico Press, 1986), 227–50.

51. Colonial authorities were particularly concerned about Spanish, mestizo, and African middlemen who intercepted Indian producers on their way to market, seizing their goods. Beginning as early as the 1520s, Spaniards were forbidden to buy from Indians for the purpose of reselling. See Charles Gibson, *The Aztecs Under Spanish Rule: A History of the Indians of the Valley of Mexico, 1519–1810* (Stanford, CA: Stanford University Press, 1964), 360; Angulo Aguirre, *Artesanado y ciudad*, 45–46. See also R. Douglas Cope, "The Underground Economy in Eighteenth-Century Mexico City" (Paper presented at the Boston Area Latin American History Workshop, David Rockefeller Center, Harvard University, March 2006), for an expanded discussion of regatonería. Colonial authorities also carefully regulated the prices of basic staples, even meat, to ensure the population's subsistence. See Enriqueta Quiroz Muñoz *Entre el lujo y la subsistencia: Mercado, abastecimiento y precios de la carne en la ciudad de México, 1750–1812* (Mexico City: El Colegio de México, 2005).

52. The tailors' guild was the largest in Mexico City in 1788. Pérez Toledo, *Los hijos del trabajo*, 75.

53. Cope, "Underground Economy"; Cope, *Limits*, 108–9; Jorge González Angulo Aguirre, "Los gremios de artesanos y la estructura urbana," in *Ciudad de México*, ed. Moreno Toscana, 25–36.

54. AGN, Cédulas, Duplicados, vol. D15, exp. 168, f. 127. The alcabala was a sales tax levied on a good each time it changed hands. For most of the colonial period, the alcabala did not apply to goods that were resold within Mexico City. This exclusion likely would have covered baratilleros dealing in second-hand goods. In all cases, the Consulado, which collected the tax on behalf of the Crown between 1644 and 1661 and again between 1673 and 1753, had broad discretion in how it collected the tax. Indians were exempt from the alcabala unless they traded in goods that originated overseas. See Robert Sidney Smith, "Sales Tax in New Spain, 1575–1700," *Hispanic American Historical Review* 28:1 (1948): 23–24. On the Consulado's administration of the alcabala, see also David Brading, *Miners and Merchants in Bourbon Mexico 1763–1810* (New York: Cambridge University Press, 1971), 113.

55. AHCM, Ayuntamiento, Rastros y Mercados, vol. 3728, exps. 2, 4. The 1635 order is referenced in Ibid., exp. 2 (1688).

56. Most guilds had two veedores, who were chosen by the masters of that guild. Those elections were overseen by the Ayuntamiento. Angulo Aguirre, *Artesanado y ciudad*, 36.

57. The tribunal of the fiel ejecutoría served as the municipal consumer protection authority, setting prices for basic staples and investigating accusations of fraud. Mexico City's corregidor, or local magistrate, and two elected alcaldes, members of the Ayuntamiento, sat on the tribunal. In the case of conviction, the corregidor determined the sentence, while the alcaldes were responsible for visiting commercial establishments and determining whether they were conforming to the regulations. See Martha Leticia Espinoza Peregrino's thesis, "El Tribunal de Fiel Ejecutoría de la Ciudad de México, 1724–1790: El control del Cabildo en el comercio urbano" (Undergraduate thesis, Escuela Nacional de Antropología e Historia, 2002), 64–65, 122.

58. AHCM, Ayuntamiento, Real Audiencia, Fiel Ejecutoría, Veedores, Gremios, vol. 3832, exp. 3, f. 6.

59. AGN, Indios, vol. 12, exp. 72, f. 201.

60. See Norman F. Martin, "La desnudez en la Nueva España del siglo XVIII," *Anuario de Estudios Americanos* 29 (1972): 275.

61. AGN, Reales Cédulas Duplicadas, vol. D45, exp. 159, fs. 302–2v.

62. AHCM, Ayuntamiento, Real Audiencia, Fiel Ejecutoría, Veedores, Gremios, vol. 3832, exp. 6, f. 1.

63. Ibid., fs. 1–1v.

64. Ibid., f. 1v. The tension between tailors and clothing vendors appears to have been a largely internecine struggle that took place within the tailor guild, as there was no separate guild for *roperos*.

65. AHCM, Ayuntamiento, Real Audiencia, Fiel Ejecutoría, Veedores, Gremios, vol. 3832, exp. 3, fs. 4, 14v.

66. Ibid., fs. 22–23.

67. Yale University, Sterling Memorial Library, Mexico Collection HM 248, Part II, 1:35:36. Here the word *sangrada* appears to refer to the process by which two pieces that have been sewn together are separated—in short, another means of illegally altering clothing from its original state. See Real Academia Española, *Diccionario de la lengua castellana* (Madrid: Viuda de Ibarra, 1803), 774, 2.

68. Pérez Toledo, *Los hijos del trabajo*, 53–54. Iñigo García-Bryce argues that artisans in Lima held onto their middling status well into the nineteenth century, occupying a largely overlooked middle strata of society that included lawyers, doctors, shopkeepers, and notaries. See García-Bryce, *Crafting the Republic: Lima's Artisans and Nation Building in Peru, 1821–1879* (Albuquerque: University of New Mexico Press, 2004), 11.

69. Historians' analysis of the guilds' decline focuses mainly on the late eighteenth and early nineteenth centuries. Pérez Toledo, for example, begins her study of artisan guilds' transformations in 1780. Felipe Castro Gutiérrez argues that

the guild system entered into crisis following the 1774 publication of Pedro Rodríguez, Conde de Campomanes's *Discurso sobre el fomento de la industria popular*, though he finds that structural problems in the guilds began slightly earlier. See Pérez Toledo, *Los hijos del trabajo*; and Castro Gutiérrez, *La extinción de la artesanía gremial* (Mexico City: UNAM, 1986), 126.

70. Juan Hernández Chapas, caught selling new clothing in the Plaza del Volador, adjacent to the Plaza Mayor, in 1707, was a master in the guild, as was Miguel Samudio, at least by the end of his appeal. AHCM, Ayuntamiento, Real Audiencia, Fiel Ejecutoría, Veedores, Gremios, vol. 3832, exps. 3, 4.

71. Ibid., exp. 42.

72. Ibid.

73. Lizardi, *El periquillo sarniento*, 274.

74. AHCM, Ayuntamiento, Real Audiencia, Fiel Ejecutoría, Veedores, Gremios, vol. 3832, exp. 14.

75. Ibid., exp. 50.

76. Ibid., exp. 42.

77. On the importance of compassion in the Spanish colonial justice system, see Scardaville, "(Hapsburg) Law," 514. The medieval legal treatise *Siete Partidas* enshrined this principle: "Although the King is bound to defend all people of his land, he should have special concern for these [the miserable ones], for they are as people abandoned and with less counsel than others.... When they appeal to him, compassion should move him." Quoted in Woodraw Borah, *Justice by Insurance: The Indian General Court of Colonial Mexico and the Legal Aides of the Half-Real* (Berkeley: University of California Press, 1983), 13.

78. AHCM, Ayuntamiento, Real Audiencia, Fiel Ejecutoría, Veedores, Gremios, vol. 3832, exp. 3, f. 26.

79. See ibid., exp. 5, for another case in which Núñez de Villavicencio ruled in favor of a ropero. Ramírez, the coauthor of the baratilleros' petition to change the ordinances regarding new clothing sales, had his merchandise confiscated again in 1710 for not bearing the *sello*, or stamp of authenticity, that the guild gave to new clothes. Nuñez de Villavicencio again sided with the ropero, forcing the overseer to return the clothes to Ramírez. AHCM, Ayuntamiento, Real Audiencia, Fiel Ejecutoría, Veedores, Gremios, vol. 3832, exp. 9.

80. Ibid., exp. 3, fs. 5–5v.

81. Ibid., exp. 50, f. 5.

82. See R. Douglas Cope, "Between Liberty and Constraint: Government Regulation of Petty Commerce in Mexico City, 1700–1780" (Paper presented at the Latin American Studies Association Meeting, Washington, DC, September 2001); and John Leddy Phelan, *The People and the King: The Comunero Revolt in Colombia, 1781* (Madison: University of Wisconsin Press, 1978), 86.

83. On baratilleros' use of a nineteenth-century discourse of public health and hygiene, see AHCM, Ayuntamiento, Rastros y Mercados, vol. 3730, exp. 161 (1842).

84. For more on tensions between corregidores and the regidores of the Ayuntamiento of Mexico City, see Alejandro Cañeque, *The King's Living Image: The*

Culture and Politics of Viceregal Power in Colonial Mexico (New York: Routledge, 2004), 60.

85. AHCM, Ayuntamiento, Hacienda, Propios y Acreedores, vol. 2230, exp. 7, fs. 3–3v.

86. Ibid., exp. 12, f. 1.

87. Ibid., fs. 1–3v.

88. Ibid., f. 75.

89. Ibid., f. 74.

90. Ibid., fs. 3–5. An ordinance from 1588 banned roperos from calling out to people on the street to attract them to their stores, perhaps in an effort to distinguish shopkeepers from mercachifles. Juan Francisco del Barrio Lorenzot, ed., *El trabajo en México durante la epoca colonial: Ordenanzas de gremios de la Nueva España* (Mexico City: Secretaría de Gobernación, 1921), 36.

91. AGN, Reales Cédulas Duplicadas, vol. D15, exp. 168, fs. 127–28.

92. AGN, Reales Cédulas Originales, vol. 22, exp. 73, f. 2

93. AHCM, Ayuntamiento, Hacienda, Propios y Acreedores, vol. 2230, exp. 12.

94. See also Fernández de Lizardi's *Alacena de Frioleras*, in which he satirizes Mexicans' desire for inexpensive goods (a *friolera* is something with little worth or little importance and an *alacena* was a small store, like those in the Baratillo Grande). See José Joaquín Fernández de Lizardi, *Obras IV—Periódicos*, ed. María Rosa Palazón M. (Mexico City: UNAM, 1970). Unfortunately, the extant documentation makes it difficult to compare prices in the Baratillo with those in the cajones of the Plaza Mayor. Few records of prices in the Baratillo survived, and those that did often group items together (e.g., "silk and stitching for two pairs of stockings at two pesos, two reales"). Other evidence, like King Charles II's claim above about jewelry prices, is anecdotal. See AGN, Indiferente Virreinal, caja 6102, exp. 46; and AHCM, Ayuntamiento, Rastros y Mercados, vol. 3729, exp. 92, fs. 15v–17.

95. Retail merchants continued to be excluded from those privileges. William J. Callahan, *Honor, Commerce, and Industry in Eighteenth-Century Spain* (Boston: Harvard Business School Press, 1972), 71. See also Callahan, "A Note on the Real y General Junta de Comercio, 1679–1814," *Economic History Review* 21:3 (1968): 519–28.

96. Solórzano y Pereyra, *Política indiana*, Book 6, ch. 14, 63.

97. Gonzalo Gómez de Cervantes, *La vida económica y social de Nueva España al finalizar el siglo XVI* (Mexico City: Antigua Librería Robredo, 1944). Quoted in Brading, *Miners and Merchants*, 95.

98. AHCM, Ayuntamiento, Rastros y Mercados, vol. 3728, exp. 1.

99. At one time, the Crown required all merchants, regardless of stature, to obtain permits to sell in public plazas. For petty vendors, this practice came to an end in 1611 when the king granted the Mexico City Ayuntamiento the right to assign specific spaces for vendors to sell and to charge them rent for that privilege. The practice continued, however, for ambulatory vendors. See for example AGN, Reales Cédulas Duplicadas, vol. D35, exp. 238 (1644); and vol. D30, exp. 360 (1675). For examples of the permits given to indigenous vendors, see AGN, General de Parte,

vol. 1, exp. 479, f. 108v (1579); AGN, General de Parte, vol. 2, exp. 287, f. 61v (1579); and AGN, General de Parte, vol. 6, exp. 327, f. 125v (1602). On the discontinuation of permits for petty vending, see AHCM, Ayuntamiento, Cédulas y Reales Órdenes, vol. 2977, exp. 10.

100. AHCM, Ayuntamiento, Hacienda, Propios y Acreedores, vol. 2230, exp. 12, fs. 22–25. Dios Anzures also noted that "selling by hand" was illegal in Castile (f. 4). For the original files on the dispute in Zacatecas, see Archivo Histórico del Estado de Zacatecas, Ayuntamiento, Comercio, caja 1, exp. 46 and caja 2, exp. 56.

101. AHCM, Ayuntamiento, Hacienda, Propios y Acreedores, vol. 2230, exp. 12, fs. 78–78v.

102. In 1729, officials at Mexico City's cathedral sought to shutter the Baratillo because it was encouraging immoral behavior at the doorstep of the church. They referenced the case that "the cajoneros are pursuing," suggesting that authorities still had not rendered a decision by then (and probably never did). The religious officials' request gained no traction because the Ayuntamiento invoked its jurisdiction over the Plaza Mayor to block it. See AHCM, Actas de Cabildo, vol. 55A, fs. 46v–50.

103. Unfortunately, no register of the Consulado's membership exists for the 1720s. Kicza writes that membership in the Consulado hovered around 200; Valle Pavón finds the average to be lower, around 130 merchants, though it fluctuated over time. Kicza, *Colonial Entrepreneurs*, 51, 107–8; and Valle Pavón, "El régimen de privilegios," 163. For the Consulado's membership requirements, see *Ordenanzas del Consulado de México: Universidad de mercaderes de la Nueva España, confirmadas por el Rey en el año de 1607, impresas, por tercera vez en 1816*, located in AGN, Indiferente Virreinal, caja 5059, exp. 74.

104. Kicza, *Colonial Entrepreneurs*, 107–8.

105. Louisa Schell Hoberman argues that because of their extensive financial dealings with the colonial government—including their long-term control over the alcabala tax farm and their loans to the Crown—merchants expected to have a say in any legislation that affected their economic interests, and enjoyed the right to an official solicitor who represented them before royal authorities. Traditional Hispanic biases against merchants, however, prevented mercantile elites from ascending to the highest ranks of colonial government. See Hoberman, *Mexico's Merchant Elite*, 156; and Valle Pavón, "El regimen de privilegios," 168.

106. We will recall that the tailor Miguel Samudio sold eighty pesos of clothing—a hefty sum—to an itinerant merchant in a single transaction and that Fianca's two stands were worth about 25,000 pesos. AHCM, Ayuntamiento, Real Audiencia, Fiel Ejecutoría, Veedores, Gremios, vol. 3832, exp. 3; and AGN, Indiferente Virreinal, caja 4520, exp. 35.

107. See, for example, AHCM, Ayuntamiento, Hacienda, Propios y Acreedores, vol. 2230, exp. 7; and AHCM, Ayuntamiento, Real Audiencia, Fiel Ejecutoría, Veedores, Gremios, vol. 3832, exp. 50. Kicza notes that by the late colonial period as much as one-third of the adult male population in Mexico City had adopted the term "don" and many mixed-race and indigenous women used its feminine equivalent. Sarah Chambers observes a similar trend in late-colonial Arequipa, Peru. See

Kicza, "The Great Families of Mexico," 431; and Chambers, *From Subjects to Citizens*, 163–64. Still, not every stand owner is referred to as "don," suggesting that the title was not meaningless, and that some of these men possessed a higher social status than others.

108. Rivalries between street vendors and shopkeepers never went away. John Cross describes street vendors in late twentieth-century Mexico City as "the bane of the commercial bourgeoisie, who claim that they represent 'disloyal competition.'" Cross, *Informal Politics*, 18.

109. Kicza, *Colonial Entrepreneurs*, 265; Manuel Miño Grijalva, *Censo de población de la Ciudad de México, 1790* (Mexico City: El Colegio de México, 2003).

110. See Cope, *Limits*, ch. 6; and Mangan, *Trading Roles*, ch. 5.

111. Kicza, *Colonial Entrepreneurs*, 107–8.

112. As other historians have shown, the downward mobility of the white middle classes worried the Bourbon government in the eighteenth century and contributed to the establishment of the Mexico City poorhouse and the Monte de Piedad in the 1770s. Francois, *Everyday Credit*, 25.

113. AHCM, Ayuntamiento, Hacienda, Propios y Acreedores, vol. 2230, exp. 7. See also the petition from the vendors in the Plaza de Santa Catarina, who in 1773 asserted the import of their commerce to the community. AHCM, Ayuntamiento, Rastros y Mercados, vol. 3728, exp. 10, fs. 5–5v and discussed in Cope, "The Marvelous and the Abominable," 7–8.

114. AHCM, Ayuntamiento, Fincas: Mercados, vol. 1100, exp. 7 (1796); AHCM, Ayuntamiento, Créditos, Compensaciones, vol. 2062, exp. 21. Olvera Ramos notes that colonial confraternities also commonly had statues of the Virgin of Guadalupe. It is not clear if the baratilleros had their own confraternity; no source this study examined mentions one. See Olvera Ramos, "El Baratillo de la Plaza Mayor," 390.

115. AGN, Indiferente Virreinal, caja 5093, exp. 2, f. 130. Like many aspects of the shadow economy, authorship of these petitions is often murky. In the fiel ejecutoría cases discussed above, the baratilleros had a lawyer, de Córdova, whose name appears on the court records. In other instances and other types of cases, including this petition, the documents do not list the name of an attorney or any other author. A wide range of individuals might have been involved in the drafting of these documents—from lawyers to unlicensed legal aides to scribes to the vendors themselves—with different actors sometimes participating in different stages of the process. One of the most striking aspects of baratilleros' petitions, from the late eighteenth century onward, is that vendors almost always signed their own names, illustrating that they were at least partially literate and suggesting that there was a good chance they had read the documents they were signing. See Bianca Premo, *The Enlightenment on Trial: Ordinary Litigants and Colonialism in the Spanish Empire* (New York: Oxford University Press, 2017), 51; chapter 1 provides an excellent overview of legal petitioning in colonial Spanish America.

116. AHCM, Ayuntamiento, Hacienda, Propios y Acreedores, vol. 2230, exp. 7. There are additional complaints in the same file from other baratilleros about vendors outside the market who were harassing them.

117. "Baratillo," *Diario de México,* November 18, 1808. The Baratillo del Factor, as the market was called, combined the vendors of the Baratillo Chico of the Plaza Mayor and the Baratillo Grande that was in the interior patio of the Parián. See also AHCM, Ayuntamiento, Fincas: Mercados, vol. 1100, exp. 11, f. 2.

118. AHCM, Ayuntamiento, Rastros y Mercados, vol. 3728, exp. 2, f. 1920.

119. AHCM, Ayuntamiento, Hacienda, Propios y Acreedores, vol. 2230, exp. 7.

120. Torre Villar, *Instrucciones,* 776.

121. AHCM, Ayuntamiento, Hacienda, Propios y Acreedores, vol. 2230, exp. 12, fs. 74–74v.

122. Recall that in the period during which the Consulado operated the tax farm in Mexico (1644–1661 and 1673–1753), it generally did not collect the alcabala from petty merchants in the capital. See Smith, "Sales Tax in New Spain." On the Consulado's broader involvement in the finances of New Spain, see Guillermina del Valle Pavón, *El Consulado de comerciantes de la Ciudad de México y las finanzas novohispanas, 1582–1827* (Mexico City: El Colegio de México, 1997).

123. AGN, Archivo Histórico de Hacienda, vol. 550, exp. 53, no pagination. For additional discussion of this episode, see Cope, "Underground Economy."

124. Ibid., exp. 54, fs. 1v–2.

125. Ibid., exp. 53.

126. By 1790, only 360 of 818 militia members came from almacenes, and these men were almost always employees, rather than owners of the warehouses. Christon I. Archer, *The Army in Bourbon Mexico, 1760–1810* (Albuquerque: University of New Mexico Press, 1977), 178–79.

127. Ibid. See AGN, Indiferente de Guerra, vol. 60B and 122a for the original documents related to this case.

CHAPTER 4. THE DICTATOR, THE AYUNTAMIENTO, AND THE BARATILLO

1. AHCM, Ayuntamiento, Rastros y Mercados, vol. 3730, exp. 162. Although the institution of the Ayuntamiento dated to the colonial period, its internal structure changed with independence and again in 1840, when the governor of the Department of Mexico implemented a new code for the capital city's municipal government. According to those regulations, the body would be comprised of six alcaldes (supervisors), twelve regidores (aldermen), and two *síndicos* (city attorneys), each elected to two-year terms. The "alcalde primero" served as a kind of president of the council, though he would not be referred to as such until the 1870s. The body normally met twice a week. See *Ordenanzas municipales del que fue el departamento de México: Sancionadas por el Gobierno y Junta Departamental en el año de 1840, y que según algunos, están vigentes en el actualidad en el Distrito Federal* (Mexico City: Imprenta del Tecpam de Santiago, 1868), ch. 2, art. 1 and ch. 5, art. 1; Warren, *Vagrants and Citizens,* 13; Rodríguez Kuri, *La experiencia olvidada,* 31.

2. Will Fowler, *Santa Anna of Mexico* (Lincoln: University of Nebraska Press, 2007), x.

3. Federalists favored a weaker national government, based roughly on the U.S. model, while centralists advocated for a strong national executive more akin to France. By the late 1840s, these camps had transformed into more ideologically oriented liberals and conservatives, respectively. The early 1840s were a period of transition.

4. The writings of Frances Calderón de la Barca, the Scottish wife of a Spanish diplomat stationed in Mexico in the late 1830s and early 1840s, who described the chaos Mexico's frequent revolts brought to the capital's streets, continues to exert an outsized influence in historians' views of daily life in nineteenth-century Mexico City. See, e.g., Mark Wasserman, *Everyday Life and Politics in Nineteenth-Century Mexico: Men, Women, and War* (Albuquerque: University of New Mexico Press, 2000), 37.

5. This chapter suggests that the popular political engagement that Richard Warren found in *Vagrants and Citizens* continued after the collapse of federalism in 1830. It builds on recent work by Vanesa Teitelbaum, Sonia Pérez Toledo, and Carlos Illades on artisanal and working-class politics in the city. None of those works, however, focuses on street vendors or shows urban popular groups engaging in the public sphere as early as 1842. See Warren, *Vagrants and Citizens*; Teitelbaum, *Entre el control y la movilización*; Pérez Toledo, "Formas de gobierno local, modelos constitucionales y cuerpo electoral, 1842–1867," in *Historia política*, ed. Rodríguez Kuri, 221–79; and Illades, *Hacia la república del trabajo*.

6. Viceroy Félix María Calleja removed the entry barriers to the guilds in an 1813 decree, ending their legal monopolies. Guilds maintained a strong sense of corporate identity well into in the middle decades of the nineteenth century, but they no longer enjoyed the same legal protections. See Pérez Toledo, *Hijos del trabajo*, introduction.

7. In October 1841, just as Santa Anna was returning to Mexico City, the Republic of Yucatan, comprising the present-day states of Yucatan, Campeche, and Quintana Roo, declared its independence from Mexico. It did not rejoin the country until 1848.

8. Cecilia Noriega Elío, *El Constituyente de 1842* (Mexico City: UNAM, 1986), 18. See also Will Fowler, *Forceful Negotiations: The Origins of the* Pronunciamiento *in Nineteenth-Century Mexico* (Lincoln: University of Nebraska Press, 2010).

9. On government efforts to raise tax revenue in the 1830s, see Barbara A. Tenenbaum, *The Politics of Penury: Debt and Taxes in Mexico, 1821–1856* (Albuquerque: University of New Mexico Press, 1986), 49. See also Costeloe, *Central Republic*, 193.

10. At one point, as many as 50 percent of the coins in circulation were believed to be counterfeit. Covarrubias, *La moneda de cobre*, 139–40. The poor quality of the government-issued coins, and the fact that their assigned value was so much higher than the value of the materials from which they were produced, made counterfeiting attractive and relatively easy. Indeed, Gabino Pérez, the *evangelista* for the vendors of the Volador market, was arrested for counterfeiting in 1835. AHAGNCM, Fondo

Antiguo, Sección Notarías Siglos XVI–XIX, Hacienda, Miguel Cabrera, vol. 3, f. 8v–9.

11. See María del Carmen Reyna, *Historia de la Casa de Moneda: Tres motines en contra de la moneda débil en la Ciudad de México, siglo XIX* (Mexico City: Departamento de Investigaciones Históricas, INAH, 1979), 27; and Richard A. Warren, "Rashomon in the Zocalo: Writing the History of Popular Political Culture in Nineteenth-Century Mexico," *MACLAS Latin American Essays* 16 (2002): 73–94.

12. Bustamante was a conservative who had alienated many of his allies by increasing taxes to try to keep the government afloat. See Fowler, *Forceful Negotiations*, 164–65.

13. Carlos María de Bustamante, *Apuntes para la historia del gobierno del general don Antonio López de Santa Anna* (1845; rpt. Mexico City: Fondo de Cultural Económica, 1986), n.p.

14. *El Estante Nacional* (Puebla), April 5, 1845, cited in Costeloe, *Central Republic*, 184.

15. Fowler notes that the 1841–1844 period was among the most stable of the era, with Santa Anna's key ministers remaining in place for all or most of the time. Cecilia Noriega calls the period between the signing of the Bases de Tacubaya and the 1842 constituent congress "a parenthesis of peace and optimism in the country." Santa Anna did not serve as president for all three years but instead followed his usual pattern of ruling temporarily and then installing someone loyal to him as president before returning to his estate in Veracruz. See Fowler, *Santa Anna of Mexico*, 214; and Noriega, *Constituyente*, 45.

16. Fowler, *Santa Anna of Mexico*, 217–18, 224.

17. Costeloe, *Central Republic*, 194.

18. AHCM, Actas de Cabildo, Sesiones Ordinarias, vol. 161A, December 7, 1841.

19. Yoma Medina and Martos López, *Dos mercados*, 86, 88, 90.

20. AHCM, Ayuntamiento, Rastros y Mercados, vol. 3730, exp. 160, fs. 2–5.

21. Olvera Ramos, *Mercados*, 199. The first reference to a rental contract between baratilleros and the Ayuntamiento appears in AHCM, Ayuntamiento, Fincas: Mercados, vol. 1100, exp. 9, f. 3v.

22. AHCM, Ayuntamiento, Rastros y Mercados, vol. 3730, exp. 160, fs. 2–6v. Unfortunately, neither this contract nor any other between vendors and the Ayuntamiento has survived, so we must take Pérez at his word.

23. See Mark Becker, "In Search of *Tinterillos*," *Latin American Research Review* 47:1 (2012): 96. Evangelistas were known as *tinterillos* in other regions of Hispanic America.

24. Fernández de Lizardi, *El periquillo sarniento*, 180, 222–23. The word *tinterillo* was also a derisive term for an unqualified lawyer. Becker, "In Search of *Tinterillos*," 97.

25. AHCM, Ayuntamiento, Rastros y Mercados, vol. 3730, exp. 160, fs. 1–2.

26. Becker argues that Ecuadorean tinterillos "represented a diffusion of the art of writing, advancing the democratization and power of literacy to marginal communities." Becker, "In Search of *Tinterillos*," 109. In doing so, they challenged, as

Christina Jiménez has argued, Ángel Rama's distinction between the "lettered," written culture of the educated classes, and the oral culture of the popular classes in Latin America. Jiménez, "Performing Their Right," 451.

27. AHAGNCM, Fondo Antiguo, Sección Notarías Siglos XVI–XIX, José López Guazo, fs. 333v–34v. When Pérez borrowed 200 pesos from Ramona Zuleta to start a business that year, he used the guantes—which is to say the market value—of that iron stand as collateral for the loan. The contract acknowledged that although traspasos were technically illegal (Revillagigedo's *Reglamento* was still in effect in 1836), the value of the guante would nonetheless suffice to cover Pérez's obligation. The document illustrates that Mexico City's street commerce continued to blur the boundaries between legality and illegality after independence.

28. AHCM, Ayuntamiento, Fincas: Mercados, vol. 1100, exp. 16, fs. 1, 20, 28.

29. The money was to be disbursed from the national treasury, paying down a 480,000-peso debt the national government had with the Ayuntamiento. The source of this debt is not specified in the file.

30. AHCM, Ayuntamiento, Fincas: Mercados, vol. 1100, exp. 16; Yoma Medina and Martos López, *Dos mercados*, 124–25.

31. This junta departamental was created by the first centralist constitution, called the *Siete Leyes* (Seven Laws), of December 1836, which turned the states formed under the federalist constitution of 1824 into departments with governors appointed directly by the Mexican president. Juntas departamentales, later called *asambleas departamentales*, took the place of state legislatures and were comprised of seven individuals, chosen by the same electors who selected congressional representatives, who were charged with overseeing the activities of the municipal governments in their departments. They were relatively independent from the president, though their members generally had conservative sympathies. Prefects and subprefects reported to governors. Warren, *Vagrants and Citizens*, 134, 144; Lucio Ernesto Maldonado Ojeda, *La Asamblea Departamental de México, 1836–1846* (Mexico City: Asamblea Legislativa del Distrito Federal, 2001), 74–76.

32. AHCM, Ayuntamiento, Fincas: Mercados, vol. 1100, exp. 16, fs. 68v–75.

33. Arrom observes a remarkable continuity from Bourbon to liberal to conservative regimes in how Mexico's ruling elites viewed the urban poor. Arrom, *Containing the Poor*, 5, 284. Other scholars have noted that paternalistic sentiments played a role nineteenth-century authorities' treatment of street vendors in Mexico. See, for example, Gamboa Ramírez, "Las finanzas municipales," 35; and Bleynat, "Taxes and Compassion."

34. *Legislación Mexicana*, December 15, 1841.

35. AHCM, Actas de Cabildo, Sesiones Ordinarias, vol. 161A, December 19, 1841.

36. AHCM, Ayuntamiento, Rastros y Mercados, vol. 3730, exp. 160, f. 21.

37. Though no newspapers reported on the clash between vendors and police at the time, several references to the event appear during the following months. See, e.g., AHCM, Ayuntamiento, Rastros y Mercados, vol. 3730, exp. 160, fs. 28–30 (in a letter from Pérez to the Ayuntamiento dated January 15, 1842); and AHCM, Ayuntamiento, Rastros y Mercados, vol. 3730, exp. 161, f. 16.

38. In the 1860s, the Austrian emperor Maximilian appointed Aguirre as prefect of Mexico City. John Musser, "The Establishment of Maximilian's Empire in Mexico" (PhD diss., University of Pennsylvania, 1918), 59.

39. AHCM, Ayuntamiento, Fincas: Mercados, vol. 1100, exp. 14; *El Siglo Diez y Nueve*, January 2, 1842. The comment about Santa Anna's twice repelling foreign aggression refers to the Spanish invasion of Tampico in 1829 and the French invasion, often called the Pastry War, in 1838.

40. AHCM, Actas de Cabildo, Sesiones Ordinarias, vol. 161A (December 27, 1841); *El Siglo Diez y Nueve*, December 30, 1841.

41. Ayuntamiento de México, *Exposición de las razones que tuvo el exmo. Ayuntamiento para contratar la nueva obra que se está haciendo de la plaza del Volador* (Mexico City: Impr. de V. García Torres, 1842), 16–18. Conservatives such as Aguirre and Mariano de Icaza joined liberals like Baz in authoring the *Exposición*. Baz was a liberal who would go on to serve as a federal deputy for the Federal District under the Restored Republic in 1869. Luis G. Salvídar, ed., *Diccionario de la legislación Mexicana* (Mexico City: La Constitución Social, 1870), xxxvii. Icaza served as prefect for the Valley of Mexico under Emperor Maximilian. Francisco de Paula de Arrangoiz y Berzábal, *Apuntes para la historia del segundo Imperio Mejicano* (Madrid: Imprenta de M. Rivadeneyra, 1889), 320.

42. The first half of the nineteenth century saw New York eclipse the Mexican capital as the largest city in the Americas. In 1800, Mexico City had roughly one hundred thousand people compared to New York's sixty thousand. By 1850, however, Mexico City's population stood somewhere between one hundred twenty thousand and two hundred thousand residents, while New York's had surged to more than five hundred thousand. See Haslip-Viera, *Crime and Punishment*, 19, for different estimates of the late-colonial population; and Frederick John Shaw Jr., "Poverty and Politics in Mexico City" (Ph.D. diss., University of Florida, 1975), 8. Sonia Pérez and Herbert Klein's analysis of the 1842 Mexico City census suggests that the city's population stood at only about 122,000 in that year, underscoring how little the city had grown since the beginning of the century. See Pérez and Klein, *Población y estructura social de la Ciudad de México, 1790–1842* (Mexico City: UAM Iztapalapa, 2004), 132–33. For U.S. population data, see Campbell Gibson, "Population of the 100 Largest Cities and Other Urban Places in the United States: 1790 to 1900," U.S. Census Bureau, Population Working Paper 27 (June 1998).

43. Brantz Mayer, *Mexico As It Was and As It Is* (New York: New World Press, 1844), 39–40.

44. In the 1820s, Mexico's federalists were divided between *escocés* (Scottish-rite) and *yorkino* (York-rite) factions associated with the Masonic lodges. On competition between those factions, see Warren, *Vagrants and Citizens*, 76–79.

45. "Costumbres: El Baratillo," *El Siglo Diez y Nueve*, February 27, 1842, 3. Another article in *El Siglo Diez y Nueve*, printed on March 12, 1842, complained that soldiers were selling their military-issued boots in the Baratillo—a practice that continued from the colonial era.

46. In May 1836, Governor José Gómez de la Cortina ordered that the Baratillo "disappear." Argos, "Comunicado," *El Mosquito Mexicano*, May 10, 1836, 1. The order does not appear to have been implemented.

47. AHCM, Ayuntamiento, Rastros y Mercados, vol. 3730, exp. 162. Unfortunately, no renderings of the Baratillo during the time it was in the Plaza del Factor seem to have survived.

48. *Diario de México*, June 25, 1811, 715.

49. *Correo de la Federación Mexicana*, May 5, 1828, 4.

50. Don Juan de la Peña, "El Evangelio de Arista," *Diario de la Revolución*, September 29, 1833, Guadalajara, Jalisco edition, 1.

51. In the aftermath of the 1828 Parián riot, the government established a bivouac in the Baratillo because officials worried another disturbance might erupt there. AHCM, Ayuntamiento, Gobierno del DF, Bandos, 1789–1925, caja 2, exp. 69; AHCM, Actas de Cabildo, vol. 149A, fs. 112–12v. On the riot, see Silvia M. Arrom, "Popular Politics in Mexico City: The Parian Riot, 1828," *Hispanic American Historical Review* 68:2 (1988): 245–68. Such criticism of the Baratillo, however, continued to compete with expressions of support for its vendors and customers. See, for example, the contributor to the newspaper *El Mosquito Mexicano* who called the Baratillo "useful and necessary so that the poor, depraved or not, have a recourse for their needs." Argos, "Comunicado," *El Mosquito Mexicano*, May 10, 1836, 1.

52. AHCM, Actas de Cabildo, Sesiones Ordinarias, vol. 162A, May 20 and 22, 1842; AHCM, Ayuntamiento, Rastros y Mercados, vol. 161, f. 4.

53. AHCM, Ayuntamiento, Rastros y Mercados, vol. 3730, exp. 161, fs. 1–2. Minutes from the June 1 city council session reference the request of one Don José María Miranda to transfer his clothing stand in the Baratillo to his son, who sold fruit. See AHCM, Actas de Cabildo, Sesiones Ordinarias, vol. 162A, June 1, 1842.

54. AHCM, Ayuntamiento, Rastros y Mercados, vol. 3730, exp. 161, fs. 3–3v; AHCM, Actas de Cabildo, Sesiones Ordinarias, vol. 162A.

55. AHCM, Ayuntamiento, Rastros y Mercados, vol. 3730, exp. 161, f. 9v.

56. "Representacion hecha al Escmo. ayuntamiento el dia 27 del corriente por los individuos que la suscriben," *El Siglo Diez y Nueve*, May 31, 1842, 2–3.

57. AHCM, Ayuntamiento, Rastros y Mercados, vol. 3730, exp. 161, fs. 4v–5v.

58. Ricardo Ortega y Pérez Gallardo, *Estudios genealógicos* (Mexico City: E. Dublán, 1902), 251.

59. AHCM, Ayuntamiento, Rastros y Mercados, vol. 3730, exp. 161, fs. 7–9v.

60. Audiences for Mexico City's newspapers in the mid-nineteenth century were still relatively small; print runs probably did not exceed 2,000 in the 1840s. Still, the political impact of a petition printed in *El Siglo Diez y Nueve* was significant, and it likely reached a larger public than the individuals who purchased the paper. See Corinna Zeltsman, "Ink Under the Fingernails: Making Print in Nineteenth-Century Mexico City" (Ph.D. diss, Duke University, 2016), 3.

61. AHCM, Ayuntamiento, Rastros y Mercados, vol. 3730, exp. 161, fs. 13–14v.

62. Ibid., f. 10.

63. Ibid., exp. 120, fs. 1–2. Colonial laws and regulations did not necessarily disappear after independence; many remained in effect for decades, until republican lawmakers replaced them.

64. Market vendors and other urban popular actors would continue to make this argument in the second half of the nineteenth century. See Jiménez, "From the Lettered City," 223; and idem, "Popular Organizing for Public Services: Residents Modernize Morelia, Mexico, 1880–1920," *Journal of Urban History* 30 (2004): 495–518; and Bleynat, "Taxes and Compassion."

65. AHCM, Ayuntamiento, Rastros y Mercados, vol. 3730, exp. 161, fs. 14–14v.

66. Ibid., fs. 16v–17.

67. Ibid., f. 16.

68. Michael P. Costeloe, "Generals versus Politicians: Santa Anna and the 1842 Congressional Elections in Mexico," *Bulletin of Latin American Research* 8:2 (1989): 262. Costeloe argues that the Mexican Congress and its elections also continued to function relatively freely in this period and that the army never exercised the same control over it that it did over the appointment of presidents. See also Pérez Toledo, "Formas de gobierno local," 250.

69. According to the 1842 census, at least twenty-eight of the forty signatories could vote. This fact suggests that these men were not career criminals, as the Baratillo's detractors often claimed, since a criminal record would have disqualified a man from voting. See Pérez Toledo and Klein, *Población*, 128–29; and Sonia Pérez Toledo, "Base de datos del Padrón de la Municipalidad de México de 1842," unpublished data set, 2005.

70. For the election results, see *El Siglo Diez y Nueve*, December 26, 1842. Richard Warren has noted that five council members refused to take their seats on the 1843 Ayuntamiento, due to various problems with the election. Richard A. Warren, "Desafío y trastorno en el gobierno municipal: El Ayuntamiento de México y la dinámica política nacional, 1821–1855," in *Ciudad de México: Instituciones, actores sociales y conflicto político, 1774–1931*, ed. Carlos Illades and Ariel Rodríguez Kurí (Zamora, Michoacán: El Colegio de Michoacán; Mexico City: UAM Azcapotzalco, 1996), 129. Icaza served as a member of the Ayuntamiento again in 1848. See *Colección de leyes, decretos, circulares, y demás documentos oficiales importantes del Supremo Gobierno de los Estados-Unidos Mexicanos que se han publicado desde 30 de mayo de 1848* (Mexico City: Imprenta de la Calle de Medinas, 1849), 134.

71. In Jürgen Habermas's original conception, the public sphere was a site of bourgeois sociability and intellectual ferment. James Sanders contends that nineteenth-century Latin America had a "public sphere of the street"—preserved mainly in newspaper articles and speeches that captured the "everyday thought and political discourse" of a much wider range of actors than the *letrados* of Latin America's cities. See Sanders, *Vanguard of the Atlantic World*, 13–14; and Habermas, *Transformation of the Public Sphere*. This chapter's findings depart from the work of other historians of Mexico City who have argued that street and market vendors did not have access to the capital's press or its public sphere, or found that they only gained access to those arenas in the last decades of the nineteenth century. See Susie S. Porter, *Work-*

ing Women in Mexico City: Public Discourses and Material Conditions, 1879–1931 (Tucson: University of Arizona Press, 2003), 191. Ingrid Bleynat echoes this interpretation in her dissertation, "Trading with Power." Christina Jiménez engages with Rama's notion of the "lettered city," rather than Habermas's public sphere, and argues that during the Porfiriato, scribes helped vendors in Morelia penetrate the "lettered" written culture of the educated classes. See Jiménez, "Performing," 451; and idem, "From the Lettered City."

72. The baratilleros' actions lend support to Richard Warren's contention that Mexico City residents continued to "voice their political opinions" in the 1830s and 1840s despite the turmoil in national politics and increasingly troubled municipal elections. However, this case shows that they did so not only through riots and crowds but also through the mechanisms of local government and the press. See Warren, *Vagrants and Citizens*, 169–70. See also Pérez Toledo's recent work on the *alcaldes del barrio* (neighborhood wardens) and the neighborhood-based network of political patronage in the middle decades of the nineteenth century. Pérez Toledo, "Formas de gobierno local."

73. The census does not specify the type of merchandise the vendors in the market were selling in 1842, only their profession, so it is not clear whether they offered mainly second-hand goods, or a mix of new and used manufactures, as was the case in the eighteenth century. On the implementation of free trade in Mexico City's food markets, see Moncada González, *La libertad comercial*.

74. Marie Francois has noted that Mexico City's vulnerable middle classes, hard hit by the copper money devaluation, stagnant wages, and rising prices, continued to rely on the city's pawnshops in order to make ends meet during the middle decades of the nineteenth century. Francois, *Everyday Credit*, ch. 3. During the colonial period, many of the Baratillo's activities would fall under modern-day definitions of the informal economy. With the formal dissolution of the guild system, that legal framework largely disappeared, so it may not be accurate to call the Baratillo part of the informal economy during this era. See de Soto, *The Other Path*, 12.

75. According to the 1842 census, 1,782 women in Mexico City worked in artisanal trades, constituting 18.6 percent of women in the workforce. Of these, the majority (76.6 percent) worked in textile production, followed by tobacco production and leatherwork. Women had only a minimal presence in other trades. Pérez Toledo and Klein, *Población*, 222.

76. See Porter, "And That It Is Custom." Written evidence like petitions and market censuses may not fully account for women's presence or labor in the market. Indeed, this was the case in late twentieth-century Mexico. See Mendiola García, *Street Democracy*, 25.

77. Twenty-one of the thirty-three signatories identified in the census were born in Mexico City. This ratio is roughly in line with the proportion of migrants in Mexico City's overall population in 1842—about one-third. See Pérez Toledo and Klein, *Población*, 178.

78. AHCM, Ayuntamiento, Rastros y Mercados, vol. 3730, exp. 161; Pérez Toledo, "Base de datos."

79. Census records from the early 1880s show that many Baratillo vendors continued to live in the immediate vicinity of the market. In his analysis of street vendor petitions in the 1910s, Mario Barbosa finds that this pattern held true more than seventy years later, when more than 90 percent of vendors lived within five blocks of where they worked. See Barbosa Cruz, *El trabajo en las calles*, 164.

80. AHAGNCM, Fondo Antiguo, Sección Notarías Siglos XVI–XIX, Antonio Pinto, vol. 3566, July 5, 1836. Puzzlingly, Villar claimed she could not write in 1836 and did not sign her will, yet her signature appears on the 1842 petition. It seems unlikely that she learned to write in her fifties, so the explanation for the discrepancy is not clear.

81. Ibid., Miguel Aristegui, vol. 295, fs. 85–86.

82. AHCM, Ayuntamiento, Justicia, Jurados de Imprenta, vol. 2740, exp. 31. Miguel Vara, Nabor Félix Rubio, Juan Álvarez, Dionisio Molina, Saturnino Guerrero, Ignacio Argumedo, and Mariano Candelario Palacio all appear on the press jury rolls of 1847. There are several other near-matches that could correspond to the signatories or their family members. Census-takers deemed all but of the two adult males who signed the letter eligible to vote in the 1842 elections, but given the relatively inclusive voting rules that Santa Anna set in the fall of 1841, which abandoned income requirements, this fact tells us little about how wealthy or poor these men were.

83. On press jury eligibility requirements, see Pablo Piccato, *The Tyranny of Opinion: Honor in the Construction of the Mexican Public Sphere* (Durham, NC: Duke University Press, 2010), 35–36. According to the 1849 census, the average annual salary of a typical wage-earner was 156 pesos. A government bureaucrat, by comparison, earned 1,080 pesos. Elected officials on the Ayuntamiento, however, were unpaid. Shaw, "Poverty and Politics," 26.

84. AHAGNCM, Francisco Bala, acta 74794, f. 55 (August 17, 1833).

85. AHCM, Ayuntamiento, Rastros y Mercados, vol. 3730, exp. 161, f. 12.

86. Most of the councilmen were indeed members of the capital's elite, often scions of political dynasties who used a position in the municipal government to launch their ascent toward more prestigious, and lucrative, positions in the national government. Several of the councilmen who were involved in this dispute in fact went on to high posts in both conservative and liberal governments in the subsequent decades. See Warren, *Vagrants and Citizens*, 86.

87. AHCM, Ayuntamiento, Rastros y Mercados, vol. 3730, exp. 161, fs. 11–13.

88. Vanesa Teitelbaum argues that between the 1840s and 1860s a new class, which she calls *gente de trabajo* (working people), comprised of artisans and other urban workers, took shape and gained some material ground in Mexico City. See *Entre el control y la movilización*, 13.

89. Carlos Illades, *Las otras ideas: Estudio sobre el primer socialismo en México, 1850–1935* (Mexico City: UAM Cuajimalpa, 2008), 34.

90. Justo Sierra, José María Gutierrez Estrada, and Mariano Otero, *Documentos de la época 1840–1850* (Mexico City: Secretaría de la Reforma Agraria, 1981), 171. For more on Otero, see Charles A. Hale, *Mexican Liberalism in the Age of Mora,*

1821–1853 (Princeton, NJ: Princeton University Press, 1968), 185–86; and idem, *The Transformation of Liberalism in Late Nineteenth-Century Mexico* (Princeton, NJ: Princeton University Press, 1989), 6–7, 186–87. Historians view Bautista Morales as more radical than Otero, but he published less, so it is difficult to say whether he might have had a hand in drafting the baratilleros' letter. *El gallo pitagórico*, his most famous work, focuses more on politics than social issues—a trait most mid-nineteenth-century liberals shared. See Juan Bautista de Morales, *El gallo pitagórico: Colección de artículos crítico-políticos y de costumbres* (Mexico City: Imprenta de Ignacio Cumplido, 1857).

91. Otero was a follower of the associative socialism of French thinkers such as Charles Fournier who saw society as an organic and progressive being, not simply a conglomeration of individuals—the vision of Mexico's orthodox liberals. Hale, *Transformation*, 6–7.

92. The precise date of their relocation is not clear from the record.

93. José Urbano Fonseca was a prominent conservative politician who served in the administrations of President Mariano Arista in the 1850s and Emperor Maximilian in the 1860s. His charitable contributions in the capital included founding a school for the deaf at the ex-convent of San Juan de Letrán. See Manuel Orozco y Berra, *Memoria para el plano de la ciudad de México: Formada de órden de Ministerio de Fomento* (Mexico City: S. White, 1867), 185–87; and AHCM, Ayuntamiento, Regidores, vol. 3841. In recent decades, scholarship on nineteenth-century Mexico has stressed the many points of convergence between liberalism and conservatism, a fact that has been obscured by a focus on the civil wars that consumed the country in the 1850s and 1860s. See, for example, Matthew D. O'Hara, *A Flock Divided: Race, Religion, and Politics in Mexico, 1749–1857* (Durham, NC: Duke University Press, 2009), 187–88; Josefina Zoraida Vázquez, "Liberales y conservadores en México: Diferencias y similitudes," *Estudios Interdisciplinarios de América Latina y el Caribe* 8:1 (1997): 153–75; and Jaime E. Rodríguez O, "Introduction: The Origins of Constitutionalism and Liberalism in Mexico," in *The Divine Charter: Constitutionalism and Liberalism in Nineteenth-Century Mexico*, ed. Jaime Rodríguez O. (New York: Rowman & Littlefield, 2005), 24.

94. AHCM, Ayuntamiento, Rastros y Mercados, vol. 3730, exp. 161; AHCM, Actas de Cabildo, Sesiones Ordinarias, vol. 162A (May 30–31, 1842).

95. AHCM, Ayuntamiento, Rastros y Mercados, vol. 3730, exp. 161, fs. 23–24.

96. *El Siglo Diez y Nueve*, February 6, 1845, remitidos.

97. Ibid. AHCM, Ayuntamiento, Rastros y Mercados, vol. 3730, exp. 161, fs. 30–36.

98. AHCM, Actas de Cabildo, vol. 170A, fs. 433–33v.

99. Susie Porter similarly found municipal authorities unwilling to fully enforce market regulations over fears of lost revenue. Porter, "And That It Is Custom," 122.

100. One such incident occurred when the Ayuntamiento lashed out at Governor José María Tornel over his establishment of a vagrants' court in 1828, which the municipal government saw as a trespass on its authority. See Ariel Rodríguez Kuri, "Política e institucionalidad: El Ayuntamiento de México y la evolución del

conflicto jurisdiccional, 1808–1850," in *La ciudad de México en la primera mitad del siglo XIX*, ed. Hernández Franyuti, 2:74. The 1824 law that created the Federal District gave Congress and the national executive control over its laws and finances. See Miranda Pacheco, "La fundación del Distrito Federal," 110.

101. *Ordenanzas municipales*, ch. 14.

102. Rodríguez Kuri, "Política e institucionalidad," 77, 80.

103. "Manifiesto al público que hace el ayuntamiento de 1840, acerca de la conducta que ha [observado] en los negocios municipales, y del estado en que quedan los ramos de su cargo," *El Cosmopolita*, January 6, 1841, 2. Speculators were also financing the daily operations of the national government. After Mexico defaulted on its loans to the British in 1827, it began borrowing heavily from wealthy individuals, called *agiotistas*, often at exorbitant interest rates. The Mexican press and public excoriated these lenders. Gabino Pérez, in his published December 1841 letter to Santa Anna, implored the president not to move forward with the construction of the new Volador market because the project was one "in which the agiotistas want to take part—the greatest enemies of our ill-fated nation." AHCM, Ayuntamiento, Rastros y Mercados, vol. 3730, exp. 160, f. 21. Barbara Tenenbaum, in *The Politics of Penury*, questions the narrative that agiotistas were parasites, noting that they financed basic infrastructure projects at a time when the government was unable to do so and even helped spur Mexico's industrialization.

104. For more on contratas, see Gisela Moncada González, "La gestión municipal: ¿Cómo administrar las plazas y los mercados de la ciudad de México? 1824–1840," *Secuencias* 95 (2016): 60. Despite this financial precariousness, the Ayuntamiento ran a deficit during only three years in the first half of the nineteenth century, casting doubt on national officials' claims that council members were incompetent managers. Gamboa Ramírez, "Las finanzas municipales," 63.

105. In the early 1840s, rent from the Parián and other public markets contributed between one-quarter and one-third of the Ayuntamiento's total yearly revenues. See AHCM, Ayuntamiento, Hacienda, Presupuestos, Ingresos y Egresos, vol. 2225, exps. 4, 5, 8. See also Moncada González, *La libertad comercial*, 106. She finds that rent from the Parián and the public market plazas produced an average of 32 percent of the city's annual revenue during the 1820s. The city generally spent little on upkeep or security for the markets, so they were major profit centers for the government. One significant cost for the Ayuntamiento, however, was the rent it paid for the land on which many of its markets stood, as a number of the market plazas were still in private hands in the mid-nineteenth century.

106. "Manifiesto al público," 2.

107. AHCM, Ayuntamiento, Rastros y Mercados, vol. 3731, exp. 180.

108. AHCM, Actas de Cabildo, Sesiones Ordinarias, vol. 162A, May 20, 1842.

109. AHCM, Ayuntamiento, Hacienda, Presupuestos, Ingresos y Egresos, vol. 2225, exps. 2–4 (municipal budgets for 1830, 1837, and 1841). See also Arrom, "Popular Politics." Brantz Mayer noted its ugliness in his travelogue, *Mexico As It Was*, 39.

110. The Ayuntamiento claimed that the Crown had declared it the owner of the building in 1703 and that it had been built with municipal funds. Santa Anna's

government countered that Spanish kings had paid for the initial construction as well as upkeep over the years, so the rightful owner was the Mexican state, as the successor to the Spanish Crown. Ayuntamiento de México, *Documentos oficiales relativos a la construccion y demolicion del Parian, y a la propiedad . . .* (Mexico City: Imprenta de Ignacio Cumplido, 1843), xi, xvi–xviii, 44, located in AHCM, Ayuntamiento, Créditos, Compensaciones, vol. 2062, exp. 21. For more on the demolition of the Parián see María Dolores Lorenzo, "Negociaciones para la modernización urbana: La demolición del mercado del Parián en la Ciudad de México, 1843," *Estudios de historia moderna y contemporánea de México* 38:38 (2009): 85–109.

111. *Documentos oficiales*, 84.

112. Manuel Carpio, the assembly's president, was a noted intellectual and conservative politician of the era.

113. *Documentos oficiales*, xiii, 97. By this time Santa Anna was on a rampage against foreign businesses: in September he banned non-Mexicans from participating in the nation's commerce and began making lists of the foreign-owned shops in Mexico City that the government intended to close. See AHCM, Ayuntamiento, Industria y Comercio, vol. 522, exp. 8.

114. See Hira de Gortari Rabiela, "Política y administración en la Ciudad de México: Relaciones entre el Ayuntamiento y el Gobierno del Distrito Federal y el Departamental, 1824–1843," in *La ciudad de México en la primera mitad del siglo XIX*, ed. Hernández Franyuti, 2:166–83; and Rodríguez Kuri, *La experiencia olvidada*, ch. 1.

115. Fowler, *Santa Anna of Mexico*, 216.

116. Costeloe, *Central Republic*, 228.

117. A statue of Santa Anna, pointing north toward Texas, was erected in the Plaza del Volador but was removed in December 1844, following his overthrow. Yoma Medina and Martos López, *Dos mercados*, 131.

118. Apart from the petitioner who urged the Ayuntamiento to banish the Baratillo to a distant plaza, Mariano de Icaza, the city's market commissioner, also insisted that the market move from the city center to the periphery. AHCM, Ayuntamiento, Rastros y Mercados, exp. 161, f. 26v.

CHAPTER 5. FREE TRADING IN THE RESTORED REPUBLIC

1. Steven B. Bunker, *Creating Mexican Consumer Culture in the Age of Porfirio Díaz* (Albuquerque: University of New Mexico Press, 2012), 20.

2. Tancredo, "Comida," *El Monitor Republicano*, March 13, 1872, 1–2.

3. In what came to be known as the Revolution of La Noria, General Porfirio Díaz rebelled after Benito Juárez violated constitutionally mandated term limits by running for and winning reelection in 1871 (the 1857 constitution limited presidents to a single four-year term). Díaz rebelled again in 1876 after Sebastián Lerdo de Tejada also violated the term limit by running again. This time, Díaz seized power in the Revolution of Tuxtepec.

4. As the historian Charles Hale wrote, liberalism went from being a combative political ideology in the mid-nineteenth century to a "unifying political myth" after 1867. Hale, *Transformation of Liberalism*, 3.

5. AHCM, Ayuntamiento, Rastros y Mercados, vol. 3734, exp. 554, f. 1.

6. The word *jardín* translates to "garden," which the Baratillo certainly was not. Lauro María Jiménez, "Proyecto higiénico administrativo para los mercados de México," *Anales de la Sociedad Humboldt*, January 1, 1872, 193; Juan Somolinos Palencia, "El Doctor Lauro María Jiménez a los 100 años de su fallecimiento," *Gaceta Médica de México* 110:6 (1975): 432.

7. AHCM, Ayuntamiento, Rastros y Mercados, vol. 3734, exp. 554, f. 1.

8. María Dolores Morales, "La expansión de la ciudad de México en el siglo XIX: El caso de los fraccionamientos," in *Ciudad de México*, ed. Moreno Toscana, 194. Morales notes that in the mid-nineteenth century, ecclesiastical corporations controlled nearly 40 percent of Mexico City's total property value, though they comprised only about 4 percent of property owners. Liberal governments, beginning in the 1860s, began breaking up the properties of hospitals, churches, and convents in order to complete the urban street grid. See Morales, "Espacio, propiedad y órganos de poder en la Ciudad de México en el siglo XIX," in *Ciudad de México*, ed. Illades and Rodríguez Kuri, 161, 182–83, 190. *Colonias* were new neighborhoods that developed outside the city's original traza.

9. The Guerrero market was the first of several new public marketplaces that the Ayuntamiento planned to build in the late 1860s and early 1870s, though it was the only one that the city managed to finish in this period, due to lack of funds. See AHCM, Ayuntamiento, Fincas: Mercados, vol. 1100, exp. 19, and D.J.G. Brito, "Mercados: Memoria del Sr. D.J.G. Brito, relativa a los de la capital en el año de 1869," *El Siglo Diez y Nueve*, January 26, 1870, 1.

10. AHCM, Ayuntamiento, Rastros y Mercados, vol. 3734, exp. 554, f. IV.

11. In the 1840s and 1850s, the Baratillo moved back and forth between the Plaza del Factor and the Plaza de Villamil several times. It was forced out of the former plaza in 1850 when the city sold the land to build the Iturbide Theater. In 1857, the Ayuntamiento evicted the vendors from the Plaza de Villamil so that a train station could be built there (it never was), and they moved to the Plaza de la Concepción. It is not clear precisely when the market migrated from that plaza to the adjacent Plaza del Jardín, though a member of the Ayuntamiento suggested it was in 1858. See AHCM, Ayuntamiento, Rastros y Mercados, vol. 3734, exp. 554, f. IV; *El Siglo Diez y Nueve*, September 1, 1850, 967; *El Monitor Republicano*, December 17, 1857, 3; *El Siglo Diez y Nueve*, February 8, 1862, 4.

12. AHCM, Ayuntamiento, Rastros y Mercados, vol. 3734, exp. 554, f. IV.

13. Ibid.

14. Ibid.; AHCM, Actas de Cabildo, vol. 202A, February 9, 1872, f. 86.

15. AHCM, Ayuntamiento, Rastros y Mercados, vol. 3734, exp. 554, fs. 2–2v; AHCM, Actas de Cabildo, vol. 202A, February 13, 1872, fs. 89v and 94.

16. AHCM, Ayuntamiento, Rastros y Mercados, vol. 3734, exp. 554, fs. 42–46.

17. Marcello Carmagnani, "Vectors of Liberal Economic Culture in Mexico," in *The Divine Charter,* ed. Rodríguez O., 285–304. See also Moncada González, *La libertad comercial.*

18. AHCM, Ayuntamiento, Hacienda, Propios y Arbitrios, vol. 2232, exp. 89.

19. AGMP, ficha 3878, tomo 197, legajo 2240, fs. 158–79. In another parallel between this baratillo and its counterpart in Mexico City, the municipal government had moved it in 1831 from the plaza where the Parián was located to a square called the Plaza del Factor.

20. AGMP, ficha 3882, tomo 197, fs. 198–99.

21. Ibid., fs. 199–200.

22. Ibid., f. 208.

23. Indeed, Steven Bunker specifically contrasts the "affluent gatherings" at the Tívoli del Eliseo with the pulquerías of Tepito—the neighborhood to which the Baratillo would move in 1902. Bunker, *Creating Mexican Consumer Culture,* 20.

24. AHCM, Ayuntamiento, Padrones, vol. 3426; AHAGNCM, Fondo Antiguo, Sección Notarías Siglos XVI–XIX, Fermín Gonzalo Cosío, vol. 1864, f. 13 (primer semestre 1875).

25. See Pérez Toledo, "Movilización social."

26. *La Iberia,* July 21, 1871, 3; *El Siglo Diez y Nueve,* May 6, 1872, 3.

27. *El Siglo Diez y Nueve,* May 6, 1872, 3; *El Ferrocarril,* May 14, 1872, 3; *El Ferrocarril,* August 7, 1872, 2–3; AHCM, Ayuntamiento, Festividades, vol. 1068, exp. 97 (1877). Rosales Gordoa may fit Carlos Illades's model of a nineteenth-century "working-class intellectual." See Illades, "Los intelectuales de la clase trabajadora del siglo XIX," in *Prácticas populares,* ed. Hanley, 465–86.

28. *Constitución Federal de los Estados Unidos Mexicanos* (Mexico City: Imprenta de Ignacio Cumplido, 1857), title 1, section 1, article 9.

29. Tancredo, "Comida," 1–2.

30. Manuel Ángel Granados Chapa, *Vicente García Torres: Monitor de la República* (Hidalgo, Mexico: Gobierno del Estado de Hidalgo, 1987), 42.

31. García Torres's relationship with his fellow councilmen was rocky almost from the start, illustrating the challenge of criticizing government while also serving in it. On March 3, 1872, only two months into his term, García Torres submitted his resignation, citing the Ayuntamiento's "hostility or indifference" to his plans for improving this city's *paseos,* or boulevards—the area of city government that he oversaw. Governor Montiel refused to accept his resignation, however, and García Torres kept his post. Later that month, his fellow councilmen censured him for his newspaper's criticism of the Ayuntamiento's handling of another matter, which involved information he had allegedly leaked from a secret cabildo session. The editors of *El Monitor* fired back at the Ayuntamiento, writing that the body "has roundly erred if it believes that because Mr. García Torres is a regidor our newspaper has been converted into an organ of the municipality." They saw the censure vote as a testament to the independence of the *Monitor* and its publisher. See *El Monitor Republicano,* March 20, 1872, 3; *El Monitor Republicano,* March 5, 1872, 3; *El Monitor Republicano,* May 23, 1872, 2.

32. "Discurso y proposición del Sr. García Torres en favor de los comerciantes que piden amparo y también de los del mercado de Guerrero," *El Monitor Republicano*, April 9, 1872, 2–3.

33. *El Monitor Republicano*, March 13, 1872, 3.

34. "Discurso y proposición del Sr. García Torres."

35. AHCM, Ayuntamiento, Rastros y Mercados, vol. 3734, exp. 554, f. 22v. The idea was not far-fetched: until Viceroy Revillagigedo banned the practice, petty vendors sold in the atrium of the both the palace and the cathedral. See Viqueira Albán, *Propriety and Permissiveness*, 100.

36. "Discurso y proposición del Sr. García Torres." Marcello Carmagnani has argued that eliminating restrictive commercial registries helped lead to the gradual unification of Mexico in a single economic space in the last decades of the nineteenth century, a necessary step for the country's rapid economic expansion that began in the 1880s. Carmagnani argues that the passage of the 1884 Civil Code of the Federal District, which formally eliminated such registries, was the watershed moment. See Carmagnani, "Vectors," 293.

37. The jurist José María Lozano wrote, "work is our most sacred property." See José María Lozano, *Estudio del derecho constitucional patrio* (Mexico City: Impr. del Comercio de Dublán y Companía, 1876), 154. See also Guillermo Prieto, *Lecciones elementales de economía política dadas en la Escuela de Jurisprudencia de México en el curso de 1871* (1871; rpt. Mexico City: UNAM, 1989), 41.

38. The freedom to work was also protected by Article 2, which banned slavery in the republic, and Article 5, which prohibited all other forms of indentured or forced service through "contracts that have as their objective the loss or irrevocable sacrifice of the freedom of man." *Constitución Federal.*

39. Elías J. Palti, *La invención de una legitimidad: Razón y retórica en el pensamiento mexicano del siglo XIX* (Mexico City: Fondo de Cultural Económica, 2005), 307; Illades, *República del trabajo*, 80.

40. "Discurso y proposición del Sr. García Torres."

41. Given the Baratillo's historical connection to artisans' guilds, this episode would appear to support Carlos Illades's argument that artisans remained closely allied with the Liberal Party in Mexico in the second half of the nineteenth century and that artisan discourse was rarely distinguishable from Liberal discourse by 1880. See Illades, *República de trabajo*, 204. Yet Illades casts doubt on whether voluntary associations provided much material benefit to their members, as only the hat makers association gained any real negotiating power in the period. Daniel Cosío Villegas goes further, arguing that the policies implemented by orthodox liberals after 1867 undid many longstanding protections for workers and that voluntary associations offered little in compensation for that loss. See Illades, *República de trabajo*, 112–13 and Cosío Villegas, *Historia moderna de México*, 9 vols. (Mexico City: Editorial Hermes, 1955–1972), 3:410–12.

42. Exact figures on the circulation of Mexico City's newspapers during the Restored Republic are elusive. In the 1870s, *El Monitor Republicano* printed somewhere between 1,000 and 10,000 copies per day. See Zeltsman, "Ink Under the

Fingernails," 3, 261. Florence Toussaint Alcaraz put *El Monitor*'s circulation at 7,000 in 1885. In 1872, the newspaper cost one-half real. Toussaint Alcaraz, *Escenario de la prensa en el Porfiriato* (Colima, Mexico: Universidad de Colima, 1989), 31.

43. AHCM, Ayuntamiento, Rastros y Mercados, vol. 3734, exp. 554, fs. 18–19. L.J. Rohlfes, "Police and Penal Correction in Mexico City, 1876–1911: A Study of Order and Progress in Porfirian Mexico" (Ph.D. diss., Tulane University, 1983), 18.

44. "El Baratillo," *El Ferrocarril*, March 12, 1872, 2.

45. *El Monitor Republicano*, March 16, 1872, 3.

46. AHCM, Ayuntamiento, Rastros y Mercados, vol. 3734, exp. 554, fs. 13, 17.

47. Ibid., f. 26v. Article 1 states that the rights of man form the basis of all social institutions, and that all laws and all authorities must respect the rights stipulated in the Constitution. Article 4 guaranteed the right to practice the profession of one's choosing. Article 9 protected freedom of association. Article 15 essentially rehashed Article 1 by outlawing "agreements and treaties" that curtailed the "rights that this Constitution gives to man and to the citizen." Finally, Article 28 banned monopolies, except for the coining of money, the mail, and temporary patents given by the government. *Constitución Federal*.

48. Timothy M. James, *Mexico's Supreme Court: Between Liberal Individual and Revolutionary Social Rights, 1861–1934* (Albuquerque: University of New Mexico Press, 2013), 6. The amendment states: "The courts of the federation shall protect any inhabitant of the republic in the exercise of the rights given him by this Constitution and all the laws enacted in accordance with it, against any encroachment by the legislative or executive branches, of either federal or state governments." It also contained the important clause limiting the scope of any amparo granted: "[Judges] shall limit themselves to giving protection in the particular case and shall not produce any general ruling with regard to the law or decree involved in the case." Lucio A. Cabrera, "History of the Mexican Judiciary," *Miami Law Quarterly* 11:4 (1957): 443. María José Rhi Sausi Garavito points out that the amparo was not, in fact, equally accessible to all, since it required the plaintiffs to hire lawyers, and because judges could fine them if they believed their cases were without merit. Nonetheless, poor groups made substantial use of this tool in the second half of the nineteenth century. See Rhi Sausi Garavito, "Las primeras tres décadas del juicio de amparo: Notas en torno a la percepción pública de un nuevo instrumento jurídico," in *Actores, espacios y debates en la historia de la esfera pública en la ciudad de México*, ed. Cristina Sacristán and Pablo Piccato (Mexico City: Instituto Mora, 2005), 138–39.

49. Folder 5143, Sons of the Republic of Texas Kathryn Stoner O'Connor Mexican Manuscript Collection, 1555–1987, MS 71, University of Texas at San Antonio Libraries Special Collections; Richard D. Baker, *Judicial Review in Mexico: A Study of the Amparo Suit* (Austin: University of Texas Press, 1971), 26–27.

50. The Spanish verb *dotar* means to endow. Thus, these were the assets that the federal government was providing to the Ayuntamiento and requiring it to administer. Manuel Dublán and José María Lozano, *Legislación mexicana ó Colección completa de las disposiciones legislativas expedidas desde la independencia de la República*, 34 vols. (Mexico City: Imprenta del Comercio, 1876–1902), 10:pt. 6169.

Bleynat describes the evolution of the Ayuntamiento's jurisdiction over markets in the nineteenth century in chapter 1 of her dissertation, "Trading with Power."

51. Rodríguez Kuri, *La experiencia olvidada*, 279; Bleynat, "Taxes and Compassion."

52. On the Ayuntamiento's purchase of the Plaza del Volador from the Marquisate of the Valley of Oaxaca, see AGN, Ayuntamientos, contenedor 6, vol. 15, no exp.

53. Morales, "Espacio, propiedad," 176–78.

54. Ayuntamiento de México, *Memoria que el Ayuntamiento Constitucional del año 1868 presenta para conocimiento de sus comitentes* (Mexico City: Imprenta de Ignacio Cumplido, 1868), 148. See also Bleynat, "Trading with Power," ch. 1.

55. Dublán y Lozano, *Legislación mexicana*, 12: 442–50. Bleynat describes the episode in detail in "Taxes and Compassion."

56. These two individuals, like most baratilleros, left little trace in the historical record beyond their signatures on petitions. At one point, Rosales Gordoa claimed that "Jesús Farfán" was a pseudonym. Indeed, it was common to write in the nineteenth-century press under a pen name. Census records show a Felix Farfán—another signatory on the 1872 letters (though on the opposite side of the conflict from Jesús)—living near the Plaza del Jardín in 1882. Ramón Escalante's name surfaces on an 1880 petition to the Ayuntamiento as part of a group of vendors requesting a place in the Merced food market. See *El Ferrocarril*, August 7, 1872, 2–3; AHCM, Ayuntamiento, Padrones, vol. 3425–26 (1882); and AHCM, Ayuntamiento, Rastros y Mercados, vol. 3736, exp. 861 (1880).

57. AHCM, Ayuntamiento, Rastros y Mercados, vol. 3734, exp. 554, fs. 44–46.

58. *El Correo del Comercio*, March 27, 1872, 3.

59. See, for example, "Baratillo," *Diario de México*, November 18, 1808.

60. AHCM, Ayuntamiento, Rastros y Mercados, vol. 3734, exp. 554, f. 13. Records from the 1860s and early 1880s show that there were, in fact, a number of pawnshops and pulquerías around the Plaza del Jardín in this era. See AHAGNCM, Fondo Antiguo, not. 55, Antonio Ferreiro, vol. 355; and AHCM, Ayuntamiento, Padrones, vol. 3426.

61. There is no record of this interaction in the press, so it probably happened in a face-to-face meeting between García Torres and the baratilleros. AHCM, Ayuntamiento, Rastros y Mercados, vol. 3734, exp. 554, f. 22v. The claim that García Torres had originally voted for the Baratillo's move to the Guerrero marketplace proved impossible to verify.

62. AHCM, Ayuntamiento, Rastros y Mercados, vol. 3734, exp. 554, fs. 22–22v.

63. *La Iberia* reported the decision on May 11, 1872, 3.

64. Sebastián Lerdo de Tejada was the younger brother of Miguel Lerdo de Tejada, for whom the Ley Lerdo was named.

65. ASCJN, 1872-05-11, CSJ-TP-TcJA-Mx-9954.

66. Tancredo, "El Ayuntamiento y los Baratilleros," *El Monitor Republicano*, May 31, 1872.

67. The word *pueblo*, in this context, means "the people" but refers to the masses, in particular.

68. Tancredo, "El Ayuntamiento."

69. For more on the role of Mexico's Supreme Court in mediating debates over individual rights in the last third of the nineteenth century, see James, *Mexico's Supreme Court*.

70. AHCM, Ayuntamiento, Rastros y Mercados, vol. 3734, exp. 554, fs. 49–51. The only regidores to vote against the order were Emilio Islas, Francisco Mejía, and Abraham Olvera. García Torres ultimately resigned from the body over a dispute involving the city's administrator of paseos. García Torres had sought to fire the administrator for his alleged ineptitude, but the governor blocked the move. García Torres was furious, claiming that the governor had dealt a major blow to the autonomy of the Ayuntamiento, and resigned in late May, this time for good. See *El Monitor Republicano*, May 23, 1872, 2.

71. AHCM, Ayuntamiento, Rastros y Mercados, vol. 3734, exp. 554, fs. 55–56v.

72. He actually filed two complaints, one with the Supreme Court and another with the district court, for reasons that are not clear from the file.

73. ASCJN, 1872–05–11, CSJ-TP-TcJA-Mx-9954.

74. Ibid.

75. Tiburcio Montiel's role in this episode is a curious one. After initially expressing concern about the impact of the move on the Baratillo's vendors, he appears to have condoned their removal by the police. Montiel went on to become a founder of the Socialist Party in Mexico and has been considered a precursor to Mexico's anarchists. Gastón García Cantú, *El socialismo en México, siglo XIX* (Mexico City: ERA, 1969), 74.

76. AHCM, Ayuntamiento, Rastros y Mercados, vol. 3734, exp. 554, f. 64.

77. "Los comerciantes del Baratillo y el ayuntamiento," *La Voz de México*, June 14, 1872, 2.

78. ASCJN, 1872–06–24, CSJ-TP-TcJA-Mx-9962.

79. AHCM, Ayuntamiento, Rastros y Mercados, vol. 3734, exp. 554, f. 70.

80. *El Ferrocarril* was a liberal newspaper that supported Porfirio Díaz.

81. *El Ferrocarril*, July 29, 1872, 3. Rosales does not seem to have had a law degree. His name appears as a witness in an 1875 case with the honorific prefix "Don," as opposed to some of the other witnesses whose names are preceded by "Lic.," the prefix for *licenciado*, the title given to attorneys in Mexico. See Juan José Baz, Gabriel María Islas, and Manuel Gómez Parada, *Causa instruida contra don Casto de Beraza sobre falsificación de firma en el juzgado 3o. del ramo criminal* (Mexico City: Imprenta de Francisco Díaz de León, 1875), 69.

82. *El Ferrocarril*, August 7, 1872, 2–3.

83. *El Ferrocarril*, July 31, 1872, 3.

84. Piccato, *Tyranny of Opinion*, 3.

85. Frank Averill Knapp Jr., *The Life of Sebastián Lerdo de Tejada, 1823–1889: A Study of Influence and Obscurity* (Austin: University of Texas Press, 1951), 225.

86. See Porter, "And That It Is Custom"; Jiménez, "From the Lettered City"; and Bleynat, "Trading with Power." Laura Gotkowitz finds that honor played an important role in court cases involving female vendors in Bolivia but does not find that

this dynamic played out in the press. Gotkowitz, "Trading Insults: Honor, Violence, and the Gendered Culture of Commerce in Cochabamba, Bolivia, 1870s–1950s," *Hispanic American Historical Review* 83:1 (2003): 83–118.

87. Jesús Farfán et al., *El Ferrocarril,* July 29, 1872, 3. Susie Porter notes that female vendors in Porfirian Mexico City stressed their poverty in petitions to authorities because "elites considered a working woman honorable if her poverty was visible." See Porter, "And That It Is Custom," 121, 139. A close examination of the petitions that the two groups sent to the Ayuntamiento or published in the press in 1872 suggests that divisions between them may have been more fluid than the language in those missives suggests. At least one vendor switched sides mid-dispute: Trinidad Aguilar initially sided with the vendors in the Guerrero market (which included one Pedro Aguilar, who may have been a relative) but then joined those who filed the writ of amparo to remain the Plaza del Jardín (where she joined a Rafael Aguilar) a month later. AHCM, Ayuntamiento, Rastros y Mercados, vol. 3734, exp. 554. A different example offers clear evidence that the split divided members of the same family. José María Escobar and his son-in-law Albino Peña found themselves on opposite sides of the debate. But the controversy does not appear to have created a lasting rift: in Escobar's 1875 will he appointed Peña to be the tutor of his two young children in the event of his death. AHAGNCM, Fondo Antiguo, Sección Notarías Siglos XVI–XIX, Fermín Gonzalo Cosío, vol. 1864, f. 13 (primer semestre 1875).

88. See, e.g., Arrom, *Containing the Poor*, 284. See also, Bleynat, "Trading with Power," which argues that the elite's duty of compassion for the poor framed relations between market vendors, the elite, and Mexico City's Ayuntamiento during the Restored Republic. This phenomenon was not unique to Mexico: female street vendors in early republican Philadelphia, known as "hucksters," similarly "sought the pity and compassion of their legislators" even as they increasingly couched their demands in the language of political equality and laissez-faire economics. See Candice Harrison, "'Free Trade and Hucksters' Rights!': Envisioning Economic Democracy in the Early Republic," *Pennsylvania Magazine of History and Biography* 137:2 (2013): 169–70.

89. "Discurso y proposición del Sr. García Torres."

90. Tancredo, "Comida," 1–2.

91. AHCM, Ayuntamiento, Rastros y Mercados, vol. 3734, exp. 558.

92. "La plazuela del Jardín," *La Voz de México,* September 25, 1872, 3; "Los baratilleros," *El Monitor Republicano,* September 27, 1872, 3.

93. Francisco G. Cosmes, *Historia de Méjico contemporánea*, Vol. 3, *Los últimos 33 años (1867–1900)* (Mexico City: Imprenta de Pedro Ortega, 1901), 746–52, 886, 1057–58.

94. Manuel Payno, *Compendio de la historia de México: Para el uso de los establecimientos de instrucción pública de la República Mexicana* (Mexico City: Imprenta de F. Díaz de León, 1876), 238–50. See also Laurens Ballard Perry, *Juárez and Díaz: Machine Politics in Mexico* (DeKalb: Northern Illinois University Press, 1978).

95. *El Monitor Republicano,* November 21, 1872, 1; Gustavo Ernesto Emmerich, "El ayuntamiento de la ciudad de México; Elecciones y política, 1834–1909," in *Las*

elecciones en la ciudad de México, ed. Emmerich, 228. *El Federalista* reported on December 19, 1871, that the municipal elections that month "were not the most pacific," with chairs and punches flying throughout the voting.

96. "La plazuela del Jardín," *La Voz de México*, September 25, 1872, 3; "Los baratilleros," *El Monitor Republicano*, September 27, 1872, 3.

97. AHCM, Ayuntamiento, Rastros y Mercados, vol. 3734, exp. 558.

98. Ibid., exp. 626.

CHAPTER 6. ORDER, PROGRESS, AND THE BLACK MARKET

1. "Una visita al Baratillo," *La Patria*, October 15, 1891, 1–2.

2. Manuel González served as president from 1880 to 1884, after Díaz's first term, but was largely subservient to his predecessor. Díaz was reelected in 1884 and held the presidency until he was ousted in the Mexican Revolution. After 1880, Mexico's economy saw significant growth under policies that lifted or rationalized internal and external trade barriers and increased foreign investment, particularly in railroads. These actions helped unify Mexico in a common market and boost its exports, particularly of raw materials, to Europe and North America during the Second Industrial Revolution. See Enrique Cárdenas Sánchez, *El largo curso de la economía mexicana: De 1780 a nuestros días* (Mexico City: Fondo de Cultura Económica/El Colegio de México, 2015), 188–291.

3. Sardín, "Las dos ciudades," *El Mundo Ilustrado,* February 15, 1903, 2, 1; Lear, *Workers*, 16.

4. *La Patria* was founded in 1877 by Ireneo Paz, a supporter of Díaz during the Rebellion of Tuxtepec and throughout his many reelections. *La Patria* at times received subsidies from Díaz's government. See Florence Toussaint Alcaraz, *Periodismo, siglo diez y nueve* (Mexico City: UNAM, 2006), 50–51; and idem, *Escenario*, 32.

5. Historians have largely overlooked this effort. Aréchiga Córdoba notes that municipal officials recognized that bringing public services to poor barrios could remedy their unsanitary conditions, but does not detail their efforts to do so. See *Tepito*, 177. The prevailing view in the historiography is that "the barrios were ignored." See Michael Johns, *The City of Mexico in the Age of Díaz* (Austin: University of Texas Press, 1997), 39.

6. John Lear, for example, describes the Porfirian state's efforts to "physically displace from the city center the prisons, tenements, hospitals, and orphanages— and therefore the populations associated with them—which detracted from the Porfirian vision of progress." See Lear, *Workers*, 34–35. Pablo Piccato describes the "ideal social map" that Porfirian officials tried to create in Mexico City, which neatly divided wealthy, modern sections from the backward neighborhoods of the poor— though he argues that authorities failed to enforce those divisions. Piccato, *City of Suspects: Crime in Mexico City, 1900–1932* (Durham, NC: Duke University Press,

2001), 14. In the realm of politics, James Sanders contends that under Díaz's rule, "excluding plebeians now trumped reforming the masses." See Sanders, *Vanguard*, 203. Susie Porter argues that street vendors, as members of *"el pueblo,"* were excluded from the respectable *"público."* See Porter, "And That It Is Custom," 122.

7. This disagreement among the capital's upper classes contradicts much of the historiography on the Porfiriato, which describes the formation of a new national elite during the period, one united, in part, by its views of the lower classes. For an example of this view, see James Alex Garza, *The Imagined Underworld: Sex, Crime, and Vice in Porfirian Mexico City* (Lincoln: University of Nebraska Press, 2007), introduction.

8. Leading Porfirian intellectuals such as Julio Guerrero and Justo Sierra believed that although Mexico's poor were plagued by atavistic instincts and habits, those traits were ultimately remediable by a technocratic state. See Guerrero, *La génesis del crimen en México: Estudio de psiquiatría social* (Mexico City: Librería de la Viuda de Ch. Bouret, 1901); and Sierra, *The Political Evolution of the Mexican People*, ed. Edmundo O'Gorman, trans. Charles Ramsdell (Austin: University of Texas Press, 1969). Porfirian technocrats focused heavily on education: during the Porfiriato, government expenditures on education increased tenfold, and the number of public primary schools doubled between 1878 and 1907. Mary Kay Vaughan, "Primary Education and Literacy in Nineteenth-Century Mexico: Research Trends, 1968–1988," *Latin American Research Review* 25:1 (1990): 42.

9. David W. Walker describes the paternalistic relations between the urban working classes in Mexico City and the Porfirian state in "Porfirian Labor Politics," 257–89. Marie Francois has observed that: "Concern with the well-being of the poor, especially the 'deserving' poor, persisted in the Mexican political culture" during the Porfiriato. Francois, *Everyday Credit*, 223. See also Arrom, *Containing the Poor*, 5. Bleynat, on the other hand, argues that while paternalistic compassion shaped relations between vendors and the Mexico City elite during the Restored Republic, the Porfiriato saw an erosion of those bonds. Bleynat, "Trading with Power," ch. 2.

10. The longer Díaz remained in office, the more he tightened his grip on power. Beginning in the 1890s, elections became more rigged and government rule more authoritarian across the country, but particularly in rural areas. Alicia Hernández Chávez, *Mexico: A Brief History*, trans. Andy Klatt (Berkeley: University of California Press, 2006), 187–92. The government also began to censor not only literal statements in the press but also innuendo. See María Elena Díaz "The Satiric Penny Press for Workers in Mexico, 1900–1910," *Journal of Latin American Studies* 22:3 (1990): 521. Rodríguez Kuri argues that the federal government "colonized" the Mexico City Ayuntamiento by stacking it with loyalists. A revolving door operated between the Ayuntamiento, high posts in the federal government, and prominent positions in the business community. See *La experiencia olivdada*, 68–73.

11. Crackdowns on political participation did not mean that the country had become entirely autocratic. Elections continued to be held throughout the country, including in the capital. In *La experiencia olvidada,* Rodríguez Kuri argues that the Ayuntamiento was an important site of political contestation throughout the

nineteenth century, despite the gradual erosion of its autonomy by the national executive. See also Fausta Gantús, "La traza del poder político y la administración de la ciudad liberal," in *Historia política*, ed. Rodríguez Kuri, 287–362. On the continuing importance of elections in rural areas of Mexico during the Porfiriato, see Leticia Reina, "Local Elections and Regime Crises: The Political Culture of Indigenous Peoples," in *Cycles of Conflict, Centuries of Change: Crisis, Reform, and Revolution in Mexico*, ed. Elisa Servín, Leticia Reina, and John Tutino (Durham, NC: Duke University Press, 2007), 91–128.

12. Rural migrants traveled to Mexico City to work in its expanding textile and tobacco industries, as domestic servants, and in other low-skill fields. See Lear, *Workers*, 58–80.

13. Morales, "La expansión de la ciudad," 194; Claudia Agostoni, *Monuments of Progress: Modernization and Public Health in Mexico City, 1876–1910* (Boulder: University Press of Colorado, 2003), 45. See also Francois, *Everyday Credit*, 318, for population estimates from additional years.

14. Lear, *Workers*, 28.

15. The term *colonia* means something akin to "section" in English, though it translates directly as "colony." The connection is not coincidental: these new sections of Mexico City were established after the enactment of the mid-century laws of the Reforma, especially the 1856 Ley Lerdo, which freed land previously held by the Church and indigenous communities to be purchased by private individuals. Mauricio Tenorio-Trillo has noted that Mexico City's expansion and renewal in this era was, in fact, a form of "frontier expansion." See *I Speak of the City: Mexico City at the Turn of the Twentieth Century* (Chicago: University of Chicago Press, 2013), 15. For a history of the relationship between Mexico City's indigenous barrios and the Spanish city, see Andrés Lira, *Comunidades indígenas frente a la ciudad de México: Tenochtitlán y Tlatelolco, sus pueblos y barrios, 1812–1919* (Mexico City: El Colegio de México, 1983).

16. Lear, *Workers*, 36.

17. Philip T. Terry, *Terry's Mexico* (New York: Houghton Mifflin, 1911), 257, cited in Lear, *Workers*, 45. Despite the increasing geographic segregation that characterized turn-of-the-century Mexico City, the boundaries that separated rich and poor sections of the city continued to be porous—just as the traza–barrios distinction was during the colonial era. Pablo Piccato has shown that the capital's poor successfully challenged such boundaries by working in the homes and businesses of the wealthy, by vending or begging in wealthy areas, and by resorting to crimes such as theft or drinking in public. Piccato, *City of Suspects*, 33. This interpretation contrasts with Lear's, who argues that a working-class identity emerged in Porfirian Mexico City out of physical and cultural separation from elites, and Johns's, which refers to the "extreme separation of the classes" in the Porfirian capital. Lear, *Workers*, 6, and Johns, *City of Mexico*, 5–6.

18. Lear, *Workers*, 20–21.

19. Ibid., 32–33.

20. "Nota editorial: El Baratillo debe ser suprimido," *El Universal*, August 9, 1898, 1.

21. "Rowdy Baratillo," *The Two Republics*, July 7, 1883, 4.

22. In 1894, of the 119 stands in the main part of the Baratillo, 48 sold *"fierros"* (literally, "iron," but may have included metal tools of any kind); 30 sold clothing or used clothing; and 20 sold shoes. There are an additional 30 names under a section of the register labeled "dais for iron and old clothing." AHCM, Ayuntamiento, Rastros y Mercados: Padrones, vol. 3750, exp. 2.

23. In the last two decades of the century, Mexico City's newspapers helped stoke fears that crime was out of control in the capital. Alberto del Castillo, "Prensa, poder y criminalidad a finales del siglo XIX en la ciudad de México," in *Hábitos, normas y escándalo: Prensa, criminalidad y drogas durante el Porfiriato tardío*, ed. Ricardo Pérez Montfort (Mexico City: CIESAS, 1997), 18–73; Piccato, *City of Suspects*, 54–55. Miguel S. Macedo reported in 1897 that Mexico City's murder rate was 100 per 100,000 inhabitants. In Madrid, by comparison, the figure was less than 8 per 100,000. Macedo, *La criminalidad en México: Medios de combatirla* (Mexico City: Oficina Tip. de la Secretaría de Fomento, 1897), 5. During the Porfiriato, circulations of major newspapers in the capital ranged from roughly 1,000 to 10,000 copies, though some periodicals that enjoyed subsidies from the federal government, particularly the semiofficial *El Imparcial*, boasted much higher numbers. As was the case earlier in the nineteenth century, exact figures are elusive. See Toussaint Alcaraz, *Escenario*, 31–32.

24. "Riña sangrienta," *La Voz de México*, January 12, 1897, 3; "Puñaladas a una mujer," *El Popular*, August 24, 1897, 2; "Gran escándalo en el Baratillo," *El Popular*, May 22, 1897, 2.

25. "El Baratillo," *México Gráfico*, February 19, 1893, 3, 6.

26. The Baratillo was also the alleged headquarters of the notorious criminal Arturo Monterrosas, which *El Mundo* called "the theater of his crimes." "Aprehensión del prófugo sentenciado a muerte Arturo Monterrosas," *El Mundo*, January 24, 1897, 1. In *Imagined Underworld*, James Garza describes how reality and myth often blurred together in the sensational reporting of the Porfirian-era Mexico City press.

27. "Peligro," *El Tiempo*, March 21, 1894; *El Imparcial*, March 1, 1901, sec. Notas de Policía; "Robo de alambre," *La Voz de México*, August 29, 1894; "Robo de cartuchos metálicos," *El Correo Español*, February 22, 1899; "Robo de rieles," *El Monitor Republicano*, June 4, 1895; "Robo en el Ferrocarril Central," *El Siglo Diez y Nueve*, August 6, 1896; "Robo en las imprentas," *La Caridad*, July 11, 1891.

28. *El Demócrata*, February 17, 1893, 4; *El Popular*, December 15, 1897, 2; and *El Popular*, November 30, 1903, in which the paper reported on the discovery of a counterfeiting operation near the Baratillo, in the neighborhood of Tepito.

29. "Il Medesimo," "Se les cayó la mollera," *La Patria*, June 28, 1893.

30. "Talento mal empleado," *La Enseñanza Objetiva*, September 3, 1892, 4.

31. Ibid.

32. "El barrio del Baratillo," *El Tiempo*, November 17, 1900, 2.

33. Piccato, *City of Suspects*, 164. Piccato notes that term *ratero* is related to the words *rata* or *ratón* (rat or mouse) and also *rastrero* (crawling, but also vile, despicable).

34. Piccato, *City of Suspects*, 41–42.

35. Ibid., 167–69.

36. Rodríguez Kuri, *La experiencia olvidada*, 61.

37. Lear, *Workers*, 41. See also Deborah Toner, *Alcohol and Nationhood in Nineteenth-Century Mexico* (Lincoln: University of Nebraska Press, 2015), and the Ayuntamiento's own essay on "La guerra contra el alcoholismo" in the official *Boletín Oficial del Consejo de Gobierno del Distrito Federal*, October 16, 1903, 481.

38. Agostoni, *Monuments of Progress*, 65–66; and Diego G. López Rosado, *Los servicios públicos de la ciudad de México* (Mexico City: Editorial Porrúa, 1976), 240.

39. "De donde vienen algunas epidemias," *El Tiempo*, July 29, 1898, 1.

40. "Una visita al Baratillo." Prominent members of Mexico's elite continued to believe that miasmas—infected airs that emanated from human waste and rotting food—were the primary causes of disease, despite the development of germ theory in the second half of the nineteenth century. See Agostoni, *Monuments of Progress*, 14.

41. *El Monitor Republicano*, November 11, 1883, 4; *La Voz de México*, December 4, 1892, 3; *La Patria*, June 16, 1893, 1.

42. "Los peligros de la ropa usada," *La Voz de México*, November 11, 1899, 3.

43. "Muy peligroso," *La Patria,* January 26, 1891, 3; "Comercio perjudicial," *El Tiempo*, June 21, 1898, 2; "El comercio de la ropa vieja," *El Tiempo*, February 27, 1901, 2.

44. Haber, *Industry and Underdevelopment*, 28. See also Edward Beatty, *Technology and the Search for Progress in Modern Mexico* (Oakland: University of California Press, 2015), 136–37; and Challú and Gómez-Galvarriato ("Mexico and Real Wages"), who find that economic growth during the Porfiriato failed to bring real wages consistently above eighteenth-century levels.

45. Beverly Lemire, "Consumerism in Preindustrial and Early Industrial England: The Trade in Secondhand Clothes," *Journal of British Studies* 27:1 (1988): 22–23.

46. In 1886 there were 77 vendors listed on the market census. In 1901, the Ayuntamiento put the total number of vendors at 128. See AHCM, Ayuntamiento, Rastros y Mercados: Padrones, vol. 3750, exp. 2; AHCM, Ayuntamiento, Rastros y Mercados, vol. 3740, exp. 1256.

47. In 1886, for example, there were eight tinglados located in the center of the market, all occupied by women who sold enchiladas, prepared meats, tamales, and quesadillas. They were four square varas in size, while most of the other stands were nine (though all paid the same six-cent daily fee). None of these women appear on any other market census. AHCM, Ayuntamiento, Rastros y Mercados: Padrones, vol. 3750, exp. 2.

48. The 1894 market roster is unique in that it indicates both owner and renter. It shows that just 20 of 119 stands had been rented out. The average value of the stalls affected by the 1888 fire was 191 pesos. This figure excludes two stalls that were valued at zero pesos (probably because they were empty at the time of the fire). AHCM, Ayuntamiento, Rastros y Mercados: Padrones, vol. 3750, exp. 2.

49. The comparison between Baratillo stands and pawnshops is an imperfect one, since pawnshops made loans with that capital, so the actual value of those businesses is somewhat more difficult to determine. See Francois, *Everyday Credit*, 200–201.

50. AHCM, Ayuntamiento, Rastros y Mercados: Padrones, vol. 3750, exp. 2.

51. The households of José de la Luz Vida and Guadalupe and Lusano Campuzano had live-in maids. See AHCM, Ayuntamiento, Padrones, vol. 3425, fs. 32 and 49v; and AHCM, Ayuntamiento, Rastros y Mercados: Padrones, vol. 3750, exp. 2.

52. Only 44 percent of men and 32 percent of women in Mexico City were literate in 1895—an overall rate of 37.7 percent. Milada Bazant de Saldaña, *Historia de la educación en el Porfiriato* (Mexico: El Colegio de México, 1993), 95. Baratilleros were also more educated than their neighbors. Just over half of the men on the blocks adjacent to the Plaza del Jardín could read (55%), in contrast to twenty-one of the twenty-three baratilleros (91%). Less than one-quarter of the women in the area could read but two of the three baratilleras could. AHCM, Ayuntamiento, Padrones, vol. 3425.

53. See, for example, AGN, Indiferente Virreinal, caja 5093, exp. 2, f. 130.

54. Among those baratilleros who lived in the one-block radius of the market in 1882 were fifteen merchants and nine tradesmen, including four cobblers, two tailors, two carpenters, one blacksmith, and one chair maker. These men did not necessarily sell the products they had been trained to make. Manuel López, whom the census identified as a tailor in 1882, operated a stand in the Baratillo in 1886, 1893, and 1894 that sold iron products. Antonio Sánchez, a carpenter by trade, sold used iron in 1886 and second-hand clothing in 1893. Whatever these men's professions were, they probably sold the goods they could obtain most easily and inexpensively. On the fluid boundaries between the artisan and merchant professions in the late nineteenth century, see Florencia Gutiérrez, *El mundo de trabajo y el poder político: Integración, consenso y resistencia en la ciudad de México a fines del siglo XIX* (Mexico City: El Colegio de México, 2011). The median age in the 1882 sample is nearly forty-five, with a range of twenty-two to sixty-two. This finding is largely consistent with the ages of baratilleros in earlier records, and contrasts with the ages of rateros, whom Piccato finds were much younger, with a median age of twenty. See AHCM, Ayuntamiento, Padrones, vol. 3425 and 3426, n.p.; AHCM, Ayuntamiento, Rastros y Mercados: Padrones, vol. 3750, exp. 2; and Piccato, *City of Suspects*, 172.

55. Judith Martí similarly finds that newspapers in Mexico had mixed feelings about street vendors. Martí, "Nineteenth-Century Views," 33.

56. "El Baratillo," *El Mundo*, January 17, 1897, 1.

57. "La traslación del Baratillo a la plazuela de Los Ángeles," *El Chisme*, March 31, 1900, 2.

58. "El palacio de la miseria: El Baratillo, lo nuevo y lo viejo," *La Patria*, March 4, 1897, 1–2.

59. *La Patria*, February 14, February 25, and March 4, 1891.

60. See, for example, the letter a baratillero sent to *La Patria*, asking for better policing of the market (June 24, 1893, 3); and a petition from a group of vendors

to the Ayuntamiento in 1899 complaining about the poor conduct of the rent collector in the Baratillo (AHCM, Ayuntamiento, Rastros y Mercados, vol. 3739, exp. 1173).

61. Francois, *Everyday Credit*, 215–16. In recent decades, historians have challenged the traditional view of the Porfiriato as a time of laissez-faire economic policies. Porfirian governments, in fact, intervened more directly in the economy than its predecessor governments in the nineteenth century. See, e.g., Sandra Kuntz Ficker, *El comercio exterior de México en la era del capitalismo liberal, 1870–1929* (Mexico City: El Colegio de México, 2007), ch. 4.1; and Richard Weiner, who calls Porfirian liberals "social engineers, not free-market ideologues" in *Race, Nation, and Market: Economic Culture in Porfirian Mexico* (Tucson: University of Arizona Press, 2004), 13, 26, and 64–69.

62. Porter, "And That It Is Custom," 120.

63. AHCM, Ayuntamiento, Gobierno del Distrito, Mercados, vol. 1737, exp. 916 (March 8, 1911). Amid the turmoil of the Mexican Revolution, the prohibition had little impact.

64. The científicos, heavily influenced by the writings of Auguste Comte, saw government not as an arbitrator, as the orthodox liberals of the Restored Republic had held, but as a powerful force in Mexican society—a pedagogue, an "inculcator of common moral and civic virtues to all citizens," as Charles Hale wrote. See Hale, *Transformation of Liberalism*, 216, 234.

65. AHCM, Ayuntamiento, Rastros y Mercados, vol. 3740, exp. 1256.

66. For details of the conference, see: John Vavasour Noel, *History of the Second Pan American Congress with Notes on the Republic of Mexico* (Baltimore: Guggenheimer, Weil & Co., 1902); and A. Curtis Wilgus, "The Second International American Conference at Mexico City," *Hispanic American Historical Review* 11:1 (1931): 27–68. While a number of historians have written about the projects that the national government undertook in Mexico City ahead of the 1910 centennial celebrations, the public works projects at the beginning of the decade have not drawn the same attention. See, e.g., Mauricio Tenorio Trillo, "1910 Mexico City: Space and Nation in the City of the Centenario," *Journal of Latin American Studies* 28:1 (1996): 75–104.

67. Ayuntamiento de México, *Discurso . . . y Memoria documentada de los trabajos municipales de 1901* (Mexico City: J. Aguilar y Compañía, 1902), 1: 15–16, 18–20, 26; "El aseo de las fachadas de las Casas," *Boletín Municipal*, July 2, 1901, 1–2. See also María Patricia Vega Amaya, "El gobierno de Ramón Corral en el Distrito Federal (1900–1903): Su impacto en la ciudad de México a través de la obra pública" (Master's thesis, Instituto Mora, 2004), 99.

68. Born to an upper-class Mexican family in 1848, Landa y Escandón was an important player in the Porfirian political machine and a fixture in Mexico City's high society. He served as a senator from both Morelos and Chihuahua before joining the Mexico City Ayuntamiento, and he was a founding member of the city's Jockey Club, the pinnacle of elite society in the capital. He also saw himself as a "protector and friend of the working classes." Hale, *Transformation of Liberalism*,

126; Rodríguez Kuri, *La experiencia olvidada*, 69; Mario Barbosa, "La política en la Ciudad de México en tiempos de cambio (1903–1929)," in *Historia política*, ed. Rodríguez Kuri, 369; Roderick A. Camp, *Mexican Political Biographies, 1884–1935* (Austin: University of Texas Press, 1991), 119; John Mraz, *Looking for Mexico: Modern Visual Culture and National Identity* (Durham, NC: Duke University Press, 2009), 199; and Porter, *Working Women*, 91–92.

69. "La transformación de los barrios de la Capital: Moción," *Boletín Municipal*, May 24, 1901, 1.

70. This approach contrasts with those taken in cities like Paris and Rio de Janeiro. See Jeffrey D. Needell, "Rio de Janeiro and Buenos Aires: Public Space and Public Consciousness in Fin-de-Siècle Latin America," *Comparative Studies in Society and History* 37:3 (1995): 519. For a discussion of Haussmann's demolition of Parisian neighborhoods, see David P. Jordan, "Haussmann and Haussmannisation: The Legacy for Paris," *French Historical Studies* 27:1 (2004): 88–89.

71. Reprinted in *Boletín Municipal*, May 28, 1901, 2.

72. Ayuntamiento de México, *Memoria de 1901*; Ayuntamiento de México, *Discurso . . . y Memoria documentada de los trabajos municipales de 1902* (Mexico City: J. Aguilar y Compañía, 1903), vol. 2; Ayuntamiento de México, *Discurso . . . y Memoria documentada de los trabajos municipales de 1903 (primer semestre)* (Mexico City: J. Aguilar Vera y Compañía, 1903).

73. "Los barrios de la Ciudad de México: El sur de la ciudad," *Boletín Municipal*, February 17, 1903, 1. See also "Los suburbios de la ciudad," *Boletín Municipal*, January 23, 1903, 1.

74. Scholars, particularly in cultural studies and anthropology, have taken a greater interest in the relationship between infrastructure and society. See, for example, the special issue on "Infrastructuralism," ed. Michael Rubenstein, Bruce Robbins, and Sophia Beal, in *Modern Fiction Studies* 61:4 (2015). For examples of empirical studies on the topic, see Beal, *Brazil Under Construction*; and Julie Kleinman, "Adventures in Infrastructure: Making an African Hub in Paris," *City & Society* 26:3 (2014): 286–307.

75. Mexican intellectuals of the era lent support to this idea. Alberto Pani, in his influential 1916 work, *La higiene en México*, argued that the state of the capital's streets, four-fifths of which were not paved with asphalt, combined with the poor's "deeply rooted practices of uncleanliness" to create dangerously unhygienic conditions. Pani, *Hygiene in Mexico: A Study of Sanitary and Educational Problems*, trans. Ernest L. de Gogorza (New York: Knickerbocker Press, 1917), 58.

76. S.v. "Miguel Ángel de Quevedo," *Diccionario Porrúa: Historia, biografía y geografía de México*, 6th ed. (Mexico City: Editorial Porrúa, 1995), 2849–50. Quevedo shared Landa y Escandón's vision of turning Mexico into a garden city with a comprehensive park system modeled on that of Paris. See Agostoni, *Monuments of Progress*, 40–41; and Emily Wakild, "Naturalizing Modernity: Urban Parks, Public Gardens, and Drainage Projects in Porfirian Mexico City," *Mexican Studies/Estudios Mexicanos* 23:1 (2007): 101–23. On Quevedo's role in the postrevolutionary regime, see Christopher R. Boyer, "Revolución y paternalismo ecológico:

Miguel Ángel de Quevedo y la política forestal en México, 1926–1940," *Historia Mexicana* 57:1 (2007): 91–138.

77. "Las mejoras en los mercados de la ciudad," *Boletín Municipal*, March 15, 1901, 1; and "Las mejoras en los mercados de la ciudad II," *Boletín Municipal,* March 19, 1901, 1.

78. AHCM, Ayuntamiento, Rastros y Mercados, vol. 3740, exp. 1256.

79. Ibid., vol. 3737, exp. 941; Ibid., vol. 3739, exp. 1182.

80. "Los comerciantes del Baratillo," *El Imparcial*, July 24, 1901, 1.

81. AHCM, Ayuntamiento, Rastros y Mercados, vol. 3740, exp. 1256. The government put the total number of vendors in the Baratillo at 128; the vendors claimed the number was between 200 and 300.

82. "El apego al rumbo," *La Patria*, August 14, 1901, 3. The editors of *La Patria* supported the vendors who sought to move the Baratillo to the Plaza de los Ángeles, which, they argued, was located in the same rumbo.

83. Piccato observes that the rumbo "combined work, nuclear and extended families, friends, and the public spaces of sociability where private life continued." See Piccato, *City of Suspects*, 48–49; and Aréchiga Córdoba, *Tepito*, 42–43.

84. See table 2 in the appendix. See also Barbosa Cruz, *El trabajo*, 164.

85. Among the 4,471 inhabitants of the four blocks adjacent to the Plaza del Jardín, the most common professions were: comerciantes (merchants) (183), *zapateros* (shoemakers/shoe sellers) (133), *carpinteros* (carpenters) (129), *albañiles* (bricklayers/construction workers) (89), sastres (tailors) (56), *domésticos* (domestic workers) (54), *panaderos* (bakers) (49), *empleados* (employees, unspecified) (49), *jornaleros* (journeymen) (48), and *herreros* (blacksmiths) (42). AHCM, Ayuntamiento, Padrones, vol. 3426.

86. Ibid. The vendors who signed the letter with Primo Giles also emphasized that the government would lose tax revenue if those businesses closed. AHCM, Ayuntamiento, Rastros y Mercados, vol. 3740, exp. 1256. On the Baratillo's association with pulque and pulquerías, see "El Baratillo—A la policía," *La Patria*, August 3, 1892, 2.

87. For the paper's first issue and mission statement, see *El Popular*, January 1, 1897, 1. On Mexico City's satirical penny press during the late Porfiriato, see Robert M. Buffington, *A Sentimental Education for the Working Man: The Mexico City Penny Press, 1900–1910* (Durham, NC: Duke University Press, 2015).

88. *El Popular*, July 23, 1901, 1.

89. *El Popular*, August 17, 1901, 1.

90. See "La supresión del Baratillo," *El Diario del Hogar*, July 21, 1901, 2. *El Hijo del Trabajo*, founded by the tailor José María González y González, similarly saw an 1883 rent increase for the vendors of the Baratillo as a part of the "war on the poor." "Siempre guerra al pobre," *El Hijo del Trabajo*, January 21, 1883, 3; Illades, "Los intelectuales," 484.

91. On the residents of working-class barrios' appropriation of the language of modernization and public health, see Ernesto Aréchiga Córdoba, "Lucha de clases en la ciudad: La disputa por el espacio urbano, ca. 1890–1930," in *Los trabajadores de*

la ciudad de México, 1860–1950: Textos en homenaje a Clara E. Lida, ed. Carlos Illades and Mario Barbosa (Mexico City: El Colegio de México, 2013), 36–46.

92. AHCM, Ayuntamiento, Rastros y Mercados, vol. 3740, exp. 1256. The Plaza de San Sebastián was on the eastern fringe of the city, southeast of Tepito. Although the Ayuntamiento's overall revenue surged in the last decades of the nineteenth century, markets continued to be an important source of income for the municipal government. Markets still constituted 5.5 percent of overall revenue in 1901, down from just over 6 percent in 1872. If the Baratillo produced roughly 9,000 pesos per year, as the vendors claimed, it would have made up slightly more than 4 percent of total market revenue. See Rodríguez Kuri, La experiencia olvidada, appendix 1, 279–83.

93. "La traslación del Baratillo," El Popular, August 12, 1901, 2.

94. "Tepito," La Patria, January 25, 1889, 3.

95. "El Baratillo y Santa Catarina," El Imparcial, July 24, 1901, 1. Over the years, various groups, including residents, vendors, newspaper editors, and government officials suggested that the Baratillo could spur economic development in peripheral areas of the city. See, for example, "La traslación del Baratillo a la plazuela de Los Ángeles," El Chisme, March 31, 1900, 2.

96. AHCM, Ayuntamiento, Rastros y Mercados, vol. 3740, exp. 1256. Vendors sometimes used the Ayuntamiento to resolve internal disputes. For example, in 1900, a group in the Plaza del Jardín asked the municipal president to remove one Rodrigo Granados and his wife from the market, whose conduct they found "completely unacceptable" and a threat to the "tranquility of our families." AHCM, Ayuntamiento, Rastros y Mercados, vol. 3739, exp. 1191. For an investigation of conflicts within the Baratillo in the early twentieth century, see Fausto Adriano Arellano Ramírez, "Conflictos, prácticas y resistencia: El mercado de Baratillo de Fray Bartolomé de las Casas, ciudad de México (1901–1918)" (undergraduate thesis, UNAM, 2017).

97. For another example of alliances between street vendors and members of the elite during the Porfiriato, see Florenica Gutiérrez and Fausta Gantús, "Los pequeños voceadores: Prácticas laborales, censura y representaciones a finales del siglo xix," in Los trabajadores de la ciudad, ed. Illades and Barbosa, 81–116.

98. AHCM, Ayuntamiento, Rastros y Mercados, vol. 3740, exp. 1256; Boletín Municipal, January 7, 1902, 2.

99. The baratilleros also pushed back against some of the negative press coverage of their market, threatening a slander suit against El Monitor Republicano in 1883. See "Se les cayó la mollera," La Patria, June 28, 1893, 2.

100. "Los comerciantes del Baratillo," El Imparcial, July 24, 1901, 1.

101. See Walker, "Porfirian Labor Politics," 267, 272; Gantús, "La traza del poder"; and Gutiérrez, El mundo de trabajo, an examination of the relationship between artisans and the Porfirian regime. Both Walker and Gutiérrez argue that Díaz effectively co-opted Mexico City's working classes in the last decades of the century, while Gantús contends that citizens continued to participate in local politics in the capital.

102. "Actas de Cabildo," *Boletín Municipal*, August 6, 1901.

103. AHCM, Ayuntamiento, Rastros y Mercados, vol. 3740, exp. 1256.

104. "La traslación del Baratillo," *El Popular*, August 12, 1901, 2. Earlier that year, another group of baratilleros had written to *El Popular*'s editor, Francisco Montes de Oca, imploring him not to support a move to the Plaza de los Ángeles. "Los comerciantes del Baratillo," *El Popular,* March 1, 1901, 1.

105. *El Popular,* July 23, 1901, 1. Ordóñez had found financial success as the owner of a cola factory, among other businesses. See David W. Walker, "Porfirian Labor Politics," 267.

106. In this regard, the baratilleros seem to have enjoyed greater access than other vendors in the capital. While previous studies have shown that vendors attempted to access and shape the Porfirian public sphere through petitions, those vendors do not appear to have had the same clout in local government or the press. See Porter, "And That It Is Custom"; Jiménez, "From the Lettered City"; and Bleynat, "Trading with Power."

107. AHCM, Ayuntamiento, Rastros y Mercados, vol. 3740, exp. 1256.

108. Indeed, although Quevedo never stated outright that the Baratillo could not return to the Plaza del Jardín, the Markets Improvement Commission proposed turning the plaza into a park in the August 2 cabildo session. "Actas de Cabildo," *Boletín Municipal*, August 6, 1901. Landa y Escandón reiterated that plan in his speech to outgoing city councilmen at the end of 1901. Ayuntamiento de México, *Memoria de 1901*, 1:25. See also AHCM, Ayuntamiento, Rastros y Mercados, vol. 3740, exp. 1256.

109. Aréchiga Córdoba, *Tepito*, 118, 128.

110. Ibid., 216.

111. Piccato, *City of Suspects*, 165.

112. *Boletín Municipal*, Actas de Cabildo, August 6, 1901.

113. "El Baratillo," *La Voz de México*, August 9, 1901, 2; "El Baratillo en Tepito: Nuevos Jardines," *El Imparcial*, January 14, 1902, 1. Beyond paving the plaza, which the Ayuntamiento apparently did quite poorly, the city was also supposed to plant trees throughout the area. "El Baratillo en Tepito: Nuevos jardines," *El Imparcial*, January 14, 1902, 1.

114. AHCM, Ayuntamiento, Gobierno del Distrito, Mercados, vol. 1729, exp. 198, f. 3.

115. One square vara is equal to approximately 0.7 square meters.

116. *Boletín Municipal*, January 28, 1902, 2.

117. "Los comerciantes del Baratillo de Tepito," *El Popular*, March 15, 1902, 1.

118. "Insalubridad en Tepito," *El Popular*, May 14, 1902, 3.

119. *La Patria*, January 14, 1903, 1; Archivo de Salud Pública, Fondo Salubridad Pública, Sección Higiene Pública, Serie Inspección de Alimentos y Bebidas, caja 1, exp. 21.

120. AHCM, Ayuntamiento, Gobierno del Distrito, Mercados, vol. 1729, exp. 224.

121. AHCM, Ayuntamiento, Policía: Salubridad, vol. 3671, exp. 217 (1903). The Ayuntamiento, in some ways, was continuing a long tradition of promising but

never building a permanent market structure for the Baratillo. The body had passed a resolution to build a market in the Plaza del Jardín in the early 1880s before reversing that decision in 1884. AHCM, Ayuntamiento, Rastros y Mercados, vol. 3736, exp. 891. The six-day nature of the market in Tepito in the early twenty-first century demonstrates that it never lost that provisional character: it all but vanishes every Tuesday. Aréchiga Córdoba also emphasizes the impermanent nature of the Baratillo's existence in Tepito. See *Tepito*, 218–22.

122. See Garza, *Imagined Underworld*, 29.

123. In December 1902, Fernando Pimental y Fagoaga, serving as interim president of the Ayuntamiento while Landa y Escandón was on a diplomatic mission in Europe, noted that the Ayuntamiento was saddled by almost 1.7 million pesos in debt service—an amount that was steadily increasing. Ayuntamiento de México, *Memoria de 1902*, 1:12.

124. The Ayuntamiento's spending on public works declined from 2,015,888 pesos in 1901 to 1,128,491 pesos in 1902. In the first half of 1903, it spent only 397,780 pesos. Ayuntamiento de México, *Memoria de 1901*, 2:37; Ayuntamiento de México, *Memoria de 1902*, 2:52; Ayuntamiento de México, *Discurso . . . Memoria del Ayuntamiento de 1903* (Mexico City: J. Aguilar Vera y Compañía, 1904), 201.

125. Ayuntamiento de México, *Memoria del Ayuntamiento de 1903*, 355–56.

126. Although many areas of central and northern Mexico held direct elections for municipal and statewide offices, Mexico City's elections continued to be indirect before the 1910 Revolution. See Rodríguez Kuri, *La experiencia olvidada*, 51–60.

127. On artisan representation on the Ayuntamiento during the colonial period, see Pérez Toledo, "Una vieja corporación y un nuevo discurso: Los gremios de la ciudad de México al finalizar la colonia," in *Construcción de la legitimidad política en México*, ed. Brian Connaughton, Carlos Illades, and Sonia Pérez Toledo (Mexico City: El Colegio de Michoacán, 1999), 97.

128. Wayne A. Cornelius has shown that residents of poor neighborhoods in Mexico City continued to rely on petitions to demand public services from the government in the twentieth century. See *Politics and the Migrant Poor in Mexico City* (Stanford, CA: Stanford University Press, 1975), 177.

129. Indeed, it may have been in Díaz's interest to allow criticism of the Ayuntamiento, as it would have it would have bolstered his case for dissolving the body and folding it into the Federal District.

130. "El palacio de la miseria," *La Patria*, March 4, 1897, 1–2.

131. Elections continued to be held for the members of the Ayuntamiento every two years. Barbosa, "La política," 367, 370.

EPILOGUE

1. See, for example, "Otros monederos falsos," *El Chisme*, April 24, 1899, 2; "Otro asalto," *El Universal*, February 10, 1901, 2; and Piccato, *City of Suspects*, 37, citing a 1908 article from *El Imparcial*.

2. The term "Baratillo" faded from use in the city's newspapers in the 1940s and 1950s. In *Children of Sanchez*, published in 1961, Oscar Lewis refers to the neighborhood's second-hand market as "Tepito," while one of his informants, speaking of the past, refers to the Baratillo. See Lewis, *Children*, xiii, 138.

3. "Quemazón en el Baratillo de Tepito," 1913, Jean Charlot Collection, University of Hawaii at Manoa Library. A rendering of the fire that appears on the broadside is reproduced in Anna Alexander, *City on Fire: Technology, Social Change, and the Hazards of Progress in Mexico City, 1860–1910* (Pittsburgh: University of Pittsburgh Press, 2016), 22. I am grateful to Alexander for sharing an image of the broadside with me.

4. "Vendía carne de caballo," *El Combate 1915*, July 7, 1915, 3; "Vendedor de baratijas," *El Diario*, June 27, 1913, 8.

5. "Tepito Radio News Company: Los ladrones organizaron una sociedad," *El Nacional*, July 16, 1931, 9; "Sobre la Marihuana," *El Nacional*, January 29, 1931, 12. The Baratillo still had connections to Mexico City's artisanal trades, as it had throughout its history, and Tepito became an important center of artisanal shoe production in the capital. See John C. Cross and Alfonso Hernández, "Place, Identity, and Deviance: A Community-Based Approach to Understanding the Relationship between Deviance and Place," *Deviant Behavior* 32 (2011): 513; and Victor Hugo Rocha Osorio, "Evolución social del barrio de Tepito como importante centro de comercio informal" (Undergraduate thesis, UNAM, 2004).

6. Lewis, *Children*, xiii.

7. For an overview of Mexico's twentieth-century economic policies, see Juan Carlos Moreno-Brid and Jaime Ros, *Development and Growth in the Mexican Economy* (New York: Oxford University Press, 2009).

8. Ana Rosas Mantecón and Guadalupe Reyes Domínguez, *Los usos de la identidad barrial: Una mirada antropológica a la lucha por la vivienda, Tepito 1970–1984* (Mexico City: UAM Iztapalapa, 1993), 39.

9. Cross and Hernández, "Place, Identity." Mexico signed the General Agreement on Tariffs and Trade (GATT) in 1986 and the North American Free Trade Agreement (NAFTA) in 1992.

10. Agustín Salgado, "Tepito: La historia de un barrio donde es caro el 'impuesto a la ingenuidad,'" *La Jornada*, March 16, 2007, http://www.jornada.unam.mx /2007/03/16/index.php?section=capital&article=041n1cap, accessed November 22, 2016.

11. Carlos Alba Vega, "La calle para quien la ocupa: Las condiciones sociopolíticas de la globalización no hegemónica en México, DF," *Nueva Sociedad* 241 (2012): 79–92.

12. Natalia Grisales Ramírez, "'En Tepito todo se vende menos la dignidad': Espacio público e informalidad económica en el barrio bravo," *Alteridades* 13:26 (2003): 69. The article's title is a reference to a common saying in the neighborhood: "In Tepito, everything is for sale except [our] dignity."

13. Although information about Tepito's consumers, like those who frequented the Baratillo, is scarce, the market is thought to serve middle-class consumers in

addition to poorer ones. See Cross and Hernández, "Place, Identity," 513; and Andrés Becerril, "La fayuca en los tiempos pre-TLC; de las chácharas a lo 'Made in USA,'" *Excélsior,* April 12, 2016, http://www.excelsior.com.mx/nacional/2016/12/04 /1132064, accessed July 19, 2017. On middle-class responses to the failure of the ISI model, see Louise E. Walker, *Waking from the Dream: Mexico's Middle Classes after 1968* (Stanford, CA: Stanford University Press, 2013).

14. Alba Vega, "La calle," 84–85. See also Sandra Alarcón, *El tianguis global* (Mexico City: Universidad Iberoamericana, 2008).

15. Barbosa, "La política."

16. Ariel Rodríguez Kuri, "Ciudad oficial, 1930–1970," in *Historia política,* ed. Rodríguez Kuri, 417–82; Diane Davis, *Urban Leviathan: Mexico City in the Twentieth Century* (Philadelphia: Temple University Press, 1994), 62–63.

17. The 1928 law that abolished the Ayuntamiento created an organ for citizen participation in the governance of the Federal District, the Consejo Consultivo, but its members were appointed, not elected. See Davis, *Urban Leviathan,* 67–68. In 1988, the Federal District held elections for local representatives in the Asamblea de Representantes del Distrito Federal. In 1997, residents of the capital elected their first *jefe de gobierno* (a position somewhere between a mayor and governor), choosing Cuauhtémoc Cárdenas, the leftist leader who lost the disputed presidential election of 1988. See Ignacio Marván Laborde, "De la ciudad del presidente al gobierno propio, 1970–2000," in *Historia política,* ed. Rodríguez Kuri, 483–563.

18. Christina Jiménez finds that vendors in the city of Morelia began unionizing in the 1920s and that by 1930 there were at least two vendor unions there. Jiménez, "From the Lettered City," 233–37. See also Davis, *Urban Leviathan,* 69–70; and Bleynat, "Trading with Power," for further discussion of vendors' organizing efforts after the Revolution.

19. "La Unión de Comerciantes en Pequeño piden se modifique el reglamento," *El Nacional,* May 16, 1931, 13.

20. "En el Antiguo Tepito," *El Nacional,* March 13, 1933, 2.

21. AHCM, Departamento del DF, Abasto y Mercados, caja 1.

22. For more on how the postrevolutionary regime sought to co-opt urban popular groups, including street vendors, see Davis, *Urban Leviathan*; and Guillermina Grisel Castro Nieto, "Intermediarismo político y sector informal: El comercio ambulante en Tepito," *Nueva Antropología. Revista de Ciencias Sociales* 1:37 (1990): 59–69. See also Mendiola García, *Street Democracy,* on how a vendor union in Puebla successfully resisted incorporation into the PRI in the 1970s and 1980s.

23. See David M. Walker, "Resisting the Neoliberalization of Space in Mexico City," in Tony Roshan Samara, Shenjing He, and Guo Chen, eds., *Locating Right to the City in the Global South,* ed. Tony Rosha Samara, Shenjing He, and Guo Chen (New York: Routledge, 2013): 171–94; John C. Cross and Sergio Peña, "Risk and Regulation in Informal and Illegal Markets," in *Out of the Shadows,* ed. Fernández-Kelly and Shefner, 49–80; and John C. Cross, "Co-optation, Competition, and Resistance: State and Street Vendors in Mexico City," *Latin American Perspectives* 25:2 (1998): 41–61.

24. Constitución Política de la Ciudad de México: Artículos aprobados por el Pleno de la Asamblea Constituyente hasta el 30 de enero de 2017, Art. 15, Section B, Numbers 12–13, http://gaceta.diputados.gob.mx/ACCM/GP/20170130-AA.pdf, accessed July 19, 2017.

25. Among the more notable interventions was the government's 2007 expropriation of the building known as "The Fortress," which served as a major distribution hub for narcotics. Police also periodically raid the neighborhood's stalls to confiscate pirated electronics and clothing. See Sánchez I., "GDF expropia"; and Alejandro González, "Realizan operativo contra la piratería en Tepito," *Milenio*, April 27, 2017, http://www.milenio.com/df/operativo-tepito-pirateria-ssp-cuauhtemoc-granaderos-cdmx-milenio-noticias_0_946105420.html, accessed June 27, 2017.

26. Alfonso Hernández, the *cronista*, or local historian, of the neighborhood and director of the Centro de Estudios Tepiteños, stated in a 2010 interview with the author that there were sixty-two vendor organizations in the neighborhood, most of which were incorporated as *asociaciones civiles* (civil society organizations). There are separate associations for vendors, many of whom no longer live in Tepito, and neighborhood residents. Alfonso Hernández Hernández, interview with the author, Mexico City, August 31, 2010. A follow-up interview on June 19, 2014, took place in Hernández's office at the Mexico City Delegación (borough hall) of Cuauhtémoc, where he was serving as vice-director of Cultural Patrimony. Hernández's position itself speaks to the extensive links between tepiteños and the government of Mexico's capital.

27. On recent tensions between vendor groups in Tepito, see "Se reactiva conflicto entre bandos de ambulantes en el DF," *Proceso*, January 14, 2015, http://www.proceso.com.mx/393109/se-reactiva-conflicto-entre-bandos-de-ambulantes-en-el-df, accessed July 27, 2017.

28. Incidents of violence include the 1692 riot, when baratilleros allegedly joined indigenous rioters in the Plaza Mayor and set fire to the markets there; when an alcalde del crimen was said to have been murdered in the market shortly thereafter; and the violent eviction of vendors during their 1872 dispute with the Ayuntamiento.

29. In recent decades, clashes between police and vendors have become more common in Tepito. The question of when those patterns began to emerge requires further investigation. In *Street Democracy*, Mendiola García traces the rise in state violence against vendors in Puebla to the 1970s and argues that it increased after Mexico's neoliberal turn in the 1980s.

BIBLIOGRAPHY

ARCHIVES

Mexico City

Acervo Histórico del Archivo General de Notarías de la Ciudad de México
Archivo Central de la Suprema Corte de Justicia de la Nación
Archivo General de la Nación
Archivo Histórico de la Ciudad de México
Archivo Histórico del Museo Nacional de Antropología
Archivo de Salud Pública
Fondo Reservado, Biblioteca Nacional de México, Universidad Nacional Autónoma
   de México

Puebla, Mexico

Archivo General Municipal de Puebla

Zacatecas, Mexico

Archivo Histórico del Estado de Zacatecas

Madrid, Spain

Archivo Histórico Nacional de España

Seville, Spain

Archivo General de Indias

New Haven, CT

Yale University, Sterling Memorial Library, Mexico Collection

San Antonio, TX

University of Texas at San Antonio Libraries Special Collections

PERIODICALS

Anales de la Sociedad Humboldt
Boletín Municipal
Boletín Oficial del Consejo Superior de Gobierno del Distrito Federal
La Caridad
El Chisme
El Combate
El Correo de Comercio
El Correo Español
Correo de la Federación Mexicana
El Cosmopolita
La Crónica
El Demócrata
Diario de México
Diario del Gobierno
El Diario
El Diario del Hogar
Diario de la Revolución
La Enseñanza Objetiva
El Estante Nacional
Excélsior
El Federalista
El Ferrocarril
Frégoli
La Gaceta Comercial
El Hijo del Trabajo
La Iberia
El Imparcial
El Informador
La Jornada
Legislación Mexicana
Los Angeles Times
México Gráfico
Milenio

El Monitor Republicano
El Mosquito Mexicano
El Mundo
El Mundo Ilustrado
El Nacional
Noticias MVS
El País
La Patria
El Popular
Proceso
El Siglo Diez y Nueve
El Tiempo
The Two Republics
El Universal
La Voz de México

INTERVIEWS

Hernández Hernández, Alfonso. Interviews by author, Mexico City, August 31, 2010, and June 19, 2014.

PUBLISHED PRIMARY SOURCES

Ajofrín, Francisco de. *Diario del viaje a la Nueva España*. Mexico City: SEP, 1986.

Ayuntamiento de México. *Discurso . . . y Memoria documentada de los trabajos municipales de 1900*. 2 vols. Mexico City: J. Aguilar y Compañía, 1901.

———. *Discurso . . . y Memoria documentada de los trabajos municipales de 1901*. 2 vols. Mexico City: J. Aguilar y Compañía, 1902.

———. *Discurso . . . y Memoria documentada de los trabajos municipales de 1902*. 2 vols. Mexico City: J. Aguilar y Compañía, 1903.

———. *Discurso . . . y Memoria documentada de los trabajos municipales de 1903 (primer semestre)*. Mexico City: J. Aguilar y Compañía, 1903.

———. *Discurso . . . Memoria del Ayuntamiento de 1903*. Mexico City: J. Aguilar Vera y Compañía, 1904.

———. *Documentos oficiales relativos a la construccion y demolicion del Parian, y a la propiedad reconocida é incontestable que tuvo el escmo. Ayuntamiento de México en aquel edificio*. Mexico City: Imprenta de Ignacio Cumplido, 1843.

———. *Exposición de las razones que tuvo el exmo. Ayuntamiento para contratar la nueva obra que se está haciendo de la plaza del Volador*. Mexico City: Impr. de V. García Torres, 1842.

———. *Memoria que el Ayuntamiento Constitucional del año 1868 presenta para conocimiento de sus comitentes*. Mexico City: Imprenta de Ignacio Cumplido, 1868.

Barrio Lorenzot, Juan Francisco del, ed. *El trabajo en México durante la época colonial: Ordenanzas de gremios de la Nueva España*. Mexico City: Secretaría de Gobernación, 1921.

Bautista de Morales, Juan. *El gallo pitagórico: Colección de artículos crítico-políticos y de costumbres*. Mexico City: Imprenta de Ignacio Cumplido, 1857.

Baz, Juan José, Gabriel María Islas, and Manuel Gómez Parada. *Causa instruida contra don Casto de Beraza sobre falsificacion de firma en el juzgado 30. del ramo criminal*. Mexico City: Impr. de Francisco Diaz de Leon, 1875.

Bustamante, Carlos María de. *Apuntes para la historia del gobierno del general don Antonio López de Santa Anna*. 1845. Reprint. Mexico City: Fondo de Cultural Económica, 1986.

Colección de leyes, decretos, circulares, y demás documentos oficiales importantes del Supremo Gobierno de los Estados-Unidos Mexicanos que se han publicado desde 30 de mayo de 1848. Mexico City: Imprenta de la Calle de Medinas, 1849.

Constitución Federal de los Estados Unidos Mexicanos. Mexico City: Imprenta de Ignacio Cumplido, 1857.

Constitución Política de la Ciudad de México: Artículos aprobados por el Pleno de la Asamblea Constituyente hasta el 30 de enero de 2017. http://gaceta.diputados.gob.mx/ACCM/GP/20170130-AA.pdf. Accessed July 19, 2017.

Cosmes, Francisco G. *Historia de Méjico contemporánea*. Vol. 3, *Los últimos 33 años (1867–1900)*. Mexico City: Imprenta de Pedro Ortega, 1901.

Díaz del Castillo, Bernal. *The History of the Conquest of New Spain*. Edited by David Carrasco. Albuquerque: University of New Mexico Press, 2008.

Dublán, Manuel, and José María Lozano. *Legislación mexicana o Colección completa de las disposiciones legislativas expedidas desde la independencia de la República*. 34 vols. Mexico City: Imprenta de E. Dublán, 1876–1902.

Fernández de Lizardi, José Joaquín. *Obras IV—Periódicos*. Edited by María Rosa Palazón M. Mexico City: UNAM, 1970.

———. *El periquillo sarniento*. Mexico City: Editorial Época, 1986.

Gómez de Cervantes, Gonzalo. *La vida económica y social de Nueva España al finalizar el siglo XVI*. Mexico City: Antigua Librería Robredo, 1944.

Güemez Pacheco de Padilla Horcasitas y Aguayo, Juan Vicente. *Informe sobre las misiones, 1793, e instrucción reservada al Marqués de Branciforte, 1794*. Mexico City: Editorial Jus, 1966.

Guerrero, Julio. *La génesis del crimen en México: Estudio de psiquiatría social*. Mexico City: Librería de la Viuda de Ch. Bouret, 1901.

Humboldt, Alexander von. *Political Essay on the Kingdom of New Spain*. New York: I. Riley, 1811.

Lozano, José María. *Estudio del derecho constitucional patrio*. Mexico City: Impr. del Comercio de Dublán y Compañía, 1876.

Macedo, Miguel S. *La criminalidad en México: Medios de combatirla*. Mexico City: Oficina Tip. de la Secretaría de Fomento, 1897.

Mayer, Brantz. *Mexico As It Was and As It Is*. New York: New World Press, 1844.

"Memorial ajustado de acusaciones, enviadas por Don Jerónimo Chacón Abarca, Alcalde del Crimen . . . " In María Pilar Gutiérrez Lorenzo, *De la corte de Castilla al virreinato de México: El conde de Galve (1653–1697)*. Guadalajara: Excma. Diputación Provincial, 1993.

Miño Grijalva, Manuel. *Censo de población de la Ciudad de México, 1790*. Mexico City: El Colegio de México, 2003.

Noel, John Vavasour. *History of the Second Pan American Congress with Notes on the Republic of Mexico*. Baltimore: Guggenheimer, Weil & Co., 1902.

Ordenanzas municipales del que fue el Departamento de México: Sancionadas por el Gobierno y Junta Departamental en el año de 1840 y que según algunos, están vigentes en el actualidad en el Distrito Federal. Mexico City: Imprenta del Tecpam de Santiago, 1868.

Orozco y Berra, Manuel. *Memoria para el plano de la ciudad de México: Formada de órden e Ministerio de Fomento*. Mexico City: S. White, 1867.

Ortega y Montañéz, Juan. *Instrucción reservada que dio a su sucesor en el mando, el Conde de Moctezuma*. Prologue and notes by Norman F. Martin. Mexico City: Editorial Jus, 1965.

Pani, Alberto. *Hygiene in Mexico: A Study of Sanitary and Educational Problems*. Translated by Ernest L. de Gogorza. New York: Knickerbocker Press, 1917.

Payno, Manuel. *Compendio de la historia de México: Para el uso de los establecimientos de instrucción pública de la República Mexicana*. Mexico City: Imprenta de F. Díaz de León, 1876.

Prieto, Guillermo. *Lecciones elementales de economía política dadas en la Escuela de Jurisprudencia de México en el curso de 1871*. 1871. Reprint. Mexico City: UNAM, 1989.

Revillagigedo, Juan Vicente Güémez Pacheco de Padilla Horcasitas y Aguayo, Conde de and Ramón Mena. *El Segundo Conde de Revilla Gigedo (juicio de residencia)*. Publicaciones del Archivo General de la Nación 22. Mexico City: Talleres Gráficos de la Nación, 1933.

Robles, Antonio de. *Diario de sucesos notables 1665–1703*. Edited by Antonio Castro Leal. Mexico City: Editorial Porrúa, 1946.

Salvídar, Luis G., ed. *Diccionario de la legislación Mexicana*. Mexico City: La Constitución Social, 1870.

Sierra, Justo. *The Political Evolution of the Mexican People*. Edited by Edmundo O'Gorman. Translated by Charles Ramsdell. Austin: University of Texas Press, 1969.

Sierra, Justo, José María Gutierrez Estrada, and Mariano Otero. *Documentos de la época 1840–1850*. Mexico City: Secretaría de la Reforma Agraria, 1981.

Sigüenza y Góngora, Carlos. *Relaciones históricas*. Mexico City: UNAM, 1940.

"Sobre los inconvenientes de vivir los indios en el centro de la ciudad. " *Boletín del Archivo General de la Nación* 9:1 (1938): 1–34.

Solórzano y Pereyra, Juan de. *Política indiana*. Madrid: Atlas, 1972.

Terry, Philip T. *Terry's Mexico*. New York: Houghton Mifflin, 1911.

Torre Villar, Ernesto de la. *Instrucciones y memorias de los virreyes novohispanos.* 2 vols. Mexico City: Editorial Porrúa, 1991.

Viera, Juan de. *Breve y compendiosa narración de la Ciudad de México.* Mexico City: Instituto Mora, 1993.

Villarroel, Hipólito. *Enfermedades políticas que padece la capital de esta Nueva España....* Mexico City: Editorial Porrúa, 1999.

SECONDARY SOURCES

Acerbi, Patricia. "'A Long Poem of Walking': Flâneurs, Vendors, and Chronicles of Post-Abolition Rio de Janeiro." *Journal of Urban History* 40:1 (2014): 97–115.

Agostoni, Claudia. *Monuments of Progress: Modernization and Public Health in Mexico City, 1876–1910.* Boulder: University Press of Colorado, 2003.

Alarcón, Sandra. *El tianguis global.* Mexico City: Universidad Iberoamericana, 2008.

Alba Vega, Carlos. "La calle para quien la ocupa: Las condiciones sociopolíticas de la globalización no hegemónica en México, DF." *Nueva Sociedad* 241 (2012): 79–92.

Alexander, Anna. *City on Fire: Technology, Social Change, and the Hazards of Progress in Mexico City, 1860–1910.* Pittsburgh: University of Pittsburgh Press, 2016.

Allerston, Patricia. "Reconstructing the Second-Hand Clothes Trade in Sixteenth- and Seventeenth-Century Venice." *Costume* 33:1 (1999): 46–56.

Andrien, Kenneth. "The Politics of Reform in Spain's Atlantic Empire during the Late Bourbon Period." *Journal of Latin American Studies* 41:4 (2009): 637–62.

Anna, Timothy E. *The Fall of the Royal Government in Mexico City.* Lincoln: University of Nebraska Press, 1978.

———. "The Finances of Mexico City during the War of Independence." *Journal of Latin American Studies* 4:1 (1972): 55–75.

Archer, Christon I. *The Army in Bourbon Mexico, 1760–1810.* Albuquerque: University of New Mexico Press, 1977.

Aréchiga Córdoba, Ernesto. "Lucha de clases en la ciudad: La disputa por el espacio urbano, ca. 1890–1930." In Illades and Barbosa, eds., *Los trabajadores de la ciudad de México,* 19–50.

———. *Tepito: Del antiguo barrio de indios al arrabal, 1868–1929, historia de una urbanización inacabada.* Mexico City: Ediciones ¡Uníos!, 2003.

Arellano Ramírez, Fausto Adriano. "Conflictos, prácticas y resistencia: El mercado de Baratillo de Fray Bartolomé de las Casas, ciudad de México (1901–1918)." Undergraduate thesis, UNAM, 2017.

Arrom, Silvia Marina. *Containing the Poor: The Mexico City Poor House, 1774–1871.* Durham, NC: Duke University Press, 2000.

———. "Popular Politics in Mexico City: The Parian Riot, 1828." *Hispanic American Historical Review* 68:2 (1988): 245–68.

Baker, Richard D. *Judicial Review in Mexico: A Study of the* Amparo *Suit.* Austin: University of Texas Press, 1971.

Bakhtin, Mikhail. *Rabelais and His World.* Translated by Hélene Iswolsky. Bloomington: Indiana University Press, 1984.

Barbosa [Cruz], Mario. "La política en la Ciudad de México en tiempos de cambio (1903–1929)." In Rodríguez Kuri, ed., *Historia política*, 363–416.

Barbosa Cruz, Mario. *El trabajo en las calles: Subsistencia y negociación política en la ciudad de México a comienzos del siglo XX.* Mexico City: El Colegio de México /UAM Cuajimalpa, 2008.

Barragán, Rossana. "Working Silver for the World: Mining Labor and Popular Economy in Colonial Potosí." *Hispanic American Historical Review* 97:2 (2017): 193–222.

Baskes, Jeremy. *Indians, Merchants, and Markets: A Reinterpretation of the* Repartimiento *and Spanish-Indian Economic Relations in Colonial Oaxaca, 1750–1821.* Stanford, CA: Stanford University Press, 2000.

Bazant de Saldaña, Milada. *Historia de la educación en el Porfiriato.* Mexico City: El Colegio de México, 1993.

Beal, Sophia. *Brazil Under Construction: Fiction and Public Works.* New York: Palgrave Macmillan, 2013.

Beatty, Edward. *Technology and the Search for Progress in Modern Mexico.* Oakland: University of California Press, 2015.

Becker, Mark. "In Search of *Tinterillos.*" *Latin American Research Review* 47:1 (2012): 95–114.

Beezley, William H., Cheryl English Martin, and William French, eds. *Rituals of Rule, Rituals of Resistance: Public Celebrations and Popular Culture in Mexico.* Wilmington, DE: Scholarly Resources, 1994.

Bleynat, Ingrid. "Taxes and Compassion: Mexico's Public Markets between 1867 and 1880." Paper presented at the Mellon Latin American History Conference, Chicago, May 2–3, 2008.

———. "Trading with Power: Mexico City's Public Markets, 1867–1958." Ph.D. diss., Harvard University, 2013.

Borah, Woodraw. *Justice by Insurance: The Indian General Court of Colonial Mexico and the Legal Aides of the Half-Real.* Berkeley: University of California Press, 1983.

Boyer, Christopher R. "Revolución y paternalismo ecológico: Miguel Ángel de Quevedo y la política forestal en México, 1926–1940." *Historia Mexicana* 57:1 (2007): 91–138.

Brading, David. "Government and Elite in Late Colonial Mexico." *Hispanic American Historical Review* 53:3 (1973): 389–414.

———. *Miners and Merchants in Bourbon Mexico 1763–1810.* Cambridge: Cambridge University Press, 1971.

Breman, Jan. "A Dualistic Labor System? A Critique of the 'Informal Sector' Concept." *Economic and Political Weekly* 11:48 (1976): 1870–76.

Bromley, Ray. "Introduction: The Urban Informal Sector: Why Is It Worth Discussing?" *World Development* 6:9/10 (1978): 1033–39.

Buffington, Robert M. *A Sentimental Education for the Working Man: The Mexico City Penny Press, 1900–1910.* Durham, NC: Duke University Press, 2015.

Bunker, Steven B. *Creating Mexican Consumer Culture in the Age of Porfirio Díaz.* Albuquerque: University of New Mexico Press, 2012.

Burns, Kathryn. *Colonial Habits: Convents and the Spiritual Economy of Cuzco, Peru.* Durham, NC: Duke University Press, 1999.

Cabrera, Lucio A. "History of the Mexican Judiciary." *Miami Law Quarterly* 11:4 (1957): 439–48.

Cabrera Siles, Esperanza, and Patricia Escandón. *Historia del Nacional Monte de Piedad, 1775–1993.* Mexico City: Nacional Monte de Piedad, 1993.

Callahan, William J. *Honor, Commerce, and Industry in Eighteenth-Century Spain.* Boston: Harvard Business School Press, 1972.

———. "A Note on the Real y General Junta de Comercio, 1679–1814." *Economic History Review* 21:3 (1968): 519–28.

Camp, Roderick A. *Mexican Political Biographies, 1884–1935.* Austin: University of Texas Press, 1991.

Cañeque, Alejandro. *The King's Living Image: The Culture and Politics of Viceregal Power in Colonial Mexico.* New York: Routledge, 2004.

Cárdenas Sánchez, Enrique. *El largo curso de la economía mexicana: De 1780 a nuestros días.* Mexico City: Fondo de Cultura Económica/El Colegio de México, 2015.

Carmagnani, Marcello. "Vectors of Liberal Economic Culture in Mexico." In Rodríguez O., ed., *The Divine Charter,* 285–304.

Castillo, Alberto del. "Prensa, poder y criminalidad a finales del siglo XIX en la ciudad de México." In Pérez Montfort, ed., *Hábitos, normas y escándalo,* 18–73.

Castro Gutiérrez, Felipe. *La extinción de la artesanía gremial.* Mexico City: UNAM, 1986.

Castro Nieto, Guillermina Grisel. "Intermediarismo político y sector informal: El comercio ambulante en Tepito." *Nueva Antropología: Revista de Ciencias Sociales* 1:37 (1990): 59–69.

Challú, Amílcar, and Aurora Gómez-Galvarriato. "Mexico's Real Wages in the Age of the Great Divergence, 1730–1930." *Revista de Historia Económica—Journal of Iberian and Latin American Economic History* 33:1 (2015): 83–122.

Chambers, Sarah. *From Subjects to Citizens: Honor, Gender, and Politics in Arequipa, Peru.* University Park: Pennsylvania State University Press, 1999.

Chazkel, Amy. *Laws of Chance: Brazil's Clandestine Lottery and the Making of Urban Public Life.* Durham, NC: Duke University Press, 2011.

Clendinnen, Inga. *Ambivalent Conquests: Maya and Spaniard in Yucatan, 1517–1570.* New York: Cambridge University Press, 2003.

Connaughton, Brian, Carlos Illades, and Sonia Pérez Toledo, eds. *Construcción de la legitimidad política en México.* Mexico City: El Colegio de Michoacán/El Colegio de México/UAM/UNAM—Instituto de Investigaciones Históricas, 1999.

Cope, R. Douglas. "Between Liberty and Constraint: Government Regulation of Petty Commerce in Mexico City, 1700–1780." Paper presented at the Latin American Studies Association Meeting, Washington, DC, September 2001.

———. *The Limits of Racial Domination: Plebeian Society in Colonial Mexico City, 1660–1720.* Madison: University of Wisconsin Press, 1994.

———. "The Marvelous and the Abominable: The Intersection of Formal and Informal Economies in Eighteenth-Century Mexico City." *Diacronie* 13:1 (2013): 1–20.

———. "The Underground Economy in Eighteenth-Century Mexico City." Paper presented at the David Rockefeller Center, Harvard University, March 2006.

Cornelius, Wayne A. *Politics and the Migrant Poor in Mexico City.* Stanford, CA: Stanford University Press, 1975.

Cosío Villegas, Daniel. *Historia moderna de México.* 9 vols. Mexico City: Editorial Hermes, 1955–1972.

Costeloe, Michael P. *The Central Republic in Mexico, 1835–1846:* Hombres de Bien in the Age of Santa Anna. New York: Cambridge University Press, 1993.

———. "Generals versus Politicians: Santa Anna and the 1842 Congressional Elections in Mexico." *Bulletin of Latin American Research* 8:2 (1989): 257–74.

Covarrubias, José Enrique. *La moneda de cobre en México, 1760–1842: Un problema administrativo.* Mexico City: UNAM/Instituto Mora, 2000.

Cross, John C. "Co-optation, Competition, and Resistance: State and Street Vendors in Mexico City." *Latin American Perspectives* 25:2 (1998): 41–61.

———. *Informal Politics: Street Vendors and the State in Mexico City.* Stanford, CA: Stanford University Press, 1998.

Cross, John C., and Alfonso Hernández. "Place, Identity, and Deviance: A Community-Based Approach to Understanding the Relationship between Deviance and Place." *Deviant Behavior* 32 (2011): 503–37.

Cross, John C., and Sergio Peña. "Risk and Regulation in Informal and Illegal Markets." In Fernández-Kelly and Shefner, eds., *Out of the Shadows,* 49–80.

Davis, Diane. *Urban Leviathan: Mexico City in the Twentieth Century.* Philadelphia: Temple University Press, 1994.

Díaz, María Elena. "The Satiric Penny Press for Workers in Mexico, 1900–1910." *Journal of Latin American Studies* 22:3 (1990): 497–526.

Diccionario Porrúa: Historia, biografía y geografía de México. 6th ed. Mexico City: Editorial Porrúa, 1995.

Elissa-Barroso, Francisco A., and Ainara Vázquez Varela, eds. *Early Bourbon Spanish America: Politics and Society in a Forgotten Era (1700–1759).* Leiden: Brill, 2013.

Elliott, J. H. *Empires of the Atlantic World: Britain and Spain in America, 1492–1830.* New Haven, CT: Yale University Press, 2007.

Emmerich, Gustavo Ernesto. "El ayuntamiento de la ciudad de México; Elecciones y política, 1834–1909." In Emmerich, ed., *Las elecciones en la ciudad de México,* 179–239.

———, ed. *Las elecciones en la Ciudad de México, 1376–2005.* Mexico City: Instituto Electoral del Distrito Federal/UAM, 2005.

Escamilla González, Iván. "Inspirados por el Espiritú Santo: Elecciones y vida política corporativa en la capital de la Nueva España." In Emmerich, ed., *Las elecciones en la ciudad de México*, 69–112.

Escamilla González, Iván, Matilde Souto Mantecón, and Guadalupe Pinzón Rios, eds. *Resonancias imperiales: El Tratado de Utrecht de 1713*. Mexico City: UNAM, 2015.

Escamilla González, Iván, and Paul Mues Orts. "Espacio real, espacio pictórico y poder: 'Vista de la Plaza Mayor de México' de Cristóbal de Villalpando." In Medina, ed., *La imagen política*, 177–204.

Espinoza Peregrino, Martha Leticia. "El Tribunal de Fiel Ejecutoria de la Ciudad de México, 1724–1790: El control del Cabildo en el comercio urbano." Undergraduate thesis, Escuela Nacional de Antropología e Historia, 2002.

Fernández-Kelly, Patricia, and Jon Shefner, eds. *Out of the Shadows: Political Action and the Informal Economy in Latin America*. State College: Pennsylvania State University Press, 2006.

Few, Martha. *Women Who Live Evil Lives: Gender, Religion, and the Politics of Power in Colonial Guatemala*. Austin: University of Texas Press, 2002.

Fischer, Brodwyn. *A Poverty of Rights: Citizenship and Inequality in Twentieth-Century Rio de Janeiro*. Stanford, CA: Stanford University Press, 2008.

Fontaine, Laurence, ed. *Alternative Exchanges: Second-Hand Circulations from the Sixteenth Century to the Present*. New York: Berghahn Books, 2008.

Fowler, Will. *Forceful Negotiations: The Origins of the* Pronunciamiento *in Nineteenth-Century Mexico*. Lincoln: University of Nebraska Press, 2010.

———. *Santa Anna of Mexico*. Lincoln: University of Nebraska Press, 2007.

Francois, Marie Eileen. *A Culture of Everyday Credit: Housekeeping, Pawnbroking, and Governance in Mexico City, 1750–1920*. Lincoln: University of Nebraska Press, 2006.

Frederick, Jake. "Without Impediment: Crossing Racial Boundaries in Colonial Mexico." *The Americas* 67:4 (2011): 495–515.

Galindo y Villa, Jesús. *La Plaza Mayor de la ciudad de México*. Mexico City: Museo Nacional de Arqueología, Historia y Etnología, 1914.

Gamboa Ramírez, Ricardo. "Las finanzas municipales de la Ciudad de México, 1800–1850." In Hernández Franyuti, ed., *La Ciudad de México en la primera mitad del siglo XIX*, 1:11–63.

Gantús, Fausta. "La traza del poder político y la administración de la ciudad liberal." In Rodríguez Kuri, ed., *Historia política*, 287–362.

García Barragán, Elisa. "El arquitecto Lorenzo de la Hidalga." *Anales del Instituto de Investigaciones Estéticas* 24:80 (2002): 101–28.

García-Brice, Iñigo. *Crafting the Republic: Lima's Artisans and Nation Building in Peru, 1821–1879*. Albuquerque: University of New Mexico Press, 2004.

García Cantú, Gastón. *El socialismo en México, siglo XIX*. Mexico City: ERA, 1969.

Garza, James Alex. *The Imagined Underworld: Sex, Crime, and Vice in Porfirian Mexico City*. Lincoln: University of Nebraska Press, 2007.

Gibson, Campbell. "Population of the 100 Largest Cities and Other Urban Places in the United States: 1790 to 1990." U.S. Census Bureau, Population Division Working Paper 27 (June 1998).

Gibson, Charles. *The Aztecs Under Spanish Rule: A History of the Indians of the Valley of Mexico, 1519–1810*. Stanford, CA: Stanford University Press, 1964.

Ginsburg, Madeleine. "Rags to Riches: The Second-Hand Clothes Trade, 1700–1978." *Costume* 14:1 (1980): 121–35.

Glasco, Sharon Bailey. *Constructing Mexico City: Colonial Conflicts over Culture, Space, and Authority*. New York: Palgrave Macmillan, 2010.

Godoy, Augusto, Teófilo Herrera, and Miguel Ulloa. *Más allá del pulque y el tepache: Las bebidas alcohólicas no destiladas indígenas de México*. Mexico City: UNAM, Instituto de Investigaciones Antropológicas, 2003.

Goldstein, Daniel. *Owners of the Sidewalk: Security and Survival in the Informal City*. Durham, NC: Duke University Press, 2016.

González Angulo Aguirre, Jorge. *Artesanado y ciudad a finales del siglo XVIII*. Mexico City: Fondo de Cultura Económica, 1983.

———. "Los gremios de artesanos y la estructura urbana." In Morena Toscana, ed., *Ciudad de México*, 25–36.

González González, Enrique. "La universidad: Estudiantes y doctores." In Rubial García, ed., *Historia de la vida cotidiana en México*, Vol. 2, *La ciudad barroca*, 261–306.

González Obregón, Luis. *México viejo*. Mexico City: Promexa Editores, 1979.

Gortari Rabiela, Hira de. "Política y administración en la Ciudad de Méxcio: Relaciones entre el Ayuntamiento y el Gobierno del Distrito Federal y el Departamental, 1824–1843." In Hernández Franyuti, ed., *La Ciudad de México en la primera mitad del siglo XIX*, 2:166–83.

Gotkowitz, Laura. "Trading Insults: Honor, Violence, and the Gendered Culture of Commerce in Cochabamba, Bolivia, 1870s–1950s." *Hispanic American Historical Review* 83:1 (2003): 83–118.

Graham, Richard A. *Feeding the City: From Street Market to Liberal Reform in Salvador, Brazil, 1780–1860*. Austin: University of Texas Press, 2010.

Granados Chapa, Manuel Ángel. *Vicente García Torres: Monitor de la República*. Hidalgo, Mexico: Gobierno del Estado de Hidalgo, 1987.

Grisales Ramírez, Natalia. "En Tepito todo se vende menos la dignidad: Espacio público e informalidad económica en el Barrio Bravo." *Alteridades* 13:26 (2003): 67–83.

Guardino, Peter. *"The Time of Liberty": Popular Political Culture in Oaxaca, 1750–1850*. Durham, NC: Duke University Press, 2005.

Guha-Khasnobis, Basudeb, Ravi Kanbur, and Elinor Ostrom. "Beyond Formality and Informality." In Guha-Khasnobis, Kanbur, and Ostrom, eds., *Linking*, 1–19.

———, eds. *Linking the Formal and Informal Economy: Concepts and Policies*. Oxford Scholarship Online, 2006.

Gutiérrez, Florencia. *El mundo de trabajo y el poder político: Integración, consenso y resistencia en la ciudad de México a fines del siglo XIX*. Mexico City: El Colegio de México, 2011.

Gutiérrez, Florenica, and Fausta Gantús. "Los pequeños voceadores: Prácticas laborales, censura y representaciones a finales del siglo XIX." In Illades and Barbosa, eds., *Los trabajadores de la ciudad de México*, 81–116.

Haber, Stephen H. *Industry and Underdevelopment: The Industrialization of Mexico, 1890–1940*. Stanford, CA: Stanford University Press, 1989.

Habermas, Jürgen. *The Structural Transformation of the Public Sphere: An Inquiry into a Category of Bourgeois Society*. Translated by Thomas Burger. Cambridge, MA: MIT Press, 1989.

Hale, Charles A. *Mexican Liberalism in the Age of Mora, 1821–1853*. Princeton, NJ: Princeton University Press, 1968.

———. *The Transformation of Liberalism in Late Nineteenth-Century Mexico*. Princeton, NJ: Princeton University Press, 1989.

Hanley, Brian Francis, ed. *Prácticas populares, cultura política y poder en México, siglo XIX*. Mexico City: Casa Juan Pablos, 2008.

Harrison, Candice. "'Free Trade and Hucksters' Rights!': Envisioning Economic Democracy in the Early Republic." *Pennsylvania Magazine of History and Biography* 137:2 (2013): 147–77.

Hart, Keith. "Informal Income Opportunities and Urban Employment in Ghana." *Journal of Modern African Studies* 11:1 (1973): 61–89.

Haslip-Viera, Gabriel. *Crime and Punishment in Late Colonial Mexico City, 1692–1810*. Albuquerque: University of New Mexico Press, 1999.

Hernández Chávez, Alicia. *Mexico: A Brief History*. Translated by Andy Klatt. Berkeley: University of California Press, 2006.

Hernández Franyuti, Regina, ed. *La Ciudad de México en la primera mitad del siglo XIX*. 2 vols. Mexico City: Instituto Mora, 1994.

———. "Ideología, proyectos y urbanización en la ciudad de México, 1760–1850." In Hernández Franyuti, ed., *La Ciudad de México en la primera mitad del siglo XIX*, 1:116–60.

———. *Ignacio de Castera: Arquitecto y urbanista de la Ciudad de México, 1777–1811*. Mexico City: Instituto Mora, 1997.

Hirth, Kenneth, and Deborah L. Nichols. "The Structure of Aztec Commerce: Markets and Merchants." In Nichols and Rodríguez-Alegría, eds., *The Oxford Handbook of the Aztecs*, 281–98.

Hoberman, Louisa Schell. *Mexico's Merchant Elite, 1590–1660: Silver, State, and Society*. Durham, NC: Duke University Press, 1991.

Hoberman, Louisa Schell, and Susan Migden Socolow, eds. *Cities and Society in Colonial Latin America*. Albuquerque: University of New Mexico Press, 1986.

Holston, James. *Insurgent Citizenship: Disjunctions of Democracy and Modernity in Brazil*. Princeton, NJ: Princeton University Press, 2008.

Illades, Carlos. *Hacia la república del trabajo: La organización artesanal en la Ciudad de México, 1853–1876*. Mexico City: El Colegio de México, 1998.

———. "Los intelectuales de la clase trabajadora del siglo XIX." In Hanley, ed., *Prácticas populares*, 465–86.

————. *Las otras ideas: Estudio sobre el primer socialismo en México, 1850–1935.* Mexico City: UAM Cuajimalpa, 2008.

Illades, Carlos, and Mario Barbosa [Cruz], eds. *Los trabajadores de la ciudad de México, 1860–1950: Textos en homenaje a Clara E. Lida.* Mexico City: El Colegio de México/UAM Cuajimalpa, 2013.

Illades, Carlos, and Ariel Rodríguez Kuri, eds. *Ciudad de México: Instituciones, actores sociales y conflicto político, 1774–1931.* Zamora, Michoacán: El Colegio de Michoacán; Mexico City: UAM Azcapotzalco, 1996.

Jacobsen, Nils, and Cristóbal Aljovín Losada, eds. *Political Cultures in the Andes, 1750–1950.* Durham, NC: Duke University Press, 2005.

James, Timothy M. *Mexico's Supreme Court: Between Liberal Individual and Revolutionary Social Rights, 1861–1934.* Albuquerque: University of New Mexico Press, 2013.

Jiménez, Christina M. "From the Lettered City to the Sellers' City: Vendor Politics and Public Space in Urban Mexico, 1880–1926." In Prakash and Kruse, eds., *The Spaces of the Modern City,* 214–46.

————. "Performing Their Right to the City: Political Uses of Public Space in a Mexican City, 1880–1910s." *Urban History* 33:3 (2006): 435–556.

————. "Popular Organizing for Public Services: Residents Modernize Morelia, Mexico, 1880–1920." *Journal of Urban History* 30 (2004): 495–518.

Johns, Michael. *The City of Mexico in the Age of Díaz.* Austin: University of Texas Press, 1997.

Johnson, Lyman. "Artisans." In Hoberman and Socolow, eds., *Cities and Society in Colonial Latin America,* 227–50.

Jordan, David P. "Haussmann and Haussmannisation: The Legacy for Paris." *French Historical Studies* 27:1 (2004): 87–113.

Kamen, Henry. *Spain in the Later Seventeenth Century, 1665–1700.* New York: Longman, 1980.

Katzew, Ilona. *Casta Painting: Images of Race in Eighteenth-Century Mexico.* New Haven, CT: Yale University Press, 2004.

Kicza, John E. *Colonial Entrepreneurs: Families and Business in Bourbon Mexico City.* Albuquerque: University of New Mexico Press, 1983.

————. "The Great Families of Mexico: Elite Maintenance and Business Practices in Late Colonial Mexico City." *Hispanic American Historical Review* 62:3 (1982): 429–57.

Kinsbrunner, Jay. *Petty Capitalism in Spanish America: The Pulperos of Puebla, Mexico City, Caracas, and Buenos Aires.* Boulder, CO: Westview Press, 1987.

Kleinman, Julie. "Adventures in Infrastructure: Making an African Hub in Paris." *City & Society* 26:3 (2014): 286–307.

Knapp, Frank Averill Jr. *The Life of Sebastián Lerdo de Tejada, 1823–1889: A Study of Influence and Obscurity.* Austin: University of Texas Press, 1951.

Konove, Andrew. "On the Cheap: The *Baratillo* Marketplace and the Shadow Economy of Eighteenth-Century Mexico City." *The Americas* 72:2 (2015): 249–78.

Kuntz Ficker, Sandra. *El comercio exterior de México en la era del capitalismo liberal, 1870–1929*. Mexico City: El Colegio de México, 2007.

Lavrin, Asunción. "The Role of the Nunneries in the Economy of Eighteenth-Century New Spain." *Hispanic American Historical Review* 46:4 (1966): 371–93.

Lear, John. *Workers, Neighbors, and Citizens: The Revolution in Mexico City*. Lincoln: University of Nebraska Press, 2001.

Lemire, Beverly. "Consumerism in Preindustrial and Early Industrial England: The Trade in Secondhand Clothes." *Journal of British Studies* 27:1 (1988): 1–24.

———. "The Theft of Clothes and Popular Consumerism in Early Modern England." *Journal of Social History* 24:2 (1990): 255–76.

León Cázares, María del Carmen. *La Plaza Mayor de la Ciudad de México en la vida cotidiana de sus habitantes (siglos XVI–XVII)*. México City: Instituto de Estudios y Documentos Históricos, 1982.

Leonard, Irving A. *Don Carlos de Sigüenza y Góngora: A Mexican Savant of the Seventeenth Century*. Berkeley: University of California Press, 1929.

Lewis, Oscar. *The Children of Sánchez: Autobiography of a Mexican Family*. New York: Random House, 1961.

Lira, Andrés. *Comunidades indígenas frente a la ciudad de México: Tenochtitlán y Tlatelolco, sus pueblos y barrios, 1812–1919*. Mexico City: El Colegio de México, 1983.

Lombardo de Ruiz, Sonia. "Ideas y proyectos urbanísticos de la Ciudad de México, 1788–1850." In Moreno Toscana, ed., *Ciudad de México*, 169–88.

———, ed. *El impacto de las reformas borbónicas en la estructura de las ciudades: Un enfoque comparativo*. Mexico City: Gobierno de la Ciudad de México, 2000.

Lombardo de Ruiz, Sonia, with Yolanda Terán Trillo. *Atlas histórico de la Ciudad de México*. Edited by Mario de la Torre. 2 vols. Mexico City: Smurfit/INAH, 1996–1997.

Lombardo de Ruiz, Sonia, Guadalupe de la Torre Villalpando, María Gayón Córdova, and María Dolores Morales Martínez. *Territorio y demarcación en los censos de población: Ciudad de México 1753, 1790, 1848 y 1882*. Mexico City: INAH, 2009.

López Rosado, Diego G. *Los servicios públicos de la ciudad de México*. Mexico City: Editorial Porrúa, 1976.

Lorenzo, María Dolores. "Negociaciones para la modernización urbana: La demolición del mercado del Parián en la Ciudad de México, 1843." *Estudios de historia moderna y contemporánea de México* 38:38 (2009): 85–109.

Low, Setha M. *On the Plaza: The Politics of Public Space and Culture*. Austin: University of Texas Press, 2000.

Lynch, John. *The Hispanic World in Crisis and Change, 1598–1700*. New York: Basil Blackwell, 1992.

Maldonado Ojeda, Lucio Ernesto. *La Asamblea Departamental de México, 1836–1846*. Mexico City: Asamblea Legislativa del Distrito Federal, 2001.

Mallon, Florencia. *Peasant and Nation: The Making of Postcolonial Mexico and Peru*. Berkeley: University of California Press, 1995.

Mangan, Jane. *Trading Roles: Gender, Ethnicity, and the Urban Economy in Potosí.* Durham, NC: Duke University Press, 2005.

Martí, Judith. "Nineteenth-Century Views of Women's Participation in Mexico's Markets." In Seligmann, ed., *Women Traders in Cross-Cultural Perspective,* 27–44.

Martin, Norman F. "La desnudez en la Nueva España del siglo XVIII." *Anuario de Estudios Americanos* 29 (1972): 261–94.

———. *Los vagabundos en la Nueva España: Siglo XVI.* Mexico City: Editorial Jus, 1957.

Martínez, María Elena. *Genealogical Fictions:* Limpieza de Sangre, *Religion, and Gender in Colonial Mexico.* Stanford, CA: Stanford University Press, 2008.

Marván Laborde, Ignacio. "De la ciudad del presidente al gobierno propio, 1970–2000." In Rodríguez Kuri, ed., *Historia política,* 483–563.

Medina, Cuauhtémoc, ed. *La imagen política.* Mexico City: Instituto de Investigaciones Estéticas, UNAM, 2006

Mendiola García, Sandra C. *Street Democracy: Vendors, Violence, and Public Space in Late Twentieth-Century Mexico.* Lincoln: University of Nebraska Press, 2017.

Miranda Pacheco, Sergio. "La fundación del Distrito Federal y los avatares de su régimen político institucional (1808–1857)." In Salinas Sandoval, Birrichaga Gardida, and Escobar Ohmstede, eds., *Poder y gobierno local en México,* 105–19.

———. *Historia de la desaparición del municipio en el Distrito Federal.* Mexico City: Unidad Obrera y Socialista, 1998.

———. "El juicio de residencia al Virrey Revillagigedo y los intereses oligárquicos en la Ciudad de México." *Estudios de Historia Novahispana* 29 (2003): 49–75.

Moncada González, Gisela. "La gestión municipal: ¿Cómo administrar las plazas y los mercados de la ciudad de México? 1824–1840." *Secuencias* 95 (2016): 39–62.

———. *La libertad comercial: El sistema de abasto de alimentos de la ciudad de México, 1810–1835.* Mexico City: Instituto Mora, 2013.

Morales, María Dolores. "Cambios en la traza de la estructura vial de la ciudad de México, 1770–1855." In Hernández Franyuti, ed., *La Ciudad de México en la primera mitad del siglo XIX,* 1:161–224.

———. "Espacio, propiedad y órganos de poder en la Ciudad de México en el siglo XIX," In Illades and Rodríguez Kuri, eds., *Ciudad de México,* 155–90.

———. "La expansión de la ciudad de México en el siglo XIX: El caso de los fraccionamientos." In Moreno Toscana, ed., *Ciudad de México,* 189–200.

More, Anna. *Baroque Sovereignty: Carlos de Sigüenza y Góngora and the Creole Archive of Colonial Mexico.* Philadelphia: University of Pennsylvania Press, 2013.

Moreno-Brid, Juan Carlos, and Jaime Ros. *Development and Growth in the Mexican Economy.* New York: Oxford University Press, 2009.

Moreno Gamboa, Olivia. "Hacia una tipología de libreros en la ciudad de México (1700–1778)." *Estudios de Historia Novohispana* 49 (2009): 121–46.

Moreno Toscana, Alejandra, ed. *Ciudad de México: Ensayo de construcción de una historia.* Mexico City: SEP/INAH, 1978.

Mott, Luiz. "Subsidios a história do pequeno comercio no Brasil." *Revista de História* 27:105 (1976): 81–106.

Mraz, John. *Looking for Mexico: Modern Visual Culture and National Identity.* Durham, NC: Duke University Press, 2009.

Mundy, Barbara. *The Death of Aztec Tenochtitlan, the Life of Mexico City.* Austin: University of Texas Press, 2015.

Muñoz, Miguel L. *Tlacos y pilones: La moneda del pueblo de México.* Mexico City: Fondo de Cultura Económica, 1976.

Musser, John. "The Establishment of Maximilian's Empire in Mexico." Ph.D. diss., University of Pennsylvania, 1918.

Needell, Jeffrey D. "Rio de Janeiro and Buenos Aires: Public Space and Public Consciousness in Fin-de-Siècle Latin America." *Comparative Studies in Society and History* 37:3 (1995): 519–40.

Nichols, Deborah L., and Enrique Rodríguez-Alegría, eds. *The Oxford Handbook of the Aztecs.* New York: Oxford University Press, 2016.

Nieto Sánchez, José. *Historia del Rastro.* Madrid: Vision Net, 2004.

Noriega Elío, Cecilia. *El Constituyente de 1842.* Mexico City: UNAM, 1986.

Ogilvie, Sheilagh. "The Economics of Guilds." *Journal of Economic Perspectives* 28:4 (2014): 169–92.

O'Hara, Matthew. *A Flock Divided: Race, Religion, and Politics in Mexico, 1749–1857.* Durham, NC: Duke University Press, 2009.

Olvera Ramos, Jorge. "El Baratillo de la Plaza Mayor: La crítica ilustrada al comercio tradicional." In Lombardo de Ruiz, ed., *El impacto de las reformas borbónicas,* 381–92.

———. *Los mercados de la Plaza Mayor en la Ciudad de México.* Mexico City: Cal y Arena, 2007.

Ortega y Pérez, Gallardo. *Estudios genealógicos.* Mexico City: E. Dublán, 1902.

Palti, Elías J. *La invención de una legitimidad: Razón y retórica en el pensamiento mexicano del siglo XIX.* Mexico City: Fondo de Cultural Económica, 2005.

Paquette, Gabriel. *Enlightenment, Governance, and Reform in Spain and Its Empire, 1759–1808.* New York: Palgrave Macmillan, 2008.

Paula de Arrangoiz y Berzábal, Francisco de. *Apuntes para la historia del segundo Imperio Mejicano.* Madrid: Imprenta de M. Rivadeneyra, 1889.

Pazos Pazos, María Luisa. *El Ayuntamiento de la Ciudad de México en el siglo XVII: Continuidad institucional y cambio social.* Seville: Diputación Provincial de Sevilla, 1999.

Pérez Montfort, Ricardo, ed. *Hábitos, normas y escándalo: Prensa, criminalidad y drogas durante el Porfiriato tardío.* Mexico City: CIESAS, 1997.

Pérez Toledo, Sonia. "Base de datos del Padrón de la Municipalidad de México de 1842." Unpublished data set, 2005.

———. "Formas de gobierno local, modelos constitucionales y cuerpo electoral, 1842–1867." In Rodríguez Kuri, ed., *Historia política,* 221–79.

———. *Los hijos del trabajo: Los artesanos de la ciudad de México, 1780–1853.* Mexico City: El Colegio de México, 1996.

———. "Movilización social y poder político en la Ciudad de México en la década de 1830." In Hanley, ed., *Prácticas populares*, 335–67.

———. "Una vieja corporación y un nuevo discurso: Los gremios de la ciudad de México al finalizar la colonia." In Connaughton, Illades, and Pérez Toldeo, eds., *Construcción de la legitimidad política en México*, 89–106.

Pérez Toledo, Sonia, and Herbert Klein. *Población y estructura social de la Ciudad de México, 1790–1842*. Mexico City: UAM Iztapalapa, 2004.

Perry, Laurens Ballard. *Juárez and Díaz: Machine Politics in Mexico*. DeKalb: Northern Illinois University Press, 1978.

Phelan, John Leddy. *The People and the King: The Comunero Revolt in Colombia, 1781*. Madison: University of Wisconsin Press, 1978.

Piccato, Pablo. *City of Suspects: Crime in Mexico City, 1900–1932*. Durham, NC: Duke University Press, 2001.

———. *The Tyranny of Opinion: Honor in the Construction of the Mexican Public Sphere*. Durham, NC: Duke University Press, 2010.

Polanyi, Karl. *The Great Transformation: The Political and Economic Origins of Our Time*. 1944. Reprint. Boston: Beacon Press, 2001.

Polanyi, Karl, Konrad Arensberg, and Harry M. Pearson, eds. *Trade and Market in the Early Empires: Economies in History and Theory*. Glencoe, IL: Free Press, 1957.

Porter, Susie. "'And That It Is Custom Makes It Law': Class Conflict and Gender Ideology in the Public Sphere, Mexico City, 1880–1910." *Social Science History* 24:1 (2000): 111–48.

———. *Working Women in Mexico City: Public Discourses and Material Conditions, 1879–1931*. Tucson: University of Arizona Press, 2003.

Prakash, Gyan, and Kevin M. Kruse, eds. *The Spaces of the Modern City: Imaginaries, Politics, and Everyday Life*. Princeton, NJ: Princeton University Press, 2008.

Premo, Bianca. *The Enlightenment on Trial: Ordinary Litigants and Colonialism in the Spanish Empire*. New York: Oxford University Press, 2017.

Priestley, Herbert Ingraham. *José de Gálvez: Visitor-General of New Spain 1765–1771*. Berkeley: University of California Press, 1916.

Quiroz Muñoz, Enriqueta. *Entre el lujo y la subsistencia: Mercado, abastecimiento y precios de la carne en la ciudad de México, 1750–1812*. Mexico City: El Colegio de México, 2005.

Rama, Ángel. *The Lettered City*. Translated by John Charles Chasteen. Durham, NC: Duke University Press, 1996.

Reina, Leticia. "Local Elections and Regime Crises: The Political Culture of Indigenous Peoples." In Servín, Reina, and Tutino, eds., *Cycles of Conflict*, 91–128. Durham, NC: Duke University Press, 2007.

Reyna, María del Carmen. *Historia de la Casa de Moneda: Tres motines en contra de la moneda débil en la Ciudad de México, siglo XIX*. Mexico City: Departamento de Investigaciones Históricas, INAH, 1979.

Rhi Sausi Garavito, María José. "Las primeras tres décadas del juicio de amparo: Notas en torno a la percepción pública de un nuevo instrumento jurídico." In Sacristán and Piccato, eds., *Actores, espacios y debates*, 121–44.

Ricard, Robert. "La Plaza Mayor en España y en América española." *Estudios geográficos* 11:39 (1950): 321–27.

Rocha Osorio, Victor Hugo. "Evolución social del barrio de Tepito como importante centro de comercio informal." Undergraduate thesis, UNAM, 2004.

Rodríguez Kuri, Ariel. "Ciudad oficial, 1930–1970." In Rodríguez Kuri, ed., *Historia política*, 417–82.

———. *La experiencia olvidada: El ayuntamiento de México: Política y gobierno, 1876–1912*. Mexico City: El Colegio de México, 1996.

———, ed. *Historia política de la Ciudad de México (Desde su fundación hasta el año 2000)*. Mexico City: El Colegio de México, 2012.

———. "Política e institucionalidad: El Ayuntamiento de México y la evolución del conflicto jurisdiccional, 1808–1850." In Hernández Franyuti, ed., *La Ciudad de México en la primera mitad del siglo XIX*, 2:51–94.

Rodríguez O., Jaime E. "Introduction: The Origins of Constitutionalism and Liberalism in Mexico." In Rodríguez O., ed., *The Divine Charter*, 1–32.

———, ed. *The Divine Charter: Constitutionalism and Liberalism in Nineteenth-Century Mexico*. New York: Rowman & Littlefield, 2005.

Rohlfes, L. J. "Police and Penal Correction in Mexico City, 1876–1911: A Study of Order and Progress in Porfirian Mexico." Ph.D. diss., Tulane University, 1983.

Rojas, Beatriz, ed. *Cuerpo político y pluralidad de derechos: Los privilegios de las corporaciones novohispanas*. Mexico City: CIDE, 2007.

Rosas Mantecón, Ana, and Guadalupe Reyes Domínguez. *Los usos de la identidad barrial: Una mirada antropológica a la lucha por la vivienda, Tepito 1970–1984*. Mexico City: UAM Iztapalapa, 1993.

Rosenthal, Anton. "Spectacle, Fear, and Protest: A Guide to the History of Public Space in Latin America." *Social Science History* 24:1 (2000): 33–73.

Rubenstein, Michael, Bruce Robbins, and Sophia Beal, eds. "Infrastructruralism." Special issue, *Modern Fiction Studies* 61:4 (2015).

Rubial García, Antonio, ed. *Historia de la vida cotidiana en México*. Vol. 2, *La ciudad barroca*. Mexico City: Fondo de Cultura Económica, 2005.

Ruiz Medrano, Carlos Rubén. *El gremio de plateros en Nueva España*. San Luis Potosí, Mexico: El Colegio de San Luis, 2001.

Sacristán, Cristina, and Pablo Piccato, eds. *Actores, espacios y debates en la historia de la esfera pública en la ciudad de México*. Mexico City: Instituto Mora, 2005.

Salinas Sandoval, María del Carmen, Diana Birrichaga Gardida, and Antonio Escobar Ohmstede, eds. *Poder y gobierno local en México, 1808–1857*. Zinacantepec, Mexico: El Colegio Mexiquense; Zamora, Mexico: El Colegio de Michoacán; Toluca, Mexico: Universidad Autónoma del Estado de México, 2011.

Salvucci, Linda. "Costumbres viejas, 'hombres nuevos': José de Gálvez y la burocracia fiscal novohispana (1754–1800)." *Historia moderna* 33:2 (1983): 224–64.

Salvucci, Richard. *Textiles and Capitalism in Mexico: An Economic History of the Obrajes, 1539–1840*. Princeton, NJ: Princeton University Press, 1987.

Samara, Tony Roshan, Shenjing He, and Guo Chen, eds. *Locating Right to the City in the Global South*. New York: Routledge, 2013.

Sánchez de Tagle, Esteban. *Los dueños de la calle: Una historia de la vía pública en la época colonial.* Mexico City: INAH, 1997.

———. "La remodelación urbana de la ciudad de México en el siglo XVIII: Una crítica de los supuestos." *Tiempos de América* 5/6 (2000): 9–19.

———. "La remodelación urbana de la ciudad de México en el siglo XVIII: Una reforma virreinal." In Lombardo de Ruiz, ed., *El impacto de las reformas borbónicas,* 129–36.

Sanders, James. *The Vanguard of the Atlantic World: Creating Modernity in Nineteenth-Century Latin America.* Durham, NC: Duke University Press, 2011.

Scardaville, Michael. "(Hapsburg) Law and (Bourbon) Order: State Authority, Popular Unrest, and the Criminal Justice System in Bourbon Mexico City." *The Americas* 50:4 (1994): 501–25.

Schwaller, Robert C. *Géneros de Gente in Early Colonial Mexico: Defining Racial Difference.* Norman: University of Oklahoma Press, 2016.

Seijas, Tatiana. *Asian Slaves in Colonial Mexico: From Chinos to Indians.* New York: Cambridge University Press, 2014.

Seligmann, Linda, ed. *Women Traders in Cross-Cultural Perspective: Mediating Identities, Marketing Wares.* Stanford, CA: Stanford University Press, 2002.

Servín, Elisa, Leticia Reina, and John Tutino, eds. *Cycles of Conflict, Centuries of Change: Crisis, Reform, and Revolution in Mexico.* Durham, NC: Duke University Press, 2007.

Shaw, Frederick John Jr. "Poverty and Politics in Mexico City." Ph.D. diss., University of Florida, 1975.

Silva Prada, Natalia. *La política de una rebelión: Los indígenas frente al tumulto de 1692 en la Ciudad de México.* Mexico City: El Colegio de México, 2007.

Smith, Benjamin T. *The Roots of Conservatism in Mexico: Catholicism, Society, and Politics in the Mixteca Baja, 1750–1962.* Albuquerque: University of New Mexico Press, 2012.

Smith, Robert Sidney. "Sales Tax in New Spain, 1575–1700." *Hispanic American Historical Review* 28:1 (1948): 2–37.

Somolinos Palencia, Juan. "El Doctor Lauro María Jiménez a los 100 años de su fallecimiento." *Gaceta Médica de México* 110:6 (1975): 429–34.

Soto, Hernando de. *The Other Path: The Invisible Revolution in the Third World.* Translated by June Abbott. New York: Harper & Row, 1989.

Storrs, Christopher. *The Resilience of the Spanish Monarchy, 1665–1700.* New York: Oxford University Press, 2006.

Teitelbaum, Vanesa E. *Entre el control y la movilización: Honor, trabajo y solidaridades artesanales en la ciudad de México a mediados del siglo XIX.* Mexico City: El Colegio de México, 2008.

Tenenbaum, Barbara A. *The Politics of Penury: Debt and Taxes in Mexico, 1821–1856.* Albuquerque: University of New Mexico Press, 1986.

Tenorio Trillo, Mauricio. "1910 Mexico City: Space and Nation in the City of the Centenario." *Journal of Latin American Studies* 28:1 (1996): 75–104.

———. *I Speak of the City: Mexico City at the Turn of the Twentieth Century.* Chicago: University of Chicago Press, 2013.

Toner, Deborah. *Alcohol and Nationhood in Nineteenth-Century Mexico.* Lincoln: University of Nebraska Press, 2015.

Toussaint Alcaraz, Florence. *Escenario de la prensa en el Porfiriato.* Colima, Mexico: Universidad de Colima, 1989.

———. *Periodismo, siglo diez y nueve.* Mexico City: UNAM, 2006.

Valle Pavón, Guillermina del. *El Consulado de comerciantes de la Ciudad de México y las finanzas novohispanas, 1582–1827.* Mexico City: El Colegio de México, 1997.

———, ed. *Mercaderes, comercio y consulados de Nueva España en el siglo XVIII.* Mexico City: Instituto Mora/CONACYT, 2003.

———. "El régimen de privilegios de la Universidad de Mercaderes de la ciudad de México." In Rojas, ed., *Cuerpo político*, 155–87.

Van Young, Eric. "Islands in the Storm: Quiet Cities and Violent Countrysides in the Mexican Independence Era." *Past & Present* 118:1 (1988): 130–55.

Vaughan, Mary Kay. "Primary Education and Literacy in Nineteenth-Century Mexico: Research Trends, 1968–1988." *Latin American Research Review* 25:1 (1990): 31–66.

Vega Amaya, María Patricia. "El gobierno de Ramón Corral en el Distrito Federal (1900–1903): Su impacto en la ciudad de México a través de la obra pública." Master's thesis, Instituto Mora, 2004.

Vilar, Pierre. *A History of Gold and Money, 1450–1920.* Translated by Judith White. London: NLB, 1969.

Viqueira-Albán, Juan. *Propriety and Permissiveness in Bourbon Mexico.* Translated by Sonya Lipsett-Rivera and Sergio Rivera Ayala. Wilmington, DE: Scholarly Resources, 1999.

Voekel, Pamela. *Alone Before God: The Religious Origins of Modernity in Mexico.* Durham, NC: Duke University Press, 2002.

———. "Peeing on the Palace: Bodily Resistance to Bourbon Reforms in Mexico City." *Journal of Historical Sociology* 5:2 (1992): 183–208.

Von Mentz, Brígida, ed. *Movilidad social de sectores medios en México: Una retrospectiva histórica (siglos XVII al XX).* Mexico City: CIESAS, 2003.

Wakild, Emily. "Naturalizing Modernity: Urban Parks, Public Gardens, and Drainage Projects in Porfirian Mexico City." *Mexican Studies/Estudios Mexicanos* 23:1 (2007): 101–23.

Walker, Charles. "Civilize or Control? The Lingering Impact of the Bourbon Urban Reforms." In Jacobsen and Aljovín Losada, eds., *Political Cultures in the Andes*, 74–95.

Walker, David M. "Resisting the Neoliberalization of Space in Mexico City." In Samara, He, and Chen, eds., *Locating Right to the City in the Global South*, 171–94.

Walker, David W. "Porfirian Labor Politics: Working-Class Organizations in Mexico City and Porfirio Díaz, 1876–1902." *The Americas* 37:3 (1981): 257–89.

Walker, Louise E. *Waking from the Dream: Mexico's Middle Classes after 1968.* Stanford, CA: Stanford University Press, 2013.

Warren, Richard A. "Desafío y trastorno en el gobierno municipal: El Ayuntamiento de México y la dinámica política nacional, 1821–1855." In Illades and Rodríguez Kuri, eds., *Ciudad de México*, 117–30.

———. "Rashomon in the Zocalo: Writing the History of Popular Political Culture in Nineteenth-Century Mexico." *MACLAS Latin American Essays* 16 (2002): 73–94.

———. *Vagrants and Citizens: Politics and the Masses in Mexico City from Colony to Republic.* Lanham, MD: Rowman & Littlefield, 2007.

Wasserman, Mark. *Everyday Life and Politics in Nineteenth-Century Mexico: Men, Women, and War.* Albuquerque: University of New Mexico Press, 2000.

Weiner, Richard. *Race, Nation, and Market: Economic Culture in Porfirian Mexico.* Tucson: University of Arizona Press, 2004.

Wilgus, A. Curtis. "The Second International American Conference at Mexico City." *Hispanic American Historical Review* 11:1 (1931): 27–68.

Woodward, Donald. "'Swords into Ploughshares': Recycling in Pre-Industrial England." *Economic History Review* 38:2 (1985): 175–91.

Yoma Medina, María Rebeca, and Luis Alberto Martos López. *Dos mercados en la historia de la ciudad de México: El Volador y La Merced.* Mexico City: Secretaría General de Desarrollo Social, Departamento del Distrito Federal/INAH, 1990.

Yuste, Carmen ed. *Comerciantes mexicanos en el siglo XVIII.* Mexico City: UNAM, 1991.

Zeltsman, Corinna. "Ink Under the Fingernails: Making Print in Nineteenth-Century Mexico City." Ph.D. diss., Duke University, 2016.

Zoraida Vázquez, Josefina. "Liberales y conservadores en México: Diferencias y similitudes." *Estudios Interdisciplinarios de América Latina y el Caribe* 8:1 (1997): 153–75.

INDEX

Africans, 21, 22, 23, 41–42

agiotistas, 228n103

Aguirre, Manuel García, 97, 222n41

Alameda: 53*map*, 102, 119, 120*map*, 145, 148, 149*map*

Albuquerque, Duke of, 33, 205n45

alcabala: and Baratillo, 72, 212n54; and Consulado, 79, 84; under Restored Republic, 127

alcaicería: 11–12, 31, 39; construction of, 26, 29, 33, 35, 58; depiction by de Villalpando, Cristóbal de, 26, 27*fig.*; etymology of, 198n46. *See also* Parián

alcaldes (on Ayuntamiento), 73–76, 194n4, 218n1

alcaldes del barrio, 225n72

alcaldes del crimen, 20, 25, 26, 196n19

Alcérreca, Ventura, 119–21

almaceneros, 80, 82, 84–85. *See also* Consulado; *mercaderes*

almacenes (import warehouses), 5, 32, 62, 80, 84–85, 210n18, 218n126

Alzate y Ramírez, José Antonio, 39, 40*fig.*

ambulatory vendors: and Ayuntamiento, 129–30; 132, 135–36; and cajoneros, 78, 80, 85; and 1857 Constitution, 122, 125; and free trade, 123; and García Torres, Vicente, 126–28; and mercantile hierarchy, 63; and paternalism, 140; permits for, 215n99; in Plaza de Villamil, 110; in Plaza Mayor, 18–20, 33, 46, 61; and police, 129, 135–36; during Porfiriato, 151; and the press, 129, 137–40; in

Puebla, 123; and Supreme Court, 134–36, and urban politics, 124–25, 142; in Zacatecas, 80

amparo, 130–31, 134, 233n48

arbitrios, 195n13. *See also propios*; superintendent of *propios* and *arbitrios*; taxes

Arteaga, Eduardo, 130, 132, 141

artisan guilds: and Baratillo, 5, 24, 69, 70–76, 105, 193n38; decline of, 74, 213n69; ethnic makeup of, 63, 209n10; and free trade, 122, 125; and middle sectors, 81, 213n68; records of, 11; in republican era, 90, 219n6, 225n74

artisans: and Ayuntamiento, 167; in Baratillo, 32–33, 70–76, 105–06, 124, 155, 192n32; colonial regulations of, 71; middling status of, 74, 89, 213n68; Liberal Party and, 232n41; in "Ordenanzas del Baratillo," 42; during Porfiriato, 246n101; republican government and, 115; in riot of 1692, 24; and shadow economy, 5, 66; and voluntary associations, 128

asamblea departamental. See departmental assembly

asientos, 45, 200n71

Audiencia of Mexico: *alcaldes del crimen* on, 20, 196n19; and Baratillo, 32, 65, 66, 84; Indians and, 21; in "Ordenanzas del Baratillo," 41; and Plaza Mayor, 34; superintendent of propios and arbitrios and, 45; and tailor guild, 73–74

Audiencia of Guadalajara, 30

avería, 64, 82

ayuntamiento (defined), 3, 186n7

Ayuntamiento (Mexico City): *alcaldes* and
regidores on, 194n4, 218n1; and artisan
guilds, 72, 213n56; and Baratillo, 3, 5, 7;
dissolution of, 167–68, 176, 250n17;
elections of, 104, 121, 140–41, 169,
225n72, 238n11; and *fiel ejecutoría*,
72–73, 213n57; finances of, 110, 166–67,
207n75, 228n104; and free trade, 123;
and Plaza Mayor, 17–19, 45–46,
216n102; and public markets, 5, 33,
44–45, 111–12, 131, 203n29, 204n44,
228n105, 246n92; relations with
national government, 6–7; and shadow
economy, 5–6, 68–70; and urban politics, 7; and urban renewal, 44, 97–98,
145–46, 157–59

ayuntamiento (Puebla), 123

baratilleros: ages of, 155, 209n9, 242n54,
181*tab.*, 183*tab.*; and ambulatory vendors, 33; and *cajoneros*, 77–83; and
Consulado merchants, 32, 84–86;
ethnicities of, 23, 63, 209n9; genders of,
8, 63, 105–06, 181*tab.*, 183*tab.*, 192n32;
literacy of, 155, 183*tab.*; in riot of 1692,
24; and urban politics, 7–9, 77, 85–87,
104, 119, 146, 177; voting eligibility of,
104, 181*tab. See also* artisans: in
Baratillo

Baratillo (in Mexico City): 2; and artisan
guilds, 70–77; and Bourbon Reforms
37–39; businesses in, 63–64; credit in,
64; crime in, 2, 20, 67–68, 150–51;
customers of, 11, 21, 64–65; factions
within, 10 122, 163, 178; and Inquisition,
68; in literature, 3; and Mexican Revolution, 172; prices in, 11, 32, 72, 77–78, 82,
215n94; rents in, 48, 54, 63–64, 110, 112,
121, 166, 204n44; and riot of 1692, 16;
and shadow economy, 4–6; in Tepito,
145, 165–66, 171–73; sources on, 10–11;
women in, 63, 105–06, 136, 137*fig.*,
154–55, 192n32, 225n76

Baratillo Chico, 31, 39–40, 40*fig.*, 52, 54,
68, 218n117

Baratillo Grande: 31, 39–41, 40*fig.*, 46,
47*fig.*; *alacenas* in, 215n94; books in, 68,
150; businesses in, 63–64, 81; consumers
in, 65; and Revillagigedo II, 54

baratillos (in other cities), 3, 19, 123,
187nn10,11

barrio bravo. See Tepito

barrios: and Baratillo, 129, 162–63; markets
in, 51; during Porfiriato, 146, 147, 151,
158, 166–67, 169; Revillagigedo II and,
49, 50*fig.*, 205n48, 207n78; and riot of
1692, 16, 23–25, 30; and *traza*, 22,
196n27, 239n15

Bases de Tacubaya, 91, 97

Bases Orgánicas, 114

Bautista Morales, Juan, 108, 226n90

Baz, José Valente, 96, 222n41

Baz, Juan José, 133

black market: defined, 5, 188n16; in Tepito,
2, 171–72; and urban politics, 3. *See also*
shadow economy

Boletín Municipal, 158

Bonavía, Bernardo, 54

Bourbon Reforms: and artisan guilds, 74;
and Ayuntamiento, 45–46, 48, 49,
208n81; and Baratillo, 37–39; and
commerce, 79; failures of, 59; Habsburg
precedents for, 12, 26, 34, 204n34; in
historiography, 38, 39, 201n7, 203n28;
objectives of, 43–44; and public markets, 44–45, 47*fig.*, 204n34; and public
space, 37, 58, 193n37; and Revillagigedo
II, 49–52; and urban politics, 39

bribes. See *gratificaciones*

Bucareli, Antonio María de, 85–86

buhoneros, 18, 20, 33, 34, 63, 79. *See also*
ambulatory vendors

Bustamante, Anastasio, 91

Cabildo, 186n7. *See also* Ayuntamiento

cacahuaterías, 63, 85

cajoneros, 33, 63, 77–82, 84–85, 216n102

cajones: in Baratillo Grande, 63–64;
defined: 20; in Plaza Mayor, 18*fig.*, 26,
33, 77; residences in, 46; in Plaza del
Volador, 51, 56; in Parián, 59, 63, 80

Calderón de la Barca, Frances, 219n4

Cameros, Francisco, 31, 45, 82, 204n33

Carranza, Venustiano, 176

castas: and Baratillo, 63, 78; in "Ordenanzas del Baratillo," 36, 41–42; in Plaza Mayor, 34; in riot of 1692, 15; and street vending, 63. See also *sistema de castas*

castizos, 22, 63

Catholic Church: and Baratillo, 2, 30, 42; conservatives and, 96; Indians and, 23; Ley Lerdo and, 239n15

census: 1788, 71; 1790, 81; 1816 commercial, 80, 209n10; 1842, 104, 105–06, 181*tab.*, 224n69, 225nn73,75,77; 1849, 226n83; 1882, 154–55, 161, 183*tab.*, 242n54

centralism, 89, 114

centralists, 91, 104, 111, 219n3, 221n31

Chalco, 64, 107

Chapultepec Park, 145

Charles I (king), 17

Charles II (king): and *alcaicería*, 26; and Baratillo, 16, 20, 30, 78, 199n59; and commerce, 79; death of, 37, 201n4; in historiography, 198n48

Charles III (king), 204n34

Children of Sanchez, The. See Lewis, Oscar

chinos, 22, 28, 63, 196–97n28

Chreslos Jache, Pedro Anselmo. *See* "Ordenanzas del Baratillo"

científicos, 151, 157, 238n8, 243n64

citizenship, 7, 89–90, 128, 138, 190n27

Civil Code of the Federal District and Territory of Baja California (1871), 131

clothing: in Baratillo, 2, 72–76, 100, 103, 119, 144, 153, 171, 240n22; and identity, 28; Indians', 16; legislation on, 72–74, 156–57, 214n79; pawning of, 64, 210n32; second-hand, 39, 54, 61, 153, 159, 171; and social mobility, 65; stands in Plaza Mayor, 70; stolen, 67–68; in Tepito, 173. *See also roperos*; tailors

Colonia de la Bolsa, 148, 149*map*, 151

colonias populares, 147–47

comerciantes, 81, 85

comercio libre, 52. *See also* free trade

common good, 7, 61, 73, 75–76

congresses, constituent: in 1842, 89, 220n15; in Mexico City, 1

Congress (Mexican), 91, 114, 141, 176, 190n23, 224n68, 227n100

Congress, Second Pan-American, 145, 157

Consejo Superior de Gobierno del Distrito Federal, 167

conservatives, 89, 95–96, 97, 118, 128, 138, 219n3

Constitution, Mexican (1824), 91, 128, 130, 221n31

Constitution, Mexican (1836), 91, 128, 221n31

Constitution, Mexican (1857), 118, 122–28, 130, 134, 229n3, 233n47

Constitution, Mexican (1917), 176

constitution, Mexico City, 1, 6, 177

Consulado: and *alcabalas*, 79, 212n54; and Baratillo, 61, 84–86; membership in, 78, 80–81, 216n103; in mercantile hierarchy, 62; and *traspasos*, 52

contraband, 2, 173–74. See also *fayuca*

contratas, 111

contratistas, 95, 111

corregidores: 45, 214n84; and Baratillo, 34, 54, 71, 73, 75–76; and *fiel ejecutoría*, 75, 213n57; and Plaza Mayor markets, 18, 22; and riot of 1692, 15

Cortés, Hernán, 17, 24, 34, 50

Council of Health, 159, 166

Council of the Indies, 56

credit, 64, 81, 84, 160

Creoles: on Ayuntamiento, 6, 34, 38, 48, 57, 203n31, 208n81; in "Ordenanzas del Baratillo," 42

crime: and Baratillo, 2; in colonial period, 20, 62, 72; during Porfiriato, 151; press coverage of, 149, 155, 240n23; and Tepito, 1, 171. *See also* Baratillo: crime in

Cumplido, Ignacio, 97, 108

departmental assembly, 112–13, 221n31

Department of Mexico, 95, 111

De Soto, Hernando, 189n18

Díaz, Porfirio: 144, 229n3, 237n2; and Ayuntamiento, 111, 146–47, 157, 167–68, 248n129; politics under, 157, 238n10, 246n101. *See also* Porfiriato

Dios Anzures, Juan de, 61, 78

education: of Indians, 21; during Porfiriato, 146, 151, 155, 158, 238n8; under Santa Anna, 91

mulattos: in Baratillo, 24, 28, 29, 42, 63, 78; and economic regulations, 72; and Indians, 23; in *sistema de castas*, 22; at university, 28

municipal government. *See* Ayuntamiento

Municipal Ordinances of 1840, 111, 218n1

natural law, 76, 196n23

newspapers: circulation of, 223n60, 232n42, 240n23; as sources, 10–11. *See also* press

Núñez, José, 129, 130, 134

Núñez de Villavicencio, Nuño, 73, 75–76, 214n79

obrajes, 20, 210n32

Obregón, Álvaro, 176

"Ordenanzas del Baratillo," 3, 36–37, 41–42, 151, 200n1

Ordóñez, Pedro, 164, 167, 247n105

Oropeza, José, 95–96

Ortega y Montañéz, Juan, 27–30

Otero, Mariano, 108, 226–27n90, 227n91

Palacio de Hierro, 145, 148

Paredes y Arrillaga, Mariano, 91, 114

Parián: and ambulatory vendors, 123; and Baratillo, 39–41, 46, 83; construction of, 26; demolition of, 112–13; in *El periquillo sarniento*, 65; and imported goods, 63; location of, 40*fig*., 53*map*, 93*map*; in Plaza Mayor, 47*fig*.; rents from, 48, 63–64, 204n44; and Revillagigedo II, 50, 54, 58–59; ownership of stores in, 80; Virgin of Guadalupe statue in, 82; in Puebla, 123. See also *alcaicería*

Parián Riot (1828), 112, 223n51

Paris, 44, 145, 153, 161, 244nn70,76

Party of the Institutional Revolution (PRI), 176, 250n22

Paseo de la Reforma, 145, 149*map*

paternalism: and baratilleros, 8, 32, 75, 84, 101, 139, 157; and street vendors, 191n30, 205n46; and urban popular groups, 96, 146, 221n33, 238n9

patronage networks: baratilleros in, 8, 84–86, 142, 169, 179; labor unions and, 176; in nineteenth century, 191n29,

225n72; petty vendors in, 33; and Porfiriato, 246n101; in Tepito, 178

pawnbroking, 64, 65, 66, 67, 210n21

pawnshops: and middle sectors, 65, 225n74; and Monte de Piedad, 210n27; and Plaza del Jardín, 133, 137, 234n60; during Porfiriato, 154, 156; and shadow economy, 5, 66

Pérez, Gabino, 92, 94–95, 96–97, 105, 107, 219n10, 221n27, 228n103

petitions: authorship of, 105, 217n115; from baratilleros, 3, 7–8, 83*fig*., 168

Philip III (king), 19, 69, 79

Philip V (king), 45, 79, 80, 201n4, 204n34

Philippines, 20, 62, 196n28

pícaros, 65, 210n22

piratería (pirated goods), 2, 13, 173, 251n25

Plaza de la Constitución, 92, 93*map*, 113*fig*., 120*map*. See also Plaza Mayor; Zócalo

Plaza de las Vizcaínas, 52, 53*map*, 64

Plaza del Factor: baratilleros evicted from, 101–03, 109; baratilleros relocated to, 52, 54, 58; location of, 53*map*; proximity to baratilleros' residences, 106; sale of, 100

Plaza del Jardín: baratilleros evicted from, 119–22, 129–31, 135–37; baratilleros relocated to, 110; proximity to baratilleros' residences, 124–25, 154–55

Plaza del Volador: 18*map*, 47*fig*., 53*map*, 149*map*; and Baratillo, 198n51; construction of market (1790), 50–51; construction of market (1841), 92, 94–98, 101, 112, 114, 228n103; *fiel ejeuctoría* raids in, 73, 75, 214n70; in *juicio de residencia*, 56; purchase of, 131; rents in, 207nn71,72,78; statue of Santa Anna in, 229n117

Plaza de los Ángeles, 149*map*, 163, 164, 245n82, 247n104

Plaza de Madrid, 100, 119–22, 124, 129, 133

Plaza de Villamil: 93*map*, 106; Baratillo in, 102, 104, 109, 115, 230n11; rents in, 110, 112, 114

Plaza Fray Bartolomé de las Casas, 172*fig*., 176

Plaza Garibaldi. *See* Plaza del Jardín

plaza judge. See *juez de plaza*

Plaza Mayor: *asiento* of, 45, 200n71, 203n33; and Ayuntamiento, 19, 33–34, 44–45, 57; Baratillo origins in, 19–20; construction of, 17; depiction by Villalpando, Cristóbal de, 27*fig*.as marketplace, 18, 22, 48; as *plaza de armas*, 37, 54; and racial mixing, 29; and Revillagigedo II, 49–50, 54–56, 58; and riot of 1692, 15, 24; urban renewal and, 16, 25–26, 33, 35, 37, 46, 47*fig*.

Polanyi, Karl, 186n8

police: and Baratillo, 109, 121, 129, 133–36, 150, 155–56, 161, 172; and informal economy, 212n49; in Plaza del Volador, 97; under Porfiriato, 151; in Tepito, 2, 251n29

Porfiriato: censorship during, 164; criminal justice reform during, 151; economic growth during, 144–45, 237n2; elites in, 145–46, 238n7; and technocrats, 151, 157, 238n8urban politics during, 8, 146–47, 157, 164–65, 169, 238n9; urban renewal during, 145, 157–59

Portal de Mercaderes, 18, 133

press: baratilleros in, 3, 7–9, 82,102–03, 104, 107–08; coverage of Baratillo in, 13, 100–101, 129, 134–35, 144, 148–55, 171, 223n51; crime reporting in, 240n23; freedom of, 118, 124, 168; in Restored Republic, 137–40. *See also* newspapers

pronunciamientos, 91

propios (rent-producing properties), 19, 33, 195n13. *See also* superintendent of *propios* and *arbitrios*

prostitution, 68

public health, 151, 160, 161. *See also* hygiene

public space: 9–10, 178, 193nn36,37; and Ayuntamiento, 122–23, 142–43; baratilleros' rights to, 76, 89, 134–35; under Bourbons, 57–59, 203n28; under Habsburgs, 35; and informal economy, 188n17; under Restored Republic, 131–32

public sphere: baratilleros in, 7, 89, 104, 138–40, 219n5; honor in, 138–39; in scholarship, 9, 192n33, 224n71, 247n106

Puebla, 123, 251n29

puestos: contracts for, 94; in Plaza del Jardín, 119, 154; in Plaza del Volador, 56; in Plaza Mayor, 20, 45–46, 51, 54, 70; rent from, 33, 204n44, 209n15; in Tepito, 165

pulperías, 63, 66, 80

pulque, 16, 33, 54, 153, 200n1, 205n45

pulquerías: 200n1; and Baratillo, 36, 88, 133, 138, 161, 234n60; and Bourbon Reforms, 201n7; and Porfiriato, 151, 166; and riot of 1692, 16

punishment: for baratilleros, 20, 29, 67, 74–75, 211n34; after riot of 1692, 16

Quevedo, Miguel Ángel de, 159–60, 162–67, 244n76, 247n108

quinto (royal tax), 66

Rabelais, François, 31

race: and Baratillo, 31, 63, 78, 81, 193n40; in colonial Mexico, 20, 22–23, 72; in "Ordenanzas del Baratillo," 41–42. *See also sistema de castas*

Rag Fair (London), 3, 187n11

Rastro (Madrid), 161, 187n11

rateros, 151, 165, 240n33, 242n54

regatonería, 71, 212n51

regidores (city councilmen), 46, 48, 69, 194n4, 218n1

república de españoles, 21–22

república de indios, 21–22

Restored Republic: Ayuntamiento and, 131–32; elites in, 142; and free trade, 131–32; newspapers in, 139, 232n42; political institutions under, 118–19, 124, 130; public space under, 131

Revillagigedo II, Count of (viceroy): 205n47; and Ayuntamiento of 1842, 98, 99*fig*.; and Baratillo, 52, 54; *juicio de residencia* of, 55–57, 59; relations with Spanish Crown, 44, 59, 208n87; Urban Commercial Regiment and, 86; urban renewal under, 37, 42, 49–52, 57–58

rights: of baratilleros, 3, 62, 69, 75–76, 88–89, 125, 142–43, 179; to the city, 7, 190n27; and Constitution of 1857, 118, 122–23, 125–30, 233n47; and Constitution of 1917, 176; of vendors in Tepito, 1, 10

riot of 1692: 15–16, 23–25, 30, 34, 194n1, 197n33; and archive, 196n24; and Urban Commercial Regiment, 85

roperos (clothes sellers), 73–74, 213n64, 215n90
Rosales Gordoa, José: 125–26, 134–36, 138–40, 143, 231n27
Rosales, Víctor, 125
Ruiz, Macedonio, 162–64
rumbos, 152fig., 161, 171, 245n83

Salamanca (school), 76
Salvatierra, Count of (viceroy), 20–21, 72, 78
Samudio, Miguel, 73, 75, 81, 214n70
San Lázaro (penitentiary), 151
Santa Anna, Antonio López de: and Ayuntamiento, 104, 110–13; and Baratillo, 88, 101–02; in 1841–1843 period, 89, 91–92, 104, 114–16, 220n15, 229nn113,117; and Parián, 112–13; and Volador market, 96–97
sastres. See tailors
second-hand markets, 3, 19, 154, 173, 187n11
shadow economy: Baratillo and, 4–6, 9, 175, 177–79; in colonial era, 61; defined, 4–5, 188n16; sources on, 10–11, 90; and the state, 6, 66–70, 86, 178
shoe sellers, 41, 58, 133, 245n85
Siete Partidas, 214n77
Sigüenza y Góngora, Carlos de, 15–16, 23–24, 26, 194n1, 197n33
sistema de castas, 22, 41, 196n28, 197n29, 202n19
slaves, 20, 22, 28
social Darwinism, 8
social mobility, 71, 78, 81, 202n19, 208n2
Spaniards: on Ayuntamiento, 203n31, 208n81; in Baratillo, 23, 29, 63, 66; in Consulado, 62; downward mobility of, 202n19; in Mexico City, 17–18, 21–22, 30, 79, 212n51; in "Ordenanzas del Baratillo," 36, 41–42; in riot of 1692, 15; in sistema de castas, 22, 42
students, 27–30, 198n51
superintendent of propios and arbitrios, 45, 54, 83fig.
Supreme Court, 13, 134–41

tailors: in Baratillo, 24, 71–75, 105, 181tab., 183tab., 192n32, 242n54, 245n85; guild, 209n10, 212n52, 213n64

taxes: and baratilleros, 5, 77, 131, 132; and Bourbon Reforms, 43, 69; and Consulado, 79, 84–85; and contratas, 111; in Tepito, 1–2. See also alcabalas; arbitrios; propios; quinto; viento
technocrats. See científicos
Tenochtitlán, 16, 17, 19, 24, 195n7, 195n12
tepacherías, 36, 200n1
tepiteños, 174, 251n26
Tepito: 1–3, 149map; Baratillo in, 162–66, 171–73; during Porfiriato, 151, 158; shadow economy in, 173–75; and urban politics, 1–3, 6–7, 176–79
textile workshops. See obrajes
tianguillo, 22–23
tianguises, 72, 195n17
tiendas mestizas, 63, 80
tinglados, 154, 241n47
tinterillos, 138, 220nn23,24,26. See also evangelistas
Tívoli del Eliseo, 117, 120map, 124, 231n23
tlacos, 41, 69–70, 201–02n15, 211n47. See also money
Tlatelolco (marketplace), 17, 195n8
Tlatelolco, Santiago de (parcialidad), 165
traspasos, 51–52, 221n27
traza, 22, 23–25, 37, 49, 50fig., 58, 196n27
Trespalacios y Escandón, Domingo de, 45–46, 47fig.

University, Royal and Pontifical, 18map, 28–29
Urban Commercial Regiment, 85–86
urban politics, 7–9, 39, 146, 157, 164, 177
urban renewal, 38, 44, 48, 58, 93map, 158, 160, 178, 201n7
Uztáriz, Gerónimo de, 79

vagabonds, 20–21, 23, 26, 28, 31, 36
Valencia, Gabriel, 91
vecindades, 147, 148, 155, 156, 166
vecinos, 90, 124
veedores (guild overseers): 72–76, 213nn56,57, 214n79. See also artisan guilds; fiel ejecutoría
Velasco, Luis de, 18–19
vendedores ambulantes. See ambulatory vendors

vendedores volantes, 46. *See also* ambulatory
   vendors
vendors: of comestibles, 18, 33, 58, 106, 110,
   120, 154, 156, 192n32; factions among,
   10, 82, 122, 163, 178; in Hispanic
   thought, 79; and labor unions, 176–77,
   250n18; organizations of, 1, 177, 178,
   251n26. *See also* ambulatory vendors;
   baratilleros
viento (tax), 125, 132
Viera, Juan de, 39–41, 65
Villalpando, Cristóbal de, 27*fig.*
Villarroel, Hipólito, 42
vinaterías, 85, 88
Viola, Vicente, 64
violence: in Baratillo, 9, 16, 109, 136, 149,
   179; in Tepito, 179, 251n29; in Volador
   market, 97

voluntary associations, 96, 128, 232n41

wages, 65, 106, 210n25, 226n83, 241n44
women: in artisanal trades, 225n75; in
   Baratillo, 63, 105–06, 135–36, 137*fig.*,
   154–55, 192n32, 225n76; in commerce,
   63–64, 81, 209n8; literacy of, 242n52; in
   "Ordenanzas del Baratillo," 41–42; in
   Plaza Mayor, 22–23; in riot of 1692,
   197n33

Zacatecas, 80
zapateros. See shoe sellers
zaramullos, 15, 16, 24. See also *baratilleros*
Zócalo: location of, 120*map*, 149*map*;
   naming of, 113*fig.*, 114; during Porfiriato,
   145, 148; shoe-sellers in, 133. *See also*
   Plaza de la Constitución; Plaza Mayor